Power Politics and State Formation in the Twentieth Century
The Dynamics of Recognition

From Kurdistan to Somaliland, Xinjiang to South Yemen, all secessionist movements hope to secure newly independent states of their own. Most will not prevail. The existing scholarly wisdom provides one explanation for success, based on authority and control within the nascent states. With the aid of an expansive new dataset and detailed case studies, this book provides an alternative account. It argues that the strongest members of the international community have a decisive influence over whether today's secessionists become countries tomorrow and that, most often, their support is conditioned on parochial political considerations.

Bridget Coggins is an International Affairs Fellow at the Council on Foreign Relations, sponsored by The Asan Institute for Policy Studies. Her research examines the intersections of domestic conflict, international security, and international order. Her work has appeared in journals including *International Organization*, *Journal of Peace Research*, *Journal of Conflict Resolution*, and *Foreign Policy* magazine, as well as in several scholarly edited volumes. She is a graduate of the University of Minnesota, where she received her BA in international relations, and of Ohio State University, where she received a PhD in political science. Previously, Coggins taught in the government department at Dartmouth College.

Power Politics and State Formation in the Twentieth Century

The Dynamics of Recognition

BRIDGET COGGINS

Council on Foreign Relations and The Asan Institute for Policy Studies

CAMBRIDGE
UNIVERSITY PRESS

CAMBRIDGE
UNIVERSITY PRESS

32 Avenue of the Americas, New York NY 10013-2473, USA

Cambridge University Press is part of the University of Cambridge.

It furthers the University's mission by disseminating knowledge in the pursuit of education, learning and research at the highest international levels of excellence.

www.cambridge.org
Information on this title: www.cambridge.org/9781107654662

© Bridget Coggins 2014

First published 2014
First paperback edition 2015

A catalogue record for this publication is available from the British Library

Library of Congress Cataloguing in Publication data
Coggins, Bridget.
Power politics and state formation in the twentieth century : the dynamics of recognition / Bridget Coggins.
    pages   cm
ISBN 978-1-107-04735-8 (hardback)
1. Secession – History – 20th century.   2. Separatist movements – History – 20th century.   3. Nation-state – History – 20th century.   4. Legitimacy of governments – History – 20th century.   5. Nationalism – History – 20th century.   6. Yugoslavia – History – Autonomy and independence movements.   7. Soviet Union – History – Autonomy and independence movements.   8. World politics – 20th century.   I. Title.
JC311.C6145   2014
320.109′04–dc23   2013044582

ISBN 978-1-107-04735-8 Hardback
ISBN 978-1-107-65466-2 Paperback

Contents

List of Maps, Figures, and Tables

Acknowledgements

I have many people to thank. This project began with my dissertation at Ohio State University with the support of a thoughtful and engaged committee: Rick Herrmann, Ted Hopf, and Alex Thompson. During that time, I was also fortunate to receive funding from the Mershon Center for International Security Studies and from the Graduate School of Arts and Sciences.

I was revising the manuscript at Dartmouth College when Kosovo formally declared independence for the second time in 2008 and when, later that same year, renewed conflict in South Ossetia sparked the Russo-Georgian war. And although it was not great timing for my project, I was not surprised that the apparent stalemates did not endure.

At Dartmouth, I would particularly like to thank Ambassador Ken Yalowitz and Christianne Wohlforth at the Dickey Center for International Understanding, both for hosting a book manuscript workshop and for their individual encouragement. I would also like to thank Charles King, Steve Saideman, and the workshop participants, whose insights and constructive feedback touched the book at a pivotal time.

I completed editing and preparing the manuscript for publication while serving as an International Affairs Fellow at the Council on Foreign Relations in residence at The Asan Institute for Policy Studies in Seoul, Korea. The Asan Institute provided a near ideal environment for finalizing the revisions. I was surrounded by interesting people doing interesting work. And Seoul is an amazing city.

The project also received valuable input along the way from audiences at "Secession as an International Phenomenon," sponsored by the Association for Research on Ethnicity and Nationalism in the Americas (ARENA), Columbia University's International Politics Seminar, and "Secession Redux: Lessons for the EU," sponsored by the EU Center for Excellence at the LBJ School of Public Affairs. I would also like to thank the countless individuals at archives and government agencies and within secessionist movements who generously shared their expertise for this research. Ishita Kala and Alannah Linkhorn served, respectively, as my research assistant and map designer in the final stages of the project. Without them, the book would certainly be less polished.

Two portions of the manuscript in Chapters 1 and 3 have previously appeared in print. I acknowledge and appreciate the permission to republish them here. Some of the basic descriptive statistics regarding secessionist movements and statehood can be found in "The History of Secession: An Overview" in Peter Radan and Aleksandar Pavkovic (Eds.). (2011). *The Ashgate Research Companion to Secession.* Surrey, UK: Ashgate Publishers, Ltd., 23–43 (Chapter 2). Additionally, some of the quantitative analysis appeared in "Friends in High Places: International Politics and the Emergence of States from Secessionism." *International Organization* 65:3 (July 2011), 433–467.

At various points when I needed advice or perspective, I was fortunate to have a group of level-headed friends and sharp colleagues. Though there are certainly more than I can list here, I am particularly thankful to Ellie Beaver, Sonu Bedi, Eileen Braman, John Carey, Jong Kun Choi, Tanisha Fazal, Cindy Frey, Paul Fritz, Yoav Gortzak, Dave and Michelle Kang, Doug Lemke, Randy Schweller, Kevin Sweeney, Srdjan Vucetic, and Bill Wohlforth. My family, Cathy Coggins, Jerry Coggins, and my brother Ted, were also important sources of moral support.

Finally, my husband Brent Strathman is an amazing person without whom I could not have completed this project. I am lucky to have him by my side.

Bridget Coggins
December 2013
Seoul, Korea

States of Uncertainty

On February 17, 2008, citizens spilled into the streets of Pristina to celebrate their independence. After nearly a decade in limbo, it seemed that the Kosovo Albanians would finally govern themselves. The United States and most of the European Union, which together upheld the region's autonomy, agreed that there were no viable alternatives to independence. Ethnic cleansing under the Slobodan Milosevic regime meant Albanians should never again be subject to Serbian authority.[1] But not everyone supported Kosovo's statehood. Serbs outside the province opposed independence because of its psychic toll on Serbian national identity, and the Serb minority within Kosovo feared Albanian domination. Farther afield, Russia, China, and others also refused to recognize the new sovereign; they insisted that Kosovo's final status be resolved with Serbia's consent or, in lieu of that, under the auspices of the United Nations Security Council (UNSC). A unilateral declaration of independence like Kosovo's thwarted the UN mandate in the region and Serbia's formal authority.[2] The Kosovars ought not to be rewarded for their regrettable choice. Moreover, Russia, China, and others believed recognition would set a dangerous precedent for secessionist movements worldwide.

Across the Black Sea, two so-called frozen conflicts reversed the Great Powers' preferences regarding state emergence. There, where Russia sees states, the United States and Europe see renegades who rightfully belong under the Georgian flag. The Georgian government had attempted to retake South Ossetia, a province legally but not effectively under its control, in August 2008. For years, the territory's de facto independence was backed by a Russian deterrent, a remnant of its stalemated war over secession there (1991–2). Russian troops,

---

[1] United States, Department of State (2008). "The Case for Kosovo," available at http://www.state.gov/p/eur/ci/kv/c24701.htm.

[2] According to UNSC Res.1244, which authorized intervention in Kosovo under Article 7 of the UN Charter.

who were ostensibly in the region to maintain a cease-fire, quickly countered what they considered an offensive Georgian attack. Accounts at the time disputed which side had reinitiated the violence.[3] But five days of combat revealed that Russia had the upper hand. Its troops restored the status quo ante and established extensive buffer zones around South Ossetia and Abkhazia, Georgia's other separatist region. Shortly thereafter, Russia formally recognized the provinces' independence.[4]

Washington and many EU members condemned Russia as an instigator and aggressor attempting to thwart Georgian sovereignty. From their perspective, President Saakashvili was well within his rights, if perhaps morally suspect, when he decided the problem in South Ossetia should be resolved by force.[5] Russian leaders, on the other hand, deemed Western support for Georgian authority hypocritical, particularly in light of their recent recognition of Kosovo.[6] South Ossetia and Abkhazia had suffered more than a decade of harsh, state-led sanctions; demonstrated strong public support for independence; and were more viable members of the international community. Even the most ambitious plans for Kosovo's transition to substantive independence required a decade of American and European assistance, whereas South Ossetia and Abkhazia had already persevered longer, and with significantly less outside help.

AN UNCERTAIN STATE OF AFFAIRS

What is a state? How and why does one emerge? These recent cases show the process is complicated and often contentious, yet international relations (IR) scholars give the politics of system membership surprisingly little thought.[7] Even though states are the foundational units of international politics, IR scholars generally defer to comparative politics and area specialists when it comes to state birth, presuming that internal, domestic-level causes predominate. Therefore, theories of international relations take states to be exogenous and the process by which they emerge is considered relatively routine.[8]

---

[3] Chivers and Barry (2008).

[4] Nauru, Nicaragua, Tuvalu, Vanuatu, and Venezuela are the only UN members to follow Russia as of this writing, although some states, including Belarus and Cuba, have indicated that they may also do so.

[5] This is true even though they had explicitly recommended against it given Russia's staunch support for the separatists and its consistent support for mediation efforts. It is also worth noting, however, that many authorities suspected Russia was attempting to annex and not secure true independence for the two.

[6] Putin (2008).

[7] Wendt (1999, p. 195) explicitly observes states' constitutions as agents have been overlooked. State creation and consolidation are considered the domain of comparative theory.

[8] Only Taiwan's, the Palestinian territories', and a handful of others' statuses are generally acknowledged as contested or problematic.

Unfortunately, our ignorance about state birth is to our own detriment; it is an important source of international change and a frequent cause of contemporary violence and war.

Adding new system members often has a profound influence on international politics. Like revolutionaries, new states install a new elite and replace governmental institutions upon achieving independence. Internal transformations like these unsettle established norms and identities, which then trigger changes in alliances, political coalitions, and trade relations.[9] New states parcel an existing state's people and territory, thereby altering regional and sometimes international distributions of power. Notably, the Soviet Union's dismemberment not only gave way to new states, but also ceded unequivocal American primacy. Finally, new states are now critical players in most international institutions, as a decisive majority of the world's states were born in the latter half of the twentieth century.

Internal violence brings additional urgency to the subject of state birth. Since the end of World War II, civil conflicts have been the most common and destructive form of war.[10] Within the set of civil wars, wars over state emergence are not only the most common, but also among the longest and most violent.[11] They are notoriously difficult to end or resolve and often relapse into conflict.[12] Furthermore, secession frequently involves violent complicating factors including ethnic cleansing or mass expulsions, gross violations of human rights, terrorism, nontraditional war fighting, and counterinsurgency campaigns. In the past century, hundreds of unique demands for independence were made, and in the second decade of the twenty-first century, more than 60 secessionist conflicts are ongoing around the world. Even an incomplete sample of twentieth-century secessionist conflicts' destructiveness – Tamil Eelam in Sri Lanka, Biafra in Nigeria, Tibet in China, the South in Sudan, the Basque Country in Spain, Mindanao in the Philippines, and various Kurdistans in the Middle East – illustrate the pressing need for strategies to reduce violence and enact durable solutions. State emergence's relative scholarly obscurity as a topic of inquiry belies its real-world significance. (See Map 1.1.)

---

[9] Walt (1985) details how revolutionary internal change influences international security and alliance politics.

[10] Sarkees (2000) and Small and Singer (1982). This claim is based on a simple comparison of frequency and cumulative war deaths for each type of war between 1945 and 1997. For a variety of reasons, it is also likely that civil war deaths are systematically underreported relative to international war deaths. Fearon (2004b) additionally notes that "the number of ongoing civil wars had been steadily, almost linearly increasing from 1945 up to 1991" (p. 275).

[11] On frequency, see Licklider (1995), Gurr (2000), and Fearon and Laitin (2003). On duration, see Fearon (2004b).

[12] Walter (1997, 2003); Posen (1993).

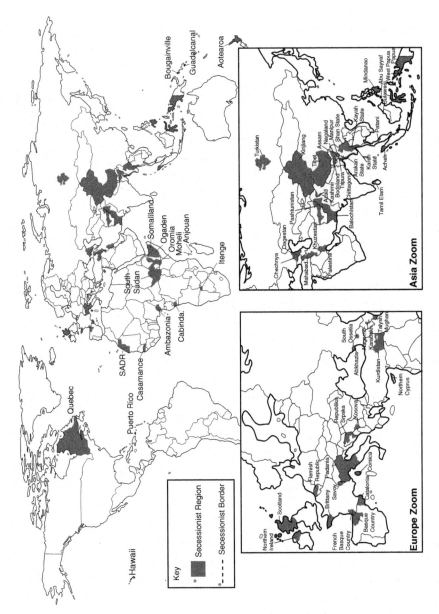

MAP 1.1 Ongoing Secessionist Movements, 2000

PATTERNS OF STATE EMERGENCE (1816–2002)

In 1816, the international system had only 25 members.[13] One hundred years later, there were still fewer than 50 states. State emergences were few and far between during the nineteenth century, and state death or violent conquest was more likely.[14] Colonial expansion did not eliminate states because conquered regimes were rarely acknowledged as legitimate sovereigns to begin with. Precolonial peoples and territories were commonly considered *terra nullius*, literally "no man's lands," and therefore deemed free for the taking. In the mid-1800s, the system reached a peak of 46 members with decolonization in the Americas, and then lost many in the following years as a result of state consolidation in Europe.

In dramatic contrast, during the twentieth century, 150 new states entered the international system, quadrupling its membership.[15] With no remaining *terras nullius*, henceforth any new state had to be born by cleaving off territory from a recognized sovereign entity. These new states were born in various ways over four periods of independence. The first two occurred after the world wars, as victors punished the vanquished and rewarded or reinstated their friends. The third occurred more gradually as empires shed their colonial holdings from the end of World War II through the 1970s. Finally, the Yugoslav and Soviet collapses created more than 20 new states from just two as the century concluded. (See Figure 1.1.)

The pattern of newly independent states should not be attributed to superficial temporal periods alone, however. Not all discontented minorities received states as President Woodrow Wilson's "Fourteen Points" speech might have implied following World War I.[16] Nor did all of the systematically oppressed achieve the independence they demanded, colonial or otherwise, when the founding members of the UN dedicated themselves to the "self-determination of peoples."[17] Several groups often vied to control the same population and territory or disputed the contours of their inherited boundaries. This meant that many more aspired to independence than actually achieved it. These patterns remain consistent today. The number of ongoing independence projects has not dipped below 50 since World War II. Among them, only a minority become states, but even unsuccessful demands typically impose high costs in lives lost, wealth destroyed or deferred, and political instability.

---

[13] Although 1816 is not the beginning of the Westphalian, state-centered order (1648), scholars generally agree that contemporary notions of sovereignty and statehood were pervasive by the nineteenth century. Krasner (1999) provides an expansive discussion.

[14] Fazal (2004), Atzili (2006/7).

[15] Correlates of War Project (2005).

[16] Wilson (1918).

[17] United Nations (2003).

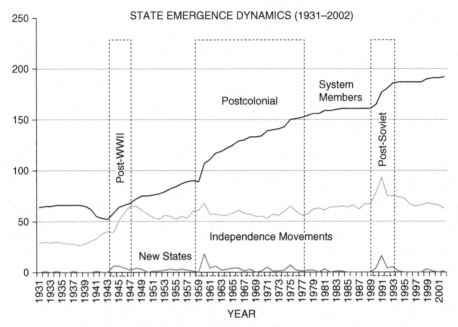

FIGURE 1.1 State Emergence Dynamics (1931–2002)

Most states born in the twentieth century became independent following internal contests over sovereignty as in anticolonial separatism or secession.[18] It is an oft-repeated claim that successful secession is exceedingly rare, yet during this time period, more than one of every three demands for independence was realized.[19] Only a particular subtype, a successful war of independence such as Eritrea's separation from Ethiopia, was uncommon. That secession's success rate is underestimated should not, however, be taken as evidence that new statehood was quickly or easily achieved. Successful demands lasted nearly 10 years (9.89) on average and were responsible for millions of deaths.[20] The French-Indochinese War alone killed 600,000 in just 9 years. Sudan's most recent civil war is reported to have killed more than 2 million people. Secessionist conflicts also frequently drew in kin countries or ideological supporters, internationalizing the violence. Moreover, the conflicts were especially fraught because they blurred the lines between civilians and combatants, wreaking havoc on civil society and stymieing post-conflict reconstruction.[21]

---

[18] For the purposes of this project, anti-colonialism and secessionism are considered equivalent. Further explanation is provided in Chapter 2.

[19] According to the dataset for this project, 95 of 259 independence movements between 1931 and 2002 became independent states (approximately 37 percent).

[20] Ibid.

[21] Walter (1997), Walter and Snyder (1999).

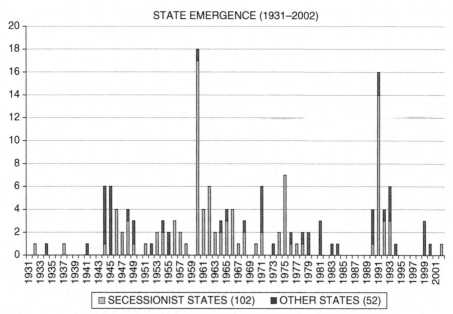

FIGURE I.2 State Emergence (1931–2002)

All cases of new independence are of interest to a study on state emergence. Nevertheless, this project limits its focus to the causes of state emergence for groups who demand independence from their legitimate governors or *home states*. Theoretical and empirical reasons inform this choice. First, some states do enter the system without prior nationalist demands, but these states-to-be could not be identified a priori. In most cases, they emerged via unilateral decolonization by an imperial power or reflected changes in territory negotiated by treaties following the world wars. Occasionally, this meant that the state preceded national identity entirely. As d'Azeglio famously exclaimed, "We have made Italy, now we must make Italians!"[22] Or instead, a state with strong national identity was occupied, destroyed in a war, and resurrected by the victorious coalition.[23] Second, as Figure 1.2 shows, the number of states born following independence demands far exceeds those born in other ways. The other, far less common forms are unilateral decolonization, when a foreign authority unilaterally devolves authority to a local one; dissolution, when a federation lawfully dissolves into its constituent parts;[24] postwar settlement,

[22] Cited in Emerson (1960, p. 95).
[23] For examples, see Fazal (2007, pp. 30–33).
[24] The line between state dissolution and secession is sometimes fuzzy. For example, it is clear that Slovenia and Croatia seceded from Yugoslavia, but it is less clear that Macedonia did. Similarly, Estonia, Latvia, and Lithuania clearly seceded from the USSR prior to its collapse, whereas states such as Kazakhstan perhaps did not and emerged as a function of the Soviet Union's dissolution.

when the victors of war determine political jurisdiction by external fiat; and union, when two or more states join to become one new state. Not every new state enters the system because of secessionism, but most in the contemporary world do. They form the subject matter for this book.

THE INTERNATIONAL POLITICS OF STATE BIRTH

I make three primary and interrelated arguments explaining when, why, and how new states emerge. First, I demonstrate that the international system's nature has been misunderstood. Statehood does not inhere in governmental control on the ground alone. Without external legitimacy, an actor is not a state. Instead, the international states system is better characterized as an international community wherein influential members determine which aspiring states will succeed and which will be left outside to founder. Therefore, an English School or soft Constructivist account provides the most accurate portrayal of statehood's essential features. The Westphalian order depends on mutual sovereign recognition among states. According to James, "The mere existence of a territorial entity which is also constitutionally independent is one thing...the extent to which it participates in international life is another matter...It depends on the number of other states which are wanting and willing to enter into relations with the state concerned."[25] Recognition by the system's members rather than – and sometimes in spite of – de facto control and authority is the pivotal distinction between states and non-state "others."

The contemporary dynamics of secession and statehood evince one of the most dramatic instances of the second image reversed; system-level factors determine not only the form and function of institutions within states, but also who those states are to begin with.[26] Tellingly, there are very few cases in recent history where new states unambiguously met the prevailing legal standards for membership, and yet states have proliferated. Legal vagaries may be partially responsible for the gap between law and practice. But the more compelling explanation for the disparity is that existing states, rather than some disinterested or unbiased arbiter, confer external legitimacy. Self-interest and power dynamics inevitably creep into the process when leaders are given the opportunity to select their own new peers.

Following from the first, my second major argument is that existing members' parochial concerns meaningfully shape their preferences for or against new states. This is an intuitively compelling, but largely untested belief.[27] International law bemoans the overtly political practice of recognition.[28] And

---

[25] James (1986, p. 147).

[26] Gourevitch (1978).

[27] Scholars including Krasner (2009) have recently suggested just this.

[28] According to the most current and widely held interpretations of international law, recognition of a new state prior to the achievement of certain objective criteria (identifiable territory and population, effective government, and the capacity to enter into international relations)

it is eminently reasonable that granting external legitimacy, like the myriad other decisions leaders make, should be politically motivated. I present three major categories of interest that influence leaders' preferences: international security concerns, domestic politics and security, and system stability. Additionally, this argument presents an alternative perspective on domestic-level theories that claim internal politics predominate when it comes to state emergence. Although it may be that internal politics or characteristics within the secessionist territory help explain whether and when state birth occurs, those factors are important because community members believe they ought to be, not because they alone constitute statehood. In short, existing theories have identified a spurious relationship; they are right about the pattern, but their causal explanations for it are incorrect.

How do powerful states' preferences figure into state birth? The dynamics of external legitimacy conform to a threshold model of sorts.[29] Many states must recognize a newcomer before it secures full membership in the international community. Unanimous recognition is not necessary, but a critical mass of acceptance must be achieved before the rights and obligations of statehood take hold.[30] All states are both members and progenitors of the system, but the Great Powers' recognition decisions are the most important. Their disproportionate material capabilities give them substantial influence over other states' recognition behavior. Often prime movers in crises of state birth, Great Power recognition serves as a focal point for others to follow, initiating a cascade of system-wide legitimacy. Further, once past the tipping point, recognized statehood is almost never revoked.[31]

Whether the Great Powers' individual preferences ultimately lead to recognition and state birth depends on their alignment with one another. Leaders do

constitutes premature recognition and carries no legal force; it is itself an illegal act (Von Glahn, 1992, pp. 87, 92).

[29] Initial articulations of threshold models can be found in Schelling (1971a, 1971b) and Finnemore and Sikkink (1998). A lay version of a threshold model also underlies Malcolm Gladwell's (2000) book *The Tipping Point: How Little Things Can Make a Big Difference*.

[30] "[U]niversal recognition is not necessary either in theory or in practice…nevertheless a 'critical mass' of recognition could said to be necessary" (Fawn and Mayall, 1996, p. 209). For example, it would be difficult, if not impossible, for a state recognized by only two other members to gain membership as a state within the United Nations or to receive a loan from the World Bank or IMF.

[31] Waltz (1979, p. 95) notes this tendency. The "stickiness" of recognition is also part of Jackson's (1990) explanation for why so-called quasi-states endure even with little domestic legitimacy. It is also noteworthy to point out that although coordinated self-interested behavior might cause state emergence initially, the threshold model implies that the same constellation of interests need not be maintained in order for statehood to endure. The legitimacy of suspending a state's sovereignty, on the other hand, is not without proponents. An example of suspended sovereignty can be seen in the U.S.-led war to overthrow the government of Iraq in 2003. Similarly, Jeffery Herbst argues that in extraordinary circumstances the international community should decertify failed states and discontinue their juridical external sovereignty (1996–7, p. 142). The *New York Times Magazine* too, in its third annual "The Year in Ideas" issue, declared "suspended nationhood" one of the most influential ideas of 2003 (Cain, 2003).

not make their choices in a vacuum; they are strategically interdependent and must anticipate how others will act and react. My third and final argument is that the international system incentivizes leaders to coordinate their recognition to (1) maintain system stability and peace among themselves, (2) ensure a critical mass of support for new members, and (3) diffuse responsibility for violating another member's sovereignty (by legitimizing a challenge to its territorial integrity) and limit the potential for its violent retribution. When the Great Powers' preferences align positively, they easily collude in favor of an aspiring state and a decisive cascade of legitimacy follows. When they align negatively, the would-be state is decisively blocked. Similarly, when their preferences do not align, leaders typically defer to the status quo and emergence does not occur. Only in extraordinary circumstances, most recently regarding Kosovo and the Georgian separatists, does the drive to coordinate lapse.

In sum, the international politics of recognition are essential to understanding which actors among the scores of potential new members will be accepted into the international community of states and to predicting when that acceptance is likely to occur. Nascent states are either elevated to state membership or excluded from it by powerful, existing members guided significantly by their own parochial interests.

THE CONSEQUENCES OF POLITICAL RECOGNITION

Collectively, these arguments have important consequences for international relations and conflict resolution. The first implication is that the politics of external legitimacy work to ensure short-term stability in the international system. Self-interests drive states' preferences, but strong states' incentives to coordinate – and not act impulsively on those preferences when they do conflict – ensure that most new members are mutually acceptable. When aspiring states advance the interests of the powerful, they will more readily be accepted as community members. When strong states' interests diverge, they avoid internationalizing the dispute among themselves by upholding the status quo. This maintains international stability because overlapping sovereignty, or the recognition of two legitimate authorities over the same territory, is avoided.

The next major implication is that the politics of external recognition may unintentionally create system-wide instability over the long run. Because new states' entries into the international system are contingent on political considerations and not necessarily on the authority and capacity of the nascent states, newcomers will generally exercise less coercive control and authority than existing models of state emergence imply; internally speaking, they are less sovereign. In the worst-case scenario, the international community is accepting new members that are bound to fail, unintentionally destabilizing the system and potentially imperilling their own security as states proliferate. Today, experts caution that a number of the world's newest states – including Bosnia and Herzegovina, East Timor, and South Sudan – are imperilled because of their equivocal sovereignty.[32] Others argue the problem is even more pervasive, so much so that external, not internal, sovereignty now sustains the majority of states in the developing world. After an initial honeymoon period, new countries may find themselves unable to or governed by regimes that are unwilling to provide even basic public goods for their people. And this may initiate a cycle of poverty, corruption, and violence that is difficult to undo. Moreover, some have linked state failure and internal weakness to international threats including terrorism, transnational crime, weapons trafficking, even the spread of disease and environmental degradation. As new states multiply, so too might weakness and international insecurity.

On the other hand, if new states can use membership's significant benefits to advance effective domestic governance through opportunities for development assistance, military cooperation, trade, and investment, then their relative weakness at birth may not have lasting adverse effects. State weakness might simply be a marker of youth. Even though this may seem overly optimistic, it is not clear that an alternative selection mechanism for new states is feasible. Nor is it certain that less politically attractive, but more effectively sovereign new members would fare any better. Requiring a certain level of capacity would initially create stronger states and slow system growth. Still, powerful states are unlikely to opt out of the opportunity to determine their new peers, and the probability of any new state's survival in the face of hostile Great Powers could not be very high.

Third, this project demonstrates that prominent models of civil war settlement and war termination significantly underestimate the influence of third parties. Although authors rightly characterize the situation between separatists and their governments as zero-sum and beset by commitment problems, they do not appreciate the extent to which conflict outcomes are dependent on powerful states' acceptance. This leaves an important variable unobserved. Secessionist wars sometimes end decisively on the battlefield but remain unresolved and continue to fester because powerful states cannot reach consensus among themselves about the outcome. Ongoing debates over Kosovo, South Ossetia, and Abkhazia are cases in point. Conversely, when they are possible, clear and credible demonstrations of support for independence or against it by the Great Powers should expedite conflict resolution. In these cases, granting legitimacy would be less costly than the intervention and peacekeeping scenarios often offered as solutions.

Finally, and relatedly, overreliance on comparative theories of state emergence has led to erroneous beliefs about potential remedies to state emergence conflicts. Specifically, scholars place undue faith in institutional configurations' and other domestic factors' abilities to prevent demands for independence and their realization.[33] The evidence presented herein demonstrates that the end of colonialism will not forestall state emergence. Nor will giving minorities

---

[32] Chopra (2003); Anderson (2004); Martell and Blomfield (2011)
[33] Roeder (2007).

autonomous political authority necessarily foment disintegration. The true causes of state birth are contingent and depend on the motives and interpretations of powerful outsiders. Attending to both the domestic and international aspects of secessionism will yield more successful policies than strategies proposed by purely domestic models.

OUTLINE AND ORGANIZATION

The book proceeds as follows: first, in Chapter 2, I review the literature within comparative politics, international law, and international relations regarding state emergence. I find that the predominant conception of state birth is oriented toward control and legitimacy within the aspiring state. However, objective measures of control and authority do not convincingly explain the pattern of state birth. Many more states emerge than domestic factors suggest should do so. I argue that international political factors best explain the gap between theory and practice when it comes to statehood. External legitimacy is the ultimate arbiter of state emergence. Therefore, understanding why states accept new members is essential to understanding the dynamics of state birth. Next, Chapter 3 lays out the project's research design and methodology.

Chapter 4 evaluates the current state of the art regarding state emergence and then adapts it for testing within the proposed new, internationally oriented framework. Among other things, it asks: are federal subunits or ethnic substates more likely to secure states than groups organized differently? Or do only the strongest separatist movements survive to become independent states? Many of the domestic-level explanations find convincing empirical support, but they are ultimately inconclusive. Most are structural and do not vary within the same case, thereby limiting their ability to explain when new states will emerge.

The chapter then introduces new hypotheses on external acceptance and tests them using an original, annual cross-sectional, time-series dataset more appropriate to international explanations. The new dependent variable is formal recognition, an executive-level decree of sovereignty, unambiguous evidence that an existing system member accepts a new peer. I then explore whether or not external politics help explain Great Power recognition decisions between 1931 and 2000. I present three major categories of political interests that should influence state preferences: external security concerns, domestic political concerns, and system stability. The new explanations improve significantly on the domestic-only theories. The quantitative evidence convincingly demonstrates that leaders accept new states with an eye toward their own interests. Furthermore, the Great Powers are each motivated by different concerns at different points in time. How those preferences align will ultimately determine patterns of state birth.

Chapters 5 and 6 use clustered case studies from the Former Yugoslavia and the Former Soviet Union to investigate support for the causal motives underlying recognition and the dynamics of recognition among the Great Powers.

Specifically, they analyze whether and how the Great Powers confront disagreements among themselves about which would-be states ought to be recognized – the alignment hypotheses regarding the causal mechanism. The cases in the Former Yugoslavia (Slovenia, Croatia, and Kosovo) demonstrate that the politics among the Great Powers themselves loom larger than most developments on the ground in secessionist conflicts. The analyses reveal that leaders consistently worked to maintain a unified front and coordinated their recognitions accordingly. Indeed, the Kosovo conflict remained unresolved for a decade, due in substantial part to the absence of an external consensus. Regarding Croatia, previous work implying that Germany unilaterally broke from the European consensus is found to overstate its case. The post-Soviet case cluster, including the secession attempts of Abkhazia and South Ossetia in Georgia, Nagorno-Karabakh in Azerbaijan, and Chechnya in Russia, traces the politics of non-recognition where Great Power interests diverged. In all of the stalemated Caucasian conflicts, despite their demonstrating significant variation in sovereign authority on the ground, no recognition was granted to the de facto independent governments. It was not until the United States and much of Europe recognized Kosovo in 2008 that Russia unilaterally recognized Abkhazia and South Ossetia in an act of retribution for its peers' violation of the recognition armistice that had so far prevailed among them over the three conflicts.

Chapter 7, the final chapter, explores the consequences of the book's main findings. The first portion synthesizes the empirical results. The latter portion explores how the dynamics of state birth will influence international politics and security in years to come, potentially – though not inevitably – creating instability long term. It also advocates a reconsideration of current policies regarding secessionist conflicts and civil war. Too many strategies for conflict prevention and resolution exclude external political factors and, therefore, underestimate the international community's potential role as a force for either good or ill.

2

Statehood in Theory and Practice

The scholarly study of international relations fixates on states. Experts study their actions and interactions; how they influence and are influenced by the system and by supra- and sub-state actors; their manners of diplomacy, trade, and war; and how they organize their internal and external affairs. Its range is exhaustive. Yet it seldom contemplates how new states enter the international community to begin with. The discipline's focus on the relations among states has unintentionally caused myopia of a sort, leading scholars to neglect foundational system dynamics like the birth and death of states. The Westphalian origin myth and the state's rise to institutional dominance within the system are well known.[1] The selection mechanism for new states is decidedly not. As a result, supposition and anecdote derived from the early European experience often substitute for theory and evidence when it comes to changes in membership.

Perhaps it is difficult to understand scholars' relative disregard for state emergence given the state's prominent place in theory, but it is easy to understand why most others might take states for granted. On any given day, distinguishing between states and non-states is straightforward. States have professional militaries, their own currencies and institutionalized bureaucracies. They are members of intergovernmental organizations, make treaties, regulate trade, and confer national citizenship. The People's Republic of China is clearly a state, whereas the Republic of Ichkeria – which most have never even heard of – is clearly not. It seems the distinction between states and non-states is obvious and tangible, requiring no further investigation.

Yet the contemporary politics of nationalism and sovereignty belie the seemingly stark contrast between the two types of actors. Ongoing controversies over the statuses of Kosovo, Somaliland, and Taiwan provide but a few examples of the many ambiguous statelike actors in existence. Statehood is also increasingly

[1] For two exemplary works, see Spruyt (1994) and Tilly (1992).

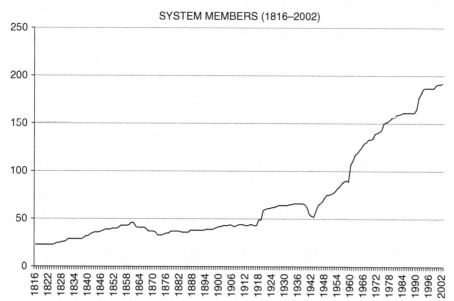

FIGURE 2.1 System Members (1816–2002)

dynamic and contested, so the rate and intensity of separatist conflicts make any ambiguities between the two types a pressing practical concern for state leaders. The system's membership has swelled to nearly two hundred states, and the international community now adds approximately two new states each year (see Figures 2.1 and 2.2).[2] A majority of those newcomers are the fruits of secessionist conflicts, in which a local movement demanded separation from its home state in order to form a new state of its own.[3] And for every successful new state, two other secessionist movements attempted to attain statehood but ultimately failed to do so.[4] An overwhelming majority of groups seeking independence never acquire it, but conflicts over demands for sovereignty are frequent, violent, and enduring.

This project seeks to remedy the disjuncture between secession's real-world import and its relative scholarly obscurity by introducing a theory of state birth. I begin by reviewing the little theory we do have regarding the dynamics of modern state emergence. I find that what we believe we know about statehood

---

[2] Correlates of War (2005). In marked contrast to the explosion in state birth, Fazal (2007) observes that 66 of 207 states have met violent deaths since 1816 (p. 20), a relatively small number. This means that the number of new states is even larger than it first appears because new states also replaced those that exited the system.

[3] During the same time period, only 58 new states entered the international community as a result of unilateral decolonization, mutual dissolution, or postwar settlement.

[4] According to the data collected for this project, 259 unique secessionist demands were made between 1931 and 2002.

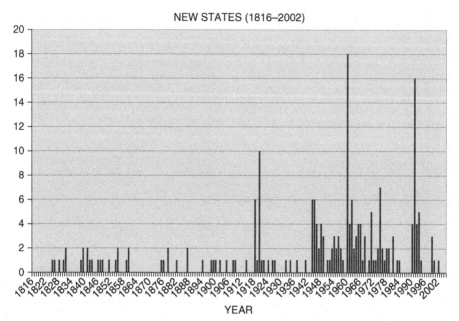

FIGURE 2.2 New States (1816–2002)

inaccurately depicts how most modern states are born. Both the presumptive model of state emergence in international relations and the normative standards prescribed by international law suggest a causal sequence to state creation that is not followed in practice. Furthermore, the gap between theory and practice is not the result of misperception or problems inherent to meeting an abstract ideal. Rather, leaders actively oppose the standards implied by law, refusing to submit to its dictates regarding a decision they maintain is uniquely within their prerogative.

Legal and scholarly consensus suggests that a monopoly of force within a territory and legitimate domestic authority comprise the necessary and sufficient characteristics of the state. The way in which an actor is received by other states has no effect on its statehood. Contrary to the existing wisdom, I put forward a social model of state emergence based in a constitutive interpretation of external legitimacy. The predominant model of state birth is not wholly inaccurate; material factors such as decisive territorial control and effective authority are often sufficient to assure a new state's entry. But they are not necessary to secure the benefits of statehood. Instead, strong states regularly elevate new members into the international community despite their tenuous claims to internal sovereignty because of external political considerations. Occasionally, even actors that convincingly assert domestic authority languish in uncertainty because the powerful refuse to embrace them as legitimate states. In opposition to its portrayal in the literature then, the international community's acceptance is not an automatic consequence of effective independence. System membership is conditioned on the judgments of existing state members who are not – and therefore cannot be assumed to be – disinterested outsiders dutifully enforcing international law or impartial interlocutors simply seeking solutions to complex conflicts. For all intents and purposes, a new state does not exist unless and until the members of the international community determine that it does.

Why do leaders deviate from established normative legal principles when it comes to accepting new peers? I argue that powerful states' parochial political motives best explain the gap between expectations and reality. Each actor seeking external legitimacy presents existing states with an opportunity to play a part in selecting their own peers, perhaps ultimately changing both the balance of power and ideas within the international system.[5] Therefore, existing states recognize new states with an eye to their own interests. At the same time, though, leaders must temper their narrowly defined, individual motives with the system's organizational imperative to coordinate their recognition with those of others, ever cognizant of their interdependence. In order to maintain stability in the state-centered Westphalian system, the members must reach a fundamental consensus regarding who is (and who is not) a state. When they cannot and recognize competing sovereign authorities within the same territory, international instability is introduced far beyond the borders of the contested region. Historically, instances of internationally contested sovereignty have been an important catalyst for Great Power war.

THEORETICAL AND SUBSTANTIVE IMPLICATIONS

If statehood is subjective and often guided by external political considerations rather than objective governmental capacity, a number of consequences follow. First, powerful states in the international system at time (t-1) are selecting the set of states that will inhabit the system at time (t). How have these socially promoted states fared relative to those with less favor? Do they populate the ranks of so-called failed or quasi states, unable to competently function in the system because of internal weakness? Or instead, are these new states relatively advantaged because of the extensive external support and legitimacy they receive? Counterfactually, would an alternative set from the pool of potential states have fared better (or worse) according to our best estimates forecasting state viability? Evaluating recognition's long-term effects on system membership will help suggest strategies for creating a more stable international order and perhaps a more legitimate and effective set of states.

---

[5] To cite but a few familiar examples, were Taiwan's statehood to be recognized, it would be among the largest economies in the world (in the top 25). Similarly, post-independence, the United States became one of the most enduringly powerful states in the history of the international system. Finally, one of the most pivotal events of the twentieth century, the dissolution of the Soviet Union, began with the secession and subsequent external recognition of the Baltic states.

Next, the external politics of legitimacy undoubtedly influence conflict dynamics but are notably absent in studies of self-determination, ethnic conflict, and civil war.[6] Perhaps the prospect of politically motivated acceptance emboldens proto-states with an otherwise slim chance of securing independence, thereby rendering difficult conflicts intractable. Conversely, a state facing a proto-state challenger without external patrons may feel emboldened to pursue aggressive tactics, secure in the knowledge that outsiders will not interfere. Isolating the conditions under which the powerful are likely to collude in a proto-state's favor may suggest novel strategies of conflict resolution. Or opponents might be able to limit the costs of conflict if they recognize early on that the international community is unsympathetic to the separatists' plight and arrive at a compromise short of war. If we hope to prevent and resolve conflicts over sovereignty and mitigate the adverse consequences borne of incentives generated by political recognition, we must consider the full range of costs and benefits facing conflict participants.

Finally, there are normative consequences to powerful states' divergence from international law. How does it affect the character of the international system? Have leaders arrived at new, mutually acceptable membership criteria? Are the foreseeable results of political recognition less desirable than those generated by adherence to the legal standards? Can our laws be modified to induce greater compliance, or are they necessarily ineffective when it comes to granting external legitimacy? The answers to each of these questions will help us understand the extent to which international law can and should play a role in the admission of new states.

IR THEORY AND THE STATE

States are the ultimate units through which politics are contested. Because no authority capable of creating and enforcing rules of international conduct exists, states themselves hold the greatest aggregate political authority.[7] Some question whether the state's dominance will continue. They foresee its gradual decline like the empires and city-states that came before.[8] But few would disagree that states

---

[6] External intervention and material assistance are analyzed, but diplomatic legitimacy in addition to or as an alternative to those factors is not. A notable exception is Fearon (2004a).

[7] Though, under certain circumstances supranational institutions have usurped the authority of state governments. The European Court of Justice (ECJ) has been particularly successful in creating binding autonomous decisions among European member states.

[8] There has been a good deal of hand wringing and investigation into the potential demise of the state. Recently the fall of the state has been attributed to the influence of globalization. Some argue that "virtual states" will replace traditional states as territory loses significance for highly developed service economies (Rosecrance 1999). Others see state erosion as a consequence of domestic deterioration and ethnic strife (Kaplan 1994, 1997; Huntington 1993, 1996). Still others envision supranational authorities usurping the state's monopoly on authority (Falk 1975; Matthews 1997; Barnett and Finnemore 2004). Further inquiries into the durability of the state include Paul, Ikenberry, and Hall (2003); Biersteker and Weber (1996), and in international law Schreuer (1993).

are and have been the primary global political actors for at least three hundred years.⁹ Much has changed during their tenure. States' capacities and functions now exceed those of their ancestors, and the breadth and depth of states' external affairs have increased. Nevertheless, the state's dominance as a unit within the system and the anarchic organization among states remain constant.¹⁰ Even if it is true that absolute sovereignty is eroding, the state's perseverance remains likely because no obvious alternative has emerged to unseat it. Furthermore, the number and scale of secessionist and revolutionary conflicts worldwide prove that access to state authority remains a particularly compelling objective for those without it and a prize worth holding onto for those facing its potential diminution or loss.

It is because scholars take their cues from real-world politics that they emphasize the politics among states.¹¹ Somewhat ironically, however, scholars' devotion to studying the interactions among states leads them to take the states themselves for granted. The most popular scholarly approaches to international politics employ a quasi-experimental logic wherein states and their preferences are held constant so that variations in system dynamics under different structural configurations can be explored.¹² Pondering state emergence is deemed superfluous to explaining the politics among fully formed states in the same way that most people's birth stories are unlikely to provide meaningful insight into their day-to-day behaviors later in life. This is especially true because scholars imagine that the process and results of state emergence are fairly similar. Regardless of the specific details, each actor became a state. From that point on, systemic pressures and competition worked to compel them to adopt similar structures and functions and, ultimately, to become "like units." In sum, states are unexamined theoretical constructs because most theories of international relations take them to be exogenous or prior. Distinguishing between state and non-state actors is presumed unambiguous and the processes by which states come to be is considered routine.¹³ Theorists differ vehemently over the nature of interactions among states but find broad consensus in the belief that states fulfill a relatively homogenous and distinguishable set of functional roles.¹⁴ This approach

---

⁹ Most credit the initiation of the interstate system to the Treaty of Westphalia of 1648. Wight (1977) argues that sovereignty was established beginning in the fifteenth century and codified during the seventeenth century at Westphalia (p. 110). Krasner notes, however, that Westphalian norms were not fully accepted within the international system until much later (around the eighteenth century) (1999, pp. 20–22).

¹⁰ Waltz (1979, pp. 88–99).

¹¹ There are certainly deviations from the state-centric model as well.

¹² This is not always the case. For example, Wendt endogenizes state preferences.

¹³ Though Wendt notes that it is most accurate to consider the components of statehood a "fuzzy set," not every typical characteristic is necessary and there are some "borderline cases" (1999, p. 202).

¹⁴ To cite but a few influential examples of this tendency: Waltz (1979, pp. 79–101, "Political Structures"); Bull (1977, p.8); Walt (1985); and Wendt (1999, pp. 202–214 and 246–312, "Three Cultures of Anarchy").

generally defers to scholars of comparative politics and history for explanations of the genesis of states (in general and particular) and the development and maintenance of the interstate system.[15]

Unfortunately, omitting dynamic aspects of the international system such as the entry and exit of states is to the detriment of international relations theory and to our understanding of many of the world's most contentious conflicts. Existing models reveal the causes and processes underlying conflict among states, but they cannot explain how or why those states came to be states in the first place. Given a world where the most important conflicts occurred between states, selective attention like this might be justified. However, when the most destructive wars are fought within countries and often over the very issue of new statehood, as they are today, the exclusion of secessionist and anti-colonial conflicts seems outmoded. If our theories and models cannot capture the fundamental dynamics of the international system, then we cannot offer insights into or explanations for the most provocative and violent conflicts of our time.

WESTPHALIA AND THE STATE

According to the established consensus, the states system began with the collection of negotiated treaties resolving the Thirty and Eighty Years Wars known as the Westphalian Peace (1648).[16] Though not fully realized or widely institutionalized at the time, the principles inherited from Westphalia, domestic authority and noninterference, have come to define the modern international system. The events at Westphalia are also significant because international relations scholars derive their models of system dynamics from conflicting interpretations of the early European experience with sovereignty and state consolidation, using their beliefs about how states originally came to be to inform their ideas about how countries continue to be born today.

Westphalia's primary legacy is the establishment of two enduring principles of international politics. The first is *domestic authority*, which implies that one unique government is deemed sovereign over the territory and population of each unit. That authority has exclusive jurisdiction over the conduct and content of governance within its borders. *Noninterference* conditions external conduct among sovereigns, requiring that they not meddle in the domestic affairs of their peers. The exclusivity of jurisdiction rests on a foundation of universal mutual acknowledgment of domestic authority among system members. Beyond these fundamental principles of organization, there is no formal hierarchy ordering

---

[15] For emblematic cases, see Gellner (1983) in comparative politics and Emerson (1960), Watson (1992), and Willoughby (1896) in comparative history.

[16] Again, Westphalian principles were not fully articulated until the end of the eighteenth century, well after the Treaty of Westphalia was signed (Krasner, 1999 pp. 20–21). Also see Murphy in Biersteker and Weber (1996, pp. 84–93). For more on the Westphalian transition, see Spruyt (1994) and Watson (1992).

international relations; states coexist in anarchy. The extent of domestic control and authority is often referred to as *internal sovereignty*, whereas the acknowledgment of exclusive legitimate authority by a state's peers is termed *external sovereignty*. Together Westphalia's twin principles constitute *sovereignty*, the foundational institution of the modern international system.[17] Put succinctly, Westphalia began to reorganize the world into political units whose internal affairs are hierarchically organized under a sovereign authority, who accept one another as independent and juridically equal, and who interact under conditions of anarchy.[18]

The basic historical details of Westphalia are not contested. In retrospect, the letter and intent of its treaties convincingly mark the end of the age of empire and foreshadow the coming sovereign states system.[19] What has remained uncertain over the centuries that have followed is the causal relationship between states and the system in which they interact. Did internally sovereign de facto states precede the system or did the mutual exchange of external recognition, foundational to the Westphalian agreements, instead create the states? Though the truth seems as irresolvable as the problematic initial relationship between chickens and eggs, it has important implications.

Scholars are of two minds when it comes to interpreting Westphalia's significance for the international system and its states. One take on Westphalia suggests states preceded the system institutionalized in 1648. These scholars view the Weberian ideal of the state, exclusive control and legitimate authority, as primary and the recognition exchanged among states as a secondary, if not trivial, consequence of its achievement. According to this way of thinking, states existed prior to the agreements at Westphalia. The peace simply established a means for productive negotiations among them. It is in this vein, focused on capacity, that Watson recounts the history, "[t]he electors and all the princes and imperial cities of the Holy Roman Empire *who were capable of conducting independent foreign policy* were represented at the negotiations."[20]

The representatives at Westphalia had fought seemingly interminable and costly wars. Their only viable alternative was a negotiated, and hopefully durable, peace among themselves. Which governments would be represented was an issue of little contest as each was a participant in a devastating war. The facts on the ground prior to the peace negotiations determined the emerging system's membership, rather than the negotiations themselves. Internal sovereignty was foundational. States came first and then they entered into relations with one another.

---

[17] Bull (1977, p. 8). In this project I use the terms "internal sovereignty" and "internal statehood," "external sovereignty" and "external statehood," and "sovereignty" and "statehood" interchangeably.

[18] Waltz (1979, pp. 88–89) is the most prominent though not exclusive proponent of this idea.

[19] Boucher (1998, p. 289); Morgenthau (1985, p. 294); Philpott (2001, pp. 82–89).

[20] Emphasis added. Watson (1992, p. 186).

The most common conceptualization of the state in international relations derives from this interpretation of Westphalia. Implicitly, the creation of new states is thought to follow a relatively uncomplicated, linear causal path. New states first consolidate their domestic authority, and then they assert themselves as sovereign independents in their interactions with other states. States' effective similarity, or likeness to other state units, forms the basis for mutual recognition and treating one another as sovereign equals. States have little choice but to acknowledge one another if they hope to peacefully and productively interact. According to this model, the achievement of external sovereignty and statehood is mostly a bottom-up, rather than a top-down, process vis-à-vis the international community. Acceptance by other states does not *cause* statehood and sovereignty from the top down. It merely reaffirms what has already been achieved in fact at the domestic level.[21] Distinguishing between states and non-states is easy because states are uniquely able to present themselves as such, much in the same way that Watson suggests the participants at Westphalia did. The Peace of Westphalia became possible only because its victors desired an anti-hegemonic order, domestic populations were exceedingly war weary, and leaders did not wish to continue fighting.[22] Equally, those who subscribe to this way of thinking believe that those states that lose the capacity to assert and defend their sovereignty will fall by the wayside as they are annexed by the strong and reincorporated into other states.[23]

A model of state emergence derived from this vision of Westphalia and a Hobbesian logic of state survival provides one potential explanation for the success and failure of nascent states today. If the state is a human community that successfully claims a monopoly on the legitimate use of force within a given territory and over a particular population, then only those groups legitimately controlling both the people and the territory they claim should achieve full statehood.[24] Proto-states incapable of asserting and defending their authority will not be accepted into the community of states, nor will those who convincingly demonstrate domestic control and authority be excluded from participation. The structure of the system instituted at Westphalia initially produced and now consistently reproduces the same pattern of state emergence. But the empirical evidence offers only qualified support for this interpretation.

---

[21] See, for example, James (1986, p. 203); Roeder (2007, p. 22).

[22] Indeed, as Parker outlines, a number of prior attempts at negotiated peace had fallen though (2001, pp. 202–207).

[23] Kaufman (1997) makes this point explicitly (pp. 117–123). This dynamic, however, is also in the spirit of most prominent Hobbesian conceptions of the international system. Each state's desire for security compels it to continually seek the power to achieve that end. States unable to compete will fail (resulting in Waltz's expectation that states will be "like units"). For examples, see Jervis (1976), Waltz (1979), Keohane (1984), and Glaser (1997). It might also be the case that states seek power, but they seek more than security seeking would dictate (Schweller 1996; Mearsheimer 2001).

[24] Weber (1919/2004).

If only those states capable of independently ensuring their own survival remained solvent, we would see a high rate of predation of the weak on behalf of the strong, including high rates of state failure among so-called quasi- and micro-states. Or perhaps these states never should have entered the system to begin with. Between 1816 and 2011, though, only 48 states exited the system whereas 220 new states entered it.[25] The exits were mostly new unions, as in Germany, Yemen, and Tanzania, or the result of destruction and reconstitution following the world wars.[26] It is not very difficult for states to survive. In actuality, they rarely "die."[27] With regard to new states in particular, we cannot explain the end of empire and the entry of postcolonial states with the bottom-up logic of self-assertion alone.[28] In a seeming paradox of the first intuitive model, many of the most viable self-asserting anti-colonial regimes faced the least acceptance from member states. For example, Katanga and Biafra waged fierce anti-colonial wars against their home states but won little to no external support in return. Nor do most other state births fit the hypothesized pattern. If self-assertion determined statehood, then Poland, Croatia, East Timor, South Sudan, and many others would not be states today. Although the relative importance of de facto control and authority is certainly worthy of further investigation, additional explanatory factors must be brought to bear in order to understand states' emergence and endurance in the contemporary world. The second, less common interpretation of the Westphalian Peace provides additional insight.

SOCIAL DETERMINANTS OF STATE EMERGENCE

The alternative understanding of Westphalia attributes greater importance to the social milieu surrounding the peace. It suggests that states did not predate Westphalia, but instead that the peace treaties simultaneously created both system and states; establishing mutual equality as rightful negotiators consecrated statehood for Westphalia's delegates. Consequently, scholarly adherents of this historical view also believe international society has an important independent effect on modern state emergence. For these scholars, "recognition of and by states operationalizes sovereignty on both sides."[29] Societal acceptance is an important cause, rather than a consequence, of statehood. States cannot be separated from the system; they are mutually, socially constituted.

---

[25] According to Correlates of War: System Membership Data. The author added South Sudan as an entrant in 2011. Fazal (2007) finds a similar pattern, but observes more entries and exits than do the COW data because she expands the set of states to include all actors that have concluded treaties with France and Britain.

[26] As in the cases of Germany, Japan, Austria, Poland, Czechoslovakia, Hungary, Greece, Yugoslavia, and a number of other states following World War II.

[27] Waltz (1979, p. 95); The term "state death" is Fazal's (2007).

[28] Emerson (1960); indeed, many note the special exception made for postcolonial states.

[29] Onuf (1994, p. 17).

By establishing a legal, anti-hegemonic order at Westphalia, representatives to the peace negotiations created both states and system. In fact, the 212 negotiators endowed with external sovereignty at Westphalia were a motley crew in terms of governmental capacity. Many of them could not and did not achieve exclusive, legitimate internal authority. It is anachronistic to assert that each delegate represented was sovereign prior to the negotiations.[30] For example, territories within the Holy Roman Empire still had obligations to it, but they were nevertheless granted equivalent participation as independent plenipotentiaries. So even though it is true that governmental structures preceded the peace, those governments' positions and roles with reference to the external environment and the populations they governed were fundamentally altered upon their mutual, Europe-wide acceptance as states.

It was at Westphalia that states, to the exclusion of other units, became the "people" of the international system.[31] And the state's personhood was determined by both preexisting features and external social acceptance. Units not acknowledged as rightful states (as non-European governments would come to discover during colonial expansion) were not afforded an equivalent standard of treatment by the community.[32] Non-states inhabited a far more dangerous external environment than states did.[33]

A number of prominent theories of international relations argue similarly that international society influences the contemporary character of international politics through institutions, regimes, systemic cultures, and/or norms.[34] Whereas states themselves are conceived of as objective units of political authority by nearly all, the social world – constructed by states themselves – is thought to affect states' characters, actions, and interactions with one another.[35] States are obvious physical realities, but they are not impenetrable or unaffected by their external environment. According to Wendt, states are "self-organizing" for the most part, but this "does not mean they are not [socially] constructed... to a significant extent."[36] Logically this should be true along both the internal and the external dimension. Alternative conceptions of the international system's dynamics like these – rooted in the less common interpretation of

---

[30] Osiander (2001).

[31] Wendt (2004, pp. 289–316). One might also think of this as the moment that endowed states with international legal personality.

[32] Nonrecognized actors' territories and populations were often considered *terra nullius*, or "no man's lands," even though this was obviously not the case. Recognition by actors other than those within the European system also did not imply statehood.

[33] Strang (1990).

[34] Krasner (1982); Krasner(1982); Onuf (1994); Giddens (1994); Rittberger (1993); Wendt (1999); Finnemore (1998); Finnemore and Sikkink (1998); Bull (1977); Buzan, Jones and Little (1993); Jackson (1990); Wight (1991).

[35] The classic articulation of this idea is Gourevitch (1978). The article argues that systemic conditions affect the character of states just as the states themselves constitute the system.

[36] Wendt (1999, pp. 73–74). Social construction occurs domestically within the state and externally vis-à-vis other states.

Westphalia – seem to provide a more descriptively accurate account of state emergence, namely, that statehood is at least partially determined by external social influences and that the requisites for external legitimacy are set by the existing community.

Social constructivists take social acceptance to be an important determinant of statehood. Philpott, for example, posits that revolutions in sovereignty have changed the character of the international system and its members over time.[37] Of particular interest to this project, he says that the criteria for state membership in international society (which he terms the *second* face of sovereignty) have changed along with each revolution. He argues that, historically, revolutionary ideas initiated systemic changes during Westphalia, decolonization, and the rise of minority protections and through the creation of the EU. And that each set of understandings significantly altered the qualities required for system membership and the new members embraced as states during their dominance. Unfortunately, little systematic evidence is provided to show that the pattern of new state members complied with the changing standards outlined.[38] Nor does the author show that most existing members of international society embraced the standards. Nevertheless, the observable implications of this theory fit the pattern of modern state emergence better than the alternative, bottom-up domestic sovereignty model does.

According to Wendt's constructivist articulation of systemic theory, state identities are shaped and reshaped by system-wide cultures via imitation and social learning in their interactions with other states.[39] State identities and interests are not "given." Instead, interests and patterns of interaction vary based on the way in which states define both themselves and others. Different dominant understandings of the social environment will, in turn, produce different patterns of relations among states. Wendt does not assume that systemic culture is perfectly and fully internalized by system members, however. Instead, different states may exhibit different degrees of internalization. In turn, it is these varied internalizations that cause variation in states' behavior, even when they face similar circumstances.

---

[37] Philpott (1995, 2001).

[38] Indeed, the author's standards for membership post-Westphalia – "a viable government, control within their territory, the ability to make and carry out treaties... [and] a Christian culture" (p. 160) – are nowhere to be found within the treaty, nor do they appear (save the Christianity requirement) in any definition of the state agreed to before 1933's Montevideo Convention on the Rights and Duties of States. As Browlie (1990) contends, "The question of the types and number of the units comprising the states system was faced in diplomatic and political practice but not as a question of principle [before the twentieth century]." This is a large temporal gap. In addition, the set of all potential states must be surveyed, not only the set of states that secured sovereign independence. The sample is biased. In order to adequately test the author's proposition, we must also ask, "Why not Biafra or Rhodesia?" The potential bias resulting from selection on the dependent variable will be discussed at length later in this chapter regarding research design.

[39] Wendt (1999).

Finally, members of the English School also propose an important social component to the interstate system. Among them, Bull argues that, although not fully formed, the elements of an international society exist within the anarchical international environment. Expanding on the Grotian international-ist position, he contends that

> states…are bound by the rules and institutions of the society they form…they are not only bound by prudence, but also by imperatives of morality and law…at no point can it be said that the conception of common interests of states, of common rules accepted and common institutions worked by them, has ceased to exert an influence.[40]

We can infer from the three examples of socially oriented theories discussed that the normative prescriptions and proscriptions of international society should influence which proto-states will succeed to become states and which will fail. According to this prospective model of contemporary state emergence, interna-tional society's acceptance is a fundamental component of any actor's realizing full statehood. Still, the mechanism by which society exerts an influence on nascent states remains unspecified, as are the norms and conventions by which that international society operates.

RECOGNITION AND STATE EMERGENCE

An institutionalist understanding of statehood provides a potential mechanism of social influence regarding new states in the form of external recognition. According to one such scholar, "States are not individually empowered sover-eign actors… who *then* establish relations with each other. Rather, notions of sovereignty imply a state society founded on mutual recognition. The status of each state is thus tied up with that of the others in a continuing process of mutual legitimation."[41] Mutual recognition is an essential component of group mem-bership according to both social theory and sociology. So if mutual recognition is essential to maintaining and reproducing the society of existing states, it should be equally, if not more, important to nascent states. In order to function as a complete member of any social group, one needs not only to identify with that group, but must also be recognized as a rightful member by other group members. Whereas mutual recognition may be less important in some social groups, for instance, those in which anyone and everyone is welcome, it is especially important in high-status groups where admission is exclusive and accorded to only a select subset of the many who desire membership. State membership in the international system is just that kind of exclusive group.

Think of Greek fraternities and sororities as an instructive analogy. Once an individual is a member of one of these social/academic clubs, it is quite easy to distinguish members from nonmembers by their behavior. Only members attend

---

[40] Bull (1977, pp. 25, 40).
[41] Strang (1990, p. 148), emphasis in orignal.

their organization's meetings, wear clothing with Greek letters on it, and participate in other common rituals. It is more difficult however, to identify who will or will not become a member by assessing a given college's entire first-year class. Some individuals will have characteristics that may predispose them to the desire to participate in fraternity or sorority life: a sibling or parent has done so, they have a particular personality type, or perhaps the group will create professional networking opportunities. But an estimate based on these characteristics would be quite rough. Once the students have actually demonstrated their intent to become associated with the organization by pledging, the odds of correctly predicting whether or not they will be permitted to join goes up, but it is still not fully determined. Some pledges will have a leg up on the others: they may be legacy admits, they may have special talents that make them more attractive to the existing members such as academic or athletic prestige, or they might have impressive endurance throughout the hazing period.

Whatever the inherent qualities of the various students, whether or not a pledge eventually becomes a member rests solely on the judgments of existing members. Indeed, even the qualities judged attractive are subject to the individual members' tastes. Pledges cannot be members based on self-identification alone, nor can their talents or personal attributes alone secure their admission; their brothers or sisters must recognize them. Once individuals do become members of the group, in subsequent years they, too, will make decisions about which new pledges will be accepted.

So it is with states in the international system. Though system membership is of far greater consequence than membership in a fraternity or sorority, we first come to know actors as states because they are recognized as such by established members of the system. Actors may demonstrate a number of qualities indicative of internal sovereignty: standing militaries, popular authority, a system of taxation, contested elections, heads of government, and other officials. Without recognition, those actors may be many things: secessionists, liberation movements, insurgents, anti-colonialists, terrorists, ethnic rebels, or indigenous peoples, but they may not be states. All aspirants believe they warrant recognition as rightful members of the community, but they lack the necessary external component. Without external recognition, even the most internally sovereign actor cannot function as a state outside of its borders.

In this vein, Strang finds, consistent with the institutionalist conception of sovereignty, that political units without status are much more likely to be preyed on and made subordinate to states than those deemed legitimate members of the international community. He observes that in the more than five centuries of Western expansion, "only 11 non-European polities recognized as sovereign have been formally subordinated as dependencies... [and] have merged or dissolved only 15 times."[42] Among those not recognized by the Western states,

---

[42] Ibid., p. 154. It should be noted that Strang observes instability only within non-European actors from 1415 to 1987.

international instability (colonization, merger, and secession) has been rampant. Strang concludes that international society mitigates the effects of Hobbesian anarchy for its members.

Based on the empirics alone though, it remains unclear *why* recognized actors are more stable than their unrecognized counterparts. It may be that recognition and membership within the international society of states provides stability and legitimacy, as Strang suggests. Or the causal relationship could be reversed; it could be the case that only internally viable actors (i.e., those capable of exercising domestic sovereignty) are recognized as states to begin with, as the more popular, bottom-up model of statehood implies. If sovereignty and viability were the primary considerations underlying recognition, the common wisdom regarding state emergence would hold and external legitimacy would merely be a consequence of stable domestic governance. Nevertheless, the formal exchange of recognition between existing states and nascent states is a useful indicator of societal acceptance. The precise causal relationship between internal and external sovereignty will receive further attention throughout the book.

INTERNATIONAL LAW, THE STATE, AND RECOGNITION

Though largely overlooked by political scientists, international law takes recognition's influence seriously. In fact, the practice is foundational to the law. The exchange of formal recognition between leaders serves as the basis for lawful diplomatic relations between states. Because recognition is consequential, its theoretical significance for statehood and its appropriate use are hotly contested.[43] The legal debate over recognition, as in international relations, consists of two opposed views of external legitimacy and its consequences for statehood. On one side are those who argue for a declaratory conception of recognition and on the other, those who support a constitutive understanding (see Figure 2.3).[44] Unlike their peers in political science though, lawyers' convictions are significantly influenced by the normative ramifications of their theories; jurists are not only seeking to explain how the world works, but are also staking their claim as to how it should work.

Advocates of the declaratory theory believe that states exist independent of their recognition as such by other states. In this sense, recognition is simply a declaration or formal acknowledgment of what already objectively is (hence *declaratory*). The other side, favoring a constitutive conception of recognition, has a more constructivist or institutionalist articulation of the state in mind. These scholars argue recognition itself is a vital component of statehood, "the

---

[43] For an excellent synopsis of the debate, see Grant (1999, chapter 1). For direct contributions to the debate, see Brownlie (1983); Crawford (1979); Lauterpacht (1947), Oppenheim (1955), and Peterson (1982). In addition, see the remaining citations in this section.

[44] More detailed discussions of the two schools of thought are Grant (1999, pp. 1–45); Crawford (1979, pp. 16–23); Brownlie (1990, pp. 87–88); Lauterpacht (1947).

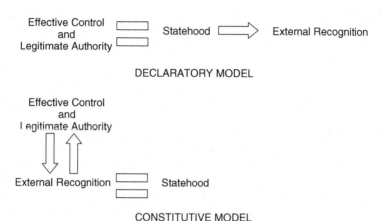

FIGURE 2.3 Two Models of State Emergence

[state is] viewed as having its genesis in recognition."[45] Without external recognition, there is no state. The theoretical differences over recognition's meaning and significance for the constitution of states inform each side's opinion about how recognition is most appropriately practiced.

Proponents of the constitutive conception of statehood see recognition as the primary demarcation between states and other, non-state actors in international affairs. Constitutive theorists do not argue issues of state capacity and popular legitimacy should be ignored, but they do argue that without recognition, these domestic factors are wielded to little effect in international relations. External sovereignty is a prerequisite for conducting much of the fundamental business of international affairs. Furthermore, constitutive theories suggest recognition should be at the unique discretion of the recognizing state. A state may choose to decide unilaterally, without reference to its peers or to the new state's capacity. Or it may choose to recognize only in consultation with other states and only once a certain level of competent authority and legitimacy has been achieved within the new state. In any case, the decision to recognize is solely that of each sovereign.

Most legal scholars find the constitutivists' prescription for recognition problematic. They see little room for the constitutive theory of recognition within international law because it ascribes a political, rather than a legal, character to recognition. If it is appropriate for each state to determine its own practice of recognition, then there is no room for external jurisdiction or oversight regarding those decisions. Accordingly, "The constitutive doctrine, casting recognition as a device of statecraft, a tool of *Realpolitik*, available to forge states out of communities at the will of the recognizing state, provides no apparent means to

[45] Grant (1999).

regulate state conduct and, in any event, no apparent code of conduct."[46] For many international jurists, constitutive scholars' conceptualization of recognition is both "unprincipled" and "morally unsatisfying."[47]

The declaratory model stands in contrast to the constitutive model's inherent politics and argues for a moral and legal doctrine of recognition rooted in objective state capacity. Advocates of a declaratory understanding see recognition as a reaction by states acknowledging another state's (already achieved) internal sovereignty and statehood. Whereas the constitutive model leaves little role for structures of supranational authority and international law, the declaratory doctrine attempts to make recognition wholly legalistic and nearly automatic upon an actor's achievement of a certain standard of domestic authority and control. Because declaratory theorists see recognition as a response to the objective existence of other states, these scholars' project includes articulating a set of universal legal conditions under which recognition of statehood is appropriate – or even required – of the international community. The motivation behind the standards is that a list of benchmarks would enable the law to discriminate between appropriate (objective and legal) and inappropriate (subjective or political and illegal) grants of recognition. This task has proven difficult.

The most widely accepted set of definitive qualities is found within the *Inter-American Convention on the Rights and Duties of States* (hereafter referred to as Montevideo).[48] The Montevideo criteria suggest that states are those actors that (1) have a permanent population, (2) occupy a permanently defined territory, (3) have an effective government, and (4) demonstrate the ability to engage in international relations with other states.[49] Additional standards have been proposed but have received only equivocal support. Some potential addenda to Montevideo include a commitment and ability to abide by international laws, independence, democracy, good governance, and special protections for minorities.[50] The definition of statehood provided by Montevideo is not unreasonable. However, its standards remain ambiguous and too easily manipulable to serve states' ulterior motives.[51] They are not explicit enough to ensure that politics does not seep into leaders' grants of recognition. Indeed, even those attempting to abide by the standards might reasonably disagree about whether or not an actor had fulfilled the requirements.[52]

---

[46] Ibid., p. 3
[47] Ibid., pp. 3–4.
[48] Organization of American States (1933), Convention on the Rights and Duties of States.
[49] Ibid.
[50] Crawford (1979); Duursma (1996); Fawcett (1968); Lehning (1998).
[51] Goldsmith and Posner (2005) argue that even state behavior consistent with the dictates of international law is often predicated on self-interest rather than normative internalization, habit, or concern for morality where the predicted outcomes are equifinal (p. 225).
[52] Kurtulus (2002, pp. 760–762) demonstrates exactly this ambiguity in his discussion of James.

Even if the efforts of declaratory theorists are not found wanting and a satisfactory operational definition of the state could be articulated, legal theories are largely normative and prescriptive rather than positive and descriptive. The most pressing difficulty for declaratory theorists comes from states' own objections to the declaratory interpretation of recognition. Most leaders do not see the criteria outlined in Montevideo as the definitive definition of statehood, nor do they agree that recognition should be anything other than a political decision. Leaders tend to see recognition as the unique purview of the recognizer and not as a legal obligation.[53] The recognition standards currently on the books are applied inconsistently and not enforced.[54] Even among the members of the Organization of American States, legally bound to the specific standards of statehood in Montevideo, there is still support for political discretion in recognition.[55] In practice, leaders are hesitant to submit to the idealistic legalism of the declaratory school.

The normative debate over recognition among legal scholars dovetails nicely with discussions of statehood in international relations. Both legal articulations of the state acknowledge a social component to statehood, manifest in recognition, but disagree about its relative causal importance. A declaratory theorist sees states as mostly self-organizing, undeniable political facts, whereas a constitutive theorist would see statehood in general, but especially external sovereignty, as a product of recognition. The argument supported by declaratory theorists is similar to bottom-up conceptualizations of the state in international relations; states are recognized because they meet the Weberian ideal. The constitutive conception, on the other hand, is more akin to socially oriented theories. Widespread external recognition constitutes external sovereignty, which is fundamental to statehood.

The argument I advance in this project is not a challenge to legal theories of statehood or the conception of the state common to international relations theory. I am agnostic with respect to the proper use of recognition among states.[56] Similarly, a static, objectivist definition of the state is useful and often necessary for theory. On any given day, there are very few actors in the international system whose statehood is uncertain once achieved. The members of the United Nations are not up for debate; their statehood is an undeniable material and social fact.

What I do suggest is that shifting our gaze to the period just prior to state emergence challenges our intuitive understanding of how and why new states enter the international system. The external legitimacy accorded to proto-states through recognition is pivotal to their eventual statehood, elevating the statuses

---

[53] Grant (1999, pp. 22–23).
[54] Halperin, Schaffer, and Small (1992, p. 46).
[55] Ibid., p. 24.
[56] In practice, the different understandings have important consequences for the character of states and the international system.

of a few and acquiescing to the subjugation of the many. Although authoritative domestic control is usually sufficient cause for an actor to realize external recognition and sovereignty, it is not necessary. And actors who might be states, but whose fates are still uncertain will realize recognition's greatest effects.

RECOGNITION IN PRACTICE

Leaders and international lawyers agree that recognition is motivated, at least in part, by political considerations rather than international law.[57] Most political scientists do not ascribe much importance to recognition though, because it is thought to carry little practical weight. Whether or not a state exists is obvious. The nonrecognition of the People's Republic of China (PRC) by the United States until 1978 did not vitiate China's domestic authority. Nor did Turkey's unilateral recognition of the Turkish Republic of Northern Cyprus secure its position as a state. By the same logic, a secessionist group that successfully demonstrates functional independent authority will be unambiguous, and recognition, though perhaps political, will not significantly influence its statehood. Among the most skeptical like Krasner, the entire institution of sovereignty is hypocritical and in practice affords few of the protections it promises in theory. It is unsurprising that leaders might attempt to use recognition to their political advantage. It is an organizing principle, but it is not particularly meaningful one.[58]

International law generally assigns more practical importance to recognition, but politically motivated recognition is both prohibited by law and not legally binding when granted. Premature recognition has no legal effect and nonrecognition is merely a matter of diplomatic relations among states. Neither determines statehood. According to the most popular, declaratory interpretation in international law, a state exists apart from its recognition as such by other states.

The contemporary dynamics of state emergence belie the superficial and subsidiary roles attributed to the politics of external recognition in international relations and law. Perhaps the declaratory theory of recognition and statehood is both technically correct and normatively right; external recognition does not and should not *legally* determine statehood. Recognition does, however, determine whether or not statehood can be exercised in any *practical* sense within the international community. Without recognition, an actor cannot even access forums such as international courts, where it might be able to vindicate its rights, because of its lack of diplomatic relations.[59]

To cite but one example, the de facto independent republic of Somaliland is beset with problems as a result of its unrecognized status. Somaliland has been independent since the ouster of former president Siad Barre and the start of

---

[57] Whether or not it should be political is contested.

[58] Krasner (1999).

[59] Witness, for example, the cases of the Baltic states, annexed illegally but nevertheless not able to assert independence because of their lack of recognized authority.

Somalia's civil war in 1991. It has been a relatively stable, domestically legitimate authority within the borders of the old British Somaliland since at least 1996. The government conducts independently monitored local and national elections, recently enacted a new constitution, has a functioning police force, and governs itself in a far more functional manner than its Somali home state.[60] Secessionist Somaliland meets the legal criteria for statehood in every respect, but it is not recognized by any other state.[61]

The problems of unrecognized proto-states such as Somaliland range from mundane day-to-day issues to matters of high politics. Even seemingly small bureaucratic arrangements between states can have large effects on the unrecognized. In a particularly telling instance, Somaliland's government revenues collapsed in 1998, dropping from $45 to $27 million USD, when Saudi Arabia banned Somaliland's livestock because the health certificates its government issued were no longer "internationally recognized."[62] Somaliland's Mohamoud Daar explains,

> To some, the lack of recognition of a nation might imply the absence of a diplomatic corps, of embassies, of VIP rooms and limousines. To the average Somalilander, however, the lack of recognition of the Republic of Somaliland means no classrooms for children, no health care facilities to ward off avoidable illnesses and pregnancy-related deaths, no street lighting and no technical assistance to de-mine the feeder roads.[63]

Though the Republic of Somaliland unambiguously meets the legal standards for statehood, so long as the states in international society are not willing to recognize its independence, Somaliland's internal sovereignty means little for its external affairs. It cannot assert itself as a state any further than it already has. Somaliland's progress toward statehood has plateaued. And yet, it is not a full member of international society. It may be able to defend itself against outside invaders (such as those from neighboring Puntland who contest the Sool and Sanaag regions), but it has no legal standing on which to do so under international law. As far as most outsiders are concerned, Somaliland is simply one of many "clan factions" in Somalia's chaotic civil war. Finally, even maintaining Somaliland's internal sovereignty is imperiled without external recognition. It will not be afforded the resources, exclusively reserved for states, that might ensure its survival. Indeed, most of the international community is effectively subverting Somaliland's authority by supporting Somalia's Transitional Federal Government (TFG) in Mogadishu.

---

[60] Bradbury (2008); Lewis (2010); Herbst (2004).

[61] This is not meant to imply that Somaliland is a strong state by any means, nor that it is without internal governance problems of its own. However, if forced to choose which actor looked more like a state according to domestic control and authority, Somalia or Somaliland, the latter is the clear choice.

[62] Schoiswohl (2004, p. 184).

[63] Daar, cited in ibid.

Alternatively, recognition has many rewards for its recipients. Recognized states benefit from advantages unavailable to the unrecognized. These benefits take the form of tangible goods and political influence. Only recognized states may make binding military, economic, or other treaties with other states.[64] Only recognized states can be full members of intergovernmental organizations (IGOs) such as the United Nations.[65] Recognized states are also uniquely able to bring grievances against other states for violations of international law at the International Court of Justice (ICJ). Similarly, only recognized states may receive loans from organizations such as the International Monetary Fund (IMF) and World Bank. Foreign direct investment (FDI) is almost exclusively limited to recognized states, and international trade flows and foreign aid tend to be filtered though recognized governments and states as well. All states benefit from their peers' recognition. Even Krasner, a vocal critic of sovereignty, agrees that external recognition confers important advantages:

> Rulers have almost universally sought...recognition. Recognition has provided them with resources and opportunities that can enhance their chances of remaining in power. Recognition can pave the way for membership within international organizations, some of which provide financial aid; can facilitate the conclusion of treaties; can increase the chances that their initiatives will not be challenged in other countries' courts because of the act of state doctrine and the principle of sovereign immunity; and can increase domestic political support. Rarely does recognition carry costs.[66]

Recognition's practical significance has gained some attention regarding African states. For example, Jackson suggests external recognition and the opportunities that come along with it allow new, weak states to consolidate their domestic power base where little existed before.[67] These states did not enter into the system fully established. Instead, many African states entered only partially formed in terms of capacity and governance, but with the external legitimacy and substantive benefits provided by membership, those states become increasingly similar to the Weberian ideal.[68] Thus in postcolonial

---

[64] Though signing a treaty with a previously unrecognized state constitutes implicit recognition according to international law, it does not occur often (Von Glahn 1992, pp. 89–90). In addition, many states object to any inference of recognition where it has not been expressly granted de jure.

[65] There are presently two non-member states of the United Nations, The Holy See (Vatican City) and the State of Palestine (http://www.un.org/en/members/nonmembers.shtml). These actors are only credited with observer status, however, and may not vote. In addition, some states (India, Philippines, Belarus, and Ukraine among them) were permitted entry into the UN and League of Nations (LN) prior to independence. These were exceptions to the norm. In some cases, like those of so-called micro-states, membership in international organizations provides far greater clout than territory and population would dictate (e.g., Luxembourg and Vanuatu).

[66] Krasner (1999, p. 223).

[67] Jackson (1990).

[68] This model also fits the pattern of new statehood (or reconstituted statehood) following the world wars. A top-down process of legitimacy preceded domestic authority and control. Orentlicher (1998) discusses this process at length as does Emerson (1960) in Chapter 2, "The Era of the Two World Wars," pp. 22–36.

regions where independent statehood is a relatively new phenomenon, borders have been highly resistant to change. New states have not emerged because of the powerful legitimating effects conferred on existing states by widespread external recognition.

Herbst, also an Africanist, agrees with Jackson's portrayal of African states as propped up by external sovereignty and internally deficient. However, in most cases he does not foresee progress toward domestic consolidation and effective sovereignty, rather he predicts that these states will languish and fail.[69] Herbst argues that Africa's relative external stability has been disastrous for many of its peoples because strict adherence to the territorial status quo has precluded the emergence of smaller, less corrupt, and more competent and responsive states. As a remedy, he suggests decertification or de-recognition for African states found unwilling or incapable of functional governance. The recommendation is extreme. It is unheard of for governments to go so far as to revoke recognition. In extraordinary circumstances, they might sever diplomatic relations or transfer recognition, but their support of that state's legal personality remains intact. When failed African states lose their legitimacy, Herbst argues, order will emerge organically to replace the current disorder. Once leaders enact decertification, he further recommends that recognition be granted only to stable, internally legitimate proto-states like Somaliland in order to ensure that Africa's failed state problem does not recur.[70]

Still others argue that Jackson's and Herbst's dualist understanding of statehood, old sovereignty premised on effective control and new sovereignty based on external legitimacy, mistakes consistency for change. Österud is emblematic, "Recognition by practical interchange was constitutive in nineteenth-century Europe, and the empirical qualities of recognized states were extremely variable and often precarious, as indeed they remain for many old states today."[71] So perhaps external acceptance is, and has been, a fundamental attribute of sovereignty for all states, not just the weak and postcolonial. He continues, "There is definitely a split between 'empirical statehood' at one end of the scale, and 'states by courtesy' at the other. But there is, as always, a fairly contingent relationship between position on this scale and admission to the state system."[72]

TOWARD A SOCIAL THEORY OF SECESSION AND STATEHOOD

After reviewing the literature on statehood in international relations and international law, it is clear both lack a full appreciation of the dynamics and

[69] Herbst (2000) argues that the European model of statehood is at odds with patterns of traditional authority in Africa, patterns more suited to Africa's population geography and natural resource availability. Some African states can successfully conform to the European ideal, but others face seemingly insurmountable obstacles.

[70] Herbst (1996–7, 2004).

[71] Österud (1997, p. 182).

[72] Ibid., p.182.

determinants of state emergence. In international relations, near exclusive use of a bottom-up model of statehood can be traced to a prevailing interest in the politics among states and an aspiration to theoretical elegance and parsimony. Though many strands of scholarship argue that international society has important, top-down effects, not one articulates a theory of state emergence incorporating that dynamic. And, as previously discussed, some suggestive theories in this vein do not provide compelling empirical tests of their claims. In international law, the potential political determinants of statehood are dismissed because of scholars' normative desire to advance legal efficacy. There is a strand of legal theory articulating a constitutive, political conception of statehood and recognition. However, jurists have largely discredited the approach because the resulting practice of recognition would not fall under the purview of international law.

In this project, I argue ignorance of top-down social influences on state emergence is to the detriment of international relations theory and the contemporary politics of nationalism. New states emerge as a result of both internal self-assertion and external acceptance. New states can and do become members of the international system that could not and did not effectively control and govern their territories beforehand. The causal model implicit to most conceptions of statehood is overly simplistic and misleading. Most states do not consolidate their authority first and then assert themselves as states on the international stage. Instead, the relationship between internal control and external sovereignty is more complex. The exchange of recognition is no mere token; it constitutes external statehood. In most every case of state emergence, the subjective understandings and political motivations of existing states factor into whether and when an aspiring actor will become a full member of the international system.

RECOGNITION DETERMINANTS

It is clear that without recognition, the pattern of modern state emergence is unintelligible. What remain unclear are the motives behind states' recognition decisions. Do leaders attempt to abide by the Weberian, legal conception of statehood, prioritizing de facto control and authority over other considerations? Do they attempt to forward their parochial political interests? Or do they attempt to satisfy both somehow? I argue that recognizing states do not disregard governmental capacity and territorial control entirely, but that they are also significantly motivated by their own self-interests. In order to add rigor to previous theories employing self-interest, I test a number of potential instantiations of interest, identifiable a priori, to explore their precise influence on states' recognition decisions.

Like the determinants, the dynamics of recognition among states are also underdeveloped. Leaders overwhelmingly agree that recognition is their sovereign right, rather than a matter of international law. However, there is reason to suspect recognition might not be wholly independent and unilateral. I propose that it is, in fact, ordered and strategically coordinated. Leaders feel compelled to coordinate external recognition in order to maintain their social standing and security, to maintain international stability, and to reproduce the state-centric international order. First, isolated recognition is risky and potentially costly. A state that unilaterally recognizes a secessionist proto-state does so in violation of the home state's external sovereignty. This is not only intervention and a breach of international law, but also a *casus belli* (cause for war). Indeed, a young United States threatened war when confronted with possible French or British recognition of the Confederacy.[73] At the very least, unilateral recognition is cause for the home state to sever diplomatic relations with the recognizer, as China routinely does for states that recognize Taiwan. More likely, the home state will seek additional, more drastic retribution. In short, the potential bene-fits flowing from relations with a new state would have to outweigh substantial costs in order to make unilateral recognition attractive.

Second, unilateral recognition is an ineffective means of securing sovereignty for the nascent state. Membership within the international community can be conceptualized as conforming to a threshold model of sorts (see Figure 2.4). Each state's recognition of an aspiring member increases the probability that the actor will become a state, but the individual recognition decisions mean little in isolation. Only once a certain threshold of recognitions has been reached is the actor endowed with the full rights and responsibilities of a state. A new state need not secure every other state's recognition, but it must receive it from a critical mass. Unilateral recognition implies legal consequences only for the

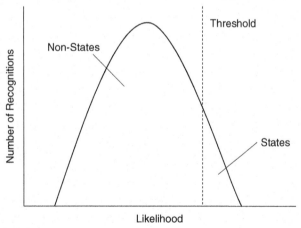

FIGURE 2.4 External Sovereignty

[73] The threat, made by Lincoln's Foreign Secretary W. H. Seward, was perhaps more bellicose than Lincoln's response would have been. See Goebel (1915, pp.180, 185–186).

single state that has conferred it. All other states will continue to support the status quo and recognize the home state's jurisdiction over the secessionists' affairs. Any recognizing state truly desiring a nascent state's success would not do so without the expectation that others would follow and that, ultimately, the critical threshold would be surpassed.[74]

Similarly, because unilateral recognition flies in the face of international consensus, it will likely cause conflict with states other than the home state. For Germany, the mere impression that it unilaterally recognized Slovenia and Croatia led to rocky relations with the rest of the European Community (EC).[75]

Finally, the system's organization creates pressures that favor the status quo, making leaders wary of contested or overlapping sovereignty, and this reluctance toward change should encourage coordination over unilateralism. Because the Westphalian order relies on the twin principles of exclusive territorial control and nonintervention, states recognizing different authorities' jurisdiction over the same territory and population are inherently destabilizing. Cases of multiple sovereignty, Kashmir and Israel-Palestine among them, constitute some of the world's most precarious conflicts. Strong states should resist destabilizing the established order, not only because it is potentially destructive for the states and non-state actors directly involved, but also because recognizing states derive significant power and authority from the dominance and stability of the Westphalian system.

In sum, states have competing impulses when it comes to recognition. One is toward unilateral, competitive recognition in service of parochial interests; the other is toward multilateral, coordinated recognition to serve both short- and longer-term goals. When states' parochial interests all point toward the same preference for or against recognition of a new member, the outcome is straightforward and coordination is easily achieved. States will recognize consistent with the international consensus. Those proto-states winning external favor will be elevated into the international community of states. Those without acceptance will remain subject to their home states.

When leaders disagree about whether or not recognition should be granted, the outcome is less certain. The most likely result is stalemate and inaction, which strongly favor the status quo. Leaders will recognize their divergent preferences, and so long as the potential benefits of unilateral recognition do not outweigh the costs of international fracture, they will uphold the home state's sovereignty. Recognition, if it occurs at all, will be delayed indefinitely

---

[74] Unless, perhaps, as India did with the nascent Bangladesh, the patron is willing to take more drastic measures to realize that state's independence, in that case, waging a full-scale war against the home state. It is also worth mentioning that in some cases, states do recognize without the expectation that others will follow, for example, Turkey's recognition of Northern Cyprus and Albania's recognition of Kosovo. In these cases, however, recognition was granted in protest or as a sign of solidarity, without the expectation that others would follow and without the expectation that the secessionist movement would be treated as a state.

[75] Libal (1997, preface).

and only be granted after the nascent state unambiguously meets the established legal criteria. Leaders may even defer recognition until the home state acquiesces to the secessionists.

In the less likely alternative, when the benefits of maintaining international unity are lower than the potential gains from relations with the secessionist state, leaders might break into two camps with one group granting the secessionists recognition and the other maintaining relations with the home state. This dynamic is destabilizing and dangerous as demonstrated in proxy wars between the Great Powers (e.g., Vietnam, Korea, and Afghanistan). Until 2008, oppositional recognition by powerful states had not occurred since the end of the Cold War. Fracture is most likely when the international order itself is contested. Because powerful states are not invested in maintaining stability in their own relations with one another under these circumstances, the costs of breaking ranks over recognition are relatively low. Sacrificing international order is more costly for status quo states, benefiting from stability and wary of raising the ire of their peers.

CORE CONCEPTS AND DEFINITIONS

Before delving into the specifics of the theory, its core concepts and objects of explanation require definitions. For instance, how do we observe recognition? Why study secessionism for a project on state emergence? And finally, how much recognition is necessary to become a state?

In a general sense, recognition is an acknowledgment of or perception of a phenomenon or condition. Oftentimes we equate recognition with simple perception. We recognize an acquaintance at our high school reunion (facial recognition) or the *Farmer's Almanac* helps us track weather conditions across time (pattern recognition). Other times, recognition has a more positive, status connotation. Individuals, for instance, receive communal prestige for achievement, *special recognition*. Unfortunately, the state and the system, indeed many of the most important concepts in IR, are not so easily seen and recognized in the traditional sense.[76] In the case of statehood, then, recognition should be equated with status.[77] *Mutual* recognition is a communication between at least two parties indicating acknowledgment of each other's status. It is social.

The recognition exchanged between states can take both implicit and explicit forms. Through normal diplomacy, leaders might implicitly acknowledge others' status as states. These practices include the extension of diplomatic privileges, such as exemption from prosecution, the signing of treaties, and the direct provision of aid according to international law.[78] In a more mundane

---

[76] Wendt (1999, p. 5).

[77] Recall, too, the inherent ambiguity in the legal standards for statehood.

[78] For an example, see Grant (1999, pp. 47–49), specifically the case of American Banana Co. v. United Fruit Co.

sense, they might also include laissez-faire behaviors such as the non-violation of territorial integrity or noninterference in domestic affairs. Most leaders, however, disagree that the extension of diplomatic privileges implies recognition when none has been formally granted. Tellingly, leaders often explicitly reaffirm that recognition has not been extended when their behavior may seem to imply otherwise. When Taiwanese President Lee Teng-hui visited his U.S. alma mater in 1995, the Clinton administration made certain that his informal visit was not misunderstood to be a diplomatic affair.[79] Lee received no reception at the White House on arrival and was not even permitted to meet with the president. The United States did not want Beijing to suspect it was supporting "creeping independence." Taiwan had not and would not receive recognition from the United States. Similarly, it was common practice during the age of colonial expansion for states to use treaties with indigenous populations to justify the transfer of their lands and treasure to Europeans. By signing treaties, the "exchange" was legitimate. Yet it is apparent that these episodes of normal diplomatic discourse were not intended to endow the indigenous peoples with sovereign equality. Instead, they were clearly temporally limited and instrumental.

Explicit formal recognition, then, rather than implicit recognition, presents the most incontrovertible evidence of international acceptance. Formal recognition can be granted by means of formal public statement or through formal documentation transmitted to the government of a new state. This method of recognition also activates a number of observable legal consequences: embassies are often established, members of diplomatic corps exchanged, and so on. It is, therefore, also easily discernable when it has or has not occurred. In most states, recognition is the unique purview of the executive, and leaders or high-level officials will make a public statement that recognition has been granted.

Deciding on a population of potential new states for this project was complicated. None of the readily available pools of actors offered as conceptually accurate and politically timely a proxy as did secessionist movements. A project on state emergence could use ethnic groups as a population of proto-states, but there are thousands of ethnic groups, many of which are without political aspirations or even a developed sense of ethnic consciousness. Additionally, many nationalist movements center on communal allegiances other than ethnicity, such as ideology (socialism or democracy) or geography (north vs. south or hills vs. plains). As the project aims to uncover why states recognize, the request or demand for recognition was a necessary prerequisite. A more limited group of ethnic identities might alleviate this problem, perhaps by selecting only "at-risk" minority communities as identified by the Minorities at Risk Project, but this population includes some of the same difficulties.[80] Not all minority

---

[79] "Clinton Assures China Ties Unchanged by Taiwan President's Visit." (Associated Press, June 9, 1995).

[80] Gurr (2000a, 2000b)

groups desire their own independent states; many prefer greater civil rights and/ or expanded autonomy. In addition, many proto-states would not fall within either the minority or the at-risk category.[81] Even separatist groups do not universally desire their own independent states. It is important to properly identify groups that want to be a part of the international community, not mere autonomy from their governments. Existing states rarely recognize actors that do not seek statehood themselves; using this population would effectively exclude variation on the dependent variable for many cases within the dataset.

As a result of the limitations in readily available datasets, I survey all movements, ethnic minority or otherwise, demanding independent statehood. This sample prioritizes national self-identification (consciousness) and the demand for statehood and external recognition. Ethnographic delineations are not synonymous with national identity. Gellner explains,

A mere category of persons (say, occupants of a given territory, or speakers of a given language, for example) becomes a nation if and when the members of the category firmly recognize certain mutual rights and duties to each other in virtue of their shared membership of it. It is their recognition of each other as fellows of this kind which turns them into a nation, and not the other shared attributes...which separate that category from non-members.[82]

Put more succinctly by Emerson, "The simplest statement that can be made about a nation is that it is a body of people who feel that they are a nation; and it may be that when all the fine-spun analysis is concluded this will be the ultimate statement as well."[83]

Finally, a study of secessionism is timely given the recent spate of deadly and highly politicized conflicts over independent statehood. Conflicts in Yugoslavia, the post-Soviet states, Somalia, China, India, Indonesia, Sri Lanka, Yemen, and Sudan have drawn international attention to the political dynamics of secession and state emergence.

A secessionist movement is a nationalist movement that seeks to wholly separate from the state of which it is formally a part (its home state) to form a newly independent state. Secessionism is distinct from other forms of civil conflict because of the group's stated goal. Groups that seek special status, increased autonomy, or additional civil rights short of formal governmental separation are not secessionist even if their message is nationalist. Similarly, movements that seek to join with other states (irredentists) or to overthrow the existing social structure or governing regime within a state (revolutionaries and putschists) are also not secessionist. Finally, movements seeking independent statehood that lack either a population (platform and human-made islands) or a

---

[81] East Bengal (Bangladesh), for example, did not meet the criteria established by Minorities At Risk as a minority-at-risk within Pakistan.

[82] Gellner (1983, p. 7).

[83] Emerson (1960, p. 102).

claim to territory (pirates and nomads) are also not considered to be secession-ist.[84] Secessionist movements can be violent or nonviolent, large or small, ethnic, geographic, or otherwise. All that they share in common is a desire for newly independent states of their own.

Thus far, the definition of secession follows its common language under-standing. In one respect however, this project departs significantly from com-mon usage because I also consider anti-colonial conflicts over independence to be instances of secessionism.[85] This project is concerned with the determinants and dynamics of new statehood. Tens of new states recently entered the interna-tional system following national separatist conflicts with their colonial gover-nors, so colonial secessions could not be excluded. Some former colonial territories gained their independence through relatively peaceful negotiations with their governors and received external recognition with little trouble, whereas other bids for independence met strong resistance from both their home states and the international community.[86] In many cases, multiple national separatist movements emerged from within a single colony, but only one group was granted authority upon independence. Similarly, colonies were split into independent states or merged together upon independence based on varied domestic circumstances. A comprehensive study of new statehood requires that all colonial bids for independence that are opposed by their imperial power be defined as secessions.[87]

This project employs Great Power recognition as a proxy for widespread external sovereignty. The Great Powers are the set of states with the greatest relative material capabilities.[88] Because of these extensive capabilities, they are also presumed to have the most relational power – or the potential to get others to do what they would not do otherwise.[89] Therefore, the Great Powers' recog-nition decisions likely exert the most influence over those of ordinary states, whose interests are not as extensive or global. The Great Powers' recognitions constitute the most critical of the critical mass required to surpass the threshold to secure external sovereignty. Additionally, because unilateral recognition is often risky and potentially costly, especially for small or weak states, most will be hesitant to recognize without Great Power endorsement. Great Power

[84] For additional information on these exclusions, see Appendix A.
[85] A dummy variable (COLONY) captures whether or not colonial secessions are significantly different from secessions in general when it comes to external recognition.
[86] Kahler (1984) provides a provocative domestic explanation for the variation in decolonization practices in Britain and France. Also see Emerson (1960).
[87] Colonies without nationalist movements prior to independence were not included in the study. The colonies excluded were primarily the new states of the former British West Indies. Britain initiated the move toward independence in the colonies omitted.
[88] Operationally, I define the Great Powers as outlined by the Correlates of War Project, see Appendix A.
[89] Dahl (1957, pp. 201–218).

recognition serves as a focal point around which the remaining states can coordinate their recognition. In short, Great Power recognition is taken to be indicative of both the direction and timing of recognition for most other states in the system. Finally, time, resources and data availability simply prohibited a more extensive survey of states' recognition decisions.

3

Research Design and Methodology

This project employs a multi-method, nested research framework in order to develop and test its theoretical propositions.[1] The project has two major parts, one quantitative and the other qualitative.[2] The large N analysis establishes broad relationships between the explanatory (interest) variables and the dependent (recognition) variable. Do leaders simply make recognition decisions consistent with their country's objective political interests? If so, which motives seem to be the most influential for each state? Do temporal dynamics influence the pattern of recognition? Following a nested approach, the quantitative tests come first. These analyses eliminate unsupported hypotheses and indicate which other, supported hypotheses are worthy of further study. Then, employing insights from the quantitative analysis, more finely tuned case studies investigate the casual process behind recognition. In particular, the cases investigate leaders' deliberations regarding recognition and the mechanisms by which state interests affect grants of recognition among the Great Powers. Together, discovering these determinants and dynamics suggest the character of the international system and help identify probable new members of international society.

Various potential motives behind recognition exist, but little scholarly attention has been directed toward the topic thus far. In this first study of its kind, I explore three broad logics that help explain Great Power recognition preferences in addition to the "facts on the ground" in a given secessionist conflict. First, leaders might recognize because of geostrategic or external security considerations. Another possibility is that leaders recognize based on considerations of

---

[1] In a nested design, large N, quantitative analyses act as a guide to case selection for small N case study research exploring the mechanism of independent variables' effects on the dependent variable(s). More information on the specific parameters of nested analysis can be found in Lieberman (2005, pp. 435–452).

[2] See King, Keohane, and Verba (1994, pp. 5–6) on the merits of multi-methodological research designs.

their own domestic politics and internal security. Finally, leaders might base their decisions on considerations of systemic stability because they are moved to coordinate their recognition with that of their peers. I examine the explanatory power of these logics for the Great Powers as a group as well as each individual country. Identical interests, after all, need not motivate the Great Powers. To echo a well-known description of the U.S. Congress, Great Powers are a "they" not an "it" and may arrive at similar preferences regarding the recognition of a secessionist movement as a result of very different circumstances and considerations.[3] Nor are the three categories of interests mutually exclusive in most cases. A number of political considerations might help form leaders' preferences for and against recognition. In fact, the interests might be complementary. Granting recognition to a nascent state might simultaneously make the recognizing country more externally secure and play well to domestic political audiences. Further, countries' motivations or priorities may change over time.

HYPOTHESES

Though extensive coding rules are detailed in Appendix A, the principal hypotheses warrant some introductory discussion. There are a number of potential explanations for the Great Powers' recognition decisions. Even if we assume the Great Powers act in their own self-interests, this singular motive can take on a number of forms. I divide the potential motives for recognition into three categories: geostrategic/external security, domestic security, and system stability. These logics (and their operational indicators) are not exhaustive; they simply represent a range of potential interest motives underlying states' preferences.

Geostrategic/External Security

One group of factors that may influence recognition decisions is geostrategic and based on concerns for external security. The core of this set of influences is a logic of strategy, alliance, and enmity. Leaders' decisions whether to recognize secessionists are based on considerations of the international security environment and the effect that the new international participant is anticipated to have on the status quo. In general, states acting on this motive will use recognition in order to weaken their competitors and solidify their own security situation vis-à-vis the rest of the international community. The existing literature suggests a number of reasons why states might lend support for insurgency movements within other states. The same determinants should reasonably apply to recognition decisions with respect to secession.[4] These motives for supporting others' challengers

---

[3] Shepsle (1992) coined this phrase in describing congressional behavior.

[4] Indeed, Saideman (2002a) posits that states will be more likely to support secessionism (material or ideological support) if they have a conflictual relationship with the home state.

include a desire to destabilize unfriendly neighbors, a desire to inculcate regime change, and the prospect of gaining favor with potentially powerful insurgents.[5]

Though some security scholars may see recognition as mere "cheap talk" in comparison with costly actions such as military intervention and/or material assistance, Horowitz rightly cautions that material support is rarely sufficient to tip the scales decisively in favor of secessionists. In the vast majority of cases, external assistance is superficial and fleeting for a number of reasons: states "have more limited motives for supporting separatists than the separatists themselves have for fighting," they have "multiple international objectives," and they have their own domestic constituencies to satisfy.[6] Moreover, the practice of states contradicts the contention that recognition is simply cheap talk. Heraclides compellingly insists, "If words are 'cheaper' than deeds...then political-diplomatic or moral support would be more readily available and at a higher level and extent than tangible support." Though diplomatic support is more frequently granted, extensive high-level support like recognition is comparatively rare. It seems that "states do not generally find the utterance of such words to be 'cheap.'"[7]

Via the logic of external security, we can deduce two hypotheses about recognition. First, it is usually to a state's advantage to weaken its enemies (or increase its own relative advantage). Similarly, even the inherent uncertainties of potential relations with a new state actor are likely to be preferred over certain, continued conflictual relations with a home state. The status quo is undesirable, especially in comparison to the prospect of more amicable relations with the newly emergent state. The geostrategic logic hypothesizes that states in conflictual relationships with a given secessionist movement's home state will be more likely to prefer recognition for that movement. In the alternative, the more congenial a state's relationship with a home state, the less likely that state is to want to violate the territorial integrity of the home state by formally recognizing its challengers. Simply put, the enemy of my enemy is my friend and the enemy of my friend is my enemy.

H1:   *Great Powers with a conflictual relationship with a home state will be more likely to recognize its secessionists.*

H2:   *Great Powers with a friendly relationship with a home state will be less likely to recognize its secessionists.*

Domestic Security

Other potential influences on state recognition are the recognizing state's domestic security concerns. According to this logic, sometimes referred to as

---

[5] Byman et al. (2001, pp. 23–40).

[6] Horowitz (1985, pp. 272–273). Fearon (2004b) also notes that military intervention seems to prolong conflict rather than hasten its decisive end.

[7] Heraclides (1990, pp. 341, 369–370).

vulnerability, states view the recognition of secessionist movements abroad as a potentially destabilizing act vis-à-vis their domestic constituency.[8] A government conferring legitimacy on a secessionist movement in a foreign state potentially sends a signal supporting secessionism's legitimacy at home. Walter's work on reputation, war, and ethnic separatism demonstrates that leaders are apprehensive about the potential reputational effects of bargaining with their domestic challengers (as opposed to standing firm). When the number of prospective challengers is large, leaders will not concede to forestall an additional onslaught of demands. When they have fewer nascent challengers though, they are more willing to negotiate.[9] If secessionist challengers at home beset a Great Power, conferring legitimacy on foreign secessionists sends a similarly dangerous signal in support of separatism's legitimacy. Or, at least, a leader might be concerned that domestic challengers would interpret it as such. This fear might be particularly acute for vulnerable states whose security concerns are more domestic than international.[10] Emblematically, one scholar asserts that the leaders of some weak states believe "even the slightest recognition of secession...would be as unwise as showing blood in the lion's cage."[11]

The potential domestic consequences of foreign policy behavior are, nonetheless, important for relatively secure states with ethnic discontents, like the Great Powers, as well. China's and Russia's responses to their separatists, China in Tibet, Taiwan, and Xinjiang and Russia in Chechnya, Dagestan, and Ingushetia, are cases in point. Embattled governments in general then, should be deterred from recognizing secessionists as a matter of domestic reputation, whereas states without much domestic acrimony should confer recognition more freely. The more acute the challenge is, the greater the reticence to recognize.

H3:   *Great Powers with secessionist challengers of their own will be less likely to recognize secessionists in other states.*

Systemic Stability

The Great Powers' expansive interests will often put their preferences regarding new members at odds. However, rather than unilaterally pursuing those interests, I argue that the Great Powers should prefer to coordinate their recognition whenever possible. Therefore, when they disagree, the most likely result is that they uphold the status quo. Only in extraordinary circumstances should state leaders openly controvert one another and recognize competing authorities' sovereignty. In that minority of cases, state emergence

---

[8] Vulnerability is the term that Saideman (1997) uses.
[9] Walter (2006, 2009).
[10] Ayoob (1995, chapter 8); Saideman (1997).
[11] Bucheit (1978, p. 103).

may ultimately occur, but only gradually because disinterested states will be hesitant to pick sides and no definitive, community-wide cascade will occur. In the meantime, those conflicts hold significant potential for destabilizing international violence.

Various pressures lead the Great Powers to prefer coordinated to unilateral recognition. When their interests and preferences align, they can easily collude to enable or thwart state emergence. But they routinely have conflicting preferences over new members, and yet they nearly always successfully resolve those disagreements without internationalizing the secessionist conflict. Why? The drive to coordinate means that most of these disagreements are resolved in favor of the status quo. Present-day Kosovo, Abkhazia, and South Ossetia are exceptions to the rule. Historically, only when overwhelming individual interests prompt states to directly intervene has the overriding preference for coordination broken down. Indeed, Heraclides reflects that even during the Cold War, the superpowers were "hardly keen to antagonize each other in the periphery on secessionist issues."[12] The Great Powers ought to prefer coordinated recognition to maintain their social standing and security, to maintain international stability, and to reproduce the state-centric international order.

If Great Power recognition is strategically coordinated, it should proceed quickly when the Great Powers' interests align in favor of a state's emergence, and a new state should not be born when strong states' interests align against it; little time should elapse between the first Great Power's recognition and the last; and recognition should become increasingly probable as additional recognitions are granted. Coordination is only unlikely when a single power is strongly invested, usually enough to compel direct military intervention, to realize a particular outcome. In these cases, states are not responding to opportunities presented to them but are actively involved in creating independence or thwarting it on the ground. When powerful states become involved in secession in this way, and their interests are not in sync, dangerous international instability and violence becomes more likely.

A major public break over recognition, as with Kosovo and Georgia, has not occurred since the Vietnam War. And even so, in the wider examples of which Abkhazia, South Osseita, and Kosovo are a part (the dissolutions of the Former Yugoslavia and the Former Soviet Union), outsiders made long-term efforts to coordinate recognition and nonrecognition before independence was imminent.[13] In most instances, these negotiations led to successful coordination among the Great Powers.

H4: *Great Powers will be more likely to recognize secessionists when another Great Power or Powers have already done so.*

---

[12] Heraclides (1990, p. 371).
[13] Rich (1993); Libal (1997).

DOMESTIC HYPOTHESES

The accumulated wisdom on state emergence runs counter to my second image reversed model rooted in international politics. Instead, it suggests a bottom-up, domestic-level model. Unfortunately, existing theories regarding recognition do not lend themselves to empirical testing. As discussed earlier, Montevideo does not outline the standards necessary to fulfill its requirements of "people, territory, effective government and the ability to conduct international affairs." The difficulty inherent to the legal criteria is evident from contemplating just one of the requirements, territory. When can we be certain that a government has control over a defined territory? The standard cannot be so high as to require undisputed control over all of the territory claimed because many states have unresolved territorial conflicts with their neighbors.[14] But how much is enough physical control, 50, 80, or even 99 percent?

Next, how is territorial control determined? Must a secessionist regime militarily occupy the territories it claims? Is control necessarily established via military means? Or is it enough that the residents of the territory agree to submit to the new regime's governance? What indicators evidence their submission? Must the population support the regime in a plebiscite on independence or voluntarily pay taxes that the new regime levies? Then again, what conclusion should be drawn if only 60 or 70 percent of the population in an area favor the new state, whereas the rest remain loyal to the home state? Each potential indicator is highly limited and whether it captures the underlying concept at all, suspect.

Even disregarding the complexity involved in arriving at reasonable operational indicators, the data necessary to construct measures of control and authority are largely unavailable. Annual cross-national data are admittedly limited, but annual, cross-national, sub-state level data are even more elusive. Secessionism is also a loaded political topic. Home states do not want to broadcast their domestic struggles to the international community, much less chart their progress. Finally, no international, third-party datasets are dedicated to this task.[15] As a result of these two difficulties – ambiguous standards and data availability – estimates of bottom-up factors' relative influence on statehood and recognition are necessarily quite rough.

However, the extant comparative politics literature offers four potential explanations for state emergence that are largely consistent with the expectations of international law: ethno-national mobilization, domestic institutions, relative strength, and negotiated consent. Each uses a bottom-up causal mechanism focused exclusively on internal politics within the home state. These arguments presume that the same factors determining domestic authority also

---

[14] India and Pakistan dispute their shared border and the territory of Kashmir, for example, but their statehood is not called into question as a consequence.

[15] Halperin, Schaffer and Small (1992).

lead to system membership. Politics between the aspiring state and its home state are decisive, and potential external- or international-level influences are deemed epiphenomenal and not explored.

National Distinctiveness and Mobilization

One common explanation for state birth is ethnic distinctiveness.[16] Ethnic minority groups are thought to be more likely to demand states of their own and more likely to achieve statehood than groups with other characteristics or other types of secessionists. It is true that secession often has an ethnic character. Of the 259 movements begun since 1931, 141 were linguistically distinct and 113 were religiously distinct from the majority.[17] Secessionist demands may be particularly acute when ethnicity coincides with sociopolitical disadvantages within the home state, and this tendency is similarly evident empirically; 138 secession attempts since 1945 were pursued by at-risk ethnic minority groups as defined by the Minorities at Risk Project.[18]

This study aspires to a general model of state emergence. Nevertheless, there are reasons to suspect that secessionist demands buttressed by mobilized minorities should be more successful than others. In the age of nationalism, groups that are ethnically and religiously distinct from the governing elite have *prima fascia* evidence that their self-determination has been thwarted or that their culture is being assimilated or destroyed. Even in democracies, groups may face permanent minority status; although allowed to participate in politics, they may lack meaningful influence over public policy. Furthermore, these groups' large-scale mobilization for independence, whether through peaceful protest or widespread counter-governmental violence, should make state emergence more likely. Mass mobilization sends a signal to government leaders that group members desire independence. At the same time, when violence is employed, it is usually employed by both sides.[19] Accordingly, large-scale violence is not only an indication of the secessionist group's mobilization, but also of their home state's counter-mobilization.[20] Greater violence might equally be associated with less success.

H5:   *Mobilized minority groups are more likely to achieve statehood.*

[16] Beissinger (2002); Bunce (1999); Hale (2000); Horowitz (1985); Lustick et al. (2004); Roeder (2007).
[17] According to the dataset for this project. Linguistic dissimilarity was indicated by language family; religious dissimilarity was indicated by the major world religions. A finer religious distinction (e.g., Sunni, Shi'a and Sufi Islam) yields 203 distinct movements.
[18] Minorities at Risk Project (2009). The dataset begins in 1945.
[19] Approximately 16 percent of secessionist conflicts became wars. More than 77 percent saw violence short of war committed by at least one party.
[20] Nonviolent counter-mobilization is rare but can occur, for example, during Quebec's 1995 referendum. Also see Ker-Lindsay (2012) on home states' attempts to prevent the recognition of contested states.

Institutional Empowerment

Some assert that it is not ethno-national mobilization per se that makes state emergence more likely, but that domestic institutions empower particular groups to make and benefit from independence demands.[21] Two common institutional explanations argue state emergence is more probable for colonies or for members of ethnic federations. Colonial arguments posit distinct causal paths. First, some argue that the imperial powers encountered trouble controlling distant territories – often an ocean away – so power projection problems worked to favor anticolonialism. Second, changing views within the home state might explain colonies' relative success. An expert at the time of African independence opined, "national self-determination is what the contemporary world expects; anticolonial movements are automatically assigned to the familiar rubric of nationalism and are assumed to be serving as the agents of nations."[22] If leaders came to believe that anticolonial movements were built on popular nationalism and that national self-determination necessarily implied independence, then state birth would be more likely as these ideas spread within home states. Coincidentally, it has been suggested that controlling far-flung territories lost strategic significance as imperial powers shifted their attention toward the technologies of war.[23] Thus anticolonial secessions were more successful because leaders did not fight as hard to keep them.[24] Collectively these arguments suggest that empires lacked the capacity to thwart colonial independence, that they gradually lost the will to do so, or both.

Existing evidence supporting the anticolonial hypothesis is mixed. Unfortunately, studies of imperial decline often mistakenly overlook unsuccessful instances of secessionism; evidence of independence at all is taken as sufficient proof of their claims.[25] Frequently, though, more than one group aspired to govern the same territory. Even granting the demonstrable tendency favoring anticolonial secessions, existing theories cannot explain the variation in success among them. It remains an open question why the Kashmiris or Sikhs or Malayali failed to gain independence from British India. Also, as colonialism has been discredited as an institution of governance, the explanation is temporally bounded. Colonialism may provide explanatory leverage on state birth through the end of the twentieth century, but it is decidedly less useful today.

Recently, more precise institutional theories have been offered by scholars such as Philip Roeder, who argues that groups empowered by internal, ethnic

---

[21] Brancati (2006); Lapidus et al. (1992); Roeder (2007).

[22] Emerson (1960, pp. 127–128).

[23] Spruyt (2005, p. 4).

[24] We might also expect that colonies without secessionist movements, and, therefore, presumably without repressed nations, would remain under colonial rule longer than their separatist peers.

[25] For example, Barkin and Cronin (1994), where selecting on successes produces misleading estimates because the number of groups demanding independence is not observed.

segment states are more likely than others to secure independence.[26] He observes that, historically, statehood has not been limited to large, mobilized minorities. In fact, little popular support for independence was necessary if elites had an institutionalized mechanism of political influence at their disposal: the titular ethnic segment state. Over the twentieth century, Roeder finds that three-quarters of new states were internally self-governing ethnic segment states just prior to independence. According to his theory, segment state leaders are encouraged to make escalating demands for autonomy to wrest material benefits from the home state on "the people's" behalf. This process routinely produces independence movements that, in turn, are likely to succeed because the institution helps leaders establish what he terms "political-identity hegemony," drowning out alternative, less-well-situated nationalist projects within their borders. The ethnic segment state theory overcomes many of the colonial hypothesis's limitations. If supported, it potentially explains variations in anticolonial secessions and provides leverage on more recent cases like the Former Yugoslavia and the Former Soviet Union.

H6:   *Institutionally empowered groups are more likely to achieve statehood.*

Decisive Relative Strength

Probably the most widely held common wisdom regarding state emergence is that more powerful (materially capable) secessionist movements are more likely to secure independence. According to this intuition, the coercive capacity sufficient to exclude any competing authorities within a territory makes the state, and where a *fait accompli* exists, it cannot be ignored.[27] Much of the literature supporting this hypothesis comes from the study of domestic violence and war.[28] Most studies concentrate on the causes and dynamics of secessionist wars instead of their termination and results.[29] But some research on civil war settlements finds that more durable peace follows wars in which one side wins conclusively, whereas negotiated resolutions are more likely to quickly relapse into violence. Definitive victory is thought to engender lasting peace because it clarifies the balance of power, advising the loser against reinitiating violence in an attempt to achieve its ends, that is, if the loser's capacity for war has not been entirely destroyed.[30] Notably, Toft finds that rebel victories are particularly likely to create long, stable peace.[31] Therefore, when the secessionist movement

[26] Roeder (2007).
[27] Crawford (1996) makes this case regarding Bangladesh's independence.
[28] Though IR specializes in the study of violence and war, this literature unambiguously presents a domestic-level model of state birth.
[29] Among them are Brancati (2006); Collier and Hoeffler (2004); Fearon (2004); Heraclides (1990); and Walter (2006b).
[30] Licklider (1995); Toft (2010).
[31] Toft (2010).

	War Win	War Loss/ Stalemate	No War	Total	All Ongoing
Success	13	4	59	76	
Failure	2	12	106	120	
	15	16	165	196	63

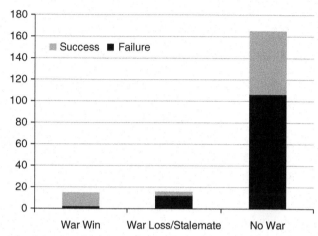

FIGURE 3.1 War Outcomes and Secessionism (1931–2000)

is disproportionately powerful, it ought to successfully secure independence and statehood.

Reviewing war outcomes provides a straightforward, albeit blunt means of testing whether definitively strong secessionists are more successful. Among conflicts that escalated to war, those ending in decisive victory for the secessionists ought to lead to state emergence (see Figure 3.1). This is what we find. Of the 41 secessionist wars between 1931 and 2000, 16 favored the home state or ended in stalemate, 15 favored the secessionists, and 10 remained active. Thirteen of the 15 secessionist victors secured independent states. Only two, the Saharawis and Chechens, did not.[32] More surprisingly, 4 of the 16 defeated groups secured system membership, and Abkhazia, although also defeated militarily, may add to that total if the international community ultimately embraces its legitimacy.

The evidence shows that relatively strong movements are decidedly more successful than their weaker peers, though it is not true that only the strongest movements become states. Most new states enter the system before securing authoritative control over their territories. Some are accepted in the midst of secessionist wars, just as many states recognized Algeria's independence as its

---

[32] An alternative coding might define Chechnya and Abkhazia as stalemates.

war raged with France.[33] Others receive external legitimacy even though they do not and cannot control the people and territory they claim, like East Timor upon its independence.[34] Overpowering the competing authorities may be a sufficient cause of state emergence, but it also appears to be an unnecessary one. Furthermore, an argument based on definitive strength is necessarily limited in its scope. Battlefield successes reliably predict state emergence for disputes that select into war but do not provide much insight when conflicts favor the home state, do not escalate to war, or end in a draw.

H7:   *Materially stronger secessionist groups are more likely to achieve statehood.*

Negotiated Consent

The final existing explanation for state birth is negotiated consent. In the post-colonial era, consent is the only fully legal means by which secession can regularly occur.[35] The consent of the home state is considered a definitive and necessary signal of state birth according to international law. The rule would not yield the most viable new system members but would best preserve the home state's sovereignty and, therefore, like coordinated recognition, would serve to maintain stability in the international order. The causal argument behind the hypothesis is normative. If the home state grants independence, the international community should defer to its decision. Unless and until it does, leaders cannot accept the newcomer because the conflict is an internal affair, and leaders are legally bound to uphold one another's sovereignty; domestic authority and nonintervention are the foundational principles of the Westphalian order. Indeed, Crawford asserts emphatically that outside of anticolonial conflicts, the international community does not recognize new states without the home state's consent.[36]

States occasionally emerge following negotiated settlements with their governments. Montenegro gained independence after a successful referendum and Serbia's consent in 2006, and many states negotiated their independences under the League of Nations Mandate and UN Trust systems. Even so, evidence supporting the consent-first requirement is equivocal. First, it is often ambiguous whether a home state willingly granted independence or was compelled into conceding. Had the UN Security Council not intervened to ensure East Timor's plebiscite, establish order, and defend its autonomy, it is unlikely that the

---

[33] Connelly (2002, p. 256).

[34] Chopra (2003) argues that East Timor lacks the fundamental bases of effective government; the international community has essentially created a new, failed state.

[35] According to a strict interpretation of sovereignty and noninterference consistent with the Helsinki Declaration (1975); O'Connell notes that decisive war victory might also constitute a legitimate basis for a demand for consensual separation (1992, p. 908 at ftn. 38).

[36] Crawford (1979). As the cases in the introduction show, if this was ever true, it is no longer accurate.

Indonesian government would have upheld its independence. More recently, something similar could be said regarding the independence of South Sudan. Second, there are as many examples of outsiders flouting home states' sovereignty as those respecting it.[37] Pakistan opposed East Pakistan's secession and the separatists might have failed had India not intervened and forced Pakistan to relinquish its control. Initially, state leaders did condemn India's behavior and withheld legitimacy for the new state. Still, nearly 50 UN members had recognized Bangladesh by February 1972 and fully half of them did before Pakistan finally accepted independence. States do not typically withhold legitimacy in deference to the home state even when international law unambiguously instructs them to do so.

Historically only around half of the states emerging from secession had their home state's consent by the time they entered the system.[38] Furthermore, according to the more detailed data collected for this project, two-thirds of Great Power states' recognition grants came before the home state acquiesced to independence.[39] Consent does not appear to be a prerequisite for state birth. Nonetheless, once a home state concedes to a secessionist demand, state emergence does typically become routine.[40] When a conflict is resolved internally, there is no reason not to accept the new member. Consequently, this project examines ongoing secessionist conflicts and admits that external legitimacy granted after a conflict's formal resolution is markedly less political. This ensures that the fundamental conflict is ongoing and presents a hard test for international-level factors because they must precede a resolution at the domestic-level.

RESEARCH PLAN AND ANALYSIS

The quantitative section of the project employs a variety of analytic techniques. I use a Cox proportional hazards regression model to explore the determinants of Great Power recognition. The first test approaches the Great Powers as a group. This test explores whether or not the domestic- and international-level hypotheses are generally supported by the Great Powers' recognition decisions. Next, I run individual models for each of the Great Powers. This tests the determinants of recognition for each of the Great Powers separately. The intuition behind the individual models is that perhaps China's decisions are highly related to its

---

[37] Indeed, Krasner (1999) dubs the entire institution "organized hypocrisy" for precisely this reason.

[38] Correlates of War Project (v.2004.1) (2005). Consent according to the data for this project.

[39] Even that deference, on closer inspection, is often not. In half of the post-consent cases, it was Beijing that did not accept the states because they had established diplomatic relations with Taiwan. Subtracting these cases leaves just 25 percent of new states with consent before membership.

[40] The only exceptions are abdications of authority like the South African Bantustans. The international community would not agree to the independence that South Africa granted because the government was deemed to have an ulterior motive, namely expelling black South Africans.

domestic security situation, whereas Britain offers recognition based on normative considerations. There is good reason to suspect powerful states will have
varied interests.

Case studies form the second major potion of the project and were selected
based on two criteria. First, clusters of cases within the same geographic and
temporal area were chosen to control for factors other than those under study. In
the Yugoslav cluster, all of the secessionists were parts of the Former Yugoslavia.
In the post-Soviet cluster, each of the home states belonged to the former Soviet
Union. The secessionist movements emerged just as their home states (Russia,
Azerbaijan, and Georgia) were asserting their own independence. Selecting cases
that are very similar except for the variables of interest – in this case domestic
control and authority and external politics – gives greater certainty that the
explanatory variables are, in fact, influencing the dependent variable.

The second criterion for case selection was variation on the domestic control
and authority (internal sovereignty) variable left unexplored in the large N
analyses. In the Yugoslav cluster, for example, Slovenia convincingly controlled
its territory and population upon recognition, Croatia's control was uncertain,
and Kosovo's was minimal. Because investigating the effects of domestic sovereignty was untenable in the large N analysis, the cases will shed light on its
weight relative to external political considerations.

4

Quantitative Analyses

Widely accepted theories in international relations and international law suggest a secessionist movement's status as a state depends on its domestic-level characteristics. Most prominently, they argue that existing states should admit only those actors with decisive internal sovereignty into their exclusive fraternity. The pattern of contemporary state emergence shows, though, that more states enter international society than convincingly meet the criteria. This means that recognition must be motivated, at least in part, by other factors or considerations. Many of these factors reside at the domestic level, but the international level should not be dismissed out of hand. Contrary to the presumptive models, but more consistent with the observed pattern of state emergence, I argue that existing states' self-interests motivate recognition, mediated by their mutual interest in preserving the international order.

Chapter 3 outlined several hypotheses about states' motives for and patterns of recognition. In this chapter, I develop operational indicators for the concepts discussed therein, provide details about the hypothesis tests, and review my quantitative findings. The analysis begins by offering evidence that the pattern of modern state emergence is unintelligible using indices of internal control and authority alone. Whereas cross-national data along these dimensions are limited and the legal requirements for statehood ambiguous, a survey of new states nevertheless reveals an important gap between the theory and practice of recognition. Recognition is not exclusively determined by domestic-level factors. Next, I explore the intuitively compelling, but so far untested, relationship between Great Power interests and recognition. Using event history techniques to test domestic factors alongside the international-level, interest hypotheses, I find that external politics systematically motivate external acceptance. Even considering domestic-level factors, each self-interested motive has a statistically significant, substantively meaningful effect on the likelihood of Great Power recognition.

Additionally, there are important periodic effects on state practice. Looking only at decisions made post-1945, recognition is increasingly associated with states' geostrategic interests and decreasingly influenced by coordination (though it still demonstrates the largest substantive effect by far). Similarly, whereas democratic states were once quite willing to recognize one another's challengers – unintentionally undermining their own security and well-being in the process – after 1945 they were not significantly more likely to do so. Taken together, these findings suggest recognition may be more beholden to external politics now than it was earlier in the twentieth century.

Modeling each country's decisions in isolation, significant differences in the Great Powers' *modus operandi* are also apparent. Whereas the United Kingdom and China were importantly motivated by their domestic politics in external recognition, the United States was in the enviable position of not having much internal instability at all and was, therefore, relatively unconstrained by domestic vulnerabilities when granting recognition. Meanwhile, the Soviet Union/Russia and France used recognition most consistently in support of their geostrategic interests. Each Great Power fit a distinct profile regarding motive. Only the systemic coordination interest had a consistently positive, statistically significant effect on every state's recognition. In fact, it was the only factor that systematically affected the likelihood of recognition for the United States. Another interesting finding regarding coordination: the two weaker powers during the study period – China and France – were the most influenced by the recognition cues of the stronger (i.e., the United States, Soviet Union/Russia, and Great Britain). This perhaps lends credibility to the project's more general assumption that weaker states often defer to more powerful states on matters of system membership.

The chapter concludes by discussing the implications of the quantitative findings and by identifying outstanding questions regarding recognition's causal process. These informational gaps provoke the content and character of the two case studies in Chapters 5 and 6. Following a nested research design, the large N analyses serve to eliminate unsupported hypotheses and delimit further study to the hypotheses receiving *prima facie* support.[1]

QUANTITATIVE APPROACH AND JUSTIFICATION

Large N analysis presents a number of advantages for the initial portion of this project. As a first cut, it allows us to discern broad patterns among the independent and dependent variables that would be untenable using more time-intensive methods.[2] By organizing instances of secessionism into panels and

---

[1] Lieberman (2005, pp. 435–452).

[2] King, Keohane, and Verba (1994, especially chapter 3, "Causality and Causal Inference"), though the value of quantitative methods relative to qualitative methods is perhaps overstated. See especially part II of Brady and Collier (2004).

measuring the same group of actors over time, we can also observe the long-term and dynamic effects of various motives on Great Power recognition. Event history analysis in particular satisfies two of the three criteria necessary to establish causality: the hypothesized cause is temporally before the effect, and correlation between cause and effect is definitively established.[3] Finally, another benefit of statistical analysis lies in its ability to eliminate unviable hypotheses, thus affording greater focus and structure to the cases.

To date, no similar study of secessionism and recognition exists to undergird my analytic approach. However, given the information available and the nature of the inquiry at hand, a Cox proportional hazard model is the most appropriate tool.[4] An initial brush-clearing test evaluates the existing domestic-level wisdom regarding state emergence by analyzing the determinants of system membership for the 259 secessionist movements active between 1931 and 2000. The domestic-level data are structured as cross-sectional time-series or CSTS; each secessionist movement has an observation for every year in which it is ongoing. The Correlates of War system membership or UN membership date are the dependent variables for these preliminary models, instead of recognition, as the domestic characteristics of secessionist conflicts do not vary by Great Power. To evaluate my own, international-level arguments, a change in approach is required. Because each Great Power faces a different constellation of interests from conflict to conflict and year to year, the international-level dataset's structure is organized into secessionist movement–Great Power dyads by conflict year, and again yields CSTS data. The dependent variable for the study is the date on which a given Great Power welcomes a movement into the international community of states (*recyear*), operationally identified by its formal grant of diplomatic recognition. For both domestic- and international-level analyses, the hazard ratio, the exponentiated form of the coefficient, is reported in the tables. The hazard ratio indicates the relative risk, or likelihood, of recognition during a given year, assuming that it has not already been granted. Rates greater than one indicate an increased annual likelihood, whereas rates less than one indicate a decrease. Greater detail accompanies the discussion of the results.

The empirical analysis expands on the existing quantitative literature in a number of ways. First, as discussed in Chapter 2, quantitative studies tend not to focus on secession per se. Instead, secession is treated as a subset of phenomena such as ethnic conflict or civil war. Secessionist conflicts are not essentially ethnic

---

[3] The final criterion for establishing causality is ruling out all other potential causes. This criterion cannot be fully satisfied in quasi-experimental research. The most a researcher can hope for is that other prominent explanations are falsified or demonstrably less credible.

[4] The Cox model is also attractive because we are not forced to make any assumption about the distribution of errors (Box-Steffensmeier and Jones 1997; Box-Steffensmeier and Zorn 2001). Other statistical approaches, though less well-suited, could also provide leverage. See Beck, Katz, and Tucker (1998) and King and Zeng (2001). Results employing alternative models are available at the author's website.

though, as the cases of Southern Sudan (spanning many ethic groups) and Somaliland (within an ethnically homogenous home state) illustrate. Nor do they inevitably stimulate wars or even violence between secessionists and their home states. A number of European political parties have platforms dedicated to secession but work within the governmental system to effect change.[5] Many secessionist conflicts remain peaceful (i.e., without fatalities) and would go virtually unnoticed in studies of sub-state violence.[6] Even then, tens of cases of violent secessionism never reach the threshold for full-scale war.[7] Slovenia's war against the Yugoslav JNA in 1991 caused fewer than 50 recorded combat fatalities.[8]

Concentrating on a conflict's ends, in this case complete independence, alters the common typology established for quantitative analyses of civil conflict. Because the project's larger aim is to explore the dynamics underlying state emergence, studying the entire range of groups that self-identify as deserving of and aspiring to statehood during a particular time period is nearly ideal. Casting a wider net, perhaps capturing all ethnic minorities, would be less ideal because the data would contain far too many groups that never aspire to self-government. Experts estimate that there are between 4,000 and 10,000 ethnic groups worldwide.[9] Only a small percentage of these groups ever seek states of their own. Individuals within them might not even identify themselves on the basis of their ethnicity. They may not have an ethnic consciousness or ethnicity might simply lack political salience. In these countries, perhaps people identify more strongly with ideological or regional identities instead. In the language of research design, selecting a wider sample of cases using ethnic groups would strain the credulity of the "possibility principle." We could not reasonably expect that most ethnic groups might experience recognition because most will

---

[5] Examples of independence parties include Vlaams Blok in Belgium (Flanders), the Independence Party in Denmark (Faroe Islands), Batasuna in France (Basque), Corsica Nazione in France (Corsica), Lega Nord in Italy (Padania), and Sinn Fein in the UK (N. Ireland). Some are associated with violent groups; some are not. Many secession attempts also experience significant periods of peace, among them the Quebecois, Catalonians, Turkish Cypriots, Somalilanders, and many of the post-Soviet secessionists.

[6] Many states seceded with little contest from the Soviet Union and Slovakia's separation from the Czech Republic was also peaceful.

[7] The dominant operationalization of war comes from the Correlates of War Project (2005), which defines it as a formally declared war with at least 1,000 combatant battle deaths during each calendar year. Some alternative measures have been created more specific to civil war (Gleditsch et al., 2001; Licklider 1995; Sambanis 2003). The 1,000-death threshold is generally consistent across studies; they differ over which deaths (only combatants or noncombatants as well) should be counted, over the appropriate time period (1,000 deaths each year or 1,000 as a cumulative count), and over absolute or relative measures (e.g., per capita deaths) (Sambanis 2003).

[8] Nine Slovenian soldiers and approximately 36 JNA soldiers were killed during the civil war.

[9] Again, Gellner (1993, p. 74) estimates there are 8,000 distinct languages in the modern world. Hannum (1990, pp. 454–455) argues there might be 5,000 states in the system if ethno-national self-determination was fully exercised.

not even make an initial demand for independence.[10] Conversely, the set of ethnic groups would also exclude too many manifest secessionist movements that span multiple ethnicities or occur within a subset of members of a single ethnic group.

As a result, this project considers secession a unique demand and observes the factors associated with the successful achievement of that end for the group making the demand.[11] This alternative perspective on sub-state conflict may yield insights into the civil war and ethnic conflict literatures. But more likely – and more consistent with this project's purposes – the results will help shed light on the system dynamics at work in secessionist conflicts. If widespread external acceptance is definitional of membership in international society, and, therefore, a necessary component of successful secession, then the determinants of recognition promise meaningful leverage on modern state emergence. The approach should uncover a preliminary set of conditions under which prospective states are likely to be accepted into international society by its most influential members.

Second, the small number of existing studies on state emergence tends to select on the dependent variable (realized independence), rather than looking at a wider range of potential states. Selection on the dependent variable like this may generate misleading conclusions. For example, a number of studies contend that as colonial rule became discredited, leaders were more likely to accept claims of self-determination as a basis for statehood. Typically, scholars infer that there was an increased probability of independence based on the observation that a large number of post-colonial states entered the international system after 1945. Yet we also know that many post-colonial claims to statehood were rejected. The Baganda preferred restoration of the Bugandan Kingdom to incorporation within the new Ugandan state, which they saw as an arbitrary colonial relic. And pan-African movements such as Katanga attempted to establish large multiethnic states but similarly failed to secure support. Finally, multiple anti-colonial regimes often vied for control over the same territory. In Ghana (formerly the Gold Coast colony), leadership was secured, to some extent, because the British did not anticipate that Nkrumah's Convention People's Party (CPP) would prevail in elections regarding independence. For many colonial peoples demanding independence, the eventual form and fate of their efforts were not assured. Moreover, a greater number of movements demanded recognition during the period of decolonization. *Ceteris paribus*, we might expect a larger number of new state members when there are simply more groups demanding independence. So even if one accepts the conclusion that the international community more readily accepted post-colonial states, significant variation remains unexplained by selecting on successful bids for statehood. In order to

---

[10] Goertz (2005); Mahoney and Goertz (2004).

[11] As opposed to other demands or ends such as autonomy, civil rights, regime change, revolution, and so on.

avoid the problems attendant to selection on the dependent variable, I sample all of the actors demanding independent statehood between 1931 and 2000.

Finally, the tests I utilize permit greater insight into the determinants of the timing of state emergence than previous studies have allowed. Duration analysis permits the use of time-varying covariates, permitting us to trace individual secessionist movements and Great Powers over time and aggregate all of the relevant observations for them.

EMPIRICAL BEGINNINGS

By any account, the twentieth century witnessed an explosion in state birth. In the less than a century since World War I, the international community's ranks have ballooned to nearly 200. The entries were primarily attributable to secession, but a number were also the result of dissolution and unilateral decolonization. Among the states entering purely as a result of decolonization, it is well established that control and authority standards were not adhered to; replacing the colonial systems with more representative, local government was given priority.[12] Some efforts were made to ensure that colonies' transitions to statehood were successful, but most colonies lacked some aspect of functional, independent governance at the point of recognized membership.[13] Yet colonial independences are widely considered exceptions to the normal course of state emergence. In most other cases, we expect that state emergence should follow a bottom-up causal path.

Patterns of secession and statehood do not conform to that expectation. To the contrary, the only newcomers entering the system between 1931 and 2002 that convincingly met the legal standards for recognition prior to receiving at least one outsider's recognition were Bangladesh, Eritrea, Slovenia, and Somaliland. Notably, Somaliland, though it meets the legal criteria, has not yet been recognized by any other state and, consequently, is not a system member. Lowering the bar just a bit, we could also add many of the so-called frozen conflicts in post-Soviet states such as Abkhazia, South Ossetia, Nagorno-Karabakh, Transniestria, and even Chechnya to the list of unrecognized and domestically sovereign actors along with Somaliland. At some point during their secession attempts, each one of these groups had close to effective sovereignty on the ground, with most falling short because of dependence on an external patron. Figure 4.1 shows the mismatch between *de facto* independence (domestic sovereignty) and *de jure* recognition (external sovereignty) among some contemporary secessionist movements. Those groups falling within the upper-left and lower-right quadrants are consistent with the bottom-up model's

---

[12] United Nations Charter (1945); United Nations Declaration on Granting of Independence to Colonial Countries and Peoples (1960).

[13] The Mandate and Trust systems were designed with this intent in mind.

	Little de facto Authority	Widespread de facto Authority
No de jure Recognition	Kashmir, Kurdistan (Turkey), Southern Cameroon, Tibet	Somaliland, Abkhazia, Anjouan, Chechnya (1996)
Widespread de jure Recognition	Bosnia-Herz, East Timor, South Sudan	Bangladesh, Slovenia, Eritrea

FIGURE 4.1 Internal and External Sovereignty

expectations, whereas the lower-left and upper-right quadrants are contrary; *de facto* control and *de jure* recognition should be perfectly correlated.

DATA COLLECTION AND RESOURCES

Various sources were referenced in creating the dataset.[14] Great Power recognition dates come directly from the foreign ministries of the countries when available.[15] Because recognition is bilateral, there is no international repository of recognition data. The Correlates of War (COW) dataset purports to use recognition as an indicator preceding the League of Nations and United Nations, but in fact it reports only the diplomatic missions established by France and Britain from 1816 to 1920.[16] During later years, including the period under study here, the COW uses League or UN membership as an indicator of statehood.[17] Although membership in these international organizations is a useful proxy for statehood in most cases, this project concerns how external

[14] Additional details are available in the codebook.
[15] When recognition dates were not available directly from the ministries, secondary sources were consulted.
[16] Small and Singer (1982). In addition, the population must be at least 500,000.
[17] The initial impetus behind the system entry variable explains this choice. Singer and Small's primary investigation sought to understand and systematize various levels of status within the international system. They were not interested in the consecration of statehood, but in delineating the strong, influential members from the weak and insignificant ones. This also explains their choice to exclude states with populations less than 500,000 (ibid.).

sovereignty comes to be granted in the first place.[18] Once embassies are built, a proto-state's progress toward statehood is usually complete.[19] For our purposes, a more fine-grained recognition measure indicating progress toward full external statehood is required.

Information regarding secessionist movements comes from a variety of sources. Unfortunately, the sensitive nature of the subject means that the data are almost certainly incomplete as a result of governments' opacity. Home states often attempt to hide their domestic challenges away. Secrecy is desirable for at least two reasons. First, states do not want to appear weak or embattled, so keeping word of their discontents quiet helps stave off additional challenges and maintain legitimacy with the rest of the population. Second, secrecy allows governments to crack down on secessionists without attracting negative publicity. Scrutiny regarding the government's methods of quelling separatism amounts to free publicity for the secessionists. No home state wants to be complicit in the success of its challengers. Fortunately, global news services and Internet resources make maintaining secrecy increasingly difficult. Still, this potential limitation should be kept in mind, especially with reference to less transparent, authoritarian home states.

The following resources contributed the bulk of information regarding secessionist movements: Minahan's *Nations Without States*; Gurr's *Minorities at Risk;* Halperin, Scheffer, and Small's *Self-Determination in the New World Order*; Emerson's *From Empire to Nation;* and Ayres's *Violent Intra-National Conflict data*. For ongoing cases, the movements' own websites or press releases were often consulted. Websites were particularly useful for discerning a movement's demands, confirming the existence of a national flag, and finding information regarding the proposed borders and population of the new state. Data on civil and international war come from the Correlates of War datasets and the Peace Research Institute Oslo's Uppsala Conflict Data Program (PRIO/UCDP). This includes onset, end, duration, and violence level. Data on militarized international conflict short of war comes from the Militarized Interstate Dispute (MID III) project and the PRIO/UCDP data. Data on governmental regime type come from the Polity IV data.

SECESSIONISM AND THE GREAT POWERS

A secessionist movement is a nationalist group dedicated to formal separation from its home state in order to form a newly independent state.[20] Groups that

[18] India was a member of the League and UN before its independence from Britain. The Philippines was also a member of the League before independence. Finally, Belarus and the Ukraine were accepted as full members of the UN prior to independence as well. A number of states were also excluded from UN membership because of Cold War politics between the United States and Soviet Union; neither League nor UN membership is perfectly correlated with statehood.
[19] In many cases, embassies are established years after diplomatic recognition has been ascribed.
[20] A note on alternative data sources: many of the secessionist movements begun since 1931 do not fall within the coding scheme of the Minorities at Risk data. In many cases, groups were colonial did not surpass the established population threshold or the national communities were not

seek to separate from their home states in order to join another preexisting state are classified as irredentist and excluded from the category.[21] Groups that do not seek statehood, but instead seek forms of autonomy short of complete independence, including civil rights or regional self-governance, are also excluded from the set of secessionist movements, although this does not mean that groups cannot transition from seeking autonomy to seeking full independence and vice versa during different periods. Finally, groups that seek to overthrow the government of an established state, as in the case of revolution or coup d'état, are also not considered to be secessionist.

Secession is also distinct from decolonization, which is characterized by the devolution of authority from an imperial government to a local one. In some cases, as in the British West Indies, the transfer of authority is driven by the imperial power rather than by nationalist demands on behalf of the colonized peoples themselves.[22] In these cases, the colonies were not secessionist because they did not demand self-rule; they were unilaterally granted or forced into it. Other cases of decolonization were, however, preceded by demands of independence and self-government on behalf of colonial peoples. Often characterized as conflicts of national liberation or extra-systemic wars, conflicts involving movements like these fit well within the conceptual definition of secession outlined earlier. It is on this basis that anticolonial secessions were included in the dataset.

Operationally, four factors dictate whether or not a group is coded as a secessionist movement. First, a group must formally declare independence from its home state at some point during its operation. In most cases, a declaration of independence is a unilateral declaration of independence (UDI) according to international law. The word "unilateral" indicates that the home state does not recognize the group's independence, in opposition to consensual or bilateral independence. Second, the group must have a flag. This requirement indicates the movement has national consciousness. Third, the group must make a claim to both a population and territory over which it presides. This qualification is meant to exclude two types of movements that do not constitute secession attempts: (1) pirate states, where a population claim is made without a territorial claim and (2) platform islands, a popular means of attempting to evade U.S. taxes in the 1960s, wherein a claim to territory is made without a permanent

---

considered to have either suffered disadvantages or received advantages because of their group affiliation. Examples of cases that do not qualify are Puerto Ricans in the United States, East Bengalis (now Bangladeshis) in Pakistan, Abu Sayyaf in the Philippines, and Macedonians in Yugoslavia.

[21] If the state the irredentists hope to join does not make an equal and opposite claim to control the secessionists' population and territory, then the group is secessionist. See the discussion regarding Nagorno-Karabakh's and South Ossetia's inclusion in Chapter 5 for a more detailed discussion on irredentist versus secessionist claims.

[22] Jamaica was the exception in that case.

population.[23] Finally, the independence movement must last at least one week, must involve at least 1,000 people, and must claim at least 100 square kilometers (km²) of territory. This requirement was levied in the name of research efficiency. It is unlikely that a very small or very short-lived movement would capture the attention of the media or, for that matter, even its own home state. Information regarding such obscure movements would not be readily available.

For each secessionist movement identified, dates were recorded indicating the beginning and end dates of each secession attempt. Some groups attempt secession multiple times. In these cases, Tibet and Chechnya among them, roman numerals indicate the sequence of attempts. It was also sometimes the case that a single secessionist movement splintered into two or more groups. When at least one of the splintering groups qualified as a secessionist movement, that group was considered to have begun on the date of the split from the larger group.

The Great Powers were coded according to their appearance and duration within the Correlates of War datasets. The Great Powers are the most materially capable states within the system during a given period. Because they are the strongest states, they are also widely believed to be the most influential. Further, their capabilities imply that they will have global, not merely regional or local, interests. According to the COW operationalization, the Great Powers between 1931 and 2000 were Great Britain, United States, and USSR/Russia: 1931–2000; China: 1950–2000; France: 1931–1940, 1945–2000; Germany: 1931–1945, 1991–2000; Italy: 1931–1943; and Japan: 1931–1945, 1991–2000. The number of Great Powers in a given year during the study period ranged from four to seven.

MODEL SPECIFICATION AND DOMESTIC LEVEL RESULTS

Recall the following seven primary hypotheses from Chapter 3:

International-Level Hypotheses

H1: *Great Powers with a conflictual relationship with a home state will be more likely to recognize its secessionists.*

H2: *Great Powers with a friendly relationship with a home state will be less likely to recognize its secessionists.*

H3: *Great Powers with secessionist challengers of their own will be less likely to recognize secessionists in other states.*

H4: *Great Powers will be more likely to recognize secessionists when another Great Power or Powers have already done so.*

Domestic-Level Hypotheses

H5: *Mobilized minority groups are more likely to achieve statehood (are more likely to receive Great Power recognition).*

---

[23] The platform island idea has also been attempted in the Gulf of Guinea. In these cases, groups have attempted to claim preexisting offshore oil facilities.

H6:   *Institutionally empowered groups are more likely to achieve statehood (are more likely to receive Great Power recognition).*

H7:   *Materially stronger groups are more likely to achieve statehood (are more likely to receive Great Power recognition)*

Domestic-Level Variables[24]

Beginning with the conventional wisdom, the domestic level, this section discusses the operational indicators devised to test the state emergence hypotheses. According to existing theories, a secessionist movement's material strength, ethnic composition, and institutional organization are the primary factors determining its successful membership in the international community.

Hypothesis 6 argues that institutionally empowered secessionists are more likely to achieve statehood and recognition. Anticolonial movements are thought to have a greater chance of gaining recognition for at least three reasons. First, as colonialism came to be seen as an illegitimate form of governance, the Great Powers should have become more sympathetic to anticolonial secessionists' plights and, therefore, more predisposed to recognize. Second, home states were subjected to social pressure to allow anticolonial secessionists to secede, especially once the United Nations was founded. And finally, imperial powers might not have tried to hold on to colonies because the cost-benefit calculus regarding far-flung territorial holdings favored their liquidation.

Colony is a dummy variable coded o if the secessionist movement claims a territory and population that is not a colony of its home state. The variable is coded 1 if the secessionist movement is anticolonial. A colony is operationally defined as a jurisdiction, composed of people and territory, governed by a state or agents of a state that is neither geographically contiguous nor within 100 miles of the home state's shoreline. If a movement has a colonial history, but is not attempting to secede from its colonial governor, then it is not considered anticolonial. Ninety-eight of the 259 secessionist movements within the dataset were identified as colonial.

Additionally, there may be a positive relationship between claims to sub-state territories (states, regions, or republics) and successful secession. Organized jurisdictional units can more easily transition to independent statehood because the rudimentary organs of government are established prior to independence; these groups need not create institutions from scratch. Internal boundaries may seem to offer the promise of a clean break between secessionists and the home state as well. Furthermore, not only significant internally, the principle of *uti possidetis juris* has recently been used by outside powers to ensure the continuity of new states' former colonial borders and to maintain stability among the states of the Former Yugoslavia and Soviet Union.[25]

---

[24] The project's codebook provides a summary of the definitions discussed in this section.

[25] The term *uti possidetis* ("as you possess") was used to communicate that state leaders could only claim the territories that they physically possessed. The more contemporary *uti possidetis juris*

Sub-state jurisdictions should be more likely to gain recognition, whereas movements attempting to form new states without internal administrative boundaries will face greater difficulties. Preexisting units are already endowed with stable boundaries and populations; they often already have the trappings of governmental authority (police, emergency services, local elections, schools, etc.) and are often presumed to have relatively homogenous populations. Because states' choices of administrative units are wide ranging, ethno-federal divisions were taken from Roeder. This definition excluded smaller intrastate organizational units such as cities, counties, and states, but ethno-federal units share the most characteristics in common with independent countries of the various types. The Roeder operationalization double counted many colonies, so colonial units were dropped from Roeder's list. The resulting dummy variable, *ethnicfed*, was coded 0 for non-ethno-federal units and 1 for ethno-federal units. Sixty-one of 259 secessionist movements within the dataset claimed territories organized as ethno-federal units.

Hypothesis 5 argues that ethnic minority groups will be more likely to achieve statehood as a result of their distinct national character and popular support demonstrated by their mobilization. Two variables were created to test this intuition. The first captured the degree to which a secessionist movement was ethnically dissimilar from its home state. The measure is an ordinal variable resulting from the summation of the linguistic and religious differences between the home state majority and the secessionists. If the groups share a language family, the linguistic indicator is coded 0; if they are different, then 1.[26] Religious dissimilarity compares the majority's religion to that of the secessionists.[27] If the two shared a religion, the religious indicator is coded 0; if they are different, then 1. The indicators were then summed to create *distinct*. Thus, a group coded 2 is linguistically and religiously dissimilar from its home state, a group coded 1 is distinct on one dimension, and a group coded 0 shares both language and religion with the majority.[28] Of the 259 secessionist movements in the dataset, 78 were distinct from the majority on both dimensions and another 86 were either linguistically or religiously distinct.

Perhaps independence is not about difference per se, but about the politicization of difference and the voicing of justifiable grievance by the secessionist

---

("as you legally possess") granted legal authority to former colonies within the totality of their former colonial borders, thereby contravening the term's original meaning.

[26] Language families, of which there are 128 worldwide, were identified using the Ethnologue database (Gordon 2005). If the majority did not share a common language, the national language or language of government was used.

[27] Differences were judged among the five major world religions: Buddhism, Christianity, Hinduism, Islam, and Judaism. This operationalization is close, but not identical, to Huntington's measure of civilizations (1993). An additional religion variable, measuring smaller distinctions such as those between Sunni, Shi'a, and Sufi Islam or Protestant, Catholic, Orthodox, and other forms of Christianity was also created but was not statistically significant.

[28] By necessity, any objectivist, system-wide measure of ethnic and religious differences only roughly approximates local understandings of meaningful social and political difference. This should be kept in mind when interpreting these results. Unfortunately, no readily available alternatives exist.

group. To test whether reasonably large, oppressed, and mobilized minorities are more likely to become states, a dichotomous variable, *MAR*, was created. It indicates whether (1) or not (0) the secessionist group is found within the minorities at risk (MAR) data in a given year.[29] MAR groups are minority communities that number at least 100,000 or constitute 1 percent of their home state's total population, suffer discrimination because of their minority status, and are politically mobilized in order to advance or defend the group's interests[30]; 115 of 259 secessionist movements claimed to represent one or more groups defined as an at-risk minority.

Finally, two variables related to violence were created to test whether materially capable challengers are more likely to become states and to confirm that secessionist war winners are likely to secure independence (hypothesis 7). The first, recording violence level (*vlevel*), comes from PRIO/UCDP. The variable codes no armed conflict (0), between 25 and 999 battle-related deaths (1), and at least 1,000 battle-related deaths (2) in a given year.[31] Forty-five conflicts reached full-scale war during at least one year, and another 23 experienced systematic, battle-related violence. The remaining 191 cases either did not experience violent conflict or saw non-combat-related violence like terrorism. The second, *warwin*, is a dichotomous variable coding the year in which a secessionist movement defeats its home state in a war for independence (1) and was taken from the COW intrastate war data. If the conflict is ongoing, ends in a stalemate, or ends in a loss, it is coded 0.[32]

Domestic-Level Results

An initial test of the domestic-level hypotheses using the COW system or UN membership as the dependent variable shows support for most of the existing scholarship (Table 4.1). Contrary to expectations, however, neither ethno-religious distinctiveness nor mobilized and oppressed minority groups had a greater chance of statehood than did groups with more in common with the majority. Other domestic-level hypotheses fared better. As anticipated, anticolonial movements and constituent members of ethnic federations were much more likely to experience system membership. In the COW system model, the hazard ratio for anticolonial movements increased more than twenty-fold. This lends support to the supposition that governments' institutionalization of ethnic difference – as in colonialism and ethno-federalism – makes membership more likely, whereas less structural markers of difference such as group discrimination

---

[29] Minorities at Risk Project (2009).
[30] For additional criteria, see the Minorities at Risk Project: http://www.cidcm.umd.edu/mar/definition.asp. Although it is possible for a MAR group to be politically advantaged by its status, none of the groups in this study were.
[31] UCDP/PRIO (2008).
[32] Secessionist conflicts often remain ongoing after combat ceases.

TABLE 4.1 *Domestic Determinants of State Emergence for 244 Secessionist Movements, 1945–2000 (Cox)* [a]

Independent Variable	Hazard Ratio COW System	Hazard Ratio UN Membership
Ethno-Religious Difference (+)	1.18 (.27)	.80 (.27)
At Risk Minority (+)	.79 (.68)	.97 (.97)
Colony (+)	20.34***	7.56**
Ethnic Federation (+)	7.65**	4.07**
Violence Level (–/+)	0.74**	.60**
War Victory (+)	15.75***	15.58***
Number of subjects	244	244
Number of failures	83	44
Time at risk	3230	3542
Number of observations	2901	3115

Notes: Hazard ratios are presented rather than coefficients because of their straightforward interpretation. The hazard ratio is the exponentiated form of the coefficient. Tests are two tailed. $p < .05$**, $p < .001$***.
[a] The Minorities at Risk data only codes groups back to 1950. If the group was considered at risk in 1950, it was considered also to be at risk at the beginning of this analysis in 1945.

or simple ethnic distinctiveness do not. Regarding relative material capability, the level of violence in a secessionist conflict in a given year negatively influenced the chance of independence. During years of higher-level violence, movements were 26 percent and 40 percent less likely to become members. As anticipated, it appears that violence levels capture both the secessionists' strength and the home states' determination and capacity to prevent their departure. Violence only increases the likelihood of system membership in a year when, as *warwin* predicts, the secessionists defeat the home state in war. And again in this case, there were consistent and strong effects on the hazard ratio. Aside from being a colony, winning a secessionist war had the greatest impact on state birth, multiplying the probability of emergence in a given year nearly 16 times. Based on the results of this initial brush clearing, the full model will incorporate the domestic-level variables that found support (institutions and relative strength) and exclude those that did not (ethnic distinctiveness and mobilization).

International-Level Variables

Although the results from the domestic-level models are instructive, they leave a number of important questions unanswered regarding the process leading up to membership. For example, why and when are the permanent five members of the UN Security Council more or less likely to recognize a secessionist movement, paving the way for its ultimate membership in the United Nations? As they all have a veto over new members, even a single non-recognizer could block a secessionist movement's transition to statehood. Furthermore, do all of the Great Powers respond to the domestic-level characteristics in a similar manner? Or are there individual patterns? And, most importantly, are the Great Powers influenced by their own parochial concerns in determining the fate of their would-be peers?

The first and second international-level hypotheses focus on enmity and amity between states. Hypothesis 1 argues that external security motivates the recognition of new states; therefore, leaders should use recognition strategically to weaken their enemies and increase their own security. The variable testing this argument, taken from the MID data, captures whether a given Great Power and a home state initiate a militarized dispute (*cwmid*) during a given conflict year; 1,006 years saw the initiation of at least one militarized dispute between a Great Power and a home state. Next, a related hypothesis (#2) argues that leaders should be less likely to recognize secessionists attempting to separate from a friendly home state because it would threaten their own security in the process. To test this hypothesis, the Polity IV data's democracy and autocracy scores were used to create two dichotomous variables. If the Great Power–home state dyad was mutually democratic (*mutualdem*) or mutually autocratic (*mutualaut*) during a conflict year, it was coded 1. Consistent with accepted practice, states with Polity scores equal to or higher than 7 were coded democracies and those with scores equal to or less than −7 were coded autocracies. If the dyad was mixed during a conflict year, the variables were coded 0.[33] In all there were 7,737 recognition years of mutual democracy and 4,530 recognition years of mutual autocracy.

Hypothesis 3 argues that leaders will be reticent to recognize secessionists' independence when they face analogous challenges at home. Domestic vulnerability should make leaders concerned for their reputation regarding secessionism writ large; they do not want to embolden their own challengers by signaling secession's legitimacy elsewhere. Two variables were created to test this claim. The first, *challengeh*, indicates whether the Great Power has an especially high number of challengers (1) or not (0) during a given year. The variable was created by taking the number of secessionist challenges for each Great Power home state in each year of the dataset and coding 1 for cases in the 90th percentile and above, which included those Great Powers with between 8 and 21 challengers in a conflict year.[34] The most domestically imperiled states were Britain in the late 1940s and mid-1950s through the early 1960s and the Soviet Union in 1991. A total of 2,023 recognition years were coded as high challenge years. The second, *vchallenge*, indicates the cumulative violence level reached in the domestic challenges that year. Perhaps it is not the raw number of challenges,

---

[33] Mixed meaning one or both of the states had Polity scores between −6 and 6, −66, −77, or −88.
[34] Another variable, *challengers*, counted the number of secessionist challenges ongoing in a given year. It did not have a significant effect in alternative specifications of the model.

but the intensity of the challenge they present to the home state that is important. The intensity of violence was measured by summing the levels of violence from the PRIO dataset for each Great Power's domestic secessionist challenges in a given year.[35] The resulting variable ranges from 0 (none) to 6 (violence equivalent to 3 full-scale civil wars). The most cumulatively violent challenges were faced by the Soviet Union from 1946 to 1948 and again in 1950.

Finally, *prec* was created as an initial test of strategically coordinated recognition in favor of systemic stability. If the Great Powers coordinate, recognition should become increasingly likely once one has granted recognition. If no coordination occurs, a single recognition should not significantly influence the probability of a second. Therefore, this variable measures whether any one of the Great Powers has recognized the secessionists' independence as of a given conflict year. It ranges from 0 to 1 and 422 recognition years were coded 1.[36]

International-Level Results

The results of the full, international and domestic, models run with *recyear* as the dependent variable are presented in Table 4.2. The left column presents results for the entire study period, 1931–2000. The right column restricts the analysis period from 1945 to 2000.[37] The models clearly demonstrate that international politics have important, underappreciated influence on recognition and, therefore, state emergence. The external politics hypotheses all had significant effects on the chance of recognition in addition to the acknowledged domestic-level effects.

The external security motive generated somewhat surprising results. A militarized dispute between a home state and a Great Power did not make recognition significantly more likely between 1931 and 2000, but post-1945, the likelihood of recognition increased significantly for groups attempting to secede from a rival. During that time, home state–Great Power hostilities increased the probability of recognition in a given year by 68 percent. The difference in findings for the post-1945 period indicates that external security considerations

---

[35] No armed conflict (0), 25–999 battle-related deaths (1), 1,000 or more battle-related deaths (2). The intensity of violence measure is rather crude. For example, two conflicts causing 300 battle-related deaths would be coded identically to one conflict with more than 1,000 battle-related deaths. Unfortunately, no better algorithm is readily available.

[36] Two additional measures were created to test the coordination hypothesis. The first, *precs*, counts the number of Great Power recognitions granted as of a given conflict year. The second, *gprecpro*, measures the proportion of the total number of Great Powers that have granted recognition as of a given conflict year. It ranges from 0 to .857. Models run with these variables also found large, positive, and significant effects.

[37] The year 1945 marks the end of World War II and the creation of the United Nations and, therefore, a time of system-wide change in international politics. It is worth examining whether the politics of recognition are significant following this important, system-wide reordering in addition to the larger dataset. To wit, perhaps the UNSC presented the Great Powers with more opportunities to coordinate their recognition.

TABLE 4.2 *Determinants of Formal Recognition, Secessionist Movement–Great Power Dyads (Cox)*

Independent Variable	Hazard Ratio (full dataset)	Hazard Ratio (post-1945)
Domestic		
Colony (+)	8.08***	8.29***
Ethnic Federation (+)	4.98***	5.35***
Violence Level (−/+)	.62***	.70***
War Victory (+)	5.21***	5.33***
International		
Hostility w/Home State (+)	1.38	1.68* [a]
Mutual Democracy (−)	1.50**	1.22
Mutual Autocracy (−)	.35***	.20***
High Challengers (−)	.89	.76
Violent Challenge (−)	.79**	.83**
Previous Recognition (+)	30.35***	28.16***
Number of subjects	1462	1334
Number of failures	276	267
Time at risk	18,388	17,863
Number of observations	18,388	16,040

Notes: Hazard ratios are presented. The hazard ratio is the exponentiated form of the coefficient. All tests are two-tailed. $p < .05^*$, $p < .01^{**}$, $p < .001^{***}$.
[a] Significant at .058.

have only recently become an influential determinant of new system members. This may be related to the precipitous decline in major violence between states.[38] Because militarized disputes have become much less common, when they do occur, they may be more meaningful. As such, interstate violence may be a better indicator of enmity between states now than it was before 1945, when it was more common. Alternatively, the pattern might be related to the Cold War, as the two time periods overlap significantly. During that time, militarized disputes often reflected ideological conflicts that pitched the two superpowers against each other. If this is correct, MIDs occurring between 1947 and 1991 should create a particularly strong increase in the likelihood of recognition for the USSR and the United States. Models for the individual Great Powers show that although this was true for the USSR, increasing the probability of its recognition by 350 percent during the Cold War, it was not true for the United States, for which no significant relationship was found (see Table 4.3).[39] Finally, the composition of the Great Powers changed after 1945 and that may be responsible for some of the difference. France reenters the group in 1945 and China joins in 1950. The individual models for China and France show that militarized

[38] Mueller (1990).
[39] These alternative, Cold War specifications of the models can be found on the author's website.

TABLE 4.3 *Determinants of Formal Recognition, Secessionist Movement–Great Power dyads, by Individual Power (Cox)*

Independent Variable	Hazard Ratio USA	UKG	FRA	USR/ RUS	CHN
Domestic					
Colony (+)	15.82***	20.67***	19.98***	17.08***	9.22**
Ethnic Federation (+)	7.27***	5.83**	12.05**	.65	1.76
Violence Level (-/+)	.51**	.62	.60	.65	1.30
War Victory (+)	4.03*	6.12*	1.07	14.60***	4.77
International					
Hostility w/H.State (+)	2.27	1.87	10.56**	2.72*	1.23
Mutual Democracy (–)	.95	.98	.69	.48	.
Mutual Autocracy (–)	.[a]	.	.	2.53	1.11
High Challengers (–)	.[b]	.41	.73	2.23	.[c]
Violent Challenge (–)	.55*	.73	.84	.17**	
Prev. Recognition (+)	29.64***	20.70***	68.65***	20.39***	62.13***
Number of subjects	250	207	222	232	200
Number of failures	82	44	55	43	24
Time at risk	3549	2975	3073	3390	2882
Number of observations	3543	2972	3065	3381	2874

Notes: Hazard ratios are presented. The hazard ratio is the exponentiated form of the coefficient. All tests are two-tailed. $p < .05$*, $p < .01$**, $p < .001$***.
[a] For the USA and UKG, where the country remained democratic and stable throughout, the *mutualaut* variable was dropped.
[b] High challengers and Violent challenge dropped because of collinearity.
[c] High challengers dropped because of collinearity.

conflict did not significantly influence China's recognition, but conflict with France caused a large increase in the probability that it would recognize that home state's challenger(s), more than ten times the likelihood in another year.

Amity between states influenced recognition differently depending on regime type. As expected, mutual autocracy made autocratic Great Powers significantly less likely to recognize a home state's challenger(s), decreasing the probability of recognition by 65 percent in a given year (by 80 percent post-1945). However, models of the two principally autocratic states in Table 4.3, the USSR and China, did not find statistically significant negative effects for mutual autocracy. More surprisingly, mutual democracy made a Great Power significantly *more* likely to recognize a home state's secessionist challengers. A democratic home state increased the likelihood of democratic Great Powers' recognition by 50 percent. What explains democratic states' willingness to grant external legitimacy to their friends' and allies' discontents? Work at the intersection of IR and law may be instructive. Some suggest democratic states are more willing to oppose one another because they operate in a "zone of legitimate difference" wherein, because of their mutual liberalism, leaders presume different policy choices simply reflect legitimate, alternative means of securing the same underlying values.[40]

Particularly during the twentieth century, the United States and democratic, imperial powers such as the UK, France, Portugal, Belgium, and the Netherlands often had different preferences regarding the fates of their overseas territories. Although recognizing other democratic states' challengers did weaken them, it simultaneously provoked the powers to become more fully aligned with liberal principles and eventually drew the mutually democratic states closer to each other. Furthermore, the strength of the American security commitment may have allayed fears that declining power, ceding control of far-off territories, would inevitably create insecurity. Still, mutually democratic recognition was not only – or even principally – attributable to the United States; the UK, France, and post-Soviet Russia all recognized the challengers of other democracies. Alternatively, this result may uncover a corollary to the democratic peace; rather than using violence to settle scores among themselves, perhaps democracies wield diplomacy and recognition to a similar effect.

Consistent with hypothesis 3, domestic insecurity decreased the probability of a power's recognition during that year (see Table 4.2). Increased levels of violence at home made a Great Power 21 percent less likely to grant recognition to foreign secessionists in that year. The more acute the domestic challenge, the more carefully the Great Powers attended to foreign recognition's potential reputational effects. This is an especially convincing finding because the operationalization of *Great Power* may have diluted the test. Specifically, states were not considered Great Powers during the years in which they were the most internally troubled (e.g., France from 1941 to 1944). If there were a significant relationship to be found between domestic insecurity and recognition, it would most likely be captured during precisely these years. The fact that the probability of recognition declined even without observations for the years in which the Great Powers were most domestically insecure can only increase confidence in the finding. Furthermore, it suggests that domestic vulnerability, contrary to the findings of other research, does influence outside states' intervention in secessionist conflicts under some conditions.[41]

Neither an unusually high number of challengers nor the absolute number of challengers decreased the likelihood of Great Power recognition. However, these measures are less compelling indicators of domestic insecurity than the intensity of internal violence is: a significant number of demands might only constitute a low-level threat, whereas a sizeable and violent movement looms larger. For example, in 1996, Russia's recognition behavior was probably more affected by its conflict in Chechnya than the United States was by its two challenges in Hawaii and Puerto Rico.

---

[40] Slaughter (1995, p. 525).
[41] Saideman (1997).

The final international-level hypothesis (#4), that the Great Powers strategically coordinate their recognition, had the largest impact on the likelihood of recognition. When one or more Great Powers granted recognition, the subsequent probability of additional recognition increased between 28 and 30 times. Moreover, alternative measures of coordination used as robustness checks all found positive and statistically significant results. Shared Great Power interests in system stability, the diffusion of responsibility, and policy efficiency convincingly explain this pattern. The Great Powers do not make their recognition decisions in a vacuum; even when their parochial interests align in favor of a particular new member, coordination helps ensure that state emergence occurs in an orderly, predictable, and minimally disruptive manner – at least insofar as the Great Powers themselves are concerned. Coordination's longer-term effects on the new countries it helps create remain an open question.

Most noteworthy among the individual models are the distinct recognition patterns from state to state (see Table 4.3). Aside from a consistent, demonstrable interest in coordinated recognition among all of the powers, there was a great deal of variation. The probability of the United Kingdom's and China's recognition was significantly decreased in times of domestic vulnerability. When the UK had many violent challengers at home, it was 45 percent less likely to recognize, whereas China was 83 percent less likely. France and the Soviet Union/Russia, though not motivated by domestic instability, were meaningfully affected by their external security concerns. France was more than twice as likely to recognize a secessionist movement with a recent enemy as its home state, and the Soviet Union/Russia was more than 10 times as likely to do the same. In contrast, American recognition was only significantly influenced by the recognition of its other Great Power peers; none of the other interest hypotheses had significant effects. The United States did not have substantial domestic secessionist movements of its own, so its reputation was not vulnerable enough to stay the impulse to recognize. In addition, it was unaffected by its camaraderie with other democratic states.

Also intriguing, the weaker states among the Great Powers during the study period – France and China – showed the greatest positive change in the likelihood of recognition according to the systemic coordination motive; the stronger states hazard ratios increased between 20 and 30 times, but those of France and China increased more than 60 times. This lends credibility to the project's supposition that weaker states look to stronger states for leadership when it comes to decisions over new members; strong states' recognition is likely to serve as a focal point for others.

In sum, all of the international-level hypotheses received significant support. External politics have important effects on the probability of recognition and the likelihood of statehood for any aspiring system member – above and beyond the domestic level. Only one finding, regarding mutual democracy's effect on the likelihood recognition produced unexpected, though still significant, results.

CASE STUDY REORIENTATION

The quantitative analysis indicates that the Great Powers' political interests influence their recognition and, therefore, state emergence. But correlational analysis precludes exploration of the mechanism by which external political considerations affect recognition. What is the process? How much weight do leaders give their own interests relative to the facts on the ground in a given case? Do they explicitly consider their own interests or do they creep in implicitly? Do leaders bargain over recognition in an effort to coordinate? And are there other, untheorized explanations why strong states might grant or withhold external legitimacy from would-be states? Answering process-related questions like these requires small N, comparative case analysis. In brief, through well-designed case studies, we can better articulate *how* it is that external political impetuses are ultimately translated into the recognition behavior we observe.

Case Selection

The criteria guiding case selection depend on the ends envisioned for the case analysis. As alluded to earlier, this project's case studies seek to uncover the relative importance of domestic sovereignty and self-interested considerations for the Great Powers and the process by which the Great Powers make their recognition decisions. Although every effort was made to capture the strength of a secessionist movement in the quantitative portion of the study using group mobilization, violence level, and war victory, none permitted sufficient leverage. The level of violence did not effectively tap into the authority or legitimacy of the nascent state, and at-risk minority mobilization, although better along the popular legitimacy dimension, did not include non-MAR secessionist groups or capture effective authority and control. Therefore, two primary considerations guided case selection for the qualitative study. First, the cases needed to exhibit wide variation on the as yet unexplored explanatory variable – domestic control and authority – and needed to demonstrate significant variation along the Great Power interest variables.[42] Second, variables other than the primary explanatory variables needed to be as similar as possible so as to induce a modicum of control; those cases in the same geographic region and occurring during the same time period received preference.

The cases selected for this portion of the project are in the Former Yugoslavia and in post-Soviet states. Slovenia, Croatia, and Kosovo all shared the same Yugoslav home state and demanded independence around the same time. In contrast, Abkhazia, Chechnya, Nagorno-Karabakh, and South Ossetia have different home states (though Abkhazia and South Ossetia are both Georgian).

---

[42] Variation on the Great Power interest variables guiding case selection was judged according to the indicators employed in the quantitative analysis. See the project's codebook for additional details. Lieberman (2005) suggests this selection technique.

These cases do share a common lineage though, because each home state was formerly a part of the Soviet Union and became independent at similar points in time. Studying cases with similar geographic locations and historical trajectories ensures that they are the "most similar" cases on the many characteristics other than those under consideration.

Within the pool of potential clustered cases of secessionism (near 70 in all), most of those not selected did not afford a high degree of leverage on the relative weight of the explanatory variables. In the remaining excluded cases, where there was substantial variation on the independent variables, the dependent variable did not vary. Isolated, non-geographically clustered cases were excluded from consideration.

The specific secessionist movements selected from within the Yugoslavia and post-Soviet case clusters are not exhaustive, but they do cover the full range of variation in domestic sovereignty. For example, at least three other cases of secession from the former Yugoslavia could have been analyzed: Bosnia and Herzegovina, FYROM/Macedonia, and Serbian Krajina. However, these cases were judged to either (1) not afford much additional leverage on the questions under study or (2) not be as data rich as the alternative, selected case. Similarly, in the post-Soviet cluster, the Transniestria secessionist movement would have induced redundant variation.

Finally, trade-offs are inherent to any research design and the logic of case selection guiding this portion of the project is no exception. In this instance, selecting cases in clusters violates independence but also induces control on a number of potentially problematic sources of variation associated with region or time period. The potential non-independence of cases implies that a Great Power's recognition decision with respect to one secessionist state might influence the likelihood of recognition for the other secessionists in the case cluster. So Kosovo's recognition may be dependent on the choices that were made in Slovenia and Croatia or Abkhazia's recognition might influence Chechnya's. Indeed, there is no doubt that the then European Community members considered the secessions of Yugoslavia's republics to be a set, not truly individual movements. Additionally, the secessionists may influence one another. In Yugoslavia, the timing of Croatia's declaration of independence was inspired by Slovenia's. As a partial fix to the issue of non-independence within the clusters, the possibility of contingent decisions and the influence of prior decisions will be explicitly addressed throughout. By straightforwardly considering dependence within the clusters, we can estimate the weight of its influence on recognition – if not rule it out entirely. The advantages of clustered cases outweigh the costs.

Two other potential limitations involve the timing of the case clusters. The first, again, is non-independence and the second involves generalizability. Because all of the cases within the case clusters occur around the same time, it is possible that there is cross-cluster dependence. For example, the EC standards for recognition that undergirded the Badinter Commission's work were derived from the experience of Soviet disintegration. And Moscow often argued that the secessionist demands in its near-abroad compared favorably to those in the Former Yugoslavia. As mentioned earlier, whenever this occurs, it is explicitly noted within the text. It is also worth pointing out, however, that the substantive implications of dependence, be it within or across clusters, for the larger argument may not be particularly acute. Where Great Power recognition does demonstrate dependence, it reinforces our belief that factors other than those on the ground are influencing state decisions.

The second potential limitation of choosing contemporaneous case clusters is their non-generalizability, in other words, that there was something distinct about the time period and that, therefore, we have reason to doubt that other recognition decisions had similar motives or dynamics. Fortunately, the results of the large N analysis – finding significant relationships between the Great Powers' interests and their recognition behavior – give us greater confidence that the 1989–2011 period was not the only time in which external politics influenced state emergence. But the possibility that the Great Powers' interests and alignment should influence whether and when new states enter the international system is one important implication of this work. If the argument is correct, different eras should yield different sets of new states.

Operational Definitions and Sources

Case study research requires rearticulating and expanding the main concepts' operational definitions.[43] *Domestic sovereignty*, according to Krasner's well-known typology, "refers to the formal organization of political authority within the state and the ability of public authorities to exercise effective control within the borders of their own polity." For the purposes of this study, Krasner's *Westphalian sovereignty*, "the exclusion of external actors from authority structures within a given territory" also fits within the domestic sovereignty concept.[44] Regimes with domestic control and authority are able, through physical force, to exclude external actors from their territory. They are also empowered to compromise that sovereignty if they so choose.

A number of factors are suggestive of the extent of control exercised by nascent states. Where secessionist conflicts took the form of formal war, we can observe the literal surrender and taking of territory and the wars' ultimate resolutions. Where there was no conflict or, as in the cases of Kosovo and most of the post-Soviet states, there is no longer conflict, the task is more complex. Because Kosovo was an international trust until its second independence declaration

---

[43] Conceptual definitions remain consistent throughout. For ease of understanding, concepts are reiterated along with the case study operationalizations.

[44] Krasner (1999, p. 3).

and recognition in 2008, reliable measures of control are widely available. In many other cases of cold secessionist conflict, this information is not readily available or highly skewed to reflect the home state's preferred view; therefore, control is more difficult to estimate. The post-Soviet cases illustrate just how variable estimates of control can be when conflicts are stalemated postwar. In these instances, a regime's control was estimated by observing whether or not the actor administered independent schools, conducted or supported legitimate trade, and provided governmental services such as those ensuring law and order or medical care; whether or not the regime collected taxes and conducted independent elections; and whether or not the government put forward an independent constitution.

In addition to physical control, the results of plebiscites, constitutional referenda, and opinion polls are reasonable indicators of popular support for secession, or the legitimacy of a particular governing regime, within the public. Other evidence of governmental legitimacy might include the establishment of cultural institutions or holidays and the return of formerly displaced or diaspora communities. When available, these indicators serve as measures of a secessionist state's popular legitimacy. Also, special care was taken to delimit the contours of the population assigning legitimacy. For example, whereas the Rugova regime was quite popular among Kosovo Albanians, Kosovo's minority Serb population was not supportive. Every effort was made to capture the nuances of the domestic political environment.

Lastly, beyond military control or voter support, domestic sovereignty was further estimated using professional external forecasts of post-secession viability conducted by Deutsche Bank, the World Bank and the U.S. State Department. These estimates suggest whether or not experts believed at the time that the secessionist states would be able to survive economically, politically, and security-wise for the foreseeable future. If a state's domestic sovereignty was fleeting or otherwise unsustainable, then the Great Powers might reasonably reject its request for recognition. Still, the instability of a nascent regime might simply be window dressing masking a leader's ulterior motives for nonrecognition. This is why expert analyses were consulted rather than accepting the justifications offered by leaders themselves. Each of the three dimensions of domestic sovereignty – (1) territorial control and effective authority, (2) popular legitimacy, and (3) projected viability – will be detailed for each secessionist movement in the two case clusters. See Table 4.4 for the secessionist movements' classification according to the three operationalizations of domestic sovereignty.

In the quantitative analysis, the political interest hypotheses regarding external security, domestic politics, and systemic stability were narrowly limited to a handful of operational indicators. The qualitative analysis allows the variables to be more inclusive. A leader motivated by domestic politics might be pressured by a powerful interest group's support of a secessionist movement, for example. Or a Great Power facing a transnational terrorist group operating in conjunction

TABLE 4.4 *Variation in Domestic Sovereignty by Case Cluster*

	Secessionist Actor	Domestic Sovereignty	Territorial Control and Effective Authority	Popular Legitimacy	Projected Viability
Former Yugoslavia	Slovenia	High	High	High	High
	Croatia	Medium	Medium	Med.-High	Medium
	Kosovo	Low	Low	High	Low
Soviet Successors	Chechnya I	Med.-High	High	High	Med.-High
	Abkhazia	Medium	Med.-High	Medium	Medium
	Nagorno-Karabakh	Medium	Med.-High	High	Medium
	South Ossetia	Medium	Medium	Medium	Low
	Chechnya II	Low	Low	Med.-High	Low

with a secessionist movement or home state could be motivated by international security concerns. Generally, when a Great Power's motives are self-regarding along the three hypothesized dimensions, it is considered evidence in favor of my argument.

The interest variables are identified by leaders' and other high-level decision makers' explicit consideration of them. One potential difficulty for this research design is the possibility that leaders have the incentive to obscure their true intentions regarding recognition. Perhaps domestic constituencies would oppose recognition for the sake of geostrategic ends but would enthusiastically support recognition to stall genocide. This, in turn, might cause leaders to portray their decision as a humanitarian response. In this example, expressed purposes may not match actual motives. Although it is difficult to guard against this possibility in any research, triangulating information sources ensures that the explanatory variables are, in fact, influencing leaders' recognition decisions; the mechanism of influence is specified. Whenever possible, public pronouncements were checked and compared with private deliberations, policy papers, multiple memoirs, and so on. More generally, the data for the case study portion of the project come from a variety of sources including transcripts, news articles, interviews, memoirs, secondary scholarly texts, and public debates.

Many potential signals indicate that others have acknowledged a new state as a member of the system. But for all of the reasons articulated at the beginning of the chapter, formal diplomatic recognition is best suited to this research. Formal recognition is typically granted through public pronouncement by a head of state or announced by a foreign secretary. This indicator is an uncontroversial sign of external acceptance; it is readily available, and it is explicit.

CASE STUDY STRUCTURE

The case studies for this project follow a loose, but structured focused comparison as described by A. L. George and Andrew Bennett.[45] Each cluster of case studies addresses the same set of questions, imposing an order to the structure of the cases in addition to the temporal order essential to any case study. Each case will discuss the following questions:

1) To what extent do the secessionists have domestic sovereignty (across time)? Domestic sovereignty includes three components: territorial control and effective authority within its borders, popular legitimacy among its people, and projected viability as a future state member.

2) To what extent are the Great Powers aware of the extent of domestic sovereignty exercised? Is domestic sovereignty an explicit consideration with respect to recognition?

3) How do leaders define their interests, broadly speaking and more narrowly vis-à-vis the secessionist movement? Do those interests coincide with the interest measures in the quantitative portion of the project?

4) How much weight do the Great Powers assign to their own interests relative to a secessionist state's domestic sovereignty when considering recognition?

5) Is recognition principally a unilateral decision? Or do the Great Powers explicitly coordinate, cooperate, or otherwise consider each other's preferences in granting recognition? And what determines the timing of their consultations?

6) Are any unhypothesized considerations entertained in discussions of possible recognition?

---

[45] As initially articulated in George (1979) and updated in George and Bennett (2004).

5

International Responses to Secession in Yugoslavia, 1989–2011

With the death of Marshall (Josip Broz) Tito, the Socialist Federal Republic of Yugoslavia (SFRY) began to show signs of the problems that ultimately destroyed it.[1] Throughout the 1980s, Yugoslavia faced constitutional crises and domestic unrest and teetered on the verge of dissolution. Somehow though, in each instance, the troubled republic persevered. It was not until 1991 that expectations of Yugoslavia's fall were finally realized. Rising expansionist nationalism among Serbs and Croats in the 1980s provoked separatist challenges in various minority regions, and those areas later secessions left the federation beyond repair. As Yugoslavia unraveled, it descended into violent civil and then international wars.

Most experts agree that Slobodan Milosevic's virulent brand of Serbian nationalism was the persistent cause behind Yugoslavia's conflicts.[2] But the reasons for Yugoslavia's destruction were not exclusively internal. Nor were the internal causes determinative. External actors were pivotal in the death of the state and Yugoslavia's collapse was not predestined. Without the specific choices made by powerful outsiders, Yugoslavia's many conflicts would not likely have reached the same conclusions.

Observers are divided over what or who bears responsibility for Yugoslavia's collapse. Many argue the Slovenian and Croatian conflicts could have been contained and need not have destroyed the state.[3] They fault external actors for their negative influence on the situation, seemingly leaving regions such as Bosnia and Herzegovina (hereafter referred to as Bosnia) and Macedonia with no choice but secession. Others argue the international community's "lack of

---

[1] Marshall Tito died on May 4, 1980.

[2] Many other responsible parties and causes underlie Yugoslavia's civil wars. These include Croatian nationalism, ethnic thugs (Mueller, 2004), federal governmental structure, and international lack of will (Gow 1997).

[3] Eyal (1993, p.49)

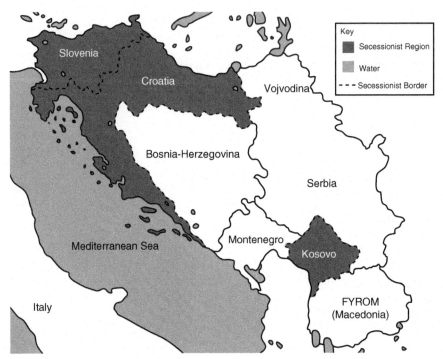

MAP 5.1 Yugoslavia Secessions

will" allowed virulent nationalism to take control of the country.[4] Once powerful states were sufficiently motivated to intervene, it was already too late. Still
others argue that it was intervention, not indifference, that doomed the embattled state. Finally, some believe Yugoslavia's bad marriage of ethnic nationalism
and federalism would have condemned any effort to keep the republic together;
it was simply a matter of time. According to this last interpretation, the dictates
of contemporary international law, specifically the Badinter Commission's
extension of *uti possidetis juris* to include internal boundaries, necessitated
Yugoslavia's disintegration.[5] If taken as established precedent, many federal
states would be vulnerable to a similar fate.

External recognition also figures prominently in the controversy surrounding
Yugoslavia's collapse.[6] As 1991 drew to a close, German officials became
convinced that the Yugoslav conflict was stalemated and, further, that Serbia
was responsible for the impasse. German leaders believed the only way to avoid

---

[4] Gow (1997); Ullman (1996).
[5] For discussions of the nature of *uti possidetis juris* and its extension beyond colonial independence
   in Yugoslavia, see Caplan (2005, pp. 68–71); Radan (1999); Lalonde (2002); Ratner (1996).
[6] Bearce (2002); Crawford (1996).

further Serb aggression was to formally recognize the secessionists, at that time Slovenia and Croatia, thereby internationalizing the conflict. As a consequence, the defenseless republics could seek the recourses afforded exclusively to states under international law. They believed that faced with the certain loss of the two republics, Serbs would be forced to give up their demands for an unaltered Yugoslavia or Greater Serbia.

Most of Europe disagreed with the Germans at first, but as the others grew frustrated with Milosevic and began to adopt Germany's point of view, Chancellor Kohl's patience ran out, and he unilaterally recognized Slovenia and Croatia. Some believe, contrary to Kohl's intentions, that Germany's decision actually provoked further Serb aggression and the subsequent war in Bosnia.[7] Seen in this manner, the decision to defect from the European Community's comprehensive settlement plan dashed any hope of salvaging Yugoslavia.[8] Perhaps Slovenia's and Croatia's secessions were unavoidable, but Macedonia and Bosnia's departures could have been prevented, as could the war in Bosnia. Finally, Germany's unilateral precedents created the potential to cause even further regional conflict as Kosovo, Macedonia, and Montenegro grappled with their own possible independence. According to this interpretation, the international community should have reigned in German sympathies in favor of greater European stability.

Recognition's possible role in the progression of Yugoslavia's wars is certainly worthy of comment, but this chapter takes an alternative approach to the question of recognition. Whether or not Germany's decision in particular catalyzed the war over Bosnia, recognition did play a decisive role in the international landscape left in Yugoslavia's wake. Why was there so much controversy surrounding Germany's choice? If Slovenia and Croatia were not yet states, why would Germany, and then the European Union (EU), recognize them as such? Specifically, why would the remaining members of the EU follow Germany's seemingly rash, unilateral example (Table 5.1). On the other hand, if Slovenia and Croatia were indeed states, why would mere recognition of an achieved fact, a *fait accompli*, cause such a fracture in European relations? How do we know that a new state has entered the international system? And in this case specifically, why didn't the Great Powers agree?

Yugoslavia's collapse has been thoroughly studied, but a reevaluation of its demise is both theoretically useful and politically timely. Scholarship has not adequately evaluated external politics' influence on the emergence of new states

---

[7] Lord Peter Carrington cited in Silber and Little (1996, pp. 199–200); Silber and Little suggest the same themselves on p. 205. Gow (1997) argues to the contrary that war preparations for Bosnia were made well in advance of EC recognition. This fact suggests that war would have come to Bosnia regardless of the international community's recognition decisions (p. 34).

[8] European Community (EC) and European Union (EU) will be used interchangeably throughout the project. The European Union formally succeeded the European Community when the Treaty of the European Union came into force on November 1, 1993.

TABLE 5.1 *Great Power Recognition*

Slovenia	Germany	December 24, 1991 (effective January 15)
	Britain	January 15, 1992
	France	January 15, 1992
	Russia	February 17, 1992
	Japan	March 17, 1992
	United States	April 7, 1992
	China	May 12, 1992
Croatia	Germany	December 24, 1991 (effective January 15)
	Britain	January 15, 1992
	France	January 15, 1992
	Russia	February 17, 1992
	Japan	March 17, 1992
	United States	April 7, 1992
	China	May 13, 1992
Kosovo	Germany	February 20, 2008
	Britain	February 18, 2008
	France	February 18, 2008
	Russia	No recognition
	Japan	March 18, 2008
	US	February 18, 2008
	China	No recognition

in the post–Cold War era. Although many scholars and diplomats expected state emergence to slow (if not stop completely) with the demise of colonialism and the fall of empires, it has not.[9] Instead, it seems the interstate system has no natural equilibrium; the desire for sovereign independence remains strong, and state emergence continues unabated. What are the causes and consequences of this counterintuitive trend? When and why does the international community accept new members without colonial grievances as it did with the Former Yugoslavia?

The politics of recognition are also of renewed relevance to the Former Yugoslavia's current politics because Kosovo's status remains uncertain. Although it unilaterally declared independence in 2008, Kosovo would likely not be able to maintain its independence without external backing. Indeed, as one headline exclaimed, Kosovo declared "something a lot like dependence" rather than true independence. Three of the five permanent Security Council members formally recognize Kosovo, but Serbian officials have no intention of revoking their claim to authority over at least part of the territory and have, until

[9] As evidence that formal colonialism is no longer practiced, the United Nations Trusteeship Council, one of the major international instruments dedicated to trust and non-self-governing territories' independence, suspended its regular meetings with the independence of Palau in 1994. Since then, Secretary General Kofi Annan had recommended that the council disband entirely.

recently, pledged to take it back by force if necessary.[10] For their part, Kosovo Albanians are unwilling to surrender even a shred of the autonomy they have enjoyed since 1999. Lastly, Russia and China do not seem willing to grant recognition to a government that unilaterally declared independence, cannot sustain itself, and sets an undesirable precedent for others. In short, the Kosovo situation may yet have repercussions for international stability; the strongest states in the international system do not often recognize competing authorities within the same territory.

Furthermore, Kosovo's final status will undoubtedly influence future majority-minority relations within the region.[11] Many Eastern European states, including those of the Former Yugoslavia, continue to struggle with ethnonational separatism and the accommodation of national minorities. Understanding the politics of recognition surrounding Yugoslavia's initial dissolution may shed light on the future of regional politics, especially in countries like Bosnia.

Unfortunately, even with the benefit of hindsight, the most important cause of Yugoslavia's wars will remain uncertain. As with most international conflicts, Yugoslavia's demise was the result of numerous inherent pathologies and avoidable missteps, ranging from long-standing ethnic hatreds to Milosevic's insidious nationalism to democratic transition to international intervention. This chapter will not do justice to every factor contributing to Yugoslavia's collapse. Instead, it concentrates on understanding the external or international forces contributing to Yugoslav dissolution and the new states that emerged in its wake. Specifically, it asks when, why, and how the Great Powers determined that Yugoslavia was no longer one state, but many.

In this chapter, I examine the international politics surrounding three very different secessionist states within the Former Yugoslavia: Slovenia, Croatia, and Kosovo.[12] The case cluster first describes the domestic and international contexts in which the secessions arose. Then, assessments of the level of internal sovereignty exercised by each proto-state are taken. Next, I explore the bilateral and multilateral politics surrounding each secession attempt, examining the Great Powers' initial preferences regarding recognition as well as their evolution

---

[10] Though Serbian demands for Kosovo have become more moderate since Milosevic's ouster, Serbs still seek a special relationship, possibly formal, with Kosovo's Serb minority.

[11] For example, authorities in Transniestria declared that they would hold a referendum on independence in the event of Kosovo independence. Yevgeny Shevchuk, speaker of the parliament in the self-proclaimed republic, argued that Kosovo independence would set a precedent for other states in the post-Soviet space, including Transniestria, Nagorno-Karabakh, and South Ossetia. ITAR-TASS (2006).

[12] Not all of Yugoslavia's constituent units will be considered in this chapter. Although the conflict in Bosnia is certainly integral to Yugoslavia's collapse, too many dynamics were simultaneously at play in that republic. As Bosnia sought independence, Croats and Serbs within Bosnia sought to join Croatia and Greater Serbia. These dynamics limited the potential insight for a case study. Macedonia was not included simply because its variation on the independent variable (authority and control) was redundant.

over time. In this portion, I evaluate how the Great Powers justify their preferences; whether the Great Powers are explicitly attempting to coordinate their
recognition with one another; and, regarding Kosovo, why nearly two decades
of coordinated nonrecognition lapsed.

HISTORICAL BACKGROUND

Yugoslavia confronted the same difficulties many Eastern European states did as
they adjusted to the post–Cold War era. Economic transition, latent ethnic
nationalisms, and political volatility made the period particularly uncertain for
the region. Rapid change, high inflation, and political unrest were commonplace. Remarkably, most countries emerged from their postwar transformations
relatively unscathed, though fundamentally altered from their Cold War selves.
Yugoslavia was not so fortunate. Yugoslavs' responses to the pressures of the
new world order were exceptional in the extent of their destruction and the
brutality of their violence.

Josip Tito had ruled Yugoslavia for nearly the entire post–World War II
period (1953–1980). Though devoutly socialist, Tito's Yugoslavia was often at
odds with the Soviet Union. First, Tito advocated domestic profit sharing for
state-owned enterprises (SOEs), which, though not well thought of in the USSR,
left Yugoslavia economically somewhat better off. Second, Tito was fiercely
independent. Under his leadership, Yugoslavia became one of the founding
members of the Non-Aligned Movement; he would not join the Warsaw Pact
states. Tito's uneasy relationship with the Soviet Union made him a Western
darling, as did what was then seen as his deft handling of Yugoslavia's difficult
minority situation. Charismatic and strong willed, Tito insisted that Communist
ideology and Yugoslav identity alone were sufficient to unite the republic.
Accordingly, his regime repressed ethnic nationalisms in favor of socialist unity.

Nevertheless, local governmental control within Yugoslavia often coincided
with a republic's ethnic majority (see Table 5.4). Slovenia's population of about
2 million was approximately 90 percent Slovene. Serbia was two-thirds Serb
(including Kosovo and Vojvodina), Montenegro was two-thirds Montenegrin,
and Macedonia was two-thirds Macedonian. Croatia, with a population around
4.7 million, was 85 percent Croat and around 12 percent Serb. Serbs constituted
local majorities in 14 of the 102 administrative districts within Croatia, however.[13] Finally, Bosnia had the most ethnically diverse population where "some
40 percent [were] Muslims, 32 percent Serbs and 18 percent Croats."[14] This
effectively meant that many of Yugoslavia's republics (Croatia, Macedonia,
Montenegro, Slovenia, and Serbia) had ethnic majorities that were politically
dominant as well.

---

[13] Weller (1992, p. 569).
[14] Ibid. It should be mentioned that the precise contours of Yugoslavia's ethnic makeup are
   contested.

At the same time, most Yugoslav states had significant minority populations. There were Serb enclaves in Bosnia, Croatia, Kosovo, and Vojvodina. Both Bosnia and Slovenia had Croat minorities. Kosovo had a small Macedonian population. Serbia had Albanians, Bosnians, Montenegrins, and Macedonians. And Montenegro had Albanians, Bosnians, Croats, and Serbs. Finally, in Macedonia there were Albanian, Montenegrin, and Serb minorities. So even though majority populations were politically dominant, state borders did not neatly coincide with ethnicity. Even Yugoslavia's constituent parts were decidedly multiethnic.

Though it had not always been the case, Yugoslav authority became significantly more diffuse and federal in the 1970s. Under the 1974 constitution, each republic essentially governed itself. Schools, police, and even territorial armies were organized under local, rather than national, authority. The diffuse governmental structure had mostly encouraged internal stability under Tito:

[T]he country lived under a relatively mild party dictatorship that guaranteed freedom of movement, the basic forms of private ownership, an effective public administration and services, and a changeable tolerance of the informal political opposition within and outside the Communist party. A relatively high degree of cultural and administrative autonomy for the various federal units made it possible for a period of greater restrictions on the freedom of the press and speech in one republic to be mitigated by a more liberal attitude on these matters adopted in another republic. In that way the effects of one-party exclusivity were to some extent neutralized.[15]

Unfortunately, it was also Yugoslavia's federal organization – along principally ethnic lines – that encouraged tensions between the republics to manifest in interethnic hostilities throughout the 1980s.

When Tito died, so did the idea that Yugoslavia's nations were indivisible and their internal boundaries arbitrary. Almost immediately, Kosovo Albanians demanded that Kosovo's status be elevated from an autonomous region to a constituent republic.[16] Serbian authorities responded badly. The Albanians were brutally repressed by Serbia, which dubbed them "hostile and counterrevolutionary."[17] Kosovar officials were purged from government, rioters were jailed, Pristina University was closed, and a state of emergency was declared. Serbian nationalism resurfaced. Threatened by the activist turn in Kosovo, and justifiably concerned for their own security, Kosovo Serbs demanded that Serbia intervene. Serbs throughout Yugoslavia advocated that Kosovo and Vojvodina have their autonomy revoked. But unrest only spread as Serb authorities placed increasingly draconian restrictions on the autonomous regions. Violence had proliferated throughout Kosovo by 1989.

[15] Pusic (1992, p. 244).
[16] Kosovo Albanians first rioted for autonomy in April and May of 1981.
[17] Pond (1981, p. 14).

It was in this tendentious ethnic and economic environment that Slobodan Milosevic ascended to power in Serbia. Milosevic politically manipulated Kosovo's unrest to stoke fears of ethnic subordination among Kosovo Serbs and Serbs in Serbia proper (though there was little evidence of systematic Serb repression in Kosovo).[18] Until then thought of as a bland technocrat, Milosevic defied expectations. He used nationalist propaganda, emotional public rhetoric, and scripted public protests to consolidate his political power. Milosevic became the leader of Serbian Communists in 1987 and proceeded on to the Serbian presidency on May 8, 1989, after ousting his former mentor, Ivan Stambolic.[19] Once in power, Milosevic set to "protecting" Serbs in Kosovo by restricting local power and asserting federal control. Time would clarify, though, that Milosevic's political ambitions did not end with protecting Serbs in the autonomous provinces.

Around the same time, Slovenia and Croatia began pushing for greater autonomy. Mounting Serb nationalism undoubtedly strengthened the desire to decentralize authority, but economic incentives figured more prominently at first.[20] Yugoslavia's six republics faced starkly different circumstances as they transitioned to an open market economy. Each state's preference for the character and pace of Yugoslavia's reforms mirrored its economic incentives. Slovenia and Croatia were relatively advantaged in liberal international markets and felt stifled by the other republics. Net contributors to the central government, they wanted to decrease their burdens and become more integrated with Europe. The difficulties of economic transition, the worldwide recession in the 1980s, Yugoslavia's huge foreign debt, and relative dependence among the republics all strained Slovenia's and Croatia's relations with the union. Though the two were economically strong, they did not want to remain bound to the struggling southern republics. To continue to live as permanent minorities within that system, under Serb dominion, was even less attractive. In contrast, Kosovo was relatively underdeveloped and benefited significantly from the contributions of other members.[21] Not eager to forgo those returns, Kosovars

---

[18] Though Kosovo Serbs were the targets of violence during the Albanian riots in Kosovo, Serbs were not systematically discriminated against in the region.

[19] Judah (1997) notes that the formal ceremony was scheduled for June 28 in order to coincide with the 600th anniversary of the Battle of Kosovo, thus heightening the nationalist sentiment behind the occasion (p. 164).

[20] Vodopivec (1992) argues contrarily that "calls for repressive measures against opposition intellectuals and for centralization in the fields of education, science and culture did more to mobilize public opinion than did the economic problems" (p. 237).

[21] As one author observed, "Slovenia, with only 8.2 percent of the [Yugoslav] population produced between 17 percent and 18 percent of Yugoslavia's GDP, 25 percent of Yugoslavia's total exports, and 33 percent of Yugoslavia's exports to hard currency markets [in the 1980s]" (Prunk, 1997, p. 27). Slovenia paid "20 percent" of the federation's income in the form of taxes and "special funds for the underdeveloped regions" (ibid., p. 28). Serbia proper and Croatia provided the greatest percentage of funds to support Yugoslavia's federal institutions (Bookman, 1992, p. 78). Bookman also notes that Croatia provided more if Kosovo and Vojvodina are considered a part of

initially preferred greater internal autonomy and political prestige to independence.

Yugoslavia's republics differed in their domestic political characters as well. Again, Slovenia and Croatia established Western-style systems, whereas the other republics followed Serbia's example more closely. Slovenia's first independent elections were held in April 1990. The major Slovenian parties campaigned on human rights, democratic governance, and economic liberalism. Milan Kucan, of the League of Communists of Slovenia (LDC), was elected president. Though Slovenia elected a Communist president and the Communists under Milosevic were also in power in Serbia, superficial continuity masked deeper differences.[22] As one observer noted, "the difference between the League of Communists of Slovenia and the League of Communists of Serbia corresponded roughly with the difference between Franz Vranitsky's Austrian Socialists and the Supreme Soviet in Azerbaijan."[23] Serbia's centralizing aspirations threatened Slovenians, and they found the popular, nationalistic fervor anachronistic. Even so, Slovenes were initially willing to pursue internal reforms along the lines of a confederation of independent states like that of the British Commonwealth. Slovenia only came to embrace secession as constitutional negotiations broke down. It became evident that the two systems, one liberal and democratic, the other centralized and nationalistic, were fundamentally incompatible.

Croatians, although similar to Slovenians in some respects, adopted a distinct political character from that of their neighbors. Like Slovenians, Croatians contributed substantial support to the less developed republics. Also like Slovenia, in the years following Tito's death, the Croatian Communist Party had ruled Croatia. And, therefore, it was widely held that Croatia's first free elections, in May, would yield a Communist Party victory. However, outsiders underestimated Croats' antipathy for Titoism and the Croatian Communist Party. Further, they incorrectly gauged the extent of Croats' insecurity and the ferocity of their own newfound nationalism. The Communists lost and were replaced with the right-wing HDZ (Christian Democratic Union).

Whereas Slovenia had transformed the Communist Party from within, Croatians transferred power to a regime they believed would lead their republic away from both Milosevic and their Communist past. Popular opinion saw the Croatian Communists as ineffectual and too moderate in their stance toward Milosevic. Also unlike Slovenia, Croatia had a significant, discontented Serbian minority. Ethnic mobilization and expansionist rhetoric among Serbian Serbs

---

Serbia. Bosnia and Slovenia contributed the next greatest proportions, followed by Vojvodina. Kosovo and Montenegro, the least developed regions, also contributed the least to central authorities. Rezun notes that even in Slovenia economic uncertainties provoked anti-migrant sentiments directed at guest workers from the southern republics (Rezun, 1995 p. 178).

[22] In January 1990, Slovenes and Croats left the Yugoslav Communist Party to form their own Communist parties.

[23] Pusic (1992, p. 242).

were potentially destabilizing in Croatia, especially in areas with local Serb majorities. The Croatian population felt threatened. Dr. Franjo Tudjman's HDZ presented a more assertive, more palatable alternative to being bullied by Serbia.

The HDZ delivered. One of the new government's first acts in office was a constitutional change affirming that Croatia was "the national state of the Croatian people," eliminating the special place formerly reserved for its Serb minority.[24] Though the change was principally a gesture, the HDZ's historical association with Nazism did little to allay fears within the Serb community. The new government touched off a spiral of insecurity between Croats and Croatian Serbs. Judah aptly notes, "Milosevic's Serbian nationalism was the greatest boost to Tudjman's Croatian nationalism, but now that the Pandora's box had been opened, there was no shutting it;" the two nationalisms would feed off of each other's hostility.[25]

Controversial in his own right, as president, Tudjman advocated a Catholic, verging on anti-Semitic, Croatian nationalism, Croatian independence, and an obliquely irredentist agenda regarding Bosnia.[26] His rallying cry was effective among Croats. By one count, seven political movements within Croatia were dedicated to secessionism by 1989.[27] In response, Croatia's significant Serb minority threatened to join Serbia in the event of independence. The domestic political situation was incredibly unstable. Though Croatia took its cues from Slovenia when it came to the future relationship among Yugoslavia's states, independence had become Croats' primary goal.

PRECIPITATING EVENTS

Yugoslavia's union was imperiled as the 1980s came to a close. And yet, none of republics or autonomous regions had demanded independence. Slovenia and Croatia both ostensibly sought a confederation of states, maintaining some degree of Yugoslav unity, and Kosovo wanted higher status within the existing union. Finally, Yugoslavia's remaining republics were satisfied with continued unity – contingent on the other republics remaining within the state as well. In

---

[24] Caplan (2005, p. 115 and n.80).

[25] Judah (1997, p. 165).

[26] Emblematically, he had been known to say that Bosnia and Croatia formed a "natural political and economic unit" and that Bosnia was historically "a Catholic kingdom, linked to Croatia" Tanner (1997, pp. 228, 242).

[27] Rezun (1995) cites the Central Committee of the Croatian League of Communists, the Croatian Catholic Community, the Croatian Liberation Movement, the Croatian National Committee, the Croatian Revolutionary Brotherhood, and Otpor "a Croatian terrorist group" (p.122). Elsewhere Otpor is described as a Serbian pro-democracy youth group turned political party. It was widely discredited within Serbia because of its strong ties to the U.S. government. Otpor was subject to a number of human rights abuses at the hands of Serb authorities leading up to the 2000 elections according to the Human Rights Watch World Report for 2001. It is unclear whether these two groups are associated with each other.

the spring of 1991, the constituent republics made their final attempt to negotiate structural reforms and salvage the federation. The negotiations were unsuccessful. A mutually agreeable solution was impossible given Milosevic's rigid
insistence on centralized authority and Slovenia's and Croatia's refusal to submit
to his or any continued Serbian authority.

In 1989, under pressure from federal authorities, Vojvodina and Kosovo lost
their autonomous statuses and their leaders were replaced with Milosevic allies.
Later, Montenegro's leaders were similarly replaced. On July 2, Kosovo's provincial assembly formally demanded that its status be elevated to a constituent
republic. Its population had been demanding this for years. Serbian authorities
reacted by dissolving Kosovo's legislative assembly. They then proceeded to
formally incorporate both autonomous provinces under Serbian authority.
Effectively, this meant Serbia now controlled four votes within the Yugoslav
Federation: Kosovo, Montenegro, Serbia, and Vojvodina. Once in control, more
than 100,000 Albanian jobs within Kosovo were eliminated. Albanians called a
general, province-wide strike to protest the new policies. Serbia retaliated by
subjecting the Kosovo Albanians to a virtual police state. Within Slovenia and
Croatia, Milosevic's treatment of Kosovo and the other provinces was taken as a
harbinger of things to come. Independence quickly became a more attractive
option.

On December 23, 1990, Slovenia held a referendum on independence.
Ninety-three percent of the electorate participated in the vote, and approximately 89 percent of voters supported secession in the event that negotiations
with the other republics failed (Table 5.2). The day before, Croatia promulgated
a new constitution nullifying federal law within the province.[28] The Yugoslav
Supreme Court quickly declared both nullifications illegal. Neither Tudjman nor
Kucan, however, demanded independence outright. Both held fast to the proposed loose confederation among Yugoslavia's states. But they also publicly
reiterated that the 1974 constitution granted a right of secession to Yugoslavia's
constituent nations, leaving open the possibility for their eventual departures.[29]

Throughout the spring, the presidents of Yugoslavia's states participated in a
series of negotiations in an attempt to maintain their union and create workable
formal relationships among the republics. Little, if anything, was accomplished.
As Silber and Little recount, the representatives simply used the occasions to
reiterate their already recalcitrant positions. In fact, there was no negotiation at
all. Milosevic granted Slovenia's and Croatia's contention that they had a
constitutional right to secede, but he countered that Croatia's minority Serb
population was entitled to the same right. Tudjman dubbed the sessions

---

[28] The Slovenian parliament had declared sovereignty on July 2 and declared federal law null on
July 27.

[29] Interestingly, the constitution also stipulated that secession could only occur with a consensus of
Yugoslavia's constituent nations. This technicality was not raised by either.

"conversations of the deaf."[30] Behind the scenes, Slovenia and Croatia quietly began preparations to secure their independence.

In early May 1991, according to established precedent, the Yugoslav federal presidency was supposed to rotate to Stjepan "Stipe" Mesic, a Croat. But the Serbian-controlled block prevented Mesic from assuming the post. They installed Borisav Jovic, a Serb, as president instead. The move proved to be the straw that broke the camel's back. Slovenia and Croatia both moved for complete, formal independence and sovereign statehood. In Croatia, a referendum held on May 19 yielded overwhelming support (93.24 percent) for independence. Predictably, Croatian Serbs boycotted the election. They had conducted their own referendum earlier that month yielding a 90 percent vote in favor of remaining within Yugoslavia (see Table 5.2). With only around 12 percent of the total Croatian population though, even a unanimous Serb vote against independence in the republic-wide referendum would not have affected the outcome. In contrast, Slovenia's independence mandate had been clear since its plebiscite in December 1990.

Slovenia's and Croatia's secessionist aspirations were now undeterrable. Central authorities' threats that declarations of independence would be forcefully opposed would not stop them. Nor would a last-minute visit by American Secretary of State James Baker, who reiterated that the international community resolutely opposed unilateral moves toward secession. Kucan's and Tudjman's decisions were not hasty; they had been coordinating their possible independence for months. On June 15, the two met to make final preparations for their formal declarations of independence; although the Slovenians believed that Croatia was far less organized, Tudjman pressed forward nonetheless.[31] Both republics declared independence on June 25, 1991.[32] Their demands were dubbed unconstitutional and illegal, first by the presidency and then by the Yugoslav Constitutional Court. The Yugoslav National Army, the JNA, quickly moved to suppress the rebellions. In October, Kosovo formally declared independence as well.

[30] Silber and Little (1996. p. 147).
[31] For a firsthand recounting of the final meeting, see ibid., pp. 149–150.
[32] On September 17 (1991), Macedonia declared independence. Kosovo came next on October 11, 1991. Finally, Bosnia declared independence on April 5, 1992. Almost immediately on word of the secessionist ambitions, minority populations in those republics declared themselves independent as well. Serbs and Croats declared themselves independent of Bosnia in 1992 (in July and October, respectively). Then, Serbs in Croatia declared themselves independent on March 1, 1992. All of the secondary secessions sought reunification with some part of the Former Yugoslavia; Serbs wanted to remain within Greater Serbia and Croats sought union with the new Croatian state. The declarations of Republika Srpska and Croatian Community of Herzeg-Bosnia were irredentist movements as their primary aim was to reunite all of Yugoslavia's predominantly Serb regions within a single independent state.

TABLE 5.2 *Independence Demands and Plebiscites*

	VOTE	INDEP.	UNION	OTHER	PERCENTAGE VOTING	TOTAL REG.
Slovenia Dec. 6/24/91	12/23/90[a]	88.5% 1,237,230	4.5% 54,000	1% Invalid	93.2% 1,398,000	1,500,000/ POP: 2 mil
Croatia Dec. 6/25/91	5/19/91	94% 2,910,240	5% 154,800	Serb Boycott: 2.7%, 100,000	86% 3,096,000	3,600,000/ POP: 5 mil
Serbian Krajina[b] Dec. 12/19/91	8/90	99%[c]	–	–		POP:
Kosovo Dec. 10/18/91[d]	9/26–30/91	99.87%	–	–	87%	POP: 2 mil
Kosovo Dec. 10/18/91	5/1992	98%	–	–	80%	POP: 2 mil
Bosnia[e] Dec. 12/20/91	3/1/92	99.4% 2,061,932	0.029% 6,037	0.25% Invalid Serb Boycott: ~33%	63.4% 2,073,500	3,200,000/ POP: 4.2 mil
Macedonia[f] Dec.9/17/91	9/8/91	95.26%		Albanian Boycott:	72.16%	1,300,000/ POP: 2 mil
Montenegro Dec. n/a	4/2006	42%[g]	35%	20%, 400,000	975,000	POP: 650,575
Montenegro Dec. 6/4/2006	5/22/06	55.4%[h]		n/a	n/a	POP: 650,000

[a] Specifically, 9 Slovenians and 37 Yugoslavs according to Spencer (1998, p. 175).

[b] UNPROFOR included 38,599 personnel at its height in March 1995. Although its mandate was initially limited to Croatia, as violence spread throughout Yugoslavia, it was expanded to include every constituent republic but Slovenia.

[c] Reproduced from "The National Composition of Yugoslavia's Population, 1991," *Yugoslav Survey* 33:1, pp. 4–13. Population for Kosovo and Vojvodina taken from Judah (1997), Appendix 4: Yugoslav Census of 1991, p. 316, who in turn cites *Statistical Pocket Book: Federal Republic of Yugoslavia* (Belgrade, 1993). Ethnic breakdown for Kosovo and Vojvodina taken from Duncan and Holman (1994, p. 27). Gray fill indicates the ethnic majority or the most numerous ethnicity within each subunit.

[d] A Kosovo census scheduled for 2005 was delayed until 2011. Kosovo had not held a census since 1981, well before international administration began. Albanians remained a majority in Kosovo, but many were internally displaced or refugees. Kosovo's total population was estimated to be more than 2 million as of 2006.

[e] Sum of Turks (4.8%), Romanies (2.7%), and Others and unknown (4.7%). Yugoslav not reported.

[f] Including Kosovo and Vojvodina.

[g] Forecast based upon a September 2005 poll conducted among Montenegrins taken from Cagorovic (2005).

[h] Summed. See original for details (ibid, p. 9).

THE INTERNATIONAL ENVIRONMENT

Outside Yugoslavia, the international system was undergoing a number of important political transitions in the late 1980s and early 1990s. In the Soviet Union, Mikhail Gorbachev had barely survived a coup attempt brought about by his institution of dramatic internal reforms. Politics and economics within the USSR were changing rapidly and the Superpower's future was uncertain. For the Yugoslav government, the Soviet Union's decline signaled the end of its geo-strategic influence and disproportionate leverage with the West. For Yugoslavia's discontented minorities, the Soviet Union's decline was viewed as an opportunity. Its subordinated minorities knew the central government's hand had been weakened with the demise of bipolar antagonisms. The superpowers might not be so quick to involve themselves in Yugoslavia's affairs because the stakes in the region were not as high as they once were. The conditions were ripe for independence.

Around the same time, discontented minorities in the USSR began secession attempts of their own. Sensing the central authorities' weakness, the Baltic states were the first to demand independence from the Soviet Union. Many others would soon follow. The coincidence of the two countries' secessionist challenges would not bode well for Yugoslavia's secessionists. Great Power leaders were acutely aware of Yugoslavia's potential influence on separatism in the USSR, and most leaders were far more concerned with the Soviet Union's disintegration than with Yugoslavia's. They were loath to set a precedent that might usher in worldwide instability.

Elsewhere in Europe, important changes were also underway. In Eastern Europe, Poland, Hungary, and Czechoslovakia were undergoing economic and political transitions in what have come to be called *refolutions* (a combination of reform and revolution). The Eastern European states' peaceful transitions away from communism toward democracy demonstrated that revolutionary change could be achieved through reform rather than violent upheaval. In these countries, where rapid reforms similar to those in Yugoslavia were occurring, violence was almost entirely averted. A peaceful transition was occurring in Western Europe as well. East and West Germany formally reunited on October 3, 1990. The new government was ushered in on a wave of euphoric satisfaction with self-determination and Western-style governance. Germany quickly stabilized and became an important player in regional politics. Neither German reunification nor the Eastern European *refolutions* inspired violence. Their successes, even in the face of dramatic change, made the Yugoslav conflict seem all the more brutal and unnecessary from the outside.

Across the Atlantic, the United States was involved in a war of its own. Gulf War I aimed to compel Iraq to withdraw from Kuwait, which it had occupied, and abandon its irredentist claims. Until the U.S.-led coalition intervened in the Iraq-Kuwait conflict, it was unclear whether the United States would assert itself as a global hegemon or whether, instead, the Soviet Union's fall would usher in a multipolar era. The war was significant for Yugoslavia because it meant much of the world, certainly the West, was preoccupied with the forces and finances they had committed in the Middle East. Most of the world was hesitant to get involved militarily in Yugoslavia's civil war.

As the Soviet Bloc was struggling through a transitional period and the United States was occupied elsewhere, Western Europe was laying the groundwork for its economic and political integration. Among its more ambitious aims, Europe hoped to create a unified European foreign policy. When conflict broke out in Yugoslavia, it was understood to be a European problem and, thus, an unprecedented opportunity for Europe to test its new initiative. As the Superpowers were otherwise engaged, they were content to oblige Europe a trial run at collective diplomacy. Still, European policy collaboration had not been tested. European leaders were no more eager than the United States to make a military commitment to Yugoslavia, so the means at the EC's disposal were limited.

As a result of the rapid changes in the international system, not all of the Great Powers were similarly interested or involved in Yugoslavia's conflicts. Initially, the European powers played the most significant role. The Soviet Union, and later the Russian Federation, mostly opted out of diplomatic intervention early on because of political turmoil and its own dissolution management. When Russia was engaged, it was in its role as a permanent member of the UN Security Council and member of the Commission on Security and Cooperation in Europe (CSCE).[33] The United States was not directly active in Yugoslavia until European leaders asked it to intervene in the mid-1990s. Finally, Yugoslavia was outside of the Asian powers' spheres of influence. China, a staunch defender of domestic sovereignty and nonintervention, played an active role in Security Council actions but was not otherwise active in the conflict. Japan, just securing its position as a global power, was even less engaged because it had no equivalent institutional position within the United Nations, nor was it particularly invested in the course of events in Yugoslavia.[34]

DOMESTIC SOVEREIGNTY

Yugoslavia's secessionists exercised various degrees of physical control within the territories they claimed, they had different levels of governmental legitimacy within their respective populations, and experts saw varied potential for each to become a viable state. Of course, any pre-independence viability estimates are subject to the somewhat unreasonable assumption that the status quo is

---

[33] Though the Soviet Union was not directly involved, concern for precedent made its disintegration a prominent consideration in the Great Powers' actions toward Yugoslavia. This was especially true within the EC. The CSCE formally changed its name to the Organization for Security and Co-operation in Europe (OSCE) on January 1, 1995.

[34] This is consistent with the expectations generated by the quantitative indicators. Japan had no security interests in Yugoslavia, faced no domestic challengers, and shared little in common with either Serbia or the secessionists.

maintained.[35] Nevertheless, according to the null hypothesis, authoritative control and effective authority should determine external recognition. Part of that estimation includes not only whether a regime is *temporarily* in control of its population and borders, but also whether it can reasonably be expected to *maintain* that control. Expert forecasts are the best, albeit imprecise, indicator of a secessionist region's potential viability.

As discussed earlier, there can be no incontrovertible evidence that a secessionist movement surpasses the established threshold for statehood. The criteria with the greatest consensus, the Montevideo standards, are inherently ambiguous, and efforts to clarify them have been unsuccessful.[36] Because the legal requirements are so unspecific, I created an index of control to guide this project's case selection. The lowest level of control, in this cluster manifest in the Kosovo case, includes secessionist regimes that clearly do not reach the standards for independence. At the medium level of control, the secessionist state arguably meets the minimum level of capacity required by law in most respects but falls short on at least one of the four required dimensions. Croatia fits within this category in the Yugoslav case. Finally, movements within the high category unambiguously meet or exceed the legal standards. In this cluster, Slovenia's domestic sovereignty was beyond reproach.[37]

SLOVENIA

Slovenia exercised the greatest degree of domestic sovereignty coincident with its declaration of independence. Although the central government mobilized JNA forces to combat its secession, the resulting civil war lasted only 10 days (Table 5.3). It is true that little force was brought to bear to maintain control over Slovenia, but Slovenia's armed forces were also proficient.[38] The regional government had a strong foundation for effective governance, partially because of Yugoslavia's loose federal structure, but additionally because Slovenes made extensive preparations for independence. Most Slovenians strongly favored independence. There was strategic ambiguity in the language of Slovenia's

---

[35] One difficulty in judging viability prior to independence is that a move for independence itself often provokes conflict (as it did in each of Yugoslavia's conflicts). Some of the costs associated with formal separation from a home state are estimable; others depend on the force brought to bear to resist the secession. As we will see, Slovenia's chances of winning its war against Yugoslav authorities did not look good ahead of time. Once the war began, however, and it was clear that Yugoslavia would not fight hard, its chances became much better. So, potential viability is often overtaken by the progress of events on the ground.

[36] See Grant (1999, pp. 30–32) on additional criteria such as "good governance," democracy, "civilizational level," and willingness and ability to observe international law.

[37] See Table 4.3.

[38] For example, many JNA forces moved into Slovenia only to find themselves surrounded by the Slovenian defense forces and cut off from their supply lines. The central government's war plans did not anticipate that the Slovenians would be so strategic.

TABLE 5.3 *Yugoslavia Conflict Statistics*

	Violence Duration	Deaths	Other	Territory	Victor	Peacekeepers
Slovenia	1991	46[a]		+100%	Slovenia	
Croatia (1)	1991–1992			−30% +70%	RSK/ Serbs	UNPROFOR[b] ENDED: 3/96
Croatia (2)	1995			+30% (100%)	Croatia	UNPROFOR/ UNCRO(6,581)/ UNTAES(5,561)/ UNPSG (110) ENDED: 10/1998
Kosovo	1998–1999		NATO	+100% international protectorate	NATO	KFOR/UNMIK (19,000) AS OF: 4/2005
Bosnia	1992–1995			+100%	Dayton Accords 1995	UNPROFOR/ UNMIBH (2,047) ENDED: 12/2002
Macedonia	n/a			+100%		UNPROFOR/ UNPREDEP (1,110) ENDED: 2/28/1999

[a] Sum of Hungarians (21%) and Others (23%).
[b] Sum of Hungarians (1.6%) and Others and unknown (4.6%).

plebiscite, but popular support for independence from Serbia was undisputed.[39] As a consequence of all these factors, few doubted Slovenia would remain viable if granted formal membership within the community of states. Slovenia had one of the most developed and open economies in Eastern Europe. And, beyond its potential conflict with Yugoslav authorities, Slovenia had no enemies or standing extraterritorial disputes.

It was plainly evident, even before its war against the JNA, that Slovenia would flourish as a state. The Great Powers did not grant Slovenia recognition immediately, however. Giving Slovenia external sovereignty implied important consequences for Great Power interests and for Yugoslavia's remaining conflicts. The circumstances on the ground were not compelling enough to overwhelm the Great Powers' other concerns in the region.

Domestic Sovereignty in Slovenia

Slovenia's June 25 declaration of independence was met with swift force, just as Serb authorities had promised only days before. The relative power balance

[39] Some argued at the time that Slovenia's referendum had not shown support for independence outright, but only support for independence in the event that negotiations among the republics failed.

favored the federal authorities. At the time, Slovenia's armed forces were estimated at 20,000 troops.[40] The JNA had 38,000 troops stationed in Slovenia
alone.[41] Somewhat surprisingly, Slovenia's state security forces quickly over-
whelmed the JNA. Post-conflict data show that only 37 JNA soldiers and 9
Slovene defenders died in the conflict, a casualty estimate much lower than
typically warrants the label "war."[42] Yet, Slovenia was decisively the victor.

The Slovenes' dramatic battlefield success was due, at least in part, to the fact
that Slobodan Milosevic was not particularly interested in keeping Slovenia
within Yugoslavia.[43] There were not enough Serbs there to make a fierce defense
worthwhile. He reasoned that federal resources were better spent in Croatia and
Bosnia. Also detracting from the federal authorities' efforts, JNA forces had low
morale and were uncertain about their mandate in Slovenia.[44] The experience
was demoralizing for the JNA. Adding further insult to injury, Slovenian authorities confiscated retreating Serbs' weapons as they withdrew. Slovenia's minister
of defense dubbed them "war reparations."[45] Though the full force of the federal
government was not brought to bear in Slovenia, Slovenes were well prepared
for the conflict. They performed well in combat and convincingly established
control over their territory afterward.

Slovenia began planning for independence well before its formal declaration.
In the spring of 1991, Slovenian authorities began withholding payments to the
federal government, recalled their numbers from the JNA, established foreign
policy institutions, created quasi-diplomatic offices abroad, and made plans for
a Slovenian army and independent currency.[46] When Slovenia nationalized
federal territorial defense forces, the authorities abolished the Yugoslav common
market in retaliation. Consequently, many economic ties between Slovenia and
the federal government were preemptively severed. Once independence was
declared, the domestic transition to functional independence was relatively
smooth. According to Silber and Little,

---

[40] *The Economist* estimated that Slovenia had a reserve force of some 68,000 men, but only enough
arms for 40,000 of them ("Slovenia's Self-Defense" 1991); Tanner (1997, p. 252) suggests
Slovenia had 40,000 troops in its militia.

[41] The JNA was estimated to have nearly 138,000 troops total on active duty. Tanner (1997, p. 252)
notes, however, that Yugoslav troops active in the Slovenian war might have numbered as few as
2,000.

[42] *The Economist* reported on July 6 that the conflict left "dozens of dead and scores of wounded,"
but precise figures were not given ("The Road to War" 1991, p. 2).

[43] In fact, Serb authorities viewed the conflict as a policing action, not a war. They told the
Slovenians when they were coming to reassert control and even disclosed the roads by which
they would arrive. There was another, more aggressive war plan, but it was not implemented
(Silber and Little 1996, p. 156).

[44] Gow (1997, p. 32) notes that the JNA miscalculated, believing a mere show of force would compel
the Slovenians to capitulate.

[45] "Slovenia's Self-Defense" (1991, p. 46).

[46] Ramet (1993, p. 873).

[Slovenians] had backed their independence legislation with executive orders, creating and staffing the independent bodies that would...assume control of the borders, the air traffic, and the port authorities. At the frontiers with Italy, Austria and Hungary, they removed the Yugoslav symbols, flags and notice boards, and replaced them with the heraldry of the new independent Republic of Slovenia. They ordered federal police and customs officials off the premises. They also began to place border posts along the 600-kilometer frontier border with neighboring Croatia.[47]

The war for Slovenia ended with the Brioni Agreement, signed on July 7, 1991. Brokered by Europe, Brioni formally resolved the military conflict between Yugoslavia and Slovenia and arranged for the JNA's withdrawal from Slovenian territory. But it also stipulated that the secessionists (at that time Slovenia and Croatia) would rescind their declarations of independence for three months pending negotiations on a comprehensive settlement. Finally, under European pressure, the Serbs agreed to allow Stipe Mesic to assume his rightful place as the president of the Federal Presidency. Perhaps contrary to its intentions, Slovenia's domestic sovereignty only became more secure during the mandated moratorium.

Slovenia's local government simply moved forward in establishing its domestic authority. Emblematically, Slovenian authorities set to creating passports for their citizenry; 150,000 were made during the moratorium period alone, and they planned to produce 100,000 more before the end of 1991. Silber and Little additionally note that "[Slovenes] took advantage of the cease-fire to strengthen their barricades. In Ljubljana, the buses and trucks that had acted as makeshift defenses were replaced by tank traps made from crisscrossed iron girders, and surrounded by barbed wire."[48] Though Slovenes acquiesced to the international community's appeal for patience in theory, they also realized their negotiations with Milosevic had reached an insurmountable impasse. In early October, as the moratorium period expired, Slovenes closed the southern frontiers connecting Slovenia with the rest of Yugoslavia.[49] From that point forward, at 34 frontier posts, Yugoslavs were considered foreign guests and not permitted entry without passports.[50]

Slovenia's domestic political authority was as apparent as its physical control. The Slovene Communist Party split from the federal party in 1989 and pro-secessionists won decisive political victories in the April 1990 elections. Slovenia's local governmental authority did not derive from its association with the central authorities in Belgrade or the Yugoslav Communist Party. Furthermore, Slovenia's December 1990 referendum demonstrated popular support for independence. The results, 89 percent in favor of independence of the 94 percent participating, gave the government an overwhelming mandate.

---

[47] Silber and Little (1996, p. 154).
[48] Ibid., p. 164.
[49] Slovenia formally re-declared independence on October 8, 1991.
[50] "Yugoslavia's rebel republics prepare to got it alone" (1991).

Finally, Slovenia even had the blessing of Milosevic, whose party announced its recognition of Slovenia's right of peaceful secession on the 4th of July.[51]

To look at the balance of power between Slovenia and federal Yugoslav authorities prior to the 10 Day War, Slovenia's prospects for forcefully asserting independence were not favorable. But retaining Slovenia was not Milosevic's priority, so effective independence was secure by October 1991.[52] Possible contagion from conflicts then underway in neighboring republics presented the only potential disruption of Slovenia's territorial control. Even that was unlikely though, because of Slovenia's geographic position in the northwestern corner of Yugoslavia and because of its homogenous ethnic makeup – leaving it somewhat physically and politically distant from the rest of the country. The only likely difficulty would be an influx of refugees fleeing conflicts in Croatia or Bosnia.

Slovenia's economy was strong relative to the other Yugoslav states, but it would be less strong relative to the universe of sovereign states. Still, Slovenia's Western orientation in the years since Tito's death had prepared it for exposure to competitive international markets. Slovenia's economic stability was most vulnerable when the international community imposed sanctions on Yugoslavia. Many observers have noted that the UN's sanctions locked the power balance among the republics in place, effectively benefiting Serbian forces (who had secured the federal army) while disadvantaging all others. This was certainly true for the more protracted conflicts in Croatia and Bosnia. For Slovenia, the sanctions' economic effects were more important than the scarcity of arms. The period between December 1990 and December 1992 saw a 30 percent decline in Slovenian living standards.[53] Once the sanctions were lifted, the economy rebounded.

The Slovenian economy's strength was demonstrated when its trade deficit had become a trade surplus by the end of 1992. In its first full year of partially recognized sovereignty, Slovenia reported a gross national product (GNP) of $6,700 per capita, on par with Argentina and Greece and more than double that of Estonia, Latvia, and Hungary.[54] Finally, Slovenian unemployment was on par with Poland's and only slightly higher than that in Hungary. Though measures from 1992 are post hoc, they are also suggestive of Slovenia's pre-independence trajectory.

---

[51] Silber and Little (1996, p.164).

[52] Although Slovenia was probably physically independent before October, because the war was over in mid-July, it did not formally reassert its independence until the Brioni moratorium had passed on October 8.

[53] Of course, Slovenia's independence was secure and widely recognized for most of 1992. This period covers more time than the duration of the sanctions ("Daily Report: Eastern Europe" 1992).

[54] Reported in nominal U.S. dollars.

CROATIA

Croatia had the second-most domestic sovereignty relative to Yugoslavia's other secessionists. It did not meet the legal standard for territorial control, but it did satisfy the popular authority and effective government criteria. Croatia steadily lost its Serb-majority territories to Serbs as its war of independence dragged on.[55] By the time a cease-fire that actually held was arranged, Croatian authorities retained only two thirds of the territory they claimed. Croatia's population was also more diverse and decidedly less supportive of the new regime than Slovenia's. Serb populations within the Krajina and on the eastern border with Serbia were steadfastly opposed to Tudjman's/Croatian authority. Croats were, however, a decisive majority in the state (near 80 percent). Finally, Croatia's potential viability hinged on a number of factors: the end of its war with Serb authorities, the extent of its involvement in the Bosnian war, and its relations with its own domestic minorities. A bright spot was that, like Slovenia, Croatia was economically advantaged and had been exposed to liberal markets.

Domestic Sovereignty in Croatia

The Croatian War began just after Slovenia's (Table 5.3).[56] Though the two states had signed a mutual defense treaty prior to their declarations of independence, Croatia did not come to Slovenia's aid. Nor did Croatians even attempt to impede the JNA's progress as it traveled through Croatia toward Slovenia. Had Croatia defended Slovenia as it had promised, Slovenians likely would have supported Croatia. Instead, Tudjman's decision left Croatia isolated. It was an important strategic mistake. Unlike Slovenia, in Milosevic's mind much of Croatia *was* worth fighting for, and he had ample resources at his disposal to pursue it. Local Croatian-Serb militias afforded the Serbian effort plausible deniability for its violence as well as a significant volunteer force.[57] Moreover, Slovenia's quick success left defeated JNA forces newly available for the Croatian confrontation. When the Brioni Agreement came into effect, JNA troops and hardware simply withdrew from Slovenia eastward into Croatia and Bosnia. As soon as a month after its declaration of independence, Serbs controlled approximately one-third of Croatia's territory. Serbs contested Croatia's territorial control in the east along the border with Serbia and in the so-called Serbian Krajina (RSK) in the south.

[55] Even some Serb minority areas such Baranja, where Serbs constituted only 25 percent of the population, were lost.

[56] Croatia experienced violence in its conflict with its Serbian provinces prior to the war as well.

[57] In the beginning of the war, Milosevic maintained that Croatia's violence was wholly attributable to Croatian Serbs rising up against Croatian independence, desiring instead to rejoin Serbia or maintain their place within the Yugoslav republic. The international community's uncertainty over who was perpetrating the violence delayed intervention.

Serbian forces were more numerous and better armed than the Croatian military. Just before the war, Croatia had a force estimated at 60,000 men. Serbs could count as many as 138,000 military personnel and thousands of Croatian-Serb irregulars. In Croatia, the UN arms embargo had a perverse effect relative to its mandate, locking in Serbs' material advantage in terms of heavy artillery and light weapons. Again, the balance of forces was clearly in favor of the central government. Finally, Serbs pursued their territorial ambitions with especially violent tactics in Croatia, further destabilizing political and territorial control.

Throughout the late summer and fall, a combination of military conquest and ethnic cleansing left much of Croatia's territory under Serb authority, depleted of its former Croatian inhabitants.[58] When Serbs would take a city, town, or village, they would force its population out with only what they could carry. This practice created a dramatic refugee problem. Captured men and Croatian military personnel were often simply murdered. Estimates show that in the five months between August and December of 1991, 80,000 Croats and Muslims were either displaced or killed.[59] Croatians suffered their worst defeats in the east. Purges of cities such as Vukovar and Dubrovnik were especially brutal. As winter began, Serb forces held and controlled virtually all of the Croatian territory that Milosevic desired. Only then did Serbia finally acquiesce to a lasting cease-fire – and only then because Milosevic anticipated it would freeze Croatia's contested map in place. Croatian Serbs, he expected, would henceforth be governed by Serbia.

In addition to the unfavorable balance of forces and the unanticipated brutality of Serbian tactics, some of Croatia's territorial losses were attributable to Croats' faith in international diplomacy. Virtually all of Croatia's losses occurred during the Brioni moratorium. Croatia initially attempted to avoid direct confrontation with Serbian forces in the hope that the EC process would ultimately yield a satisfactory agreement. For example, the authorities waited until September, well after the war in Croatia had begun in earnest, to have the National Guard surround and attempt to capture the JNA's barracks. Luca Bebic, the Croatian defense minister, remarked at the time, "bit by bit we are losing control over our territory, waiting for the results of the EC peace initiative. Now we have no illusions about getting help and are undertaking an offensive."[60] Unfortunately, Croatia had already lost much of its territory.

---

[58] Though the majority of the refugees were Croats, Croatia's other minority populations were also victimized by the Serbs.

[59] Tanner (1997, p. 278) recounts, "Officially 6,651 deaths were accounted for [in total]. But another 13,700 were 'missing,' the majority of which [were dead]."

[60] From the article "Europe may use force in Yugoslavia" in The Independent September 17, 1991. Cited in Tanner (1997, p. 256).

Croatia was unable to reclaim its losses until after the Great Powers had formally recognized it.[61] Even at that point, Croatian forces could not have regained the territories without powerful external advocates. Croatia's territorial defense forces had been disarmed under the Brioni agreement, and within the Croatian police, "half were Serbs and hostile to the HDZ."[62] Croatia's newfound military capabilities were a function of illegal imports and clandestine military training. Military equipment was imported in violation of the still-standing UN arms embargo, and a private American security company with ties to the Defense Department conducted tactical military training. American officials were rumored to be complicit in both the arms transfers and the training.[63]

Croatia's governmental authority was similarly less established than Slovenia's. Aside from the regime's unpopularity in majority Serb regions, its preparations for independence were deficient. In fact, by the summer of 1991, Croatia had done little beyond holding its referendum and nationalizing some services and industries.[64] In their final meeting before the Slovenian and Croatian declarations of independence on June 15, one participant recalled, "There was almost a conflict between Tudjman and one of his ministers, Franjo Greguric, because Tudjman said 'we have everything ready too, all the laws, everything [customs, police, airports, boundaries] is prepared.' And Greguric said 'No Mr. President, this is not true.'"[65] Nevertheless, Tudjman insisted Croatia declare independence at the same time as Slovenia. Tudjman encouraged Croatia's association with Slovenia, believing it would bolster his claim. Slovenians however, actively discouraged packaging the two secessions together, sometimes pointing to Croatia's weakness in order to support a Slovenia-first argument for independence.

On the other hand, Croatia did have substantial autonomy as a function of its status as a constitutive republic within Yugoslavia. The Croatian government ran its own schools, police force, and territorial defense. Also like the Slovenians, the Croatian Communists had severed their relationship with the Yugoslav Communists (even though the Croatian Communists were no longer in power). Similarly, when Serbia abolished the Yugoslav common market, Croatia's trade became quasi-independent. Croatia also introduced its own currency, the Croatian dinar, asserting a certain amount of financial control over the economy. So even though Croatia's domestic authority was less than

---

[61] In 1993 and 1995, Croatia took back most, but not all, of its prewar territory. Some areas along the Croatian border with Serbia remained in dispute.

[62] Tanner (1997, p. 231).

[63] Cowell cited in Ullman (1996, p. 16 at n.11); Silber and Little (1996, pp. 349, 352).

[64] For example, on becoming president, Tudjman nationalized radio, television, and the local news agency. He also created an airline to rival Yugoslavia's and began rewriting the Croatian constitution (Tanner 1997, p. 229).

[65] Bavcar, cited in Silber and Little (1996, pp. 148–149).

Slovenia's, it was still mostly independent. Only its territorial control was severely compromised.

Internal opposition from Croatia's Serbs complicated issues of sovereign authority on the ground, but the new regime's legitimacy was generally strong. In Serb majority areas, the Republic of Serbian Krajina (RSK) declared its opposition to Croatia's secession from Yugoslavia. Rather than seeking an independent state of their own, Croatia's Serbs demanded to remain within Yugoslavia. Genuine opposition within Croatia's Serbian population was also effectively exploited by Yugoslav authorities who militarily and financially supported them. As a result, what began as a minimally armed local resistance became a well-armed force that defied international attempts to broker cease-fires. Nevertheless, Serbs constituted only a small minority within Croatia. Solid support from Croatians alone would provide a popular mandate.

In Croatian-majority territories, support for independence and the new regime was less contentious but somewhat unconsolidated. Croatia's April referendum yielded more than 90 percent favoring independence. General support for independence was stronger and more consistent than that for Tudjman, however. Tudjman's authority was solid before the war but declined with time. As the conflict progressed, strategic missteps and unpopular domestic policies significantly eroded his popularity, on both the left and right.

Some Croatians displayed their dissatisfaction with Tudjman with radical tactics. A right-wing paramilitary organization, Hos, raised a significant challenge to the HDZ's authority, at one point suggesting the possibility that civil war would erupt among Croatians themselves.[66] Hos's popular support did not rival Tudjman's, but their extreme tactics and fascistic ideology did appeal to a violent fraction of the Croatian populace. Tudjman eliminated Hos by jailing its participants and confiscating their property. Despite its sometimes contentious politics, the new regime's popular authority was generally solid. It was certainly greater than support for remaining within Yugoslavia.

Before the war began, Croatia's prospects for enduring, independent governance were fairly good. Croatia's economic potential was on par with that of most Eastern European states, and support for the regime was generally strong. Even after much of the war was fought and the Carrington cease-fire arranged, the Croatian economy remained viable. What made Croatia's future prospects uncertain was the possibility that Croatian nationalism would interact badly with competing nationalisms in neighboring states and/or the minority populations within them. In particular, the war with Serbia and the Croatian Serbs was stalemated but unresolved; a war in Bosnia, with a significant Croat population, had just begun; and the HDZ's policies had the potential to further aggravate hostilities with Serbs in and around Croatia.

---

[66] Tanner (1997, pp. 267–298); Hos, an acronym for Hrvatske Obrambene Snage, translates to Croat Defense Forces.

Croatians were said to have paid the highest price among Yugoslavia's states for their potential independence. Croatia's economy remained strong, though damaged, throughout the war. In August, the government introduced the Croatian dinar: "[I]n spite of the dramatic expense of the war, [its new currency] turned out to be less inflationary than the old Yugoslav dinar."[67] Croatia's war did have negative effects on the economy, however. According to one estimate, more than 10 percent of Croatia's housing stock had been ruined, 30 percent of its industrial infrastructure had been destroyed or lost, and 37 percent of the railway was damaged or in Serb hands. Croatia also had nearly 330,000 internally displaced refugees. Croatia's economy would take much longer to rebound than Slovenia's; its prewar economic strength and relatively open economy were its saving grace.

Croatia's ethnic relations presented the greatest potential challenge to its continued stability. The future of Croatia's conflict with its rebel Serb population, though stalemated, had the potential to disrupt Croatian governance again. The Croatian government did not revoke its claim to its lost territory. As a consequence, violence would likely recur within the southern and eastern territories. Indeed, just that occurred when the Croatian military retook the areas in 1993 and 1995. Second, a significant population of ethnic Croats, approximately 17 percent of the total population, lay just across the border in Bosnia, where violence had just broken out (Table 5.4). Nationalism and popular sympathies made the Bosnian Croats' plight difficult for Croatia to ignore. Military involvement or monetary aid would put further strain on an already weakened Croatian government and economy. Finally, even if there was no further military confrontation with the Croatian Serbs, Tudjman's policies inspired a great deal of consternation in the Serbian community. Like they had after Tito's death, poor minority relations antagonized by a chauvinistic regime had the potential to be disruptive for Croatia's future domestic minority relations. Its minorities needed assurances that should they be brought back under Croatian authority, they would be safe. It would be difficult to dissuade Croatian Serbs of their well-founded fear.

KOSOVO

On October 11, 1991, three days after Slovenia and Croatia reiterated their demands for statehood, Kosovo Albanians declared their independence from Serbia. Kosovars had been pushing for formal autonomy the longest but were slow to declare full independence. This was due in part to the restrictive policies imposed on the region, which left few political opportunities available for Kosovars to exploit. But it was also because their demands were moderate, their pursuit of those demands was peaceful, and their potential for functional independence remote. Besides its leader Ibrahim Rugova's pacifism, Kosovo was

---

[67] Ibid., p. 253.

TABLE 5.4 *Yugoslavia Ethnic Demographics (1991)*[a]

Territory Population	Albanian	Bosnian Muslim	Croat	Mac.	Mont.	Serb	Slov.	Other/ Yugoslav
Bosnia 4,364,574	0	43.7%	17.3%	0	0	31.4%	0	2.1%/5.5%
Croatia 4,760,344	0.3%	1%	77.9%	0	0.2%	12.2%	0.5%	~4%/2.2%
Kosovo (1991) 1,954,744	90%							10%
Kosovo (2006)[b] 2,000,000+								
Macedonia 2,033,964	21%	0	0	64.6%	0	2.2%	0	12.2%[c]
Montenegro 615,276	6.6%	14.6%	0	0	61.8%	9.3%	0	4%/2.7%
Serbia[d] 9,791,475	17.2%	2.4%	1.1%	0.4%	1.4%	65.8%	0	3.2%
Slovenia 1,962,606	0.1%	1.4%	2.7%	0.2%	0.2%	2.4%	88%	4.8%[e]/0.6%
Vojvodina 2,012,605						56%		44%[f]
Yugoslavia 23,528,230	9.3%	10%	19.2%	5.8%	2.3%	36.2%	7.5%	6.2%[g]/3%

[a] Prunk recounts, "of the 92 percent of the electorate who voted, 88 percent voted for a free and independent Slovenia" (1997, p. 29). Weller notes, "88.5 percent of the Slovenian voters opted for independence" (1992, p. 569). Regardless of the specifics, independence won an overwhelming majority of the vote.

[b] Vote on SAD Krajina remaining with Yugoslavia. Milosevic cancelled a referendum on Krajina independence.

[c] Referendum on Serbian autonomy that only polled Serbs and was declared illegal by Croatian authorities.

[d] On July 2, 1990, Kosovo's provincial assembly formally declared independence from Serbia contending its status was rightfully that of a constituent republic of the Yugoslav Federation; it was not a declaration of secession.

[e] "Are you for a sovereign and independent Bosnia and Hercegovina, a state of equal citizens, nations of Bosnia and Hercegovina – Muslims, Serbs, Croats and other nations that live in it?"

[f] "Are you in favor of a sovereign and autonomous Macedonia with the right to join a future alliance of sovereign states of Yugoslavia?"

[g] The referendum on independence required a vote of 55% in favor to pass. The Montenegrin diaspora, which accounted for 3% of the electorate, was widely viewed as the decisive factor in the election result (Wood 2006).

landlocked and could not easily accrue the weaponry or personnel necessary to confront the Yugoslav central authorities. By 1991, Serbs had extensive experience repressing the Kosovo Albanians, and the Albanians recognized their own weakness.[68]

Of the three Yugoslav secessions, Kosovo had the lowest degree of control over its territory, and the least potential for viable independent governance, though it rivaled Slovenia in its popular legitimacy. Kosovo's governmental authority was moderate, but not strong, because much of Kosovo's formal governmental power had been stripped away in the 1980s. Serbia's reactions to Albanian activism left Kosovo's infrastructure weakened and under Serbian control. Albanian authorities established a parallel, shadow government in response to counter the legitimate government. Ibrahim Rugova became president of the shadow regime in 1992 with a convincing mandate among Albanians. His support declined somewhat with the dissolution of the SFRY and the rise of Albanian militarism in the late 1990s.

Domestic Sovereignty in Kosovo

Albanians did not convincingly control much of Kosovo's territory if military and police control alone is taken to be decisive evidence. Before Yugoslavia's conflicts began, Slovenia, Croatia, and Kosovo were not so different in terms of the authority they exercised. Within Yugoslavia, the statuses of the republics and the autonomous regions were essentially similar, though perhaps endowed with differential prestige as a consequence of the constitutional order. Kosovo and Vojvodina had votes equivalent to those of the republics within the collective presidency. They also had their own constitutions and court systems. And, just like the republics, they had authority over their own territorial defense forces, police, and schools. Both autonomous regions were nominally under Serbian control but had many of the trappings of independent statehood.

When Milosevic assumed the presidency in 1989, he revoked this effective control. He replaced indigenous authorities with his own supporters and abolished the region's autonomy. Kosovo became a virtual police state for Albanians.[69] Albanians could not buy property without the authorities' permission; tens of thousands lost their jobs; students could not enter Pristina University; its remaining students could only receive education in Serbian; and arbitrary arrest and police violence were commonplace.[70] As recounted at the time by a Kosovar in Judah:

---

[68] Judah (1997, p.306) notes that the Albanians were torn over the earlier Yugoslav wars. Although they yearned for the Serbs to suffer defeats in Slovenia and Croatia, they also hoped that the RSK separatists would find success in their conflict with Croatian authorities. They believed RSK independence would set a precedent for Kosovo independence or unification with Albania.

[69] The imposition of martial law in Kosovo began as the suppression of a mining strike in February 1989.

[70] Caplan (2005, p. 141).

The pressure is continuous. Police expeditions, raids on villages, armed civilians parading around. They always use weapon searches as excuses. They harass families and beat parents in front of their children...They use fiscal controls to break the Albanian shop owners. They surround one part of the town and search everyone to collect hard currency. No one dares react. There is no contact between the citizens and the government.[71]

Rugova, president of the underground government, sought Albanian independence quietly, somehow without raising the ire of Serbian authorities.[72]

Dissatisfied, in 1995–1996, the Kosovo Liberation Army (KLA) clandestinely formed and began a violent campaign against Serb authorities and moderate Albanian "co-conspirators" in the province. By 1998, KLA paramilitaries claimed they held approximately 25 percent of the province, principally in the Drenica region. The KLA was not conventionally strong but pursued an opportunistic insurgency. Like the shadow government, the KLA was subject to Kosovo's difficult geography, landlocked with few means of acquiring sufficient weaponry to compel Serbia to leave.[73] Numbering 10,000 to 20,000, armed with light weapons and disorganized, the KLA was no match for the force of the Serbian government and the JNA. On February 28, 1998, Serbia began a major military offensive against the Kosovo Albanians. The campaign's ostensible purpose was suppression of the KLA. It turned out to include ethnic cleansing and indiscriminate violence against Albanian civilians.

Both secession and the Rugova government enjoyed overwhelming popular support among Albanians even as dissent mounted over the best means of achieving statehood. Kosovo's illegal referendum on independence yielded a 99.7 percent favorable vote, though approximately 200,000 Serbs boycotted (see Table 5.2). The Rugova government, which had been in power in Kosovo since Tito's death, was immensely popular among Albanians. As in Slovenia, Kosovo's population was relatively homogenous, at approximately 90 percent Albanian (Table 5.4). As a result, the government and its drive for independence had a strong popular mandate, stronger than that of Croatia, even without the support of Kosovo Serbs.

Under Rugova's leadership, the shadow government provided social services, schools, and hospitals to the Albanian population. The Albanian government also successfully collected taxes within the province and from the Kosovo Albanian diaspora.[74] The shadow government was so legitimate – and Serbia so illegitimate – in the eyes of Kosovo Albanians that there was very little

---

[71] Human Rights Watch, "Open Wounds: Human Rights Abuses in Kosovo" cited in Judah (1997, p. 305).

[72] Judah (1999, p. 11) implies Rugova was tolerated by Serbian authorities because they feared driving popular support to the KLA.

[73] With the collapse of the Albanian state in 1998, weapons became more readily available. Indeed, rising violence on the part of the KLA was the proximate cause of the 1998 Serbian offensives in Kosovo.

[74] See Judah (1997, p. 305) on domestic taxation in Kosovo and Judah (1999, pp. 11–12) on the 3 percent income tax collected from Kosovo Albanians abroad.

interaction between Albanians and the official Serb-led government. Albanians themselves provided all essential governmental services. Of course, the level of service provided by the Albanian government was also lower than the official government's had been before its authority was taken away.

Events in Yugoslavia overtook Rugova's quiet diplomatic efforts in the latter half of the decade. When the Dayton Peace Accords were signed in 1995 and Milosevic conceded to the international community's demands in Croatia and Bosnia, it confirmed that Kosovo's pacifistic means to independence had failed. As a reward for Kosovo's patience and respect for international law, the international community would recognize the Federal Republic of Yugoslavia (FRY) as the rightful successor to Yugoslavia and Kosovo Albanians would remain subject to Serbian rule. Local support for violent resistance exploded, and thousands of Albanian émigrés flocked to join the KLA when Albania's government collapsed in 1997. The KLA was suddenly better organized, better armed, and better funded than ever before.

Kosovo had low potential for stable economic and political life post-secession. It was the least developed of all Yugoslavia's provinces and had minimal potential to support its own independent economy, even before the conflict with Serbian authorities.[75] Among Kosovo Albanians, domestic governance would undoubtedly remain stable. But the challenge to Kosovo's authority would not be internal. Instead, it would come from Serbia. Kosovo's special place within Serbian national mythology gave its minority Serb population disproportionate political significance. The plight of Kosovo's Serbs was central to Milosevic's rhetoric and he would not be easily dissuaded.

Kosovo was heavily dependent on the contributions of the other Yugoslav republics for its economic security. Kosovo Albanians argued Serbs purposefully retarded their efforts to develop while they were a part of Yugoslavia. Under Serb jurisdiction, Kosovo's natural resources were overexploited while investments in infrastructure and education were curbed. Throughout the 1990s, most Albanians did not have work. They were forced into subsistence agriculture or black market trade. For their part, Albanians claimed Kosovo's independent economy would be stronger; the industriousness demonstrated by the shadow government and parallel economy proved their potential to form a stable, viable state. Serbs argued contrarily that Albanians had mismanaged the province in the 1980s. They were ungrateful to the republics that had supported them, backward, and ultimately responsible for their own unfortunate circumstances.

Many Kosovo Albanians initially hoped that they might join Albania proper post-independence. But that aspiration's realization was unlikely. The Albanian diaspora certainly supported their ethnic kin in Kosovo, but the Albanian government harbored no irredentist ambitions toward the province. With the collapse of the Albanian state, even the prospect of a special relationship between Kosovo and Albania post-independence would not promise much by

---

[75] Ding (2002); Bookman (1992, pp. 155–156).

way of material resources or increased political legitimacy. Albania, Kosovo's greatest patron, formally recognized Kosovo's independence in October 1991, but no other states followed until more than a decade later.[76]

A DIPLOMATIC PRELUDE

Initially, none of the Great Powers supported the secessionists. Just prior to the declarations of independence, the international community actively lobbied against both Slovenia's and Croatia's demands. The European Community (EC) and the United States took special care to convey to Slovenian and Croatian leaders that external support and recognition would not be forthcoming. There would be no reward for unilateralism or for the use violent tactics. James Baker, then U.S. secretary of state, visited on June 21, met with each of the Yugoslav presidents, and assured them the United States did not condone secession. The EC similarly sent a representative, who argued that Slovenia and Croatia were too small and too weak to survive as independent states. The EC could not support them, nor would its members recognize their statehood should they decide to follow through with their independence claims.[77] Privately, some European diplomats, notably the Germans and Italians, expressed their support for the secessionist regimes. Nevertheless, their support was conditioned on the higher priority that European unity be maintained. The Maastricht Summit, to be held in December, would formally create the European Union and initiate economic and foreign policy coordination among Europe's states. The stakes were too high to break ranks. None of the important players were prepared to unilaterally recognize Slovenia's or Croatia's independence.

Some members of the international community were concerned that a Slovenian or Croatian secession attempt would spill over, creating violence throughout the region. In the EC, Yugoslavia's neighbors were especially sensitive to potential violence or fleeing refugees. Similarly, the Great Powers foresaw the potential for demonstration effects among the Yugoslav republics themselves. If Slovenia and Croatia were to secede, what would become of Bosnia, Macedonia, and Kosovo? If there were conflicts in Macedonia or Kosovo, would Greece, Turkey, or Albania feel obliged to intervene? No one could predict the

---

[76] Some observers characterize Kosovo's relationship with Albania as irredentist. Albania's recognition of Kosovo demonstrates convincingly that while deeply interested in the fates of their kin in Yugoslavia, Albanians did not hope to acquire the territory. See Rezun (1995, p. 118) for a discussion of Hoxha's reservations about Kosovo and its Albanian population. Similarly, Judah (2001) argued that, "there is considerably less to Greater Albanian nationalism than meets the eye" (p. 8). Also see Judah (1997, pp. 307–308).

[77] Ironically, the European dispatched to counsel Slovenians and Croatians that they were too small and too weak was the representative from Luxembourg, one of the smallest, weakest (though wealthy) states in the world (population: ~450,000, territory: ~1,000 mi²).

secessions' effects on the rest of Yugoslavia or its immediate neighbors. They only agreed that none of the possible contingencies were good.

On the other hand, the Great Powers saw little potential for Yugoslavia's conflict to extend far beyond its immediate borders. Yugoslavia was known to be a hotbed for international war, but Great Power interests in the Balkans had shifted dramatically at the end of the Cold War. The United States and the Soviet Union were no longer inclined to contest every ideological battle in the periphery. None of the important players believed that their interests were so imperiled that military intervention was immediately necessary.[78]

At the same time, the Great Power leaders were not wholly disinterested in Yugoslavia. They had significant political interests in the outcome of Yugoslavia's wars. The SFRY was within the European sphere of influence. Russia had strong ties of identity with Serbs and strong secessionist challengers at home. France wanted U.S. influence in Europe to diminish as Europeans reasserted control on the continent. China and Russia wanted to forestall the erosion of sovereignty. Britain saw its quagmire in Northern Ireland in Yugoslavia's wars and preferred to remain on the sidelines. Both France and Britain, however, wanted to temper Germany's new assertive demeanor. Finally, Germany had domestic political and ideological reasons for supporting self-determination. Each Great Power had material and ideational interests that might have influenced its preferences regarding recognition.

THE EUROPEAN COMMUNITY

The EC was eager to try its hand at collective diplomacy. Its first initiative was dispatching a task force to negotiate a peaceful, low-cost solution to the secessionist hostilities. The CSCE offered to send a mission and called for a cease-fire as well. But European leaders were divided over their policy toward Yugoslavia's secessionists from the start. For months, as the Europeans tried to negotiate a Yugoslav peace, they also tried to find a mutually agreeable solution among themselves. And for months, Germany acquiesced to French and British demands that any settlement be comprehensive and acceptable to all of Yugoslavia's states. Unfortunately, there was no diplomatic middle ground to be had. Either the secessionists would be recognized and enter international society, or they would be reincorporated by force into a Yugoslavia dominated by Serbia. The Europeans realized this too late.

As Europe grappled with maintaining a united front, events on the ground were rendering preventive diplomacy useless. As soon as Slovenia and Croatia declared independence on June 25, the Yugoslav wars were underway. Europe tried to establish cease-fires between Serbian authorities and the secessionists, but Slovenians won their war almost as soon as it began. Somewhat surprisingly, in September, Milosevic agreed to participate in European-backed negotiations

---

[78] Ullman (1996, p. 3).

regarding Croatia, where conflict was still underway.[79] Unfortunately, the offer was disingenuous. The negotiations accomplished nothing. Milosevic planned to earn goodwill in Europe by appearing to negotiate, in turn buying time for Serb forces to gain control of Western Slavonia and the Krajina. In much of Europe and the United States, the strategy worked and contributed to the fog of war. For most of the summer and early fall, the Great Powers were uncertain that culpability for the violence lay with Milosevic. Croatia's war intensified.

As the Brioni moratorium went on, and the negotiations made no progress, it slowly became clear to the Europeans that their initial impression of the Yugoslav conflict was incorrect. Milosevic was not an embattled, somewhat objectionable leader struggling to hold on to a multiethnic state. Not all of the parties were equally responsible for the conflict. Instead, Milosevic was a staunch Serbian nationalist attempting to create a Serb homeland at any cost. At first, Serbia's political domination of Yugoslavia seemed the best means to achieve that end. But as time went on and Slovenia and Croatia refused to submit to Milosevic's will, he altered his vision. He would have to carve a smaller Serbian homeland (Greater Serbia) out of the Yugoslav republics. Once Milosevic suppressed the secessionists with force and began targeting civilians, Europeans finally started to see the Serbs as aggressors. However, by the time the Europeans changed their view, Serbo-Croatian paramilitaries and the JNA had already altered the lines of control on the ground to suit their preferences.

The EC was in a difficult position. By fall, its members recognized the Former Yugoslavia would not survive intact, but they disagreed about the future form it should take. Three strategies of conflict resolution were advocated by three sets of states. Each strategy corresponded not necessarily with the extent of domestic sovereignty exercised or the secessionists' potential for successful statehood, but with the states' own political interests. Britain and the United States preferred a comprehensive settlement. France preferred military intervention followed by negotiation. And Germany wanted the EC to consider recognizing Slovenia and Croatia. Potential fractures in European unity appeared.

In an attempt to maintain consensus following a string of diplomatic failures, the EC convened the Arbitration Commission for Yugoslavia. Often referred to after its head, Robert Badinter, the commission's mandate was to advise the EC on two issues related to Yugoslavia. First, in the commission's expert opinion, was Yugoslavia in the process of dissolution? On November 29, Badinter replied that "yes," Yugoslavia "was in the process of dissolution."[80] As a result, the Carrington initiative, convened under the auspices of the EC and focused on negotiating a comprehensive settlement, was abandoned.[81] There would be no

---

[79] Led by Carrington, the first negotiations occurred on September 7, 1991, at The Hague. Afterward there was a precipitous increase in the level of violence within Croatia.

[80] Opinion No.1, November 29, 1991.

[81] The Carrington negotiations were held under the auspices of the EC, led by Lord Peter Carrington, and involved Slovenian, Croatian, and Serbian leaders.

mutually agreeable solution for Yugoslavia's states; Yugoslavia functionally ceased to exist. Instead, the Europeans would consider recognition for any Yugoslav state desiring independence. At its ministerial meeting on December 16, the European Community announced its conditions for granting recognition.

Badinter's second task was to evaluate whether the states requesting European recognition met the slate of EC standards.[82] Badinter's recommendations, in turn, would form the basis on which the EC would act. Though they could not successfully avert the secessions, the Europeans could salvage their attempt at a unified foreign policy.

What was remarkable about the EC standards was their complete disregard for the legal requisites of statehood. International law suggests each state is free to impose *additional* standards or contingencies for recognition. However, physical control, authority, and the ability to engage in international affairs are recognition's legal prerequisites. The EC did not demand any of the Montevideo standards be met. Badinter's requirements read that to receive European recognition, a state would have to accept the "Helsinki norms." First and foremost, the states had to be constituted on a democratic basis. They also had to accept the principles of the UN Charter, the Helsinki Final Act, and the Charter of Paris (of the CSCE), all of which included human rights standards and norms including the rule of law, democratic governance, and the peaceful settlement of conflicts. Finally, the prospective states would have to formally demonstrate provisions for the protection of minorities and renounce any territorial claims on neighboring states.[83] Perhaps the legal standards were implied. The commission's recommendations were similarly not based on whether or not the Yugoslav republics met the Montevideo criteria though, so this possibility is not well supported by the evidence.[84]

Even though Slovenia was fully independent by December 1991, Slovenian leaders harbored no illusions that external recognition would come easily. They abided by Europe's rules. Slovenia and Croatia requested EC recognition on December 19 and Bosnia and Macedonia requested recognition the next day. It

---

[82] Not every republic desired recognition. First, Serbia objected that the secessions were illegal and the arbitration commission illegitimate. Later Serbia and Montenegro argued it was the legitimate successor to the SFRY and, therefore, required no new recognition from the international community.

[83] "Guidelines on the Recognition of New States in Eastern Europe and the Soviet Union" and "Declaration on Yugoslavia" EPC – European Community December 16, 1991. The "denouncing of territorial claims" applied specifically to Macedonia. Greece believed Macedonia would attempt to annex some of its territory because its name implied a greater territory than it occupied. Macedonian leaders assured the EU that it had no irredentist ambitions, but Greece could not be dissuaded.

[84] It is noteworthy that Badinter's recommendations would have conformed to a Montevideo-based analysis, that is, Slovenia and Macedonia met the standards for statehood, whereas the other Yugoslav republics did not.

was Bosnia's first formal declaration of independence.[85] Kosovo's submission for recognition, which arrived on December 21, was not even considered.[86]

When Badinter's conclusions were finally handed down on January 11, the commission supported EC recognition for Slovenia and Macedonia alone. Croatia's recognition was not recommended. The commission cited the Croatian constitution's insufficient individual and minority protections as its rationale for withholding support. Bosnia received an unfavorable recommendation as well. No plebiscite demonstrating the will of its people accompanied its application.

In addition to its recognition advice, Badinter recommended that Yugoslavia's former internal administrative borders serve as the borders of the newly independent states.[87] This border delimitation would stand unless negotiated otherwise by the new governments themselves. In doing so, Badinter was extending the notion of *uti posseditis* beyond its traditional application to postcolonial states. The decision also provided official justification for the commission's rejection of Kosovo's application. Because it was only an autonomous region, rather than a constitutive republic, Kosovo was not eligible for recognition. Kosovo Albanians would have to remain under Serbia's jurisdiction.

BRITAIN

Europe's most powerful state did not look favorably on recognition for Slovenia and Croatia. Indeed, Britain's foreign minister was among the first to reaffirm support for Yugoslavia's territorial integrity following the declarations of independence. The British did not want to intervene militarily in Yugoslavia, and they did not support independence for the secessionists. It was important that European stability and unity be maintained, however. Britain saw its role as that of a moderator, reigning in rash or aggressive policies such as those favored by Germany and France. Even though British leaders "vehemently opposed recognition," they did not want to prioritize Yugoslavia's conflicts over European unity.[88] Consequently, Britain would reluctantly acquiesce to whatever European consensus might be reached.

The British saw their own domestic quagmire in Yugoslavia's conflict and did not want to be bogged down with another state's insurgents. Early on, Britain quashed French efforts to send a Western European Union (WEU) interposition force to Croatia for just that reason. Similar to the Russians, domestic political

---

[85] Bosnia would again declare independence following its independence referendum on April 5, 1992.

[86] Letter dated December 21, 1991, from the government of the Republic of Kosovo cited in Caplan (2005, p. 139 at n.184).

[87] Decision 1, November 29, 1991.

[88] Silber and Little (1996, p. 199).

strife loomed large in the British imagination. British leaders invoked the Northern Irish analogy on multiple occasions.[89] Unlike their Russian colleagues, though, the British were not concerned about setting a precedent at home. Their own domestic challenge was manageable. Instead, the British were concerned that any involvement in Yugoslavia would require an international commitment of personnel and money analogous to their own in Northern Ireland. That possibility was to be avoided at all costs. Salvaging Yugoslav unity was not worth the potential cost.

The British shared little in common with Yugoslavia's states in terms of ethnic or religious affinity. No strong ties of identity had been forged between their peoples. Slovenia, Croatia, and Kosovo voiced support for democratic principles and free trade. But those ideals were not as important in the post–Cold War era as they might have been to Britain only a few years earlier, when seemingly every potentially non-Communist regime received support. If identity considerations played any role, it was again by analogy to Northern Ireland. Among the British, Yugoslavia's conflicts were seen through the prism of Protestants' own conflict with Catholics, namely, that the conflicts were ethnic, historically based, and intractable. British affinities did not lay with one side or the other.[90] Rather, their own experience with ethnic conflict, and what they understood to be the root cause of the violence in Yugoslavia, led them to conclude intervention would be fruitless.

When the British did entertain intervention in Yugoslavia, it was security driven, rather than moralistic. As reports of widespread human rights violations proliferated, and calls for Britain to stop the indiscriminate violence began, British leaders were unmoved.[91] Defense Secretary Malcolm Rifkind agreed with critics of British policy that Britain had a "special" interest in Yugoslavia. But he argued that the special interest was a selfish interest in security. It was not an interest in advancing a moral code. Indeed, if Britain were to intervene in Yugoslavia on the basis of self-determination or human rights, it might be expected to support those mores in other cases too.[92] He argued that to advance intervention in Yugoslavia on a universal, moral basis via the UN would require Britain to support UN intervention in *every* case. The British did not reject a system-wide norm of self-determination per se, but they were concerned that, through practice, they might inadvertently create the mistaken expectation that Britain would consistently enforce that norm. British leaders preferred to enforce self-determination on a discretionary, case-by-case basis rather than be branded

---

[89] Hurd, quoted in Usborne (1991).

[90] Tanner (1997) suggests to the contrary that Britons had an "almost instinctive Protestant fear of Catholicism." He argues the English favored Serbs because they were English speaking, represented a greater portion of the English population, and were better politically organized than the Croats (p. 273). Other authors cite no evidence of these motives within Britain.

[91] One striking departure from that consensus was Margaret Thatcher, who advocated intervention.

[92] Simms (2002, p. 23).

hypocrites when their policies would inevitably fail to conform to the stated ideal.

British policy preferences were informed by Lord Carrington's warning that recognition without a comprehensive settlement would bring chaos to Yugoslavia. This belief led Britain to drag its feet when other states were seen to be making rash or unilateral moves that imperiled the Carrington peace talks.[93] This explains why Britain opposed the French proposal to send a peace-making force to Croatia and why Britain did not support German moves toward recognition. Though Britain had little interest in Yugoslavia, other than an extended security interest in European stability, maintaining consensus within the EC was a high priority.

FRANCE

French diplomats were the most pro-European among the European powers. France was determined that Europe had a chance, independent of the United States, to successfully resolve Yugoslavia's conflicts. By working through their differences in Yugoslavia, the French thought the European Community would forge a strong foundation for its nascent economic and political union. At the same time, French and German policy disagreements constituted the primary obstacle to European unity. French leaders did not concede to Yugoslavia's dissolution until much later than many of their European colleagues. But French opposition was not based on principle or fact so much as a reticence to concede to German preferences or its renewed strength in European affairs.

The French were alone in their support for military intervention in Yugoslavia. Early on, France proposed that the WEU send an interposition force to ensure that Croatia's cease-fires would, in fact, hold. Many had already failed. Britain disagreed with the policy. The WEU was not invited to intervene by Serbia, so the idea was a non-starter.[94] French diplomats' effort to send military support under the auspices of the WEU was seen by many as an attempt to consolidate nascent security cooperation in Europe. Unfortunately, their proposal was premature. Europe was not yet capable of pursuing collaborative military action.

As a result of its failure in the EC, France turned to the Security Council, another venue in which it wielded substantial influence. French decision makers hoped that by corralling diplomatic efforts into the EC and UN, France would have a significant voice in the policy process. French leaders did not support what they saw as unnecessary involvement by the United States in an exclusively European affair. NATO, an institution France considered U.S. dominated, should be invited to participate only as a last resort. The longer the U.S.-led

---

[93] Recall the Carrington talks began on September 7, 1991, and aimed to find a comprehensive settlement for Yugoslavia among the six republics. The talks were sponsored by the EC.

[94] Hoffmann (1996, p. 108).

alliance remained a prominent figure in European diplomacy, the longer its power would persist in Europe.[95]

France opposed the Slovenian and Croatian secessions. According to some, French diplomats prioritized maintenance of the Yugoslav state over self-determination as a result of their own historical experience with statehood. Because the French state was created through conquest prior to the consolidation of the French nation, the French simply would not accept the Yugoslav secessions or the concept of secession in general. Nationalism was always secondary to state integrity and national consensus was not required to justify statehood. The Slovenian and Croatian justifications for independence were, therefore, considered ill conceived.

Another, less primordial explanation for France's initial support of Serbia was its concern for domestic and regional security. The French had secessionists of their own, notably Corsica, and recognized Europe's potential vulnerability to self-determination claims: "From the French perspective, there was inherent in the German policy toward self-determination and recognition an almost cavalier disregard for the stability of the European state system."[96] Its own secessionist troubles were not acute, but regional security was at stake.

France was also interested in tempering Germany's resurgence in Europe; their historical animosities resurfaced over EC policy toward Yugoslavia. France had become accustomed to its position as one of only two important powers in Europe while Germany was weak and divided throughout the Cold War. German assertiveness in Yugoslavia surprised French decision makers. They believed German behavior was out of place and threatening. That Germany in particular was advocating recognition for Slovenia and Croatia only made the French more resistant to reconsidering their position.

If France was swayed by ideological affinities or ethno-religious considerations, it was not apparent. France's initial support for Serbia stemmed from its preference for European stability and state integrity rather than an identity-based affinity. France is a Catholic country like Slovenia and Croatia, but there was no outpouring of sympathy from the Catholic Church or French Catholics as witnessed in Germany. Similarly, there was little public discussion of ideological support for the nascent democracies in Slovenia, Croatia, or Kosovo.

Late in 1991 and in early 1992, as French public opinion became mobilized in favor of humanitarian intervention, the French position became more flexible. It was also increasingly apparent that France's decision to support Milosevic and Yugoslav unity was ill founded as Milosevic's regime was perpetrating ethnic

---

[95] Gow (1997, pp. 158–159). To clarify, France believed U.S. influence was unavoidable, but that the proper institutional venue could ensure that other, European preferences were also considered – the less U.S. influence the better.

[96] Campbell and Seymour (1997, p. 306).

cleansing in Croatia and Bosnia. Still, France held fast to its belief in the uniquely European character of the conflict and its desire for European-centered policy.

GERMANY

German involvement in Yugoslavia's collapse is notorious. Initially, the German government did not support Slovenia's and Croatia's secessions, though one might not know it from the popular press. German support for recognition came about gradually, once it became clear that there was no comprehensive agreement to be had. Unfortunately for European unity, German certitude came about before it had convinced the rest of the EC. By November 1991, no fewer than 12 cease-fires had been agreed upon and failed in Croatia. Only then did German leaders openly advocate recognition as a means to break the stalemate.[97]

Germany had vested interests in the resolution of Yugoslavia's wars. It was the Great Power most geographically proximate to Yugoslavia, it had the closest ties to Yugoslavia among the European states, and its population was resolutely sympathetic to the secessionists' plight. Most factors suggested Germany would prefer recognition for Slovenia and Croatia. German action was stayed, however, by the desire to maintain European unity in light of the upcoming Maastricht Summit and the nascent European Union. Germans believed that if they could persuade the other members of the EC to their way of thinking, then perhaps European unity could be maintained *and* Germany could pursue its preferred policy. Some suggest that German decision makers went so far as to make *quid pro quo* demands for European recognition in exchange for Germany's support of Maastricht, but scant evidence supports this claim.[98] Nonetheless, German leaders did lobby hard for European recognition.

Germany was Yugoslavia's largest trade partner and primary foreign aid donor. At the time, much was made (especially by Serbia) of the possibility that Germany preferred independent Slovenia and Croatia to Yugoslav unity for economic reasons. But the evidence belies a German economic interest in Yugoslav disintegration. Though Germany was economically important for Yugoslavia, Yugoslavia was not of reciprocal economic importance to Germany. Germany was the largest investor in much of Eastern Europe simply because of its economic strength. In fact, Germany actually stood to lose if Yugoslavia fell apart. Yugoslavia had substantial debt with Germany, and it was not clear how or whether the debt would be repaid should the Yugoslav Federation cease to exist.[99] Similarly, the Germans had no standing quarrel with Serbs that might have given them an advantage in the event that Yugoslavia dissolved. In its economic affairs, Germany would have been content to maintain

---

[97] Eyal (1993, p. 43).
[98] Tanner (1997, p. 272) suggests Genscher did demand a *quid pro quo* but identifies no source.
[99] Maull (1995–1996, p. 118).

the Yugoslav status quo. Many other factors were pushing Germany to prefer recognition, however.

Germans had a number of important social ties to Slovenia and Croatia. Like Germany, both Slovenia and Croatia were majority Catholic republics, though Slovenia significantly less so than Croatia.[100] German Catholics in Bavaria, a powerful political block, lobbied strongly in favor of their coreligionists. Pro-Croatian sentiment was especially strong because Serbs, in contrast, were understood to be communist and decidedly antireligious. The Catholic Church gave support for recognition as well. Tanner recounts that "the German and Austrian Catholic bishops had close ties to their Croat counterparts. [And] Croat *Gastarbeiters* [guest workers] formed a numerous and influential community in Munich and Vienna."[101] At the same time, German guest workers did not vote, so their influence on German diplomacy should not be overstated.[102] But religious identity was not all that the Germans shared in common with the secessionists.

In truth, popular support for recognition was widespread from the beginning, certainly prior to Foreign Minister Genscher's or Chancellor Kohl's vocal diplomatic support. Germans' defense of secession was not based on ethnic or religious affinities though. The average German saw Slovenia's and Croatia's plights (and later Kosovo's) as similar to their own. In the post–Cold War era, the two republics were throwing off the yoke of communism, embracing democratic norms, and pursuing their rights of self-determination. Yugoslavia's situation was not dissimilar to the reunification of West and East Germany. The German public's support was normative, in that it was resolutely in favor of self-determination. It was ideological, in that the secessionists were seen as rejecting communism. And it was sympathetic because Germany had just successfully achieved what its people believed was a goal similar to that of the secessionists. Ullman explains: "The most persuasive argument in German politics seems to have been that, since the reunification of Germany had come about through the international community's willingness to take seriously the principle of national self-determinations, the breakaway Yugoslav republics should enjoy no less an opportunity."[103] Even though it was true that Germans had ethno-religious and ideological reasons for supporting Slovenia's and Croatia's independence, the most influential of the factors was a normative belief in the principle of self-determination.[104]

---

[100] It is perhaps more accurate to say that Catholics were a dominant minority within Germany as there was no simple majority religion. Croatia's Roman Catholic majority constituted approximately 80 percent of the population, whereas Slovenia's Catholic majority was just over 50 percent.

[101] Tanner (1997, p. 254).

[102] Caplan (2005, p. 46).

[103] Ullman (1996, p. 18).

[104] Ibid.

Political incentives, prompting Kohl and Genscher to favor recognition, arose as a consequence of the secessionists' domestic support. Local German politicians overwhelmingly supported recognition for Slovenia and Croatia. All four parties, the Christian Democratic Union (CDU), Social Democratic Party (SPD), Free Democratic Party (FDP), and the Greens went so far as to issue a joint statement recommending the national government push for recognition for those demanding independence.[105] Kohl was criticized for supporting the communist Serbs at the expense of the emerging democracies in Slovenia and Croatia.[106] As the Croatian conflict dragged on without decisive European action, domestic criticism of Kohl's (and Europe's) policies only grew.

Finally, adding urgency to the German initiative, Germans' ethno-religious ties to the secessionists also meant that Germany received the largest share of Croatian refugees once the war began. It was estimated that 100,000 Croatian refugees had traveled to Germany by 1994.[107] The influx of refugees strained the German economy, already occupied with raising living standards among former East Germans. It also created some anti-immigrant sentiment within the German population. The desire to stem the tide of Yugoslav refugees might be the only parochial interest (domestic security) underlying German policy.[108]

As the summer and fall of 1991 passed and violence in Croatia only intensified, German decision makers became vocal and resolute in their support for recognition and independence. They reasoned that if the international community could not stop the conflict through negotiation, then the Slovenians and Croatians should at least have the opportunity to defend themselves. Recognition implied the secessionists' right to legal self-defense, so the embargo could be lifted and states could legitimately send aid. Finally, recognition might convince the Serbs that the international community would never ratify its conquest of Croatia and prompt them to concede. German leaders' desire to recognize was stayed only by a sincere desire to maintain European consensus.

THE ABSENT SUPERPOWERS

The United States and the Soviet Union, though initially not deeply involved in Yugoslavia, would come to play important roles in the later phases of the conflict. In the early 1990s, both had more pressing interests elsewhere. And, in any case, Europe did not want them to interfere. Only as the Yugoslav conflict dragged on and the violence mounted were the United States and Russia compelled to become involved. Both states opposed independence. Russian interests were more significantly engaged than were those in the United States, however.

---

[105] Caplan (2005, p. 45).
[106] Gow (1997, pp. 167–168).
[107] "Deserters face deportation to Croatia" (1994).
[108] Ullman (1996, p. 18).

UNITED STATES

The conflict in Yugoslavia did not catch the United States unaware. American intelligence agencies had been predicting ethnic conflict and disintegration in the Balkans since Tito's death.[109] Nevertheless, the United States was not eager to become involved. Many in George H. W. Bush's administration viewed Yugoslavia as a no-win situation for the United States; there was no obvious aggressor, no clear military solution, and no vital American interest at stake. Further stymieing the initiative, the United States was occupied with Gulf War I and had just emerged from protracted Cold War antagonisms with the Soviet Union. With Europe eager to cut its newly consolidated teeth on the conflict, it was easy for the United States to remain disengaged at first.

Two prominent accounts describe the U.S. decision to distance itself from Yugoslavia's conflicts. They attribute U.S. motives to either (1) a desire to see Europe flounder or (2) a self-preservationist instinct, informed by the realization that Yugoslavia was a potential quagmire. Some within the Bush administration certainly believed Europe's "bluff should be called." The Europeans were so eager to take charge in Yugoslavia and so naïve about the political and material costs of intervention; it was an opportunity to allow the EC's unitary foreign policy to fail. Lawrence Eagleburger, at least, was convinced that the Europeans would struggle in the Balkans and that only afterward, humbled, would they learn to burden share.[110]

Some evidence does show that the Bush administration was unsympathetic to the EC's situation, but much more evidence points to the United States' own fears of being bogged down in Yugoslavia. National Security Advisor Brent Scowcroft recalls Secretary of States James Baker arguing that the United States "didn't have a dog in [Yugoslavia's] fight."[111] Like some of their European peers, many in the Bush administration did not initially see a connection between Milosevic and the Croatian and Bosnian Serb insurgencies. They thought that the resistance movements were indigenous, and perhaps unaided by Milosevic. So again, the fog of war contributed to difficulties in attributing responsibility for the violence.[112] With no apparent solution and complex minority relations, Yugoslavia seemed like an intractable situation. U.S. decision makers essentially shared the British view of the conflict.

The United States did not want recognition for Slovenia or Croatia. It supported maintaining the status quo. But the United States would not go out of its

---

[109] Duncan and Holman (1994, p. 34); Larrabee (1997, p. 280).
[110] Simms (2002, p. 54). Eagleburger was deputy secretary of sate at the time and Bush's primary political advisor regarding Yugoslavia. His expertise in Yugoslav affairs derived from his time as U.S. ambassador to Yugoslavia during the Carter administration (1977–1980).
[111] Silber and Little (1996, p. 201); see also Gow (1997, p. 203).
[112] Larrabee (1997, p. 35).

way to stop the secessions either. If recognition was to come for Yugoslavia's republics, the primary concern of the United States was precedent. The Americans did not want Yugoslav recognition to serve as an exemplar for the USSR. So far as the United States was concerned, recognition of the secessionists would have to wait until a gradual dissolution could be negotiated for the Soviet Union. If the USSR dissolved violently, there would be worldwide repercussions. U.S. concern for the dissolution of its former rival was more pressing than the plight of Yugoslavia's states, which could wait. On December 25, 1991, the Soviet Union dissolved and Yugoslavia's precedent-setting potential became a moot point.

Though the United States had domestic challengers, U.S. policy makers were unconcerned that recognition might set precedents for their own secessionists. Minority demands in the United States would likely not lead to independence for the Hawaiians, Puerto Ricans, or other domestic discontents. Nor were U.S. secessionist claims accompanied by violence or widespread political unrest. Domestic secessionists presented little challenge to U.S. legitimacy on the whole. America's secessionists were not powerful enough to influence its foreign policy agenda.

At home, there was scant political pressure regarding Yugoslavia. There were small, active ethnic lobbies within the United States, but their influence on policy was debatable. Direct monetary support for ethnic kin in Yugoslavia was far more influential in the conflicts than political mobilization in the United States. The greater American public was not strongly in favor of either intervention or recognition; it was entirely uninformed.

Finally, identity concerns did not play an obvious role in U.S. decision making toward Yugoslavia's secessions. It is noteworthy that although both Slovenia and Croatia emphasized their modern, Western orientation when explaining the rationale behind their desire to separate from Yugoslavia, their argument did not persuade the Bush administration.

When the 1992 campaign season began, Yugoslavia belatedly became an important topic in U.S. domestic politics. William "Bill" Clinton, Bush's presidential challenger, sharply critiqued the administration's decision to turn a blind eye to Yugoslavia's human costs. Clinton's analysis put pressure on the Bush administration to alter its approach and generally raised public awareness regarding Yugoslavia. As a result, U.S. policy toward the Balkans became more assertive, but not until Clinton had replaced Bush and Yugoslavia's wars had already gone on for nearly two years. Recognition was not a priority for the United States until it intervened diplomatically in the Bosnian war, when the United States traded its recognition of Slovenia and Croatia for European recognition of Bosnia.[113]

---

[113] U.S.-EU recognition of Bosnia was coordinated to occur at the same time, April 7, 1992.

SOVIET UNION/RUSSIA

Domestic instability precluded active Russian participation in Yugoslavia, at first. Nevertheless, the Soviet Union was among the most important factors influencing many states' recognition decisions. Potential Soviet dissolution loomed large in the American and European imagination. Minimal though it was, Russian policy toward Yugoslavia favored Serbs and opposed the secessions. Russians had a special relationship with Yugoslavia's Serbs, both in terms of ideological affinity and ethno-religious makeup. And with the Soviet Union's domestic unrest came numerous secessionist movements challenging the USSR's domestic authority. Like their Western counterparts, Russians were concerned Yugoslavia might serve as an unwanted precedent for their own union's demise. Finally, like China, the Soviet Union had a long track record of opposition to external intervention into other states' sovereign affairs. The secession problem was internal and best left to Yugoslav (read: Serbian) authorities. Once Russia's domestic politics had stabilized though, Russians sought out a middle ground between maintaining its noninterventionist stance and beginning to engage the West.

Soviet decision makers' concern for their own internal security troubles would have been sufficient cause for the Russians to oppose recognition. There were other reasons too. For instance, Russians and Serbs share a Slavic heritage. Many observers argue Soviet leaders' perceptions and policies toward the conflict were colored by their shared heritage with the Serbs. Indeed, Russian leaders and Western officials reiterated exactly that on numerous occasions throughout Yugoslavia's war. Goble submits to the contrary, however, that although ethnic identity is "mentioned most often," it is also the "most overrated" and "least understood" explanation for Russian behavior toward the Yugoslav wars.[114] He explains that Soviet politicians saw their shared Slavic identity as a double-edged sword. Whereas Russians were predisposed to be sympathetic to the Serbs, they also feared Western perceptions that the two states were perfect analogs, and that an event in one forecasted things to come in the other.[115] Consequently, Soviet pronouncements of Serbian affinity were likely crafted for domestic consumption and not indicative of actual policy influence.

Many Russian citizens did support the Serbian position based on their shared ethno-religious and ideological identity, however. Russian corporations and private citizens violated the UN embargo to lend material support to the Serbian effort. Support of this kind was common among Russian nationalists, for example, who were decidedly motivated by shared Slavic identity.[116] In addition, anti-American sentiment was still common among citizens in the early 1990s. Opposition to the West then, rather than ethnic affinity with the

[114] Goble (1996, p. 183).
[115] Ibid.
[116] Rezun (1995, p. 178).

Serbs, may further explain domestic mobilization in favor of communist Serbia.[117] Public support for Serbia among Russians did not translate into assertive foreign policy. Russian leaders did not want to encourage their association with the Serbs.

If we assume the preceding analysis of U.S. and European decision making is correct, Russians had good reason for their concern that the Russo-Serb analogy had been taken too seriously by the West. Western leaders *were* preoccupied with Yugoslavia's potential to influence Soviet dissolution.[118] But the Yugoslav-Soviet analogy was imperfect. Ullman explains that even though there were obvious parallels between the situations Russian Soviets and Yugoslav Serbs faced, there were important differences as well.

On December 24, when the Soviet Union formally dissolved, its Russian population was fragmented into the various successor states left in its wake, exactly the fate Yugoslavia's Serbs feared. In addition, Russians, like the Serbs, were not majorities in any of the USSR's successor states. Russians pursued a different political strategy than Serbs did, though, because of significant differences between the two situations: "By virtue of its geographic expanse, the size of its population, the relatively advanced state of its economy and even its imperial status during the era preceding the revolutions of 1917, Russia could plausibly aspire to something like a hegemonic role in what was once its undisputed domain."[119] Russia lost most of its territory at the end of 1991 but maintained its potential to influence the former republics with significant Russian minorities, in what came to be known as the Russian near-abroad. The same was not true for Serbs, whose dominance within Yugoslavia derived largely from political power. The two also differed because Russia could not play the nationalist card that Serbs did. Russian nationalism was historically revisionist, "[seeking] to recover something that has been lost, rather than to glory in what has been achieved."[120] For Russia, blatant nationalism would have threatened its immediate neighbors. They had just become its "something lost."

As Russia moved beyond its own political transition, it began seeking a more constructive relationship with the other Great Powers. Therefore, Russians wanted to disassociate themselves from the example set by Yugoslavia's Serbs.[121] Though Cold War tensions remained, Russia's formal diplomatic role in Yugoslavia was described as "extremely prudent":

American journalistic reporting tends to play up instances when Russia has cast a vote in the UN Security Council opposed to actions or policies that Washington prefers. Yet in

---

[117] Gow (1997, p. 189).
[118] In hindsight, the reverse causal story is more likely true, that is, that events in the Soviet Union affected events in Yugoslavia.
[119] Ullman (1996, p. 28).
[120] Goble (1996, p. 187).
[121] Ibid., p. 183.

every instance but one (and that one a relatively unimportant instance), the United Kingdom and France have been on the same side as Russia.[122]

In the early 1990s, Russia did not want to antagonize the United States by becoming more active in Yugoslavia, nor did it want to forfeit the special financial assistance the United States provided at the Cold War's end. Russian opposition to recognition was overdetermined. Some of Russia's interests dictated support for the Serbs, but intervention on their behalf was ruled out by Russia's instability and later desire to engage the West.

THE ASIAN POWERS

China and Japan were less involved in Yugoslavia's conflicts than their European and American counterparts. The conflict in Europe was outside their region and of little interest except in the abstract. Japan was just beginning to assert itself as a Great Power with global interests and had little institutional authority. China, with both power and expansive interests, was involved in Yugoslav diplomacy because of its UNSC membership and its vested interest in maintaining a strong norm of sovereignty throughout the system. China's interest in Yugoslavia was not motivated by its own secessionists, but rather by its leaders' strong belief in maintaining domestic sovereignty. Relative to the other Great Powers, however, its engagement was limited.

China was reticent to support independence for Yugoslavia's secessionists, but even more wary of setting a precedent for intervention in states' internal affairs. Both China and Russia were likely to oppose intervention or force under the auspices of the UN.[123] Nevertheless, it was important to Chinese decision makers that they be involved and consulted by the other Great Powers. When NATO intervened in Kosovo on the Albanians' behalf in 1999, the Chinese government strenuously objected both to its contravention of domestic sovereignty and to NATO's thwarting of the Security Council's authority as the sole guarantor of global legitimacy.[124] Though, earlier in the decade, China had been content to follow Europe's lead, maintaining the option of a UNSC veto when necessary.

China's leaders wanted global influence and its Security Council position was a useful means by which to assert it. Beijing objected to the U.S.-led alliance taking action against Serbia because it had not been privy to the decision making. China was (and continues to be) concerned about creeping American imperialism. If the United States were simply allowed to "forum shop" for the international institution most likely to submit to its will, China's strength and the

---

[122] Ullman (1996, pp. 29–30).
[123] China abstained in many instances when Yugoslav policies and declarations were adopted within the Security Council.
[124] It did not help matters much when, on May 7, 1998, NATO forces accidentally bombed the Chinese Embassy in Belgrade.

strength of the Security Council would be weakened. In this way, the Chinese position was similar to the French position, as it preferred policy coordination through the WEU or UN to NATO.

Additionally, the norm of nonintervention in states' internal affairs was an important determinant of China's policy preferences. China had domestic challengers of its own and did not welcome international meddling in its internal affairs. That sensitivity to external intervention was especially acute in the wake of the Tiananmen Square massacre and the international criticism it provoked.[125] Most of China's secessionists were unlikely to succeed. China was still, however, a weak state in many ways. Its vast territory, huge and diverse population, and uneven development made domestic instability an important concern.

Then again, there were some signs that China's stance on interventionism had moderated. Once steadfastly opposed to intervention in any circumstance, China began participating in UN peacekeeping efforts in 1991.[126] Still, its standards were quite restrictive and China would only participate given two conditions. First, the host country had to acquiesce to intervention, and second, the UNSC had to approve the mission.[127] NATO did not meet either condition in Kosovo.

As late as December 1991, Japanese authorities declared that they were not contemplating recognition for either Slovenia or Croatia and reiterated their support for the multilateral talks under Cyrus Vance and John Owen (later of the Vance-Owen Peace Plan). Like China, Japan had little interest in Yugoslavia's wars. But unlike China, Japan had just begun to play an active role in power politics outside of Asia. Japanese influence was further limited by its lack of a formal role in the primary institutions involved. Japan had no seat on the UN Security Council, nor did it belong to NATO or the EC.

RECOGNITION AND NONRECOGNITION

When the Badinter recommendations were handed down in January, Croatia's nonrecognition was not the commission's only controversial decision. It also supported Macedonia's recognition, which infuriated Greece. Furthermore, Badinter demanded that Bosnia adhere to a standard higher than that required

---

[125] The Tiananmen Square, pro-democracy protests occurred between April and June of 1989. Hundreds of nonviolent protestors were killed when the Chinese government cracked down and declared martial law on June 3 and 4.

[126] As of 2000, China had participated in the UN missions to Iraq-Kuwait (UNIKOM 1991), Western Sahara (MINURSO 1991), Mozambique (ONUMOZ 1993), Cambodia (UNAMIC and UNTAC 1991 and 1992), Liberia (UNOMIL 1993), Sierra Leone (UNAMISL 1999), and East Timor (UNTAET 2000).

[127] Gill and Reilly (2000, p. 46). Gill and Reilly note, however, that China refused to participate in any peacekeeping operation in which the state maintains diplomatic ties with Taiwan, "apparently regardless of the broader security issues involved."

of the other republics – namely, that it hold a referendum in order to demonstrate its democratic constitution. Though Slovenia and Croatia had submitted plebiscite results, Badinter's guidelines did not require them. At the time, one commentator remarked that "[the] only opinion relative to recognition that was not contentious was the commission's judgment that Slovenia had satisfied the EC's requirements."[128] Badinter's decisions, if uniformly followed, would strain European relations as much as they would create a foundation for a unified foreign policy; Germany strongly favored recognition for both Slovenia and Croatia, and Greece resolutely opposed recognition for Macedonia.

In addition, European leaders made plain their plan to deviate from international law. Douglas Hogg, the British minister of state, remarked during parliamentary debates over Yugoslavia that "The traditional criteria that we adopt for the recognition of states probably apply to Slovenia. They do not apply in the case of Croatia in the same way, but...one of the reasons why...is that Croatian territory has been invaded by the JNA and Serbian irregulars."[129] Though the inherent uncertainties of war certainly made it difficult to attribute responsibility for Croatia's and Bosnia's violence, the amount of control exercised by each secessionist regime was apparent. Slovenia met the legal requirements for domestic sovereignty and statehood. Croatia and Kosovo did not. Hogg's argument shows that leaders acknowledged Croatia's lack of capacity but prioritized other factors in granting recognition and casting the JNA as a foreign occupier.

When recognition did come to Yugoslavia's secessionists, it did not conform to the Montevideo criteria. Nor did it follow Badinter's ad hoc recommendations.[130] Instead, recognition adhered to a dual logic of European unity and self-interest. Most held fast to their commitment to European consensus until the very end. But their unity was a function of bandwagoning rather than a true expression of their preferences. Once the EC's comprehensive settlement initiative was abandoned, and one state had granted recognition, the rest of Europe followed suit. The superpowers and the Asian powers then followed the European lead.

Within Europe, Germany was alone in its strong preference for Slovenia's and Croatia's recognition. Some leaders had softened their opposition, specifically to what they saw as premature recognition for Croatia, but they consistently favored a united European policy. Outside of Europe, Russia was most opposed to recognition, but its own domestic turmoil precluded an assertive diplomatic role. The United States, like much of Europe, also did not prefer recognition, but unlike its European counterparts, the United States had no vested interest in policy coordination. Finally, the Asian powers were peripherally engaged in

---

[128] Caplan (2005, p. 38).
[129] Quoted in ibid., p. 65 at n.58.
[130] Both would have dictated that Slovenia would receive recognition, and Croatia and Kosovo would not.

Yugoslav diplomacy, though China was generally concerned that domestic sovereignty not be violated.

Germany announced its recognition of Slovenia and Croatia first, on December 24. Though, in a move feigning deference to European consensus, its recognition would not come into force until January 15 (see Table 5.1). The rest of the EC granted recognition on January 15 as planned. German policy adhered to the letter of its agreement with the other European states, but not to its spirit.[131] German authorities granted recognition so quickly after the December 16 decision to consider recognition that it was nearly impossible that Badinter's advice could have influenced their choice.[132] Even so, German defection from the other European states was not as profound as it might seem.

In fact, there was wide consensus within Europe that recognition would eventually come to Slovenia and Croatia as early as July, once Milosevic began to forcibly oppose the secessions. Leaders only disagreed about when and how recognition should occur.[133] If Germany had withheld its recognition for another three weeks, Europe would have recognized Slovenia and Croatia in concert. Germany's lobbying efforts would have been partially responsible for the timing of Europe's choice, but even without German influence, recognition would have come eventually. Ultimately, the outcome would have been the same.

So far as Germany's unilateralism is concerned, Campbell and Seymour make a persuasive argument that recognition did not presage an era of German unilateralism, as the French and British had feared. Instead, Germany's recognition "was evidence of [its] faith in the efficacy of decisions taken and actions sanctioned by multilateral institutions."[134] German decision makers were convinced that recognition and international legitimacy alone would compel Serbia to acknowledge its defeat. The French foreign minister asserted afterward that Germany had pushed the EC into recognition, that it was a mistake and that maintaining Yugoslavia would have been wiser.[135] But the evidence contradicts that European leaders believed maintaining Yugoslavia was a viable option after Badinter's November 29 decision on dissolution.

[131] Ironically, Germany (and France) had divined the idea for and standards of conditional recognition in the first place (Caplan 2005, p. 23).

[132] Interestingly, the Germans had some reason to be confident that Croatia would meet the Badinter standards because they had sent a legal scholar to advise them on achieving them. Caplan notes, "At the end of November, the German Foreign Ministry had dispatched the legal scholar Christian Tomuschat to Zagreb...Tomuschat, particularly satisfied with the results of his efforts [on minority protections], declared that the legally anchored protection of minorities in Croatia 'should serve as a role model for the further development of minority rights in Europe'" (2005, p. 39 at n.103).

[133] Ibid., p. 18.

[134] Campbell and Seymour (1997, p. 300).

[135] Cited in Hoffmann (1996, p. 105 at n.17).

The remaining Great Powers followed the European lead. Russia, Japan, the United States, and China recognized Slovenia and Croatia in the winter and spring of 1992. Russian recognition came just after it recognized its own former republics and the threat of a Yugoslav precedent had diminished. The United States recognized Slovenia and Croatia in exchange for European recognition of Bosnia, which, along with Kosovo, the United States now saw as more pressing concerns for regional security and stability. Finally, China deferentially withheld recognition until after Serbia recognized the two new states, maintaining its insistence that secession was an internal affair and a matter of sovereign discretion; China would not recognize without the consent of their home state.

POST MORTEM

Recognition was not the panacea German authorities imagined it would be. Croatia's war with Serbia and the RSK did not end. And for some time, the facts on the ground did not change. On the other hand, in time, widespread support for Croatia's legitimate authority allowed its successive military campaigns to take back territory from Serbia later in the 1990s. Slovenia's recognition helped its economy stabilize and paved the way for its membership in the EU. In Kosovo, nonrecognition only led to greater problems as Serbia shifted its attention away from the other republics and toward its internal, Albanian enemies.

Recognition's consequences varied based on the extent of domestic sovereignty the secessionists exercised. Recognition did not much influence domestic sovereignty in Slovenia, where violence had ceased months before and normal governance had taken hold. Its primary impact was providing entry into prestigious, international governmental institutions and furthering economic development. It was more important for Croatia, though, whose territorial control suffered considerably under the weight of sanctions and continued conflict with Serbian insurgents. The political and military advantages that flowed from external recognition improved the government's ability to consolidate political power. U.S. support and arms transfers buoyed its material capacity significantly. Finally, Kosovo, which had attempted in vein to garner consideration for its independence alongside the constituent republics, struggled to maintain what little authority it did have. Its government received no recognition and would face only higher-intensity violence and civilian slaughter as the conflict in the Former Yugoslavia continued.

DEVELOPMENTS IN KOSOVO

Throughout the mid-1990s, Kosovo had suffered under what Alex Bellamy describes as "malign non-engagement." The international community believed sacrificing Kosovo was necessary to save Bosnia, where full-scale war had broken out between Serbs, Croats, and Bosnian Muslims. Kosovo's problems, though, continued to fester.[136] The KLA was a mixed blessing for Kosovo's independence. On one hand, the group pacified Albanians who might have otherwise defected from the parallel government. On the other hand, the KLA was considered a terrorist organization, not only by Serbia, but also by the United States, Russia, and other external actors whose support would be critical to Kosovo's ultimate success.

As the KLA had anticipated, the Serbian government responded to its campaign with overwhelming force, cracking down with even greater military and police control than before. Reports of human rights abuses, expulsions, and mass killings were widespread. The new violence quickly made Kosovo an international priority. Western leaders realized that unrest in Kosovo, unlike that in Slovenia and Croatia, had real potential to spill over into neighboring states and create instability throughout Eastern Europe. More importantly, Greece and Turkey, both NATO members, might be compelled to intervene on opposing sides.[137] Throughout 1998 and early 1999, the international community tried in vein to negotiate a settlement to end the violence. Each seemingly cooperative move by Milosevic was later renounced and resisted until March 24, 1999, when NATO finally initiated air strikes to compel Serbs to withdraw from the province (Table 5.3).

Despite their apparent support for the Kosovo Albanians, as NATO began bombing, the Great Powers still opposed independence. Russian Prime Minister Yevgeniy Primakov argued in 1998 that Albanians' violent, independence-only stance was the primary impediment to conflict resolution. It was inevitable that Kosovars accept autonomy short of independence. He further indicated that China shared a similar perspective on the situation.[138] French Foreign Minister Hubert Vedrine asserted that "a partition of the Serb province of Kosovo [was] out of the question" but did not rule out international "protection."[139] The British ambassador to Russia stated simply that "Great Britain [was] against Kosovo becoming an independent republic."[140] Finally, the United States also reaffirmed Serbian authority over Kosovo, even though it disagreed strongly with Serbia's means of asserting that control.

Milosevic relented to NATO's demands on June 3. Serbian troops would withdraw and allow the international community to administer the province. NATO halted military operations on June 10. The same day, the Security Council authorized the United Nations to create an interim authority for Kosovo.[141] Abbreviated UNMIK, United Nations Interim Administration Mission in Kosovo, the mission's mandate was to provide functional self-

---

[136] Bellamy (2002, pp. 65–66).
[137] Kaufman (2002, pp. 156–157).
[138] "Russia: Russian Foreign Minister Opposes Independence for Kosovo" (1998).
[139] "Vedrine Rules Out Partition, Independence for Kosovo" (1999).
[140] "Russia: UK Against Kosovo Gaining Independence" (1999).
[141] S/RES/1244 (1999) June 10, 1999.

government within the territory. Self-government included the reconstruction of its infrastructure, support of humanitarian relief, and the protection of human rights and facilitation in the determination of Kosovo's final status. The Serbian government no longer had authority within Kosovo, retaining only nominal sovereignty in the region. Instead, the Special Representative of the Secretary General (SRSG) was Kosovo's highest authority. The EU ran the Kosovo economy. The Kosovo Force (KFOR) controlled Kosovo's airspace and borders, and UNMIK issued passports and organized the police force. However, UNSC Resolution 1244 reassured Serbia that any final settlement to the Kosovo conflict would necessarily require its consent; no matter how proscribed its exercise of authority, Serbia remained the *de jure* government.[142] Additionally, majority Serbian enclaves in Northern Kosovo remained effectively under a Serb-controlled parallel government protected by NATO.

After the KLA's 1998–1999 conflict with Serbian authorities, Kosovo's potential for a viable economy and successful governance was decimated. More than half of Kosovo's population was displaced following NATO's intervention. Conservative estimates suggest 25,000 Albanians were displaced outside of Kosovo; some estimated as many as 300,000 refugees had fled Serb authorities and the war. Most production activities within the region were disrupted or stopped entirely, sometimes for as much as a year. Finally, much of Kosovo's housing stock had been destroyed. Kosovo relied principally on international donors and the Albanian diaspora for economic support. The Kosovo economy began transitioning to a market economy under UN guidance, but unemployment in Kosovo was still estimated to be 50 percent as late as 2005.[143] However, Serbia was also weaker and did not offer much greater hope of viability were Kosovo to be reincorporated into its territory. The American CIA estimated that Serbia's and Montenegro's economies in 1999 were only half of what they were in 1990, before the UN sanctions and NATO bombings.

Five years into the UNMIK/KFOR administration, on March 17 and 18, 2004 large, violent anti-Serb riots beginning in Mitrovica and spreading to other cities in Kosovo reinvigorated international efforts to arrive at an enduring solution. At this time, Kosovo Albanians potential use of force against Serbs and other smaller minority populations in the region were a primary international concern. The UN and NATO did not want to suborn additional ethnic cleansing. Yet the conditions at that time seemed even less favorable to a negotiated settlement than in 1999, not just on the ground, but also internationally.

Russia was no longer facing high levels of domestic instability at home that would occupy its attention and had become actively involved in Kosovo. It became a member of the "contact group" – an informal group of states with vested interests in the conflict – along with Britain, France, Germany, Italy, and

---

[142] Ibid.
[143] "Serbia and Montenegro" (2006).

the United States. And although Russia had initially appeared to betray Serbia by agreeing to the group's guiding principles – "no return of Kosovo to the pre-1999 situation, no partition of Kosovo, and no union of Kosovo with any or part of another country" – which seemed to leave only independence of some sort on the table, it quickly changed its position.[144] Less than three months into the process, President Vladimir Putin began advocating a universal solution for Kosovo, linking any determination of its final status to unresolved conflicts along the Russian periphery, remarking, "Not all the conflicts are settled in the post-Soviet territory. We cannot follow the way when we use some principles in one place and other principles in another one".[145] In response, some of the other members of the contact group, including Britain, began vocally supporting independence in their meetings with Kosovo authorities.[146] Further negotiations did not break the stalemate, and by the fall of 2006, Russia seemed prepared to use its veto if the issue of independence without Serbia's consent came to the Security Council. NATO extended Partnership for Peace membership to Serbia in an attempt to undermine Serbian nationalists in the 2007 parliamentary elections and potentially shift the political landscape, but little change regarding Kosovo occurred.

By the summer of 2007, the most important axis of negotiations was Washington-Moscow, not Belgrade-Pristina. The negotiations between Albanians and Serbs continued, but the most important developments were occurring among the Great Powers. Early in the year, the Ahtisaari Plan had deferred the question of Kosovo's status to the Security Council.[147] Russia demanded that any Kosovo solution ought to remain true to Resolution 1244, whereas the United States and much of Europe were attempting to find a way to justify independence without establishing a new precedent threatening fellow EU members with secessionists as in Greece, Spain, and Italy. Yet, the pressure for intra-European consensus was not nearly so great now that the European Union was well established and its members had let the United States take the lead on Kosovo.

After Russia asserted that the Kosovo decision ought to be universal and not "unprecedented," U.S. decision makers started talking openly about a unilateral declaration of independence, assuring Kosovars that their recognition would be forthcoming. This was a rhetorical strategy aimed at Russia. Although a gradual, UNSC-sanctioned transition to independence would be bad for Moscow, a unilateral independence gained without Russian consent was undoubtedly worse; seeing this, surely Moscow would moderate its stance. Russian leaders

---

[144] "Contact Group Guiding Principles," November 2005.

[145] REGNUM News Agency (2006).

[146] "Envoy Assures Kosovo President of British Support on Final Status Issue" (2006); "Serbia's Draskovic Says UK Straw's Comment on Kosovo Violates International Law" (2006); "EU Downplays Comments on Kosovo Independence" (2006).

[147] In March, Ahtisaari did send a confidential communication to UN Secretary General Ban Ki Moon recommending independence as the only viable solution for Kosovo (Lynch 2007).

did not interpret the situation that way or at least did not respond as the Americans hoped they would. Whatever slim chance there was for a final status resolution had been lost by the fall. The final talks between Belgrade and Pristina collapsed in December.

On February 17, 2008, frustrated with the stalemated negotiations and at the urging of the United States and much of Europe, Kosovo unilaterally declared its independence. Three of the five Great Powers quickly granted recognition, but Europe was not united. A number of states did not want to embolden their own discontents at home. Russia and, to a slightly lesser extent, China remained steadfast in their opposition to full independence. Russia also seized the opportunity for the Kosovo decision to serve as a precedent in the post-Soviet space where its interests were more directly at stake.[148] Still, only around 54 percent of the international community's members have recognized Kosovo as of this writing.[149] It would seem that the tipping point has not been reached and many state leaders remain uncertain about how to interpret the fracture among the Great Powers.

CONCLUSION

This analysis of Great Power decision making regarding recognition in Slovenia, Croatia, and Kosovo clearly demonstrates that considerations other than domestic sovereignty and viability played an important role. Regarding Slovenia, the Great Powers withheld external sovereignty for months in favor of a comprehensive Yugoslav settlement that never came to pass. Whereas what might be termed premature recognition – and the potential for legitimate military force that came with it – retroactively allowed Croatia to adjust its borders to include territory and people that were clearly not under its effective control or willing to submit to its political authority. Finally, though Kosovo had a strong popular mandate for independence, its effective control and authority were very limited. However, these characteristics were not even considered because the Great Powers would not countenance a non-republic's statehood. Later, sustained primarily by an interim international administration, Kosovo's ultimate fate remained uncertain. Furthermore, that limbo was as much a function of the political impasse among the Great Powers as it was intransigence on the part of leaders in Kosovo and Serbia. Indeed, the domestic-level politics are hard to disentangle from the international. In each of the three cases, external politics influenced the granting and timing of Great Power recognition; membership cannot be explained with reference only to domestic-level politics. Moreover, Great Power leaders were making a conscious choice to subordinate questions of sovereignty to other more parochial concerns of their own.

[148] The details of the Russian response will be discussed in greater detail in Chapter 6.
[149] One hundred and five of the 193 members of the United Nations formally recognized Kosovo as of October 10, 2013.

Slovenia clearly met the highest legal standards for statehood. Probably following its decisive 10 Day War with Serb authorities, but certainly after the Brioni moratorium had passed, Slovenia was more stable, politically independent, and economically viable than many existing members of the international community. Even before it was recognized, Slovenia met and surpassed the additional recognition standards required by the EC. By any account, Slovenia's domestic sovereignty was beyond reproach.

There, recognition was not immediately granted because the Great Powers had interests running contrary to Slovene independence. When German decision makers decided to recognize Slovenia, it was in conjunction with Croatian recognition. The "package deal" that Croatians had encouraged by seceding at the same time helped legitimate their independence even though Slovenia discouraged the association. Slovenian recognition was stalled for five months while Europe and the Serbs jockeyed over Croatia. In terms of this project, Slovenia exemplifies low Great Power interest and high domestic sovereignty. Slovenia's domestic sovereignty alone would have been sufficient for it to gain recognition as a state eventually, but the Great Powers withheld recognition until it became a politically attractive alternative and a means to preserve a united European foreign policy. Somewhat ironically, Slovenia's relative stability and lack of violence made recognition a less pressing concern for the international community; it was the wheel that did not squeak.

Croatia had strong governmental authority and popular support, but its control over the territory it claimed was severely compromised. Many states have border disputes or some contested areas of control within their territories, but Croatia's territorial control was highly contentious. In addition, the Croatian constitution lacked the personal and minority protections that the EC demanded before it would grant recognition. The regime fell short according to at least two criteria, one legal and one political.

In spite of these shortcomings, Croatia received recognition alongside Slovenia within its Yugoslav borders. Germany was overwhelmingly sympathetic to the secessionists' cause in general and particularly motivated to grant Croatia recognition. German recognition stemmed from a belief that Croatia's war would subside in the face of external recognition, rather than an empirical claim that Croatia already met, or would meet, the legal standards. Because Europeans were consumed with presenting a unified front regarding Yugoslavia, they followed Germany's lead. In some cases, states prioritized European unity over their own individual preferences against recognition. Croatian recognition, then, is a case in which equivocal domestic-level sovereignty translated into external sovereignty as a function of the Great Powers' interest in coordination. Under typical circumstances, the strong interest of a single state is not enough to compel other states to recognize. But in this particular case, Britain's and France's overriding interest in maintaining European unity drove them to follow the German precedent and paper over the apparent difference regarding timing.

Finally, Kosovo had little domestic sovereignty when it first declared independence in October 1991. It did not meet the Montevideo standards nor did it meet the standard for a hearing by Badinter. The Great Powers also had few interests in Kosovo. And like Slovenia, Kosovo was not violent in the early 1990s, so the Great Powers were not motivated to involve themselves in the Albanians' struggle. Only once violence exploded in the province, as the KLA became active and Serbian authorities began to ethnically cleanse the territory, did the international community intervene.

At the time of the Yugoslav secessions, many of the Great Powers had problems with secession and domestic instability. Britain faced secessionists in Northern Ireland and Scotland, and France had separatists in Corsica, the Alsace, and the Basque country. These movements were not as strong or as destabilizing as those faced by Russia or China, however. Russia would fight and lose a war with Chechen rebels in 1994–1995 and lost most of its territory during the Soviet Union's dissolution in 1991. And, though this time more successfully, it entered into a second, anti-terrorism action in Chechnya from 1999 to 2000.[150] China faced extensive unrest in Taiwan, Tibet, and Xinjiang as events in Yugoslavia unfolded between 1990 and 2008. Adding to its domestic instability, though not secessionist, China came under intense international scrutiny for its repression of pro-democracy protestors in 1989. Finally, beginning in 1998, Hong Kong would also become a potential secessionist threat.

Great Power behavior regarding Yugoslavia suggests that strong states may be better able than weaker states to manage domestic unrest, and that their foreign policy will not be influenced by domestic unrest until the level of discontent is quite high. Insights from the quantitative results on domestic insecurity are largely confirmed by Russian behavior regarding Yugoslavia, but not in exactly the manner predicted. Although domestic insecurity did stay Russian recognition during the earlier Slovenian and Croatian secessions, this occurred indirectly because the Soviet Union mostly opted out of diplomacy and conflict resolution. When the Russian position was more secure in the later Kosovo conflict, Russia also became more engaged and assertive in its opposition to Kosovo's independence. And this was especially true after Chechnya had been pacified. Even though the Soviet Union/Russia never lost its Great Power status, it behavior war similar to the World War II French and German cases in that it was not actively involved in decision making. So an embattled state is less likely to recognize secessionists' independence, but a deeply unstable regime also loses its capacity to weigh in and attempt to influence the other Great Powers.

Geostrategically, Yugoslavia had lost its centrality at the end of the Cold War. Russia and the United States, which might have deemed Yugoslavia's governmental stability of pivotal importance only years before, were not eager to intervene. Yugoslav authorities had no conflicts with the powerful to sour

[150] Lower intensity, but still large-scale Russian counterterrorism operations continued in Chechnya through April 2009.

their relations early in the conflict, so the Great Powers favored maintaining the status quo. As time and the conflicts wore on, however, Serbia was increasingly at odds with NATO. Even with Milosevic's departure in 2000, Kosovo probably had better prospects for independence because Serbia had come to be seen as an enemy by the United States, Britain, Germany, and France. Furthermore (and discussed in greater detail in Chapter 6, NATO expansion – specifically into Georgia – and lingering Cold War suspicions indirectly influenced Russia's stance on Kosovo. Russia saw the opportunity to exploit the Kosovo situation for its own ends in Georgia, Moldova, and Azerbaijan while maintaining its support of Serbia. Its improved domestic security situation did not pay dividends to Kosovo but certainly did to South Ossetia and Abkhazia.

Finally, belief in democratic self-determination was an important, though not hypothesized, motive behind German support for recognition of Slovenia and Croatia. Germans saw their own recent experience with self-determination in the Croatian case, perhaps evidence in favor of the amity hypotheses, though not unambiguously so. Support for self-determination did not, however, move most of the Great Powers away from their initial preference for the status quo. Moreover, when the Great Powers did recognize Slovenia and Croatia, they did not appear motivated by a change regarding self-determination. Indeed, Russia, China, and France all favored maintaining Yugoslavia's territorial integrity when it came to the secessionists (and secessionism in general) and roundly criticized Germany.

SELECTED YUGOSLAVIA TIMELINE (1989–2011)

	1989
February	Constitutional amendments within Serbia began reintegrating Kosovo.
July	
5	Yugoslavia revokes Kosovo's and Vojvodina's status as autonomous provinces.
October	
13	President Bush meets with Yugoslav Prime Minister Ante Markovic.
November	
9	The Berlin Wall falls.

	1990
April	Franjo Tudjman's CDU government comes to power in Croatia. Slovenia holds its first democratic elections since World War II (Demos Coalition wins 55%).
July	
2	Slovenian Assembly declares sovereignty and declares federal law null.
September	Kosovo and Vojvodina are formally incorporated into Serbia.
27	Slovenia's parliament declares Yugoslav federal law void within Slovenia.

December

22	Croatia declares supremacy of Croatian law over federal Yugoslav law.
23	Slovenes vote for independence should accommodation within Yugoslavia prove impossible (88.5% in favor).

1991

January

10	Yugoslav Constitutional Court declares regional nullifications illegal.
February	U.S.-Russian–led talks between Croatia and Croatian Serbs take place.

May

12	Krajina Serbs vote for independence from Croatia; 90% vote to remain in Yugoslavia.
15	Croat Stipe Mesic blocked from assuming the Federal presidency; Serb Borisav Jovic assumes the presidency instead.
19	Croatia votes for independence; 93% vote in favor; Serbs boycott.
20	United States quietly suspends aid to Yugoslavia.
24	U.S. aid to Yugoslavia restored.

June

19	Meeting of the OSCE declares support for Yugoslavia's territorial integrity.
21	U.S. Secretary of State Baker reasserts support for maintaining the territorial integrity of Yugoslavia while visiting Belgrade.
24	Slovenia formally declares independence.
25	Croatia formally declares independence.
26	Yugoslavia (JNA) begins a war to secure Slovenia's borders.
	Croatia formally recognizes Slovenia (though not recognized itself).

July

2	Kosovo Albanians declare independence from Serbia and federal equality
	(Albanian riots demanding the same began as early as 1981).
4	Slovenia defeats Yugoslavia in its war of independence (10 days).
	Committee of Senior Officials begins negotiating a cease-fire under the auspices of the Organization for Security and Co-operation in Europe.
5	EC bans arms exports to Yugoslavia and revokes nearly $1 billion in aid.
7	Slovenia, SFRY, and EC issue Brioni Declaration. The agreement includes a three-month moratorium on independence claims, Slovene disarmament, withdrawal of JNA, and a mission of 50 international observers.

August

18	Serbs in Croatia hold an unofficial referendum on autonomy for RSK.
19	Knin Serbs (within Krajina) declare the Republic of Serbian Krajina (RSK).
22	Coup attempt fails to unseat Gorbachev in USSR.
27	EC establishes the Conference on Yugoslavia led by Lord Carrington.

September
2   United States says it has no plans to recognize Slovenia and Croatia
                 should fighting continue.[151]
                 Yugoslav presidency votes 7–1 to approve EC brokered plan to end
                 fighting in Croatia (Montenegro votes No).
7   Peace Conference on Yugoslavia opens at The Hague.
8   Macedonia votes for independence.
17   Macedonia formally declares independence.
26   Kosovo Albanians secretly vote for independence.
October
8   Slovenia formally re-declares independence (Brioni moratorium
                 expires).
11   Kosovo formally declares independence.
18   EC Agreement on Yugoslavia is the first to involve United States
                 and USSR.
November   NATO announces a "new strategic concept" focused on local
                 instabilities in Europe.
13   Germany announces it will recognize Slovenia and Croatia by
                 Christmas.
29   EC Arbitration Commission (Badinter) concludes SFRY is "in the
                 process of dissolution."
December
9–10   Maastricht Summit yields draft Treaty on the European Union (signed
                 December 11).
15   Security Council votes to send an observer mission to Croatia.
16   EC ministers decide to extend recognition to those Yugoslav republics
                 desiring independence and meeting specified conditions.
19   Serb Krajina formally declares independence.
19–20   Four constituent republics and Kosovo request recognition under
                 EC Arbitration Commission guidelines (Serbia and Montenegro
                 do not).
23   Germany announces its formal recognition of Slovenia and Croatia
                 (effective January 15).
                 Slovenia proclaims a new constitution.
25   Gorbachev resigns, ending the Soviet Union.

                                          1992

January
8   Republika Srpska proclaims its independence from Bosnia.
11   EC Arbitration Commission delivers its recommendations for
                 recognition: Slovenia and Macedonia are found to meet the EC
                 standards; Croatia and Bosnia do not.
15   The remaining members of the EC formally recognize Slovenia and
                 Croatia.

[151] Bush (1991).

February

3	EC "adopts positive measures" toward states of the Former Yugoslavia.
28	Republika Srpska formally declares independence.

March

1	Bosnia votes for independence.
	Montenegro votes for union with Serbia.
16	President Bush publicly remarks "positive consideration" given to "[formal] recognition of Slovenia and Croatia."[152]

April

5	Bosnia formally declares independence (though it applied for EC recognition on December 20, 1991).
7	Bosnia formally recognized by the United States and EC.
	Slovenia and Croatia formally recognized by the United States.
	United States lifts economic sanctions from Slovenia, Croatia, Bosnia, and Macedonia.

May

30	United States declares national emergency regarding Yugoslavia (initial sanctions).

August

6	United States announces intent to establish full diplomatic relations with Slovenia, Croatia, and Bosnia by appointing ambassadors.
23	James Baker resigns as secretary of state, becomes chief of staff.
25	United States normalizes trade relations with Slovenia, Croatia, Bosnia, and Macedonia.
	International Conference on the Former Yugoslavia opens in London.

September

17	United States establishes full diplomatic relations with Slovenia, Croatia, and Bosnia.

December

20	Elections held in Serbia-Montenegro.

1993–2011

January 1993	Croatian forces take back the straits of Maslenica linking Zagreb to Split and the rest of the Dalmatian Coast.
January 20, 1993	U.S. President William Jefferson Clinton enters office; George H. W. Bush exits.
March 1, 1994	Federation of Bosnia and Herzegovina is created (Muslims and Croats).
May 1995	Croatian forces take back western Slavonia.
November 21, 1995	Dayton Peace Accords are signed (final version signed December 14).
April 1996	The KLA begins attacks in the Federal Republic of Yugoslavia (FRY).

---

[152] Bush (1992).

April 9, 1996	The EU formally recognizes the FRY consisting of Serbia and Montenegro.
March–Sept. 1998	Insurgent vs. government violence and large-scale civilian targeting and expulsions occur across Kosovo.
March 24, 1999	Talks between Serbia and Kosovars break down; NATO begins 78-day bombing campaign against the FRY.
June 10, 1999	NATO's bombing campaign ends; the UNSC authorizes the creation of United Nations Mission in Kosovo (UNMIK).
June 21, 1999	KLA agrees to disarm (completed effective September 20, 1999).
February 2002	Ibrahim Rugova is elected president by Kosovo's Parliament (and is reelected in 2004).
March 17–18, 2004	Albanians riot in Kosovo.
February 2006	UN-sponsored talks on Kosovo's final status begin.
April 1, 2006	Montenegro holds independence referendum on association with Serbia.
July 24, 2006	First direct talks between Serbian and Kosovar leaders since 1999 occur in Vienna, Austria.
December 2006	NATO extends Partnership for Peace membership to Serbia.
February 2, 2007	UN's Ahtisaari Plan recommends Kosovo's transition to independence.
January 9, 2008	Kosovo parliament elects Hashim Thaci, a former KLA member, prime minister.
February 17, 2008	Kosovo formally declares independence.
October 8, 2008	At Serbia's urging, the United Nations General Assembly asks the International Court of Justice for an advisory opinion regarding the legality of Kosovo's declaration of independence.
December 9, 2008	European Union Rule of Law Mission (EULEX) takes over Kosovo mission from UN (mandate through June 14, 2012).
July 22, 2010	ICJ rules Kosovo's independence demand is not illegal under international law; Kosovar politicians are not acting in their official capacity in interim administration when declaration is made.

6

International Responses to the Wars of Soviet Succession

When the Soviet Union fell, it defied expectations of a tumultuous, violent demise and arrived at a relatively peaceful, negotiated conclusion. But Soviet succession was not without conflict entirely. Six regional clashes in the post-Soviet space erupted into full-scale civil wars.[1] Historically, the USSR had maintained a precarious balance of power among its numerous and varied minorities. With the future of that balance imperiled as the Soviet Union disintegrated, uncertainty provoked violent contests for hegemony and survival among some of its various ethnic minorities. Most of the secessionist conflicts emerging during that time remain unresolved to date.

In the 1980s, Soviet President Mikhail Gorbachev instituted dramatic reforms, including processes of economic and political liberalization, with the hope of Westernizing and modernizing the state. Contrary to his intentions, the transitions also strained the staid Soviet system and it began to collapse. The rapid, unanticipated changes were especially difficult for the Soviet public, who had not yet grappled with the complex identity issues that accompanied the reforms. As the country disintegrated, it quickly became apparent that the Soviet people could not be divided into 15 easy pieces (the number of constituent republics in the USSR). Rising chauvinistic nationalism within Azerbaijan, Georgia, Moldova, and to a lesser extent Russia provoked independence demands from their newly disenfranchised or otherwise discontented minorities.

---

[1] "Full-scale civil war" in this context does not conform to the 1,000 battle-death threshold used in the quantitative segment of this project, but it indicates widespread violence between a governing regime and at least one other non-state corporate actor. According to this definition, five of the six post-Soviet wars were also secessionist: Abkhazia (Georgia), Chechnya (Russia), Nagorno-Karabakh (Azerbaijan), South Ossetia (Georgia), and Transnistria (Moldova). Only the war in Tajikistan was not.

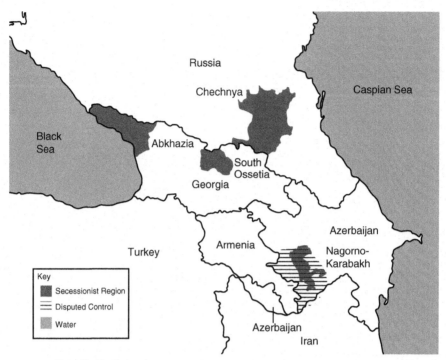

MAP 6.1 Post-Soviet Secessions

Anticipatory violence erupted in some even before the union republics' own independences had been secured.

The international community quickly recognized and consecrated the constitutive republics' (Soviet Socialist Republics or SSRs) independence and statehood. Again, as in Yugoslavia, extending *uti posseditis juris* with seeming disregard for the tenuous sovereignty demonstrated within many of the territories. With their newfound external legitimacy, all of the Soviet successor states, weak but buoyed by nationalism, determined that they would suppress their internal challengers. However, instead of restoring order, many of the policing actions ignited wars of independence that the young home states ultimately lost. For most, the people, territory, and resources surrendered in the fighting significantly hampered state consolidation.

In time, the new states rebounded economically and militarily and could effectively govern the secessionist regions if they were to regain control. Yet Russia alone has recouped its secessionist territory, and the Chechen terrorism problem that justified its intervention there has declined, but persists. Given the stalemates in the Caucasus, one cannot help but wonder whether the international community's rush to recognize the SSRs, but refusal to even consider their challengers' demands, precluded negotiated – or otherwise more durable – settlements between the parties.

Two decades after the Soviet collapse, five proto-states in the Caucasus maintain secessionist demands for statehood. All fought and secured their effective independence (or in the Chechen case, previously did); all have most of the external trappings of statehood, including flags, coats of arms, anthems, and national myths; and all have independent governments providing effective governmental control and authority and a military or national guard. In most cases, the status quo has endured for more than a decade.[2] Still, the secessionist regions lack some other aspects of functional capacity because of their extended isolation from the protections and benefits of international society. The regimes often do not fully provide for their own security; their governments do not support their own currencies; significant portions of their annual budgets come from foreign aid, humanitarian contributions, and remittances; and many of the regimes struggle to maintain law and order. Somewhat surprisingly, their home states exhibited many of the same shortcomings, especially early in the 1990s, but were nevertheless acknowledged as the only legitimate bearers of statehood. Further, external legitimacy ensured that those countries received extensive diplomatic and material support that ultimately helped them overcome those deficits.

The post-Soviet secessions pose a number of interesting questions for bottom-up, domestic-level conceptions of statehood. First, why was the Soviet Union's initial dissolution uncontroversial if some of the newly emergent states were incapable of effectively governing the territory and population they claimed? This is especially pertinent for Georgia because, in addition to its two secessionist wars, it also went through a civil war and military coup during the 1990s. Early in its own experience with statehood, Tbilisi did not legitimately govern even Georgia's *uncontested* territory. Second, why has the international community not conferred recognition when the secessionist regions have not been in the successor states' control for such an extended period? We might expect leaders to be conservative in their appraisals of secessionist regimes – that is, that there will be a lag between a nascent state's achievement of de facto independence and its *de jure* recognition – but after years of relatively stable independence, why do most of the Great Powers still not see states in Abkhazia, South Ossetia, and Nagorno-Karabakh? Why did they not recognize Chechnya, effectively condemning it to Russian reconquest? And why did Moscow break ranks with its Great Power peers by establishing diplomatic relations with Georgia's secessionists in 2008?

Additionally, the unresolved wars of Soviet succession remain an important problem for the region. Most significantly, three of the five secessions have relapsed into war – two of them international – and another is increasingly

---

[2] Chechnya's war with Russia is an exception. Hostilities reemerged in 1999 and conditions no longer favor the Chechen separatists.

volatile. Both sides of these secessionist conflicts have also used, and continue to use, brutal tactics in their attempts to control the contested regions. State policies include assassination, "disappearance," arbitrary imprisonment, embargo, and other human rights abuses.[3] The secessionists have used bombings, kidnappings, crime, forced migration, and violence against civilians in their efforts to repel their home states' claims and ethnically homogenize their territories. Hundreds of thousands people have fled their homes to escape the violence, creating serious refugee and internally displaced persons problems. Finally, the conflicts have retarded social relations in every case.

Regionally, the conflicts are also sources of deep-seated criminal instability. The secessionist areas, though not internally lawless, have an uncertain legal status domestically and internationally that makes them attractive locales for illegal trade in everything from weapons and drugs to medical supplies and even mundane goods like chicken.[4] In many, the shadow economy's trade approximates that of the legitimate market. Some of the republics, such as Nagorno-Karabakh and Abkhazia, which have been under embargo for years, have created black market trade as a matter of survival.[5] For others, illicit trade was born out of opportunism. Aside from the illegal goods passing through the de facto states, the regions also have porous borders permissive to human trafficking.[6] The secessionists' and home states' weak border controls allow the territories to be utilized as safe havens for international terrorists and rebels from other nearby Caucasian conflicts.[7] Without formal recognition, the greater international community loses potential allies, or at least those to hold culpable, in its efforts against international crime and political violence. And without meaningful control on the ground, the home states in the region cannot effectively follow through on their promises to implement law and order.[8] Ironically, because both the secessionists and home states claim control over the territories, neither is truly responsible.[9]

This chapter traces events in four of the five post-Soviet secessions: Chechnya in Russia, Abkhazia and South Ossetia in the Republic of Georgia, and

---

[3] Embargo is not necessarily a human rights violation, but it does constitute one when levied in the manner that Georgia did against the South Ossetians, purposefully attempting to starve and freeze the population during the winter. Details follow within the chapter.

[4] The Moldovan and Ukrainian governments discovered a frozen chicken smuggling ring in Transniestria. The chickens arrived legally to the secessionist region and were smuggled illegally into Ukraine at a profit of nearly $1,000 per ton. An estimated 40,000 tons were smuggled during one 6-month period. Myers (2006).

[5] Nagorno-Karabakh's geographic position and fortified borders makes it undesirable for illegal trafficking except for trade bound for Nagorno-Karabakh itself.

[6] United States, Department of State (2009).

[7] This is not true in Nagorno-Karabakh, where the borders are strictly monitored.

[8] The home states sometimes use the uncertainty to their advantage as in the 2002 Georgia-Russia crisis over Chechen insurgents in the Upper Pankisi Gorge.

[9] Charles King's work often makes this point.

Nagorno-Karabakh (NK) in Azerbaijan.[10] The cases first survey the historical background between the secessionists and their home states and describe the events leading up to the independence demands and wars in the four regions. Because the secession attempts occurred in different countries and at different times, the contextual details are succinct to allow greater discussion surrounding the Great Powers and recognition. Next, relative measures of domestic sovereignty for the secessionists and home states are taken. The cases then examine the bilateral and international politics of recognition, estimating the impacts of domestic sovereignty and political considerations for each of the Great Powers. The chapter closes with recent conflict developments including the Second Russo-Chechen War, the 2008 Russo-Georgian War, and Moscow's 2008 decision to break with the consensus over nonrecognition for South Ossetia and Abkhazia.

Unlike the Former Yugoslavia, where all of the secessionist movements eventually secured recognition from at least some Great Power states, none of the post-Soviet secessionists have received widespread recognition and membership in the international system.[11] Although this fact complicates the analysis somewhat because the dependent variable only varies for one Great Power (and only in two cases), it also permits prediction without the benefit of hindsight, a clear benefit.[12] If my argument is correct, most of the post-Soviet secessionist

---

[10] South Ossetia and Nagorno-Karabakh are sometimes considered irredentist, and not secessionist, because their goals are difficult to discern. South Ossetia fits the definition for this project: it formally declared independence from Georgia, it claimed both a territory and population, and it has its own flag. Though South Ossetians assert a desire to be associated with Russia, the regime declared independence. It did not declare itself a part of the Russian Federation and Russia has not claimed South Ossetia for Russia. Nagorno-Karabakh's "true position is ambiguous. While, on the one hand, they have insisted on being granted de jure recognition and on being made a subject of international law, on the other they speak of their 'unification' with Armenia" (Potier 2001, p. 86). Of course, the two are not mutually exclusive; independent states are free to relinquish their sovereignty in whole or part and/or to join into federative arrangements with other states. Independence may be a means rather than an end. This project codes the NK movement as secessionist because the Armenian government does not claim Nagorno-Karabakh. Similar to Northern Ireland and Ireland, a territory cannot join a state without its approval/claim. It remains unclear whether Armenia would absorb NK. The project's operational criteria are met: Nagorno-Karabakh declared independence on January 6, 1992, it claims the former autonomous oblast of Nagorno-Karabakh and the largely Armenian population therein, and it has its own flag.

[11] Among the Great Powers, only Russia has recognized South Ossetia and Abkhazia.

[12] A lack of variation on the dependent variable is problematic when attempting to draw causal inferences because it creates selection bias (King et al. 1994, pp.129–130). In each of these cases, the secessionists currently met the minimal criteria for statehood, so there is no variation on the alternative explanatory factor. However, the potential for variation on the dependent variable still exists. All of the post-Soviet cases under study should have been very likely to receive recognition, if the domestic model is descriptively accurate, but none has. Van Evera (1997) suggests that this constellation of variation (where variation on the dependent variable theoretically should have occurred, but did not) can isolate unidentified antecedent conditions (p. 23). Great Power interests are the as yet unidentified explanatory variable, but we may also identify other candidate causes in the post-Soviet cases (ibid.).

regions could still be states. Each successfully defeated its home state in a war of independence and has experienced years of self-government. The external politics surrounding the demands, however, dictate that some are more likely than others to be recognized. These are difficult cases for the political recognition theory because the effective control standards outlined by Montevideo were accomplished in each proto-state; we are most likely to find that those factors are driving recognition.[13] Further, unlike Yugoslavia, there is no ongoing crisis in the Caucasus to compel Great Power attention, and there are no regional, ulterior motives for Great Power coordination as there were for the European governments surrounding Maastricht. As a result, the post-Soviet secessions will more definitively demonstrate whether coordination is routinely an important factor in Great Power recognition or merely an idiosyncratic factor particular to Yugoslavia.

The cases in the Caucasus demonstrate that self-interested considerations do not merely color leaders' interpretations of secessionist regimes' sovereignty in ambiguous cases, as they did for Germany regarding Croatia. They may also cause leaders to withhold recognition from regimes that otherwise meet the legal standards. Comparative politics scholars are incredulous that external legitimacy can reverse domestic authority, but the Chechen case makes the power of nonrecognition readily apparent.[14] It isn't recognition per se, but its social and material consequences that make the difference for emerging states. Governments without external legitimacy are significantly more vulnerable to annexation or reincorporation and, if and when it does occur, significantly less likely to draw protests from outsiders. In many respects, recognition and non-recognition create self-fulfilling prophecies for secessionist movements on the precipice of statehood.

HISTORICAL BACKGROUND

The Soviet Union rejected ethno-religious differentiation on an ideological basis, yet many of its policies intensified and politicized ethno-religious affiliation in the end. Soviet leaders believed communist ideology would gradually supplant popular ethnic and religious affiliations within the state. But their plans were unevenly realized after seven decades of Soviet rule because their regime used ethnic hegemony and dependency as organizing principles for its constituent parts, effectively maintaining, not eroding, the importance of nationality. Internal boundaries were purposefully created to divide concentrated ethnic minorities, thereby easing the complications associated with their governance for the state. And when presented with an unfavorable ethnic demographic within an administrative unit, officials often systematically expelled local minorities and moved in ethnic Russians.

[13] Eckstein (1975).
[14] Roeder (2007, pp. 34–35).

Once Soviet rule was established, demographic reengineering remained an important political tool.[15] To pacify agitated peoples, many of them forcibly annexed, the Soviet government granted various forms of local autonomy. Some became titular minorities with their own self-titled union republics, including Azerbaijan, Georgia, and Armenia in the Caucasus. Others received more limited autonomy as autonomous oblasts (AOs) or autonomous Soviet Socialist Republics (ASSRs) within the titular union republics – for example, Nagorno-Karabakh, South Ossetia, Chechnya, and Abkhazia.[16] Even minority populations not granted titular status experienced some freedoms, had the opportunity to attend schools in their native languages, and had some special protections at the national level.[17] Consequently, where ethnic groups were not accommodated or faced discrimination by local authorities, centralized Soviet rule was able to unite minority populations across administrative boundaries. Ultimately, the USSR's internal borders were formal, but largely ineffectual divisions insofar as day-to-day life was concerned, and the complex network of autonomy arrangements created a somewhat arbitrary, though rather stable, union for many years.

Ethnic nationalism only reemerged as a significant force in Soviet politics as authoritarianism relaxed. Beginning in the late 1980s, President Gorbachev's liberalizing political and economic reforms, *glasnost* and *perestroika*, provoked two types of secessionist challenges. The first and more common were secessionist demands made by the union republics, capitalizing on Moscow's weakness to declare or reclaim independence as the USSR disintegrated.[18] The remaining secessions emerged in response to the SSRs' demands because non-titular minorities feared subjugation in the event that the union republics successfully realized independence.

Each union republic was multiethnic, but with the new freedoms of glasnost, many SSR leaders adopted exclusionary nationalism to rally the majority's support for independence. This new rhetoric understandably threatened minority communities, uncertain about what life within an independent and oppressive Georgia or Azerbaijan might hold. For some groups, repression at the hands of the republic's titular nationality became more threatening than the prospect of

---

[15] Accommodation was by no means the only tool utilized to gain demographic advantage; the Stalinist purges of minorities during the 1930s were also a Soviet population management technique.

[16] Nagorno-Karabakh and South Ossetia were autonomous oblasts whereas Abkhazia and Chechnya were ASSRs. The terms "union republic" and "Soviet Socialist Republic (SSR)" will be used interchangeably throughout the chapter. Autonomous oblast may appear as AO and Autonomous Soviet Socialist Republic may appear as ASSR. SSR and ASSR should not be confused; ASSRs had lower status than the union republics.

[17] It should be noted, however, that self-rule was also universally subject to a local Russian authority.

[18] Some of the republics, such as the Baltics, had been forcefully annexed, whereas others had no history of independence.

remaining within the Soviet Union. For others, who had not come to identify as closely with Soviet ideology, declaring their own independent state, breaking from both the USSR and their newly independent home state simultaneously, presented the more appealing choice.[19] When the Soviet Union disbanded at the end of 1991, many non-titular minorities' worst fears were realized; all of the union republics became independent countries and none of the autonomous territories (AOs or ASSRs) did.

The ultimate conclusion of the Soviet Empire belied the international community's expectations. The Great Powers had been preoccupied with the course of the Soviet demise, but when it did disband, it caused little violence between Russia and the union republics.[20] U.S. and European leaders in particular were surprised at the relative ease with which such a large and diverse country devolved into independent units. The European Union's guidelines for recognition, which had been so controversial in Yugoslavia, were largely unnecessary for the Soviet Union because, in the end, the union republics' departures were mutual and relatively amicable. The Great Powers quickly recognized the new states' formal independence.[21]

The dearth of international controversy over recognition in the Soviet Union obscures the fact that many of the post-Soviet states were, like Kosovo or Bosnia, quite unable to independently perform many functions of governance on securing recognition. The non-titular minorities knew that their new home states were weak, however, and seized the opportunity to counter-declare independence. Beneath the façades of national unity in the post-Soviet states lay complex issues of effective governance that the new regimes had not yet confronted. Most significantly, the states did not have established militaries or doctrines of their own; they could neither secure their own borders nor afford the expenses associated with large-scale uprisings and civil war.

Somewhat regardless of their weakness, the nationalistic regimes in the new states were unwilling to part with their newfound authority and violently countered the secessionists. The first four wars of Soviet succession began in Azerbaijan, Georgia, and Moldova, and a fifth began later in Russia. Transniestria (PMR), in the former Republic of Moldova, declared its Slavic

[19] So where the Ossetians' shared Christianity permitted extensive Russification, the Abkhaz and Chechens' Islamic heritage separated them from their home states and encouraged maintenance of their distinctive cultures. These secessions were not unlike that of the RSK in Croatia where the demand for independence emanated from a fear of Croatia's potential independence from Yugoslavia.
[20] Note, for example, the Soviet Union's influence on Great Power intervention and recognition in the Yugoslav conflicts as evidence of their preoccupation. Though there was "little violence," there was still violence. Soviet forces did militarily intervene in Lithuania (in March 1990).
[21] On December 17, 1991, European leaders signed the Energy Charter Treaty with former union republics of the Soviet Union, effectively recognizing their independence. It is also noteworthy that the United States recognized the Ukraine before it was clear that Moscow would approve of its independence.

majority province independent of Romanian Moldova.[22] In Georgia, the Abkhaz of Abkhazia and the Ossets of South Ossetia sought independence. In Azerbaijan, the Nagorno-Karabakh Armenians attempted to secede. Finally, Chechnya, as it had many times before, demanded a state of its own – independent of Russia – for the people of the North Caucasus.

The wars of independence, though effectively stalemated in favor of the secessionists (except for Chechnya), all continue today. None of the fundamental political conflicts have been resolved. Like the wars in the Former Yugoslavia, and secessionist wars in general, the post-Soviet conflicts occurred almost exclusively within the secessionist states' claimed territory, leaving the rump of the home state's territory relatively unscathed. This fact devastated infrastructure within the separatist regions, halted economic activities, and forced their populations to relocate. Circumstances within the secessionist areas were not good.

On the other hand, the secessionists, and not their home states, emerged victorious from each war. In most cases, sovereign authority seems to lie with the de facto governments rather than the regimes in Baku, Tbilisi, or Moscow.[23] The kidnapping, crime, and illegal traffic in drugs and weapons so common to the secessionist regions is similarly endemic to their home states. Indeed, there is often a symbiotic relationship between them.[24] Further, political corruption is rampant in the home states as well. Notably, not one of Azerbaijan's elections since independence has been judged either free or fair by international observers.[25] And in recent years, tens of thousands of protestors have taken to the streets to pressure Georgian President Mikhail Saakashvili to resign on corruption charges. Lastly, the secessionist governments sometimes afford a higher standard of living – at least in some respects – than do their home states.[26] Still, external recognition eludes the Caucasian proto-states.

CHECHNYA'S HISTORY AND BACKGROUND

The Chechen people were never easy for Russia to govern. Chechen and Chechen-Ingush resistance to Russian authority is an enduring feature of their

---

[22] PMR is the acronym for the self-declared republic's formal name, Pridnestrovskaia Moldavskia Respublica. It is also known as the Trans Dniester Republic. Though Transniestria's search for recognition is certainly of interest, it will not be formally included in this analysis. See the section on Case Selection in Chapter 3 for an explanation of its omission.

[23] Though this was true for Chechnya following the 1994–1996 war, the situation there changed dramatically. A discussion of the recent hostilities follows later in the chapter.

[24] For example, in Abkhazia's ethnic Georgian majority, Gali district.

[25] Most recently, the November 7, 2010, elections were judged inconsistent with democratic commitments by the OSCE (2011).

[26] King (2001) explains that "for most people life in an unrecognized [Eurasian] state is not significantly different from life in a recognized one." He continues, "In some cases, it is better. Citizens of Sukhumi, the capital of Abkhazia, have better access to electricity than those of most provincial Georgian cities. Citizens of South Ossetia have easier access to consumer goods. . .than many other Georgians."

shared history.[27] Systematically exterminated and expelled by successive governments, the Chechen people struggled to survive and to repel occupying forces from their homelands. All told, they have sought independence from three separate Russian governments.[28] Never acquiescing fully to foreign rule, historically Chechen resistance was characterized by opportunism and arose during times of Russian instability and conflict.[29] The most recent case of secessionism fit a similar pattern except that, in the middle 1990s, the Chechens experienced a victory of sorts.

Chechnya is located in southwestern Russia in the North Caucasus. The republic borders Ingushetia and Dagestan in Russia and is situated near the Pankisi Gorge in neighboring Georgia. Chechens pride themselves on their ability to persevere against all odds and consider themselves part of a larger, Caucasian mountainous people, united with the Ingush, some Georgians, and the Chechen diaspora. Within their republic, Chechens are a numerical majority, constituting more than two-thirds of the population in 1989 and an overwhelming 93.47 percent according to the 2002 census (Table 6.1).[30] The Chechens are a predominantly Muslim, mostly Sunni, people. Another facet of Chechen social identity, markedly distinct from the other national groups under analysis here, is its clan-based (*tiep*) structure. This traditional structure is sometimes faulted for Chechens' characterization as "backward" or "tribal" among Russians and Westerners. It also, however, permitted a massive and unanticipated popular resistance to Russian military actions during the 1994–1996 war.[31] Within the Soviet Union, Chechnya was joined together with Ingushetia to form the Chechen-Ingush Autonomous Republic, a subunit of the Russian SSR, in 1937. The Russians dealt harshly with the Chechens. As a non-titular minority, with no titular republic or ethnic homeland elsewhere, the Chechens experienced extensive "Russification," which they resisted and resented.

Chechens responded to their circumstances by opportunistically attempting to escape Soviet control. During World War II, Chechens appealed to German invaders to grant them their own independent state. Stalin responded to Chechens' treasonous behavior by dissolving the republic and deporting nearly 500,000 people; a quarter, or approximately 125,000, died in transit. Chechens

---

[27] The Russian Empire first took control of Chechnya in the early 1800s with the retreat of the Ottomans.

[28] Imperial Russia, the Bolsheviks, and most recently the Russian Federation.

[29] For example, rebellions occurred during the 1905 and 1917 revolutions and again during the Russian Civil War.

[30] The earlier Chechen figure is approximate as Chechnya was united with Ingushetia within the USSR. The 2002 figure comes from Twigg (2005, p. 134). The data come from the 2002 Russian census, which, Twigg notes, has been widely criticized for its methods and outright fabrication of data, particularly in Chechnya.

[31] Though Chechnya had no organized, modern military, its clan structure effectively organized local resistance to Russian military tactics throughout the first war. However, the importance of Chechnya's clan structure should not be overestimated. Many Chechens received training from the Russian military and were skilled fighters.

TABLE 6.1 *Soviet Successor Ethnic Demographics (1989)[a]*

	Russian	Georg.	Chechen	Abkhaz	Azeri	Osset	Armen.	Other/ Unknown
Russia Pop. 140 mil[b]	80%	–	–	–	–	–	–	Tatar 4% Ukrainian 2% Other 12%
Chechnya Pop. 865,000	25%	–	66%	–	–	–	–	
Georgia[c] Pop. 5,500,000 Unknown	6%	70%	–	2%	6%	3%	8%	5%
Abkhazia Pop. 100,000		46%					18%	
South Ossetia Pop. 99,000	2%	29%				66%		
Azerbaijan Pop. 6,800,000	4%				83%		2%	Dagestani 2% Other 4%
Nagorno-Karabakh Pop. 189,000					22%		77%	

[a] Compiled from Zickel (1991); data on South Ossetia and Nagorno-Karabakh come from Kolstø and Blakkisrud (2008). Percentages are rounded to the nearest whole point.
[b] January 2006 estimate from Central Intelligence Agency, "Russia." World Factbook Online, available at http://www.cia.gov/cia/publications/factbook/geos/rs.html.
[c] King (2001, pp. 530–531).

were not allowed to return to Chechnya until 1956, when Khrushchev announced the rehabilitation of the deported minorities. When permitted, the Chechens returned en masse, though numerically depleted, to Chechnya, bringing with them a new determination not to be forced from their ancestral lands.

Like many non-titular minorities within the Soviet system, the Chechens were again subject to homogenization efforts on their return. Chechnya was also one of the most underdeveloped and socioeconomically depressed regions within Russia. Strong central control imposed by Moscow suppressed Chechens' drive for political reform and autonomy during the 1960s and early 1970s. But by the late 1970s and 1980s, the Chechens and Ingush renewed their nationalist demands on Soviet authorities.

Liberalization in the 1980s presented another chance for Chechnya to reach for the illusive goal of self-government. Limited public protests quickly transformed and expanded to include demands for linguistic, cultural, and religious rights. Many local Russian officials were forced to resign because of popular criticism in the wake of the unrest. In addition, the Ingush, who had been administratively joined to the Chechens for decades, called for their own ASSR, separate from Chechnya.[32] By 1991, Chechens were calling on Moscow to raise their status to a union republic, a peer to, rather than a subject of, Russia.

PRECIPITATING EVENTS: CHECHNYA

Rampant instability seized the Soviet Union and the Russian republic – its seat of government – in the late 1980s and early 1990s. Chechen demands and their subsequent revolt were neither particularly pressing nor threatening to Russian leaders compared to the prospect of revolution, economic ruin, and disintegration. Moscow had successfully confronted and suppressed its restive Chechen populace before. Russian authorities were not willing to elevate Chechnya's status to that of an SSR. Russia reaped important benefits from its authority over Chechnya, most significantly, energy resources. Though Chechnya itself was no longer an important source of oil, it traversed a strategically important transportation route and processed a large portion of Russia's oil.

Chechnya's location was strategically important for Russia in other ways as well. Specifically, officials saw the region as a potential "first domino" that might cause a cascade of instability throughout the already restive Caucasus, biting into the territory of Russia proper. Still, the specter of internal instability only arose later, in the mid-1990s, once the Soviet Union and Russia's more pressing problems had passed. Moscow's initial response to Chechnya's autonomy demand was virtually no response at all. Somewhat ironically, Russian restraint and isolation might have eventually destroyed Chechnya's secessionist ambitions if they had continued. But Moscow's later militancy rallied Chechen support for independence to previously unseen heights.

When the prospect of Soviet dissolution emerged, Chechnya's future status was unclear. Russia argued that Chechnya should automatically become part of its new state, the Russian Federation (RF). Chechens argued to the contrary, that in order for Chechnya to become a part of the RF, Russians needed Chechens' explicit agreement. Chechnya had, after all, declared itself a union republic and was, therefore, Russia's equal. The attempt to negotiate new bilateral relations with Moscow was in vein. Because Russia insisted their relationship had not changed, leaders rebuffed Chechnya's requests to reconsider their future association.[33] Chechens were left with two options, either acquiesce to what they saw as Moscow's illegitimate rule or seek independence.

---

[32] Later, on the Chechen declaration of independence and the formation of the Chechen Republic of Ichkeria, Ingushetia decided to remain within the Soviet Union (then Russia).

[33] Chechen officials, therefore, refused to sign the 1992 Federal Treaty and the 1993 Constitution of the Russian Federation.

Dzhokhar Dudayev, a staunch Chechen nationalist, became president of the republic on October 27, 1991. Just a few days later, Chechnya's parliament declared independence.[34] The new republic was named the Chechen Republic of Ichkeria. While Russian leaders weighed their response to Chechnya's demand, Dudayev began consolidating power: "[He] took control of the police and their weapons and [bought, stole, or extorted] weapons from Soviet troops."[35] On November 8, Yeltsin declared a state of emergency. Dudayev countered by also declaring a state of emergency and imposed martial law in Chechnya. Only Yeltsin's decision was quickly overturned. Two days after declaring the state of emergency, Russia's Supreme Soviet denounced his decision. This forced Yeltsin to revoke the declaration and withdraw Russian troops from the area, effectively ceding control to the Chechens.

In retrospect, what Dudayev and his parliament meant by Chechen independence was open to interpretation. According to at least one expert, the Chechens viewed their territory and sovereignty as indivisible and were not open to negotiation.[36] Others contend that Dudayev was open to an arrangement short of complete independence from Moscow. Some evidence does suggest a more moderate Chechen demand. Tellingly perhaps, after declaring independence, Chechnya did not break economic or political ties with Russia and did not introduce its own currency.[37] In fact, Chechnya's eventual substantial monetary independence was the result of a proposal *offered to it* by the Russian Central Bank; Chechnya did not demand it.[38] Regardless of Chechens' true intentions, independence or autonomy, Moscow interpreted the declaration as attempted secession.

For two years following Chechnya's declaration, Russia muddled through in its relations with the breakaway republic. During that time, fairly disparate policies were pursued because Russia's internal instability rendered it incapable of functioning as a unitary actor.[39] Various Russian officials sought to exploit Chechnya's faltering political and economic situation to assist Dudayev's pro-Russian rivals. For instance, Moscow imposed an economic and travel blockade

---

[34] Dudayev came to power when his party, the National Congress of Chechen People, forced out the Communist, Chechen-Ingush Supreme Soviet on September 6, 1991. Dudayev was also later reported as having won 85 percent of an October 1991 vote within Chechnya (though irregularities were reported). Parliament formally declared Chechen independence on November 1, 1991.

[35] Lieven (1998, p. 61).

[36] Toft (2003, p. 86).

[37] Lapidus (1998, p. 26).

[38] Emphasis added. Berger (1997).

[39] In August 1991, President Gorbachev survived a three-day coup attempt by members of his government attempting to thwart the signing of the Union Treaty (which transformed the Union into the CIS). By the end of 1991, the Union had disintegrated and Gorbachev had resigned. Though little violence immediately followed, rampant economic and social instability plagued the Russian Federation as a result of Yeltsin's new economic policies through 1992. In 1993, Yeltsin's opponents attempted to impeach him; he was ousted as president; and he subsequently regained control, in part, by bombing his own parliament.

on Chechnya, hoping that poor economic performance would erode public support for independence. The blockade was largely ineffectual though, because Russia could not organize to enforce the ban.[40] The most influential sanction was Russia's suspension of Chechens' pensions, which proved to be a painful economic punishment.[41] Meanwhile, other officials negotiated openly with the Dudayev regime. And besides official contact, criminal ties forged between Moscow and Chechnya also became particularly strong during the uncertain transitional period. Trafficking oil, weapons, and drugs out of the former Soviet Union became a stable and profitable source of income on both sides of the border. Oftentimes, weapons trafficking was facilitated or even encouraged by Russian officials.[42] Ingush-Osset clashes in the fall of 1992 drew Russian troops to Chechnya's border, but this was Russia's only military mobilization toward the rebellious province from 1991 until 1994.[43]

Russian neglect of Chechnya during the early years eroded popular support for Dudayev.[44] Indeed, Dudayev's own ill-fated policies and controversial personal style might have eventually proved to be his undoing. Years of de facto independence and relative isolation left Chechens dissatisfied with their economic situation and frustrated by Dudayev's overly confrontational style. Moscow failed to capitalize on Dudayev's weakness though, because Yeltsin's own struggle for authority consumed the elite's attention. When Russian officials finally decided to change their hands-off policies and militarily suppress independence, Chechens "rallied around the flag" to support Dudayev.[45]

After a number of bus hijackings in Russia in the summer of 1993, tensions between Moscow and Chechnya increased. Yeltsin had consolidated his power and began to step up pressure on Dudayev's regime. Recalcitrant, Dudayev refused to sign the Union Treaty (on the reformation of the Soviet Union) and would no longer entertain anything short of complete Chechen independence, if he ever was willing to do so.[46] When Russian authorities traced various hijackers

---

[40] As Lieven (1998, p. 75) recounts, between 1991 and 1994, Chechnya exported 20 million tons of Russian oil (most likely much more because of corruption) that was estimated at between $300 million and $1 billion USD.

[41] Russia's refusal to pay Chechen pensions, though again unevenly enforced (about half were withheld), was a significant source of income for the republic (ibid.).

[42] Lapidus (1998, p. 17 at n.21).

[43] Ibid., p. 74.

[44] Lieven (1998, p. 75) suggests Dudayev was losing Chechen support by April 1993.

[45] Experts attribute Russia's policy change to a number of factors. First, in 1994 Russian authorities concluded an autonomy agreement with Tatarstan, leaving Chechnya as the only remaining internal Russian conflict. Second, Yeltsin and other Russian officials had turned away from the liberal perspective toward a more hard-line stance. Finally, Russia feared Western encroachment into the Russian near-abroad and the loss of Chechnya's substantial oil resources. Lapidus (1998, p. 17). The term "rally 'round the flag" was coined by John E. Mueller (1970).

[46] As to Dudayev's state of mind, when Russia stepped up pressure on Chechnya, Dudayev realized any agreement short of independence would mean continued attacks on his power from Russia and the pro-Russian, Chechen opposition. In an independent Chechnya, the threat to Dudayev's

to Chechnya, Dudayev would not extradite them nor would he allow Russian authorities to extricate them. Moscow attempted to seize a Chechen airport in response, but the operation was botched and left one Russian soldier dead. And again, on November 26, 1994, pro-Russian Chechens (with Russian support) advanced on Grozny. They anticipated that the pro-Dudayev forces would fold quickly. Those calculations proved incorrect. Dudayev's forces won a decisive victory, seized a number of Russian tanks and captured a number of Russian soldiers (whom the Russian government had previously denied were involved).[47]

Rather than staying Russia's hand, the growing list of embarrassments had the opposite effect. Russian leaders, incensed by the loss in Chechnya, turned to increasingly coercive measures. In order to justify intervention, Yeltsin cast it as an arbitration effort to quell hostilities between Dudayev and the pro-Russian opposition. But this was obviously not his true intention. Neither Yeltsin nor military action to retake Chechnya was popular among the public.[48] Yet military actions had already begun at Yeltsin's command. On December 2, Russia began bombing locations within Chechnya and on December 11, the first Russian ground troops crossed into Chechen territory. The Russo-Chechen war had begun.

ABKHAZIA AND SOUTH OSSETIA, HISTORY AND BACKGROUND

Georgia was one of the wealthiest, most well educated, and successful union republics within the USSR. Its economy was primarily agricultural, but also benefited significantly from Black Sea tourism and the transportation of oil resources. Georgia's relative affluence, though, did not protect it from the lure of exclusionary nationalism. The Soviet Union's liberalizing reforms simultaneously encouraged Georgia to buck against Soviet control externally and to subjugate its own minorities to secure internal control. Georgians paradoxically embraced multiparty democracy, free markets, and a pro-Western orientation alongside exclusionary "Georgianization" policies for the Abkhaz, Osset, and Ajar minorities within their borders. Late in the 1980s, Georgia's potential independence threatened its minorities to such an extent that secession and independence were preferable to increasingly repressive Georgian rule.

Georgia had experienced independence before, beginning in 1918, but its sovereignty was short lived.[49] After succumbing to the Red Army in 1921, the former Transcaucasian Federation, including Georgia, Azerbaijan, and

---

control would certainly be less. Lieven suggests Dudayev's decision was subject to his own political longevity rather than any greater Chechen cause (Lieven 1998, p. 84).

[47] Ibid., p. 19; Toft (2003, p. 79).

[48] For greater depth on the Russian public's reaction to Chechnya, see: Evangelista (2002); Lieven (1998, p. 125); Lyall (2006).

[49] Bolshevik forces invaded Georgia only months after Russia (May 2, 1920) and the Allies (January 27, 1921) had recognized its independence. By 1924, Soviet troops had total control over Georgia's territory.

Armenia, joined the Soviet Union on December 30, 1922, and later became the Transcaucasian SFSR. South Ossetia was made an autonomous oblast within Georgia. Georgia had trouble asserting control over Abkhazia, which had de facto SSR status equivalent to Georgia's until 1931. Soviet forces were stronger. They revoked Abkhazia's status in 1931 and made it an ASSR within Georgia. In 1936, each of the three former Transcaucasian republics was granted equivalent status as SSRs.

Though ethnic Georgians were the largest population within their republic, at around 69 percent, its minorities were of a significant size (Table 6.1).[50] The republic's Georgian population was also quite concentrated, leaving pockets of minorities in non-Georgian regions. Approximately 95 percent of ethnic Georgians lived within their titular republic alongside ethnic minorities including the Abkhaz, Ajars, Jews, Kurds, Ossets, and Russians. Three minorities had their own autonomous regions: the Ajars and Abkhaz had ASSRs and the South Ossetians had an AO.

South Ossetia is a small territory in the southern Caucasus approximately the size of Rhode Island. It shares a border with North Ossetia, a Russian territory whose majority inhabitants are the southerners' ethnic kin. Postwar, Ossets comprised a majority of the population within the South Ossetian AO, but the population was evenly split between Georgians and Ossets for most of its time under Soviet authority. Ossets speak a Persian derivative and are mostly Orthodox, whereas Georgians speak Georgian and Russian and are principally Georgian Orthodox.

The Abkhaz autonomous republic is approximately the size of Delaware, situated on the southwest edge of Georgia bordering the Black Sea. The Abkhaz, a tiny minority within Georgia, numbered approximately 100,000 (of Georgia's population of 5.5 million) in 1989.[51] Even within the Abkhazia ASSR, the Abkhaz were a minority, constituting only around 18 percent of the population. The Abkhaz consider themselves ethnically distinct from Georgians.[52] According to their national history, the Abkhaz are members of the greater Caucasian peoples. Islam is the most commonly practiced religion among Abkhaz.

Within the Soviet Union, both Abkhazia and South Ossetia performed well economically. Abkhazia was an attractive tourist destination because of its long Black Sea coast. It was also an important producer of hazelnuts and fruit. South Ossetia had an active mining industry and was a significant producer of wood, beer, and fruits. The Abkhaz and Osset peoples, however, were not allowed to thrive under Soviet Georgian rule. Georgians resented the Abkhaz and Ossets,

---

[50] Russian Census 1989.

[51] Ibid.

[52] A great deal of controversy surrounds this assertion. Georgians argue Abkhazians belong to the Iberian-Caucasian family of which Georgians are a primary lineage. See Arbatov et al. (1997, p. 348) for further discussion on this point.

believing they were unduly advantaged under the Soviet system. When opportunities arose for the Georgians to assert greater control over the minorities, they seized them.

Like many repressed ethnic groups before them, the ethnic Georgian majority responded to its own loss of sovereignty and status by imposing on its minority populations. The Abkhaz and Ossets had few advantages within Soviet Georgia; Georgians were the republic's predominant political and economic elite. Georgia's policies in Abkhazia included forced emigration, closure of Abkhaz schools, and an Abkhaz language ban. Fewer Georgians immigrated into South Ossetia because it had little industry to speak of. Or, more accurately, what industry it did have was propped up by the Soviet Union and now sat decaying. Further, South Ossetians' close relationship with Russians across the border buffered them somewhat from repressive policies levied elsewhere in the USSR. But Georgianization policies resurfaced in South Ossetia during the 1980s, including Georgian-only language policies and the exclusion of non-Georgian-speaking students from its universities.

PRECIPITATING EVENTS: SOUTH OSSETIA AND ABKHAZIA

During perestroika, rapid change and mounting calls for Georgian independence intensified feelings of threat among Georgia's minority populations. Nationalist political campaigns championing "Georgia for Georgians" indicated Georgian independence would be less accommodating to its minority communities. Like the Krajina Serbs in Croatia, the Abkhaz and Ossets feared becoming isolated within an independent, and increasingly chauvinistic, Georgian state.[53] This was especially important for the Georgian Ossets, a majority of whom lived outside the South Ossetian AO. For their part, Georgian leaders viewed the minorities' political opposition as traitorous; their requests for assured representation and higher political status within Georgia were denied.

To remedy their situation, the Abkhaz requested their leave of Georgia. They hoped to secede and join Russia, remaining within the Soviet Union.[54] The Georgian government again refused the Abkhaz' request. So Abkhaz leaders revised their demands. Rather than join the Russian republic, they would seek their own SSR – a status equivalent to Georgia's within the Soviet Union.[55] By 1989, the situation in Georgia had deteriorated so significantly that the local government could not keep peace among its ethnic groups. The Soviet Army intervened on the Georgian government's behalf with disastrous consequences.

[53] In addition to the Abkhaz and Ossetians, Azeri and Armenian populations in the south also protested the government's treatment of their people and suggested they might also secede.

[54] Abkhazia's request to join Russia was first made in an open letter to the 29th Conference of the Soviet Communist Party. It requested subordination to Russia again on July 8, 1989 (Toft 2003, p. 95).

[55] Abkhazia had been a Soviet Socialist Republic previously during a 10-year period between 1921 and 1931.

Hundreds were injured when the army used nerve gas to quell the protests. The intervention provoked a backlash from both sides and demands for independence multiplied (for Georgia from the Soviet Union and for Abkhazia and South Ossetia from Georgia).

From that point on, Georgia descended into a centrifugal spiral of battling nationalisms. In 1990, South Ossetia's regional administration declared itself a republic (SSR) of the Soviet Union, equal to Georgia. In response, the Georgian Supreme Soviet revoked South Ossetia's autonomous (AO) status and declared a state of emergency.[56] In Abkhazia, the Abkhaz Supreme Soviet declared itself an SSR, independent of Georgia, on August 25. Again, Georgia revoked Abkhazia's ASSR status and declared it a subject of Georgia. Georgia's first multiparty elections, on October 28, 1990, barred Abkhaz and Osset parties from participating because their platforms intended to "violate the territorial integrity of Georgia." Zviad Gamsakhurdia's Society of Saint Ilia the Righteous (SSIR) party joined an opposition government that constituted Georgia's first non-Communist government. The new regime advocated Georgian independence. In December 1990, Georgia announced it would boycott the upcoming Soviet referendum on the Union Treaty. It did not consider itself a part of the USSR.

Regardless, the Soviet referendum on whether the Soviet Union would remain intact took place in March 1991. In addition to Georgia, a number of SSRs did not participate.[57] Instead, Georgia held a referendum on independence. Ninety-one percent of eligible voters participated in the election, and an overwhelming 98.93 percent of those voted in favor of independence. The Republic of Georgia formally declared independence on April 9, 1991. Georgia was the fourth union republic to claim statehood and the first non-Baltic state to do so; its parliament chose Gamsakhurdia as its president.

President Gamsakhurdia was aggressive toward Georgia's already restive minorities. He promised property rights would flow only to those who had voted for Georgia's independence and that only native Georgians would be granted citizenship.[58] The president seemed unaware of the apparent hypocrisy in his government's declaration of independence and demand for recognition while he "routinely [dismissed] Ossetian complaints as 'lies,'" refusing to recognize their legitimate fear of Georgian independence.[59] Gamsakhurdia regarded the South Ossetian revolt as a foreign Russian plot, a fifth column

[56] Georgia declared a state of emergency for South Ossetia in December 1990. It was not until late November 1991 that Georgia's parliament rescinded its declaration, recognizing it was "useless" ("Georgia lifts state of emergency in South Ossetia" 1991).

[57] Abkhazia did participate, however. More than 60 percent of those eligible voted and 97.65 percent supported maintaining the Soviet Union (Arbatov et al. 1997, pp. 376–377).

[58] Recall that Osset and Abkhaz parties could not contest Georgia's elections. Citizenship would be restricted to those who could prove Georgian residency prior to Russian annexation of the territory in 1801 (Brooke 1991, Section A, p. 3).

[59] Ibid.

intended only to destabilize Georgia. The Abkhaz were similarly viewed as complicit with Georgia's enemies.

Georgia's transition to independence was fraught with instability and violence. South Ossetia declared independence from Georgia on December 21, 1991. The day after, President Gamsakhurdia was deposed in a coup d'état, and the state descended into civil war. Military leaders installed Eduard Shevardnadze as the new head of state. Three days after that, the Soviet Union formally dissolved and Georgia was granted independence. A number of states already recognized Georgian sovereignty. By January, South Ossetia and Georgia were at war.

Abkhazia's parliament declared independence on July 23, 1992. It argued that Georgia and Abkhazia should remain associated, but by a treaty negotiated between equals. On August 14, a Georgian military unit dispatched to retrieve hostages taken in Abkhazia ignited tensions between the two. Abkhazia decried Georgia's violation of its sovereignty. Georgian officials countered that their sovereign rights extended throughout Abkhazia and that the military could come and go as it pleased. Abkhaz guardsmen fired on the Georgian troops. Under Russian pressure, the Abkhaz leadership acquiesced to a cease-fire on September 3 and promised to remain under Georgian authority. But the agreement did not last. Abkhazians had no intention of following through on a commitment they had made under duress. Fighting resumed on October 1, with an Abkhaz offensive.

NAGORNO-KARABAKH HISTORY AND BACKGROUND

Armenia and Azerbaijan began contesting control over Nagorno-Karabakh following World War I and never fully resolved their competing claims.[60] The Soviets granted control over NK to Azerbaijan even though much of its population was ethnically Armenian. Armenians never accepted the decision's legitimacy. NK Armenians maintained close ties to their kin in Armenia proper while Moscow maintained strong centralized control over its constituent parts. When Soviet control relaxed and Azeri nationalism became more vocal during the 1980s, the NK Armenians determined that they would attempt to rejoin Armenia. Initially, it seemed that Gorbachev might fulfill their request, but the dissolution of the Soviet Union left the NK Armenians stranded under Azeri control, without recourse to a higher authority.[61]

Azerbaijan, like Armenia and Georgia, was part of the Transcaucasian Federated Republic, which quickly disintegrated. When the Soviets took control

---

[60] At that time, the two disputed where the boundary between them should rightly lie when the Bolsheviks took control. In November 1920, the Soviets placed all of the Caucasus republics within the Transcaucasian Republic. When the federation dissolved, the Soviets determined where the borders would be.

[61] Gorbachev intended to change Nagorno-Karabakh's status to that of a union republic. This would have given NK independence from Azerbaijan and increased its status within the Soviet system (Cornell 2001, p. 79).

in the early 1920s, the statuses of Nagorno-Karabakh and a few other regions were left unresolved.[62] The Soviets originally intended for NK to remain within Armenia but reversed the decision and made NK an autonomous oblast of Azerbaijan. The decision was formalized in November 1924. In 1936, when Transcaucasia's republics became SSRs, the Russians reaffirmed that NK should remain within Azerbaijan. Nagorno-Karabakh's status was a point of contention for Armenia and Azerbaijan from then on.

Nagorno-Karabakh is a mostly mountainous, forested region slightly larger than Rhode Island (4,400 km²). Located in western Azerbaijan, NK shares no border with Armenia but is fully surrounded by Azerbaijan.[63] It is unique among all secessionist territories for this fact. A thin strip of Azerbaijani territory, the Lachin Corridor, lies between NK and Armenia proper. Armenians constituted more than 75 percent of the population within Karabakh in 1989 (Table 6.1). The region also had a significant Azeri population (22 percent) and small Russian and Kurdish minorities. Karabakh Armenians speak Armenian and belong to the Armenian Apostolic Church, a Christian Orthodox religion. Azerbaijan's majority, in contrast, was nearly 90 percent ethnic Azeri, Azerbaijani speaking, and Muslim.[64]

Armenian leaders' frequent attempts to reverse the Soviet decision on NK through diplomatic means were unsuccessful. In the 1930s, when the Transcaucas SFSR separated into its constituent parts, the NK Armenians petitioned their return to Armenia. Again in the 1960s, with Azeri nationalism on the rise, Armenians protested to Khrushchev that the Azeris were neglecting NK's social and economic development. Strict central control during the 1970s precluded much protest, but the latent contest between Azerbaijan and Armenia over Nagorno-Karabakh reemerged in the late 1980s. As had been done in many SSRs during Soviet liberalization, the Azeri majority initiated strong nationalist programs en route to independence. Sporadic attacks and skirmishes between Armenians and Azeris began during that time, foretelling the violence to come.

The Karabakh Armenians faced especially brutal policies within Azerbaijan, including Soviet-style pogroms meant to intimidate, and perhaps ultimately eliminate, the group. Economic and political control within Azerbaijan was exclusive to ethnic Azeris, leaving the Armenian minority few opportunities. The NK Armenians were subject to extensive "Azerification" beginning in the

[62] Zangezur was ceded to Armenia. Nakhchivan, a mixed Armenian-Azerbaijani autonomous republic (ASSR), was eventually ceded to Azerbaijan along with Karabakh.

[63] This was most likely the result of Soviet efforts to divide and rule the Armenian population in the South Caucasus. Early Soviet maps show Nagorno-Karabakh sharing a border with Armenia, but by 1930, the borders had shifted to the territorial boundaries recognized today (Cornell 2001, p. 74).

[64] Ethnic Azeris are the majority in Azerbaijan and were the majority in the Azerbaijani SSR within the Soviet Union. Azeris once made up a majority within Karabakh, but they no longer do. Population transfers in the late 1980s and early 1990s left most Karabakh Azeris within Azerbaijan and Nagorno-Karabakh predominantly Armenian.

late 1960s: schools and churches were closed, cultural institutions were abolished, and the Armenian language was discriminated against. Azeri authorities systematically replaced Armenians with Azeris in law enforcement and economic positions.[65] Policies also included Azeri in-migration and the attenuation of Armenian power and influence within Nagorno-Karabakh. Under the Soviet umbrella, though, the NK Armenians remained strongly connected to their kin in neighboring Armenia. The Armenian diaspora provided extensive support to their brethren, viewing the NK Armenians' status as a collective injustice. The Soviet system's flexibility, allowing extensive contact across formal borders, probably forestalled conflict over Nagorno-Karabakh that otherwise might have ignited much earlier. When it became apparent that NK might be permanently isolated within an exclusionary, independent Azerbaijan after the Soviet Union fell, Armenians rebelled.

PRECIPITATING EVENTS: NAGORNO-KARABAKH

Glasnost initially raised Armenian hopes that authority over NK would change hands. By 1987, rumors were widespread that President Gorbachev intended to transfer sovereignty for Nagorno-Karabakh and Nakhchivan (another autonomous region) to Armenia. Though Gorbachev had, in fact, come to favor raising NK's status to that of an SSR, his decision came too late to deter conflict in NK. A skirmish between Azeris and Armenians over environmental concerns initiated the first widespread violence between the two republics under Soviet rule. The situation declined precipitously from there. Following increasingly violent measures on both sides, the NK Armenians declared independence from Azerbaijan.

Azeri nationalism intensified as Moscow loosened its grip on the SSRs. The Nagorno-Karabakh Armenians, justifiably threatened, appealed to Moscow for a change in their status.[66] Extensive Armenian protests in February 1988 prompted Moscow to consider adjusting the authority structure in exchange for a moratorium on the unrest. Before Gorbachev could respond, Azeri authorities launched a Soviet-style pogrom against Armenians throughout Azerbaijan.[67] In March, Gorbachev, under increasing pressure in Moscow, announced that there would be no change in Nagorno-Karabakh's status: it would remain within Azerbaijan. Armenians were outraged.

Fall brought mass expulsions of Armenians from Azerbaijan and vice versa. By November, interethnic relations had declined so much that martial law was declared in Armenia. In 1989, Armenia's Supreme Soviet and local

[65] Papazian in Chorbajian (2001, p. 65).

[66] February 13, 1988, the Nagorno-Karabakh Supreme Soviet requested that Moscow transfer authority for the region to Armenia.

[67] Sumgait, a Caspian seaside city close to Baku but far from Nagorno-Karabakh, was the scene of an especially brutal campaign against the Armenians. In only a few days beginning in February 1988, tens of Armenians and Azeris were killed and nearly the entire Armenian population fled the city.

representatives in Nagorno-Karabakh declared the region's intention to secede from the Azerbaijan SSR to join Armenia. Azeris instituted new pogroms against the Armenians in January 1990. Moscow had unambiguously granted Azerbaijani control over NK, and Baku was emboldened to use the most efficient tactics at its disposal. Violent Armenian protests broke out in response and Moscow dispatched troops to quell the unrest. Russian troops met the violence with violence of their own, killing at least 100. By this time, Moscow had been thoroughly discredited as an Armenian ally or impartial arbiter.

When the USSR held its March referendum on the Union Treaty, Armenia boycotted and Azerbaijan voted in favor of maintaining the republic. Armenians declared independence on September 21, 1991, after holding their own referendum on sovereignty. Three months later, on December 10, a referendum on Nagorno-Karabakh's independence, boycotted by Azeris, yielded overwhelming support for the establishment of a new country. According to the secessionist regime, 82.2 percent of eligible voters participated and 99.9 percent voted in favor of independence.[68] Azerbaijan revoked Nagorno-Karabakh's autonomous status on November 21, 1991. On January 6, 1992, just two weeks after the Soviet Union dissolved, Nagorno-Karabakh formally declared its independence from Azerbaijan.

THE INTERNATIONAL ENVIRONMENT

The Soviet and Yugoslav secessions emerged during the same historical moment, so they shared the same international political context. As the Soviet Union grappled with its own transformation, others attempted to anticipate dissolution's effects. The fall of the Soviet empire and the end of the bipolar order weighed heavily on world leaders' minds. Some pundits saw the potential for democracy and free markets in the post-Soviet states, whereas others, more skeptical of wholesale change following decades of authoritarianism, saw the potential for widespread ethno-political conflict, state failure, and economic chaos.[69] Events unfolded so quickly that no one could be sure what the future would hold.

During the early years post-disintegration, politics in the former Soviet states remained unsettled; the new states had not yet consolidated their authority, nor had they settled their future relationships with Moscow. Furthermore, the international order was in flux. Would the United States emerge as a hegemonic power or would a new era of multipolarity emerge, characterized by more traditional spheres of influence among the remaining Great Powers? Finally,

---

[68] Petrossian (1991) notes 108,736 of 132,328 eligible voters participated. An estimated 22,747 Azeris in NK boycotted the vote; 95 ballots (0.09 percent) were declared invalid.

[69] For examples, see Fukuyama (1992); Huntington (1993); Jervis (1993); Kaplan (1994); Layne (1993); Mearsheimer (1990).

how would the most powerful states attempt to influence the course of events in the region?

Events such as the 1991 Gulf War and negotiations over the European Union, which drew attention away from Yugoslavia's emerging conflicts, did not have the same effect on the post-Soviet conflicts. Instead, the Great Powers, especially the United States, the European powers, and Russia, were keenly aware of events in the new states. The United States was especially engaged in Georgia and Azerbaijan, which had adopted decidedly pro-Western orientations. European leaders became increasingly engaged in peacemaking and humanitarian operations. And once Russia stabilized, it energetically reasserted itself in its near-abroad. Aside from Russia, the Great Powers' interests aligned against the secessionists and remained that way.

The conflicts in Yugoslavia and the Russian periphery inspired fears of centrifugal disintegration throughout the international community. Between 1989 and 1994, 30 new states entered international society. Most of those new states were the fruits of secession.[70] The international community readily consecrated the independence of the USSR's former union republics but was reticent to accept any additional partitions. On achieving independence, the post-Soviet states were left with the armaments of a powerful military, including some with nuclear weapons, and their stability was of the utmost importance. The new states also had important strategic resources, including oil and gas, which required relative stability for their extraction and trade.[71] Finally, the former Soviet states lay in important strategic locations. But even with the international community's considerable material and moral support, the new states were too weak to deter or suppress the secessionist efforts within their borders.

CIVIL WAR AND STALEMATE IN THE POST-SOVIET STATES

The wars over Chechnya, Abkhazia, South Ossetia, and Nagorno-Karabakh began under similar, but distinct circumstances, and they would all end in the same way. In each instance, the separatist regions and their volunteer defense forces defied their home states' low expectations, seizing on the conventional militaries' weaknesses by using flexible, guerrilla tactics and retreating into the civilian population. They were surprisingly well armed and trained, and their home states were strikingly unprepared for combat. The separatist forces were in their homelands: they had popular support, were familiar with the terrain, and were willing to persevere until their home states withdrew. Lastly, each of the secessionist wars reached similar end points: they had compelled their home states' departures and relative peace had set in, they were de facto sovereign, and

[70] See Figure 1.2.
[71] Oil resources and pipelines were a factor in most of the secessionist conflicts.

TABLE 6.2 *Soviet Successor Conflict Statistics*

	Start Date	End Date	Deaths[a]	Displaced[b]	Peacekeepers
Abkhazia Declared 7/23/92	Aug. 14, 1992	May 14, 1994	10,000[c]	140,000–300,000	CIS (RUS)/ UNOMIG
Chechnya Declared 11/2/91	Dec. 2, 1994	Aug. 31, 1996	81,500[d]	200,000	OSCE[e]
Chechnya II	Sept. 23, 1999	April 16, 2009	65,651 +[f]	200,000–400,000	
Nagorno-Karabakh Declared 1/6/92	Jan. 1, 1992	May 12, 1994	30,000	528,000–950,000[g]	UN/OSCE (1/3 RUS)
South Ossetia Declared 12/12/90	Jan. 22, 1991	June 24, 1992	1,000	39,000–100,000[h]	RUS/OSCE
South Ossetia II Referendum 11/12/2006	Aug. 7, 2008	Aug. 16, 2008	621[i]	158,000	
Abkhazia II	Aug. 9, 2008	Aug. 16, 2008	<100	Unavailable	

[a] Estimated combatant deaths were reported when possible. Some estimates may include civilian casualties when they could not be distinguished.

[b] Displaced figures reflect the lowest and highest estimates of internally displaced persons and/or refugees during the conflict period.

[c] Some reports suggest figures as high as 11,000 for the Georgian National Guard alone, though they are likely inflated.

[d] Lacina and Gleditsch (2005); see Dunlop (2000) for an insightful discussion regarding the number of combatants and civilians killed during the first Russo-Chechen war. Civilian deaths for the first war are estimated to be 35,000.

[e] This was an OSCE observer mission, rather than a peacekeeping force.

[f] Lacina and Gleditsch (2005) give a best estimate of 45,651 battle related deaths for 1999 to 2007. Dunlop (2002) "very tentatively" estimated between 20,000 and 25,000 civilians were killed over the same time period.

[g] High estimate includes IDPs and refugees expelled from both Armenia and Azerbaijan throughout the 1989–1994 violence.

[h] A North Ossetian refugee committee estimated that half of Georgia's Ossetian population (83,000) had fled the province by October 1991. (Note that this is before Georgian independence from the Soviet Union.) See Brooke (1991, Section A, p. 3).

[i] Lacina and Gleditsch (2005).

peacekeepers had been agreed to in every case but one. Yet the wars differed significantly in the extent of violence employed, in the destruction left behind, and in the character of the new de facto governments.

Separatist hostilities ignited war first in South Ossetia, breaking out in January 1991, nearly a year before the Soviet Union dissolved (Table 6.2). Georgian-Osset violence reached a durable conclusion in the summer of 1992 with the signing of the Sochi Agreement.[72] The conflict over Nagorno-Karabakh's status reemerged in the late 1980s but did not escalate to full-scale war until January 1992. The Karabakh war, which included both Azerbaijani and Armenian forces, continued until 1994.[73] Georgia's war with the Abkhaz began in August 1992, shortly after its declaration of independence and just after the South Ossetia cease-fire agreement. The Abkhaz war ended with a cease-fire agreement in May 1994.[74] Lastly, the Russo-Chechen war began once the other wars had reached enduring stalemates, in December 1994. By summer's end in 1996, the Chechens had compelled Russia's withdrawal, and they agreed to resolve Chechnya's final status in five years.[75] Each war lasted approximately two years.

All of the conflicts caused a significant loss of life and property, but the wars in Nagorno-Karabakh and Chechnya had the highest human tolls (see Table 6.2). Experts estimate that in the course of the 28-month war, more than 30,000 individuals were killed and well over a half million people were displaced by the violence in NK.[76] The conflict there was especially disruptive to civilian populations because both Armenia and Azerbaijan used mass expulsions as means to secure demographic superiority. The Azeris (and initially the Soviets) expelled Armenians from their territory, whereas the Armenians expelled Azeris from Armenia proper, NK, and its neighboring territories. The best estimate of battle-related casualties in Chechnya counts 46,500 and 35,000 additional civilians.[77] In contrast, Georgia's short war against South Ossetia resulted in only approximately 1,000 deaths and between 39,000 and 100,000 displaced persons, and the Georgian-Abkhaz war caused approximately 2,500 casualties.[78]

---

[72] The Sochi Agreement, signed on June 24, 1992, established a cease-fire, a security corridor, a peacekeeping force, and OSCE monitors.

[73] A cease-fire in Azerbaijan, Armenia, and Nagorno-Karabakh was established on May 12, 1994, with Russian support. Although the cease-fire holds to this day, Nagorno-Karabakh is not without violence. OSCE observers estimate an average of one person a day died between the initiation of the cease-fire and their mission report in 1999, approximately 1,600 individuals. More recently, violence across the border has increased, killing approximately 30 people annually according to the International Crisis Group (2011).

[74] Russian-brokered talks in 1994 led to the cessation of major hostilities, a cease-fire agreement and the dispatch of a CIS peacekeeping force. Though the peacekeepers were nominally under the purview of the CIS, they were, in fact, all Russian.

[75] The Khasavyurt Agreement, signed October 30, 1996, formally ended the war and set a deadline of December 31, 2001, for the resolution of the Russo-Chechen relationship. The agreement states that the parties would seek a mutually acceptable political solution to the military conflict. And that the negotiations would "[proceed] from the universally recognized right of nations to self-determination, the principles of equality, free will and the freedom of expressing one's will, strengthening interethnic accord and security of nations" ("Text of Peace Agreements, Rebel Leader Comments" 1996).

[76] Lacina and Gleditsch (2005) estimate approximately 5,000 battle-related deaths occurred in three years of fighting.

[77] Ibid., 2005; Dunlop (2000).

[78] Lacina and Gleditsch (2005) estimate between 500 and 1,000 battle-related deaths occurred in South Ossetia's conflict and a best estimate of 2,500 battle-related deaths in Abkhazia.

Though the post-Soviet wars were small in scale compared to many other civil wars, for example, those in Sudan or Cambodia, much of their destructive impact lay in their concentration within a compact geographic region. Civilians fleeing one war often ended up in a territory where another conflict was underway; there was little respite for the victims of the Caucasus wars. There was a synergy to the violence for the secessionists who would capitalize on their neighbors' lack of control by taking shelter within their borders. Russian and Georgian authorities clashed over Georgia's permissive attitude toward Chechen fighters in the Pankisi Gorge and Russia's assistance to the Osset and Abkhaz secessionists. In many respects, one conflict could not be disentangled from the others.

By 1996, all of the conflicts were exhausted and the secessionists had prevailed militarily. But each of the separatist regions ended up in very different circumstances than when they first demanded independence. Abkhazia and South Ossetia were relatively advantaged under Soviet control, but the wars had destroyed much of their infrastructure. Abkhazia, which previously had a booming tourist industry, could no longer attract vacationers because of its violent instability and wrecked infrastructure. Postwar, the two Georgian regions looked more similar to their economically disadvantaged colleagues in Nagorno-Karabakh and Chechnya. In fact, Abkhazia emerged from the conflict as one of Georgia's most economically depressed regions.

The secessionist republics also had different political characters than when the wars began. In some cases, they had new leaders. Chechen President Dudayev, for instance, was killed in a Russian attack on or around April 22, 1996, and was replaced by Aslan Maskhadov, a moderate, former Russian army colonel.[79] In other cases, the political regimes had transformed over the course of the war. In NK, the military had taken on a prominent role in all aspects of political life, playing on Armenians fears by inducing a permanent siege mentality within the republic.[80] Similarly, Chechnya's war elevated the status of Wahhabist fighters within Chechen social and political life, infusing religion into what had been a secular nationalist conflict.[81]

Although violence between the secessionists and their home states had dwindled to almost nothing, true peace eluded them. The de facto regimes, without a negotiated settlement, remained highly suspicious of their home states. At the behest of both the home states and the secessionists, peacekeeping forces were dispatched to three of the regions.[82] In South Ossetia, Russian peacekeepers were sent and later came under the supervision of the Organization for

---

[79] Some questioned whether the Chechen independence movement would survive Dudayev's death, but a massive attack and the seizure of Grozny on the day before Yeltsin's inauguration ended rumors of a Chechen collapse (Lapidus 1998, p. 23).

[80] Lynch (2002, p. 836).

[81] I use the terms "Wahhabi" and "Wahhabist" recognizing their inaccuracy in describing the ideological topography of the Caucasus (Markedonov 2010, pp. 6–9).

[82] Russia refused to allow external intervention in Chechnya.

Security and Co-operation in Europe (OSCE). In October 1993, Russian peace-keepers were also the first to arrive in Abkhazia, but with their legitimacy in question, the UN became involved.[83] The United Nations Observer Mission in Georgia (UNOMIG) was dispatched in short order to verify the cease-fire. In 1994, the UN Security Council expanded UNOMIG's mandate to include monitoring and verification of the cease-fire (the first cease-fire had already been violated and invalidated), investigation of alleged crimes by the combatants, and assistance in the safe return of the conflict's refugees.[84] Peace talks under the auspices of the United Nations and the OSCE's Minsk Group regarding Nagorno-Karabakh made little progress throughout 1992–1993. The OSCE dispatched peacekeepers, one-third of whom were Russian, to Nagorno-Karabakh following the May 12, 1994, agreement. The peacekeepers in the republics effectively served two purposes: they helped maintain the peace in the three conflict zones, and they preserved the de facto control of the separatist regimes.

INTERNAL SOVEREIGNTY IN THE POST-SOVIET PROTO-STATES

Although the secessionists secured battlefield victories, their struggles to consolidate domestic sovereignty and gain international recognition had just begun. Immediately following the first Russo-Chechen war, the Maskhadov regime provided a relatively high level of domestic control and authority, had extensive popular support, and appeared viable because of Russia's military retreat from Chechen territory and abdication of authority there. But as time went on, the Chechen regime's domestic sovereignty plummeted. Without the legitimacy afforded by external recognition, Chechnya languished under Russian sanctions. By the time Russian forces invaded Chechnya in 1999, the Maskhadov regime maintained little effective authority within its borders and its viability was dubious.

All of the remaining secessionist states – Abkhazia, South Ossetia, and Nagorno-Karabakh – demonstrate an organized political authority and popular support and provide basic services for their populations. They have all held popular elections and/or referenda on sovereignty and have put forward their own independent constitutions. At the same time, the secessionist governments have "poorly developed party structures" and "personalistic," "centralized"

---

[83] After its requests for unbiased intervention were rebuffed by the OSCE and the United Nations, Georgia had few alternatives. In October 1993, Shevardnadze requested that Russia intervene to quell the Zviadist (pro-Gamsakhurdia) violence in Abkhazia. Russian-brokered talks in 1994 led to the cessation of major hostilities, a cease-fire agreement, and the dispatch of a CIS peacekeeping force.

[84] During the intense fighting of 1993, UNOMIG was suspended save for 15 observers. UNSC Resolution 881, passed on November 4, 1993, established an interim mandate that was later expanded, in July 1994, on the recommendation of the secretary general.

presidential systems, perhaps calling into question their long-term viability.[85] Each meets the criteria for recognition established by international law but lacks convincing sovereignty on at least one of the three dimensions outlined in Chapter 4 or is not likely to remain viable long term (see Table 4.4). Nagorno-Karabakh's military development is much stronger than that in Abkhazia or South Ossetia. Abkhazia receives a great deal of external humanitarian support from international organizations (IOs) and international non-governmental organizations (INGOs), whereas the other secessionist states receive significantly less. Abkhazia also has greater potential for economic viability than do Chechnya, Karabakh, or South Ossetia. South Ossetia and NK receive significant remittances from their diasporas, underwriting their viability, but simultaneously calling into question their political independence from Russia and Armenia. Finally, each of the governments provides qualitatively different effective authority. The Karabakh and Chechen regimes are essentially military, whereas the South Ossetian and Abkhaz governments are civilian.

DOMESTIC SOVEREIGNTY IN CHECHNYA, 1996–1999

Chechnya's territorial control and effective authority at the end of its war were high by any standard. Though the Chechens' means of achieving that control, principally guerrilla war, were less orthodox than one might expect from a state, Chechen authorities successfully compelled Russia's retreat. Because the war was tremendously destructive, the regime had a number of obstacles to overcome before normal governance could be established. Chechnya had been less developed than other Russian regions before the war and had become even less so by 1996. Russia also attempted to undermine Chechen domestic authority through embargoes and strangulation of its economy. Nevertheless, some experts suggest Chechnya had a credible claim to statehood according to international law.[86]

Interestingly, many of Chechnya's difficulties were shared by Russia, including economic troubles and a breakdown in law and order. An attempted coup against Yeltsin in 1993, for instance, was brutally suppressed, signaling substantial domestic instability and discontent. Later, in 1998, Russia experienced a financial crisis that initiated an economic decline more severe than the Great Depression. Afterward, Russia saw a tremendous population decline, rapidly decreasing life expectancy, political instability, and a precipitous fall in living standards. Indeed, it is worthwhile to ponder whether or not Russia would have had the ability to maintain domestic sovereignty within its substantially reduced

---

[85] Lynch (2002, p. 836).

[86] Hollis (1995); Tappe (1995, p. 255). Tappe includes a number of additional normative criteria in his analysis of Chehnya's claim.

borders without the support afforded to it by the international community.[87] It is certainly true that Boris Yeltsin's government would likely not have survived to govern a second term had it not been for unequivocal U.S. support.[88]

Territorial Control and Effective Authority

Even considering its relative weakness following Soviet dissolution, the balance of power between Chechnya and Russia favored Russia prior to the war. By December 15, 1993, an estimated 600 tanks and 40,000 Russian soldiers advanced on Grozny.[89] The number of Chechen combatants was estimated at 5,000 to 10,000.[90] The Russians were also overwhelmingly better armed. One observer noted that "At the peak of the war the Chechen commander-in-chief had no more than 6,000 'full-time' fighters, not because of a lack of volunteers but because of a shortage of weapons."[91] Throughout the war, the Russian government consistently reported that the Chechens were near defeat. And it was true that Russian forces dealt harsh blows on the Chechen resistance and its civilian population – Russian and Chechen alike.[92] Still, at the war's end, Chechen forces controlled Grozny and had retaken the formerly Russian-occupied portions of Chechnya.

Unlike Afghanistan, Chechnya avoided civil war on Russia's departure. In September 1997, Chechen authorities, now under Maskhadov, expelled all of Moscow's representatives. The expulsions effectively established Chechnya's complete independence. Later that fall, Russia, Chechnya, and Azerbaijan signed a tripartite agreement on the opening of a pipeline between the Caspian Sea and the Black Sea. For Chechens (and some observers), the agreement signaled Russia's implicit recognition of Chechen independence and its ability to engage in international affairs as outlined by Montevideo. Moscow had acknowledged the Maskhadov regime's "ability to keep [the pipeline] well-maintained and secure" of its own volition.[93] Russia sent another signal in seeming acquiescence to independence when it granted the Grozny airport international status.[94]

---

[87] At the time, some believed the Russian Federation would meet a fate similar to the USSR. See Stern (1994, pp. 54–55, in particular). Lapidus (1998) notes that international financial support for Russia remained strong throughout the Chechen conflict whereas the Russian government was able to collect only 70 percent of the taxes owed it (p. 40). The Russian Federation might reasonably have been called a failed state in the early to mid-1990s and again during the 1998 financial crisis.

[88] Goldgeier and McFaul (2003).

[89] Though additional Russian troops were dispatched to Chechnya, their numbers remained relatively stable throughout the war. Felgenhauer (2002, pp. 158–159) notes, "The overall strength of Russian forces in Chechnya never exceeded 45,000 during the 20-month campaign."

[90] Bennigsen (1999, p. 541).

[91] Ibid.

[92] Human Rights Watch (1996); Dunlop (2000, 2002).

[93] Clark (1997).

[94] Kalashnikova (1997).

Chechnya won significant financial independence as well. An agreement between the Russian Central Bank and the National Bank of Chechnya signed in May 1997 stipulated that "cash circulation and non-cash transactions [would] be organized by the Chechen government." In addition, the Russian Central Bank no longer had offices in Chechnya nor did it consider the Chechen bank its subsidiary.[95] The only remaining monetary vestige of Russian authority within Chechnya was the Russian ruble, which remained its official currency.[96] Otherwise, the republic was financially independent and recognized as such by Russian authorities. Especially surprising was the fact that the Russian Central Bank, not the Chechens, had initiated the negotiations. Said one banker, "We are realists and we simply put in the agreement what has long arisen in practice."[97]

However, the Chechen republic remained very poor and suffered from a lack of infrastructure and development. Under the weight of Russian sanctions from 1991 to 1993, Chechnya's GNP "declined by some 65.3 percent, [and] per capita income fell to one-fourth its 1991 level."[98] The unemployment problem was exacerbated after the war because Chechens could no longer travel to other countries to work (a once common practice) without internationally recognized passports and documentation. Because no governments – besides the other Caucasian secessionists – recognized the new Chechen Republic, illegal migration was the only option. Nevertheless, Chechens' effective control and authority after the 1994–1996 war were redoubtable.

Popular Legitimacy

Chechnya held its first independent presidential elections on January 27, 1997. Observers from the OSCE and other foreign organizations were present, at least in part to secure international legitimacy.[99] Chechens within Chechnya and members of the diaspora, many displaced because of the war, were invited to participate.[100] All five of the major presidential contenders were active in the

---

[95] Berger (1997).

[96] Stern (1994) notes that Chechnya had in fact "demanded the right to float [its] own [currency] and to collect [its] own taxes" (p. 57), but other sources contradict this account. Stern cites a Russian Federation deputy premier.

[97] Ibid.

[98] Galeotti cited in Toft (2003, p. 76).

[99] The U.S. State Department heralded the elections as "an important part of the process of reconciliation and...[a potential] step toward establishing democratic institutions and legitimate government in Chechnya." However, it is unclear how the elections could possibly be a step toward both reconciliation and legitimate, independent institutions (Burns 1997).

[100] Chechen officials said 513,000 people registered to vote (including refugees). The Chechens did not permit polling outside the borders of the republic for fear of election fraud but did bus refugees into Chechnya to participate in the election (Smith 1997).

Chechen resistance and dedicated to independence. Maskhadov won the presidency with 59.3 percent of the vote.[101] According to one source, Russians within Chechnya were disinterested in the election but were not barred from participating, nor did they actively boycott.[102] Beyond a peaceful internal power transition, the elections did not have their intended effect. The OSCE's head of mission in Grozny remarked that there was no reason why elections should change the international community's position on Chechnya, reiterating that the conflict was internal and needed to be settled by Russia and Chechnya alone.[103] External observers' positions did not change despite the demonstrable will of the Chechen people.

The Chechen population is one of only five titular nationalities among the 21 Russian republics to constitute a majority within its borders.[104] At the outset of the war, approximately 66 percent of Chechnya's population was Chechen, around 720,000 people, whereas 25 percent were Russian.[105] At war's end, Chechnya's absolute population had fallen, but Chechens made up a greater percentage of the populace. Even though support for Dudayev's regime eroded within parliament during the early 1990s, his popular legitimacy remained strong.[106] Once the war was over, and Dudayev had been assassinated, popular support for Maskhadov was relatively strong as well.

Finally, the Chechen government quickly went about the task of creating the domestic trappings of statehood. The new Chechen constitution was put forward in 1992, before the war with Russia had even begun. In July 1997, Chechnya began raising a military. In August, its parliament declared Chechen its official language. By October, Maskhadov's regime was preparing to distribute more than 500,000 passports to its people, and an additional 200 passports were sent to foreign governments so that they would be able to authenticate Chechen documentation.[107]

Popular support for independence among Chechens remained strong following the war. Economic difficulties plagued the Chechen proto-state, yet regular elections and normal, albeit low-level, governance set in. Maskhadov's regime came to be seen as too moderate by those who favored Islamic government, but his support within the general population was high. Rampant criminality called into question the regime's ability to maintain law and order. Still, the Maskhadov regime did manage to establish a medium to high level of popular legitimacy.

---

[101] Ibid. Other reported totals were Shamil Basaev 23.5 percent and Zelimkhan Yandarbiev 10.1 percent. Mowladi Udugov and Ahmad Zakaev received smaller shares.
[102] Bennigsen (1999, p. 546).
[103] "No foreign backing for Chechen independence bid without Russia's consent – OSCE" (1997).
[104] The other four republics are Chuvashia, Ingushetia, Tuva, and North Ossetia.
[105] Smith (1999, p. 137).
[106] Toft (2003, pp. 76–77).
[107] Isayev (1997).

Projected Viability

Challenges to Chechnya's future viability arose as an indirect consequence of the war with Russia. Chechnya's population declined following the war, and its economic situation was dire, yet these problems could be remedied with the lifting of sanctions and the restoration of peace and security within the republic. Indeed, Chechens felt a certain nobility in their struggle against Russia; displaced Russians might not return, but displaced Chechens would. The most consequential postwar development for Chechen viability was rising support for Wahhabism. Though religious Chechens were predominantly Muslim, the conflict with Russia had a secular nationalist character. As Wahhabis were some of the most successful fighters in the war, they became a cause célèbre within Chechnya, altering the ideological landscape. Initially, many Chechens were attracted to Wahhabism and the prospect of a country governed by Shari'a law. Over time, though, Wahhabism's ascendance generated internal instability for Chechnya and negatively affected its interactions with the international community.

The Russo-Chechen war had a number of adverse consequences for the de facto government and its people. Chechnya experienced a relatively small loss of life among its combatants, but its civilians suffered greatly during the war.[108] The total number of Russian and Chechen civilian deaths "probably exceeded 35,000."[109] Many Chechens were displaced within Russia or became refugees. Just before the war, in January 1994, Chechnya's population was approximately 865,000.[110] By war's end, more than 200,000 people, or nearly 25 percent of Chechnya's entire population, had been displaced by the violence.

Chechnya's economic outlook was similarly bleak. The war of independence was disastrous for its economy. The republic rebuilt somewhat with profits from oil sales and monetary support from the Chechen diaspora, as the oppressive economic circumstances led many Chechens to flee illegally in search of work. Still, the economic situation was undeniably difficult; most of Chechnya's infrastructure and its major cities were destroyed. Postwar, Moscow had promised Chechnya large-scale reconstruction aid, but it never materialized, and the limited aid that was sent had little impact on Chechnya's recovery.[111] What reconstruction did occur was internally driven.

The Chechen people as a whole, having been expelled from their land and left with little to survive on during previous Soviet purges, had become accustomed

[108] The best casualty estimates for the war suggest 11,500 soldiers were killed during the conflict. Around 7,500 Russian troops died during the war as opposed to about 4,000 Chechen fighters (Dunlop 2000). Lacina and Gleditsch (2005) arrive at a much higher, best estimate of battle related deaths: 45,651 total.

[109] Dunlop (2000, p. 338).

[110] Smith (1999, p. 137); Lapidus (1998, p. 21) suggests the war caused 100,000 casualties and forced nearly 400,000 people to become refugees.

[111] Kramer (2004/5, p. 6).

to lives of struggle. They remained dedicated to independence no matter the cost; what they lacked in material comforts, they made up for in resolve. Some observers saw cause for optimism. Bennigsen noted that in 1997,

The roads and bridges have been rebuilt; new ones have been added. Trees have been planted. The carcasses of burnt-out tanks and vehicles have gone. The centre of Grozny has been cleaned up and the most dangerous ruins pulled down. A new garden has been laid in front of the former presidential palace...In the suburbs all private houses have been rebuilt. The markets were full...Small businesses were appearing and although unemployment was extremely high, one did not see bands of idle young men...In short, the country gave the impression of great dynamism.[112]

More important for Chechnya's viability was Wahhabism's increasing prominence. During the war, defense of Chechnya became an international rallying cry among Islamists, many of whom traveled to Chechnya to fight alongside the Chechens. The outsiders had a powerful influence on the course of the war: "By the end...the Wahhabis basked in popularity. Their appeals for an Islamic state were well received by a majority of Chechens...Shari'a law was seen as a means to avoid chaos and impose discipline."[113]

The Wahhabis' popular support did not last. Chechens strong nationalism and more moderate Sufi tradition, coupled with the Wahhabists' disinterest in rebuilding or securing international legitimacy for Chechnya, decimated their popular support and credibility by the end of 1998.[114] Nevertheless, Wahhabi terrorism's effects reverberated, undermining Chechnya's domestic stability and eroding international support.[115] The havoc Wahhabi elements wreaked in Chechnya inhibited its economic revival; slowed foreign aid and non-governmental organizations' (NGO) assistance; and fomented violence within the neighboring republics, especially Dagestan.

Chechnya's difficult economic and political hurdles were not insurmountable. Russia's attempt to "wait the Chechens out" in anticipation of the 2001 final status talks had effectively stalled Chechnya's economic development. And as Russia had not formally conceded to Chechnya's independence after the war, foreign aid and international assistance were not forthcoming. These hurdles, though estimable, could have been overcome with the substantial benefits of external legitimacy and statehood. The greatest threat to Chechnya's long-term viability came from the domestic and international disquiet associated with foreign Wahhabis, Islamist politics, and terrorism. The outsiders destabilized

---

[112] Bennigsen (1999, p. 553).
[113] Ibid., p. 549.
[114] The foreign fighters viewed Chechnya as one front in a greater Islamic war against the West. Most Chechens were simply interested in winning their independence; they were not generally supportive of the global holy war.
[115] Non-conventional tactics were a persistent feature of the war, but the introduction of terrorism, particularly bombings and assassinations in Russia proper after the war, renewed concerns about Chechnya in Moscow and abroad.

Chechnya internally and decimated external support with their wanton targeting of civilians.

DOMESTIC SOVEREIGNTY IN ABKHAZIA, 1994–2008

At the close of its war in 1994, the independent Abkhaz regime convincingly
demonstrated territorial control and effective authority within Abkhazia. The
republic has experienced more than a decade and a half of self-rule since then.
Though still economically depressed as a result of sanctions and the war, the
Abkhaz economy rebounded somewhat and the regime established regular,
effective governance within its borders.[116] Abkhazia briefly relapsed into violence in 1998, but unlike Chechnya, the level of violence in the early 1990s never
returned.[117] Abkhazia's substantial autonomy within the Soviet Union lent itself
to establishing domestic sovereignty, as did its close ties to Russia. The
Georgian-Abkhaz War also attracted much more international attention than
did South Ossetia's. That international attention had a stabilizing effect on
Abkhazia through the provision of humanitarian aid, peacekeepers, and economic assistance to repair its infrastructure. Still, it is unclear whether the
Abkhaz regime was strong enough to survive as a state; it did not have an
independent currency, it provided few social services, and the possible repatriation of the Georgian majority seemed likely to reignite violence.

Territorial Control and Effective Authority

Prior to the Georgian-Abkhaz conflict, the balance of forces decisively favored
Georgia. The Abkhaz, a tiny minority constituting fewer than 3 percent of the
Georgian population, did not seem capable of defeating a country dedicating
more than 2 percent of its GNP to military expenditures. However, external and
internal factors conspired against the Georgian government in its conflict with
Abkhazia. First, the Abkhaz's secessionist ambitions garnered significant outside
assistance from Russia and inspired foreign volunteers from the greater
Caucasus region. Internally, Georgia's attention was also divided as it faced a
war in South Ossetia, a violent coup against President Gamsakhurdia, and his
later drive to retake power, nearly all at the same time. Over the course of three
short years, international intervention and domestic instability combined to
create a capability deficit from which Tbilisi could not recover.

---

[116] Sanctions, including a Black Sea blockade and closure of the Abkhaz-Russian border, were
leveled against Abkhazia in 1997 by the CIS. CIS members blamed Abkhaz authorities for the
failure of peace talks with Georgia. Though not well enforced, the sanctions did impose economic
costs on the secessionists (Khachican 2001, p. 22). The Russian blockade on Abkhazia was lifted
in 1999 at Georgia's request.

[117] The 1998 action was to counter the White Legion and Forest Brethren paramilitary groups
(Kolstø and Blakkisrud 2008, p. 490).

The final throes of the Abkhaz-Georgian war came in April 1994 when trilateral negotiations among Georgia, Russia, and the Abkhaz led to an enduring cease-fire. Georgian troops had already begun to withdraw in August 1993, redeployed elsewhere in Georgia's civil war. Abkhaz forces performed surprisingly well on the battlefield and were well armed considering that a Georgian embargo against the region had been in place since 1989. By 1994, Abkhazia had nearly exclusive control over its territory, albeit with the Russian military's assistance.[118] Russia's intervention in Abkhazia, although ostensibly nonpartisan, effectively locked in Abkhaz authority and kept Georgia out. Sixteen hundred peacekeepers under the auspices of the Commonwealth of Independent States (CIS), arriving in June 1994, ensured that the stalemate would endure.[119]

In independent Abkhazia, leaders set about building state capacity. They established an Abkhaz-only national guard and a standing army consisting of approximately 5,000 troops by 2000.[120] Four years later, they claimed to have an army of approximately 20,000 men organized after the fashion of the Swiss, living at home but prepared for rapid mobilization to defensive positions. At the time, Defense Minister Vyacheslav Eshba bragged that Abkhazia was "always ready for war." Although the balance of power between Abkhazia and Georgia was unfavorable in 1990, by 2004, Abkhazia had a truly capable military: "We have weapons, armored equipment, aircraft, troops of every kind...We buy seagoing ships from dealers and refit them ourselves...Weapons can always be bought some way, including through third countries."[121] In general, Abkhazia's forces became more functionally independent postwar.

New Abkhaz institutions also emerged during the years of Georgian blockade. Specifically, Abkhazia came to operate its own internal administrative affairs, its own schools, and its own hospitals. However, it was unlikely that Abkhazia would continue to provide public goods at such a high level. In 2002, an expert remarked that the de facto regime in Abkhazia "maintains the daily operation of legislative, executive and judicial institutions, but performs very few services for its population." IOs and INGOs provided most social services

---

[118] The only substantial portion of Abkhaz territory not controlled by Abkhaz forces in 1993 was the upper Kodori Gorge. UNOMIG Resolution 937, in 1994, planned for troops' withdrawal from the region. Moscow supported the Abkhaz rebels with troops and military equipment. Additional fighters, mostly Russian Cossacks and other Caucasian peoples (including Chechen forces under the authority of Shamil Basayev and the Confederation of the Mountain Peoples of the Caucasus (CMPC)), helped the rebel army secure its territory. Abkhazia's forces were also backed by Russian fighter bombers in February and March 1993. Most of Abkhazia's armaments came from Russia. Georgian authorities argued the equipment came directly from Moscow, but it might just as likely have arrived via the extensive black market trade in weapons ("President Shevardnadze defends concept for strengthening state sovereignty" 1997).

[119] Again, while the peacekeepers were in Abkhazia under the auspices of the OSCE, they were all Russian troops.

[120] *The Military Balance, 2000–2001*, cited in King (2001, p. 535).

[121] "We are always ready for war" (2004).

within the republic.[122] In fact, according to one source, "international aid [was] several times larger than the budget of the breakaway state," at approximately $15 million per year.[123] The republic had no postal service and no national currency, and its hospitals were operated by foreign aid.[124] Still, there was some evidence of growth; Abkhazia's state budget doubled between 2004 and 2007.[125]

In addition to international humanitarian aid, Abkhazia's economic well-being was significantly dependent on Russia. Russia provided financial support and subsidized energy imports to Abkhazia, and Russian military bases (there despite Georgian authorities' protests) propped up the surrounding local economies.[126] Furthermore, elderly Abkhaz who were willing to take Russian citizenship were eligible to receive Russian pensions in addition to their Abkhaz ones.[127] When Tbilisi introduced its new currency, the *Kupon Lari*, in 1993, Abkhazia opted to remain within the ruble zone.

Nevertheless, experts deemed Abkhazia economically viable, judging it self-sufficient in food and energy and economically independent of Tbilisi.[128] Abkhazia's industries rebounded, too, especially agriculture and its scrap metal trade. In fact, the robberies and gang activities so pervasive throughout Georgia "[tended] to be seasonal, centered around the attempts by bandits to steal [Abkhaz] hazelnut shipments in the late summer and early autumn."[129] Similarly, in 2004, Abkhazia's tourist industry served an estimated 350,000 visitors. Although substantially below the several million who traveled to its Black Sea beaches prior to the war, the signs of rebuilding were unmistakable.[130]

Each of the newfound income streams benefited from Moscow's liberal visa regime toward the Abkhaz (and Osset) population, an advantage not afforded to ethnic Georgians.[131] Since the change, Abkhazians have acquired Russian citizenship in droves. It is estimated that some "170,000 of Abkhazia's 320,000 residents had become citizens of Russia, and 70,000 others had applications pending [by summer 2004]."[132]

---

[122] Lynch (2002, p. 836).

[123] Ibid., p. 847; see also Chivers (2004).

[124] Lynch (2002, p. 847).

[125] Kolstø and Blakkisrud (2008, p. 493).

[126] King (2004, p. 4).

[127] German (2007, p. 23) notes that the practice was not restricted to Russian passport holders prior to 2005.

[128] Cornell (2001, p. 179).

[129] King (2001, p. 537).

[130] Chivers (2004).

[131] The new visa regime was highly detrimental to the Georgian economy where "as many as 500,000 Georgians" took home between "$500 million to $1 billion a year" from Russia Frantz (2000).

[132] Chivers (2004).

Popular Legitimacy

On November 30, 1994, just after the war, Abkhazia adopted a new, independent constitution reaffirming Abkhaz sovereignty. Abkhazia's domestic politics were characterized by high levels of democratic freedom; active opposition parties; and stable, clan-based political legitimacy.[133] In its years of independence, Abkhazia created its own educational and cultural institutions including universities and new national holidays.[134] Yet Abkhaz politics were somewhat personalistic and very much centered on President Vladislav Ardzinba, the republic's first independent leader, until 2005. Sergei Bagapsh, the former prime minister, succeeded Ardzinba following a chaotic election result; violent aftermath; political realignment; and second election with Raul Khadjimba, his former rival, as vice president on the ticket.[135] Although that particular election and Ardzinba's decline caused significant political tumult, it was also evidence of Abkhazia's independence from Russia as Khadjimba had been the Moscow-backed candidate. Support for the independent Abkhaz authorities is still quite high, according to a survey of Abkhaz residents in 2010. Some 4.3 percent favored remaining within Georgia, 24.4 percent favored incorporation into Russia, and 62.6 percent favored Abkhazia's independence.[136] Furthermore, in that same survey, 73.7 percent of respondents said that things in Abkhazia were "moving in the right direction" even though their support for specific Abkhaz institutions such as the police and the laws and courts was equivocal (just under 50 percent expressed support for each).[137]

Insofar as Abkhazia's non-Abkhaz populations were concerned, an estimated 30 percent of those who died in the war of independence were not ethnically Abkhaz, indicating that there was at least some support for secession among non-Abkhaz.[138] Further, though the resettlement of Georgians remains very problematic, Abkhaz leaders claim that 70,000 Georgians had returned to Abkhazia as of 2006.[139] To be sure, some Georgians have felt safe enough to return to Abkhazia postwar.

---

[133] Skakov (2005, p. 160); Kolstø and Blakkisrud (2008, p. 499) concur that freedom of the press and civil society are relatively well developed but counter that Abkhazia's party system is not.

[134] King (2001, p. 543).

[135] Caspersen (2012).

[136] Two percent of respondents refused to answer and 6.7 percent responded it was "difficult to say" (Bakke, O'Laughlin, and Ward 2011, p. 15).

[137] Ibid., pp. 15–16.

[138] Kolstø and Blakkisrud (2008, p. 499).

[139] Fuller (2006) cited in Kolstø and Blakkisrud (2008, pp. 498–499); the authors also note that officials in Tbilisi did not agree.

PROJECTED VIABILITY

Abkhazia's economy rebounded following the war, but it remained fragile. The violence caused an estimated 500 billion rubles of damage to Abkhazia's infrastructure and housing stock. With Russian tourists returning, Abkhazia showed that its seaside resorts and beautiful scenery could still draw crowds. Yet Abkhazia received a significant amount, as much as $4 or $5 million (USD) annually according to one source, from humanitarian organizations dispatched to the war zone.[140] The de facto republic was by no means prosperous. As late as 2004, Sukhumi, Abkhazia's capital city, was still 60 percent destroyed from the war.[141] Abkhazia was politically and economically viable at a low level, but it had to resolve outstanding conflicts with Georgia to be sustainable long term.

The most important factor endangering Abkhazia's viability was not economics or politics, but its outstanding conflict with Georgia. In 13 months, the Abkhaz war killed approximately 10,000 people and left hundreds of thousands displaced within Georgia and abroad. More than 100,000 people fled Abkhazia during the war; most were ethnic Georgians who fled to other parts of Georgia. The potential repatriation of ethnic Georgians, once the most populous ethnic group within Abkhazia, remained a contentious matter between the regime and Georgian authorities, who also created a regime-in-exile in Abkhazia:

Since the war, the Georgian government has subsidized structures of government for "Abkhazia in exile." Tbilisi supports an executive council of the Autonomous Republic of Abkhazia, which has 25 delegates and a supreme presidium. The ethnically Georgian government-in-exile maintains eleven ministries, thirteen state committees, nine general offices and five inspectorates.[142]

Additionally, the Saakashvili regime was approaching the secessionists in an increasingly assertive manner in the latter 2000s. In September 2006, Georgian forces took the Kodori Gorge that, though in Abkhazia, had been under the autonomous control of the Svan community. Zayavlenie reported that the Abkhaz believed that the action might have been a "test balloon" for taking back Abkhazia altogether.[143] With the benefit of hindsight, they might have been right. Finally, continuing Georgian sanctions left Abkhazia's economy, once among the most prosperous, severely depressed.

---

[140] The income comes from rents, services, and the organizations' payments to local staff. Interview with anonymous United Nations Office for the Coordination of Humanitarian Assistance official, cited in King (2001, p. 549).

[141] Chivers (2004).

[142] Lynch (2002, p. 844).

[143] cited in Kolstø and Blakkisrud (2008, p. 489).

DOMESTIC SOVEREIGNTY IN SOUTH OSSETIA, 1992–2008

South Ossetia's conflict with Georgia had fewer human and material costs than the other post-Soviet secessions. But even though South Ossetia was spared some of the destruction visited on the other post-Soviet secessionists, it was not able to parlay that advantage into a sustainable economic and governmental regime. Widespread violence did not reemerge in de facto independent South Ossetia, but it remained dependent on North Ossetia and Russia with little prospect for sustainable authority because of its lack of economic potential. In 2004, the Sochi Agreement broke down into violence, but it was quickly replaced by a new cease-fire that August. Still, South Ossetian control became increasingly tenuous when the Saakashvili regime entered office, as it enacted increasingly assertive policies there. Nevertheless, the regime remained extraordinarily popular among Ossets on both sides of the Russo-Georgian border.

Territorial Control and Effective Authority

South Ossetians' disadvantage before the war was greater than the imbalance of capabilities between Abkhazia and Georgia. Just after declaring independence, South Ossetia "mobilized all men between the ages of 18 and 60 [from its population of 99,000]" in preparation for the Georgian offensive.[144] An estimated 17,000 Georgian troops were involved in the siege of Tskhinvali (South Ossetia's capital) alone.[145] Ossetians did not so much win the war against Georgia as Georgia defeated itself. Once the Sochi Agreement had been signed, and durable peace had set in, the Ossets had uncontested physical, though not political, control over their territory. But the territorial claim was quite complicated. South Ossetia claimed only about 85 percent of the territory within the former AO. The 15 percent that it did not claim consisted mostly of Georgian villages. This created a twisting and turning permeable border that was difficult to defend.[146]

South Ossetia had created its own national guard when Tbilisi decided to form a military in its bid for secession in 1991.[147] Its standing army had troops that numbered around 2,000 in 2000.[148] The South Ossetian military received support from its North Ossetian kin in the form of military equipment and armaments. The de facto government also attempted to form economic and diplomatic relations with friendly regimes so as to establish an independent foreign policy consistent with Montevideo.[149]

---

[144] "South Ossetia mobilizes" (1991).
[145] "South Ossetia forms national guard" (1991).
[146] Kolstø and Blakkisrud (2008, p. 492).
[147] Ibid.
[148] *The Military Balance, 2000–2001*, cited in King (2001, p. 535).
[149] Potier (2001, p.137); on November 9, 1996, for example, the South Ossetian government signed a treaty of "friendship and cooperation" with North Ossetia.

Georgia's blockade of South Ossetia was especially disastrous to its economy. In winter, with impassable roads, South Ossetia was completely cut off from Russia, its major source of both trade and foreign aid. In February 1991, during the war, Georgia had cut off both water and electricity. Minorities at Risk reported that, in August 1995, some workers in South Ossetia had not been paid for more than two years as a result of poor economic conditions within the republic.[150] South Ossetia was without major industry to speak of, but its location along a major conduit of trade between Georgia and Russia was an important source of income for the regime. The OSCE estimated that as of 2004 "some $60-$70 million in goods pass through the tunnel [between North and South Ossetia] each year, compared with the official South Ossetian budget of roughly $1 million."[151] South Ossetia, also like Abkhazia, had many Russian passport holders who received Russian pensions as well as pensions from the secessionist authorities.[152]

Early in its de facto independence, during the Shevardnadze years, relations between the secessionists and their home state were stable. South Ossetian President Lyudvig Chibirov met directly with Shevardnadze on multiple occasions and negotiated agreements on matters ranging from economics to policing.[153] However, relations shifted precipitously under Saakashvili who, among other things, in 2004, put a stop to an illegal South Ossetian roadside taxation operation along one of only two roads linking Georgia to Russia across the Caucasus mountains, a practice that had, until then, been a significant source of income.[154] Generally, South Ossetia's economic situation worsened in the later 2000s, though, as of 2008, very few specific figures were publicly available to indicate the territory's economic well-being.[155]

Popular Legitimacy

In South Ossetia, much like Abkhazia, educational and cultural institutions were among the first undertakings of the new regime. Popular elections held in South Ossetia received wide participation within the electorate but were not recognized by Georgia or other outside authorities. Though popular authority seems to reside with the secessionist regime, it remains unclear whether the average South Ossetian's goal is independent statehood or reintegration with North Ossetian kin in Russia. Still, support for independence became stronger as Georgia's policies became more assertive.

---

[150] "Chronology for Ossetians (South) in Georgia" (2004).
[151] Ibid.
[152] Kolstø and Blakkisrud (2008, p. 497).
[153] Ibid., 2008, p. 492.
[154] Ibid., 2008, p. 497.
[155] Ibid.

On November 12, 2006, South Ossetia held a second popular referendum returning a vote 99.9 percent in favor of independence. During the same elections, the third such presidential election in South Ossetia, 98 percent of voters reelected Eduard Kokoity as president. At the same time, there was a counter-referendum in the former AO's Georgian-controlled areas. And in April the following year, Saakashvili recognized the counter-regime as legitimate representatives with whom Georgia would negotiate a settlement for South Ossetia.[156] According to an interview with a South Ossetian woman, relations between Ossets and Georgians were deteriorating:

Memories of that pre-war era are fading fast. "We used to live pretty well with Georgia. We were peaceful neighbors," said Lamsira, a 30ish Ossetian woman, married to a Georgian and the mother of two elementary-school-age boys, who sells beer out of her house in Tskhinvali. "But the younger generation does not know them as neighbors, but as enemies, because they've seen so many murders and killings."[157]

Projected Viability

Though reliable data were difficult to come by, South Ossetia had the least prospective viability of the Caucasian secessionists because of its economic situation and dependence on Russia. Even though its conflict with Georgia was the smallest of the post-Soviet secessions, South Ossetia's potential economic independence was low at the end of the war and remained low in the years to follow.[158] The government, too reliant on aid and trade with North Ossetia, had no developed industry to speak of; did not have its own currency; and was unable to support a sustainable, independent economy. Additionally, Georgia never offered South Ossetia autonomy equivalent to what it offered Abkhazia; the government insisted that South Ossetia remain within Georgia.[159] And whereas support for independence was strong among Ossets, there was significantly less support for the secessionist agenda among Georgians living in the former AO, and in the latter 2000s, those Georgians were increasingly confrontational with the separatist regime.

---

[156] Ibid., 2008, p. 504.
[157] Owen (2006).
[158] Cornell (2002, p. 190).
[159] President Saakashvili offered autonomy to South Ossetia early in 2005. He proposed that South Ossetia control education, cultural policy (including language), and public order, and Tbilisi would control security, defense, foreign policy, and fiscal policy (Buckley and Ostrovsky 2005). South Ossetian leaders declined his offer; it would have significantly reduced South Ossetian sovereignty.

DOMESTIC SOVEREIGNTY IN NAGORNO-KARABAKH, 1994–2011

Nagorno-Karabakh's sovereignty situation was somewhat different from that of the other Caucasian secessions because of its close relationship with its Armenian benefactor. Armenian politics were significantly more intertwined with NK than Russia's with South Ossetia or Abkhazia. The Karabakh Armenians displayed a relatively high level of domestic sovereignty but, like the South Ossetians, their desire for independence was not clearly demonstrated, as they were slow to create fully independent institutions. Nevertheless, Nagorno-Karabakh reasonably met the standards for statehood. NK prevailed in a war of independence, it convincingly controlled the territory and population it claimed, and its governing regime had a relatively high degree of popular legitimacy. Again like South Ossetia, however, Nagorno-Karabakh's economic and political solvency were not guaranteed. NK's geographic location, surrounded on all sides by Azerbaijan, would make it difficult to maintain territorial sovereignty if it returned the Azerbaijani territories connecting it to Armenia.[160] Additionally, and related to the first problem, hundreds of thousands of Azeris remain displaced because of the Karabakh Armenians' ongoing occupation of their lands, and the outstanding conflict still has the potential to be highly disruptive to Armenian control in Karabakh. Internally displaced persons (IDP) numbers are substantially higher than those of Georgians displaced from Abkhazia and a frequent political propaganda tool for the regime in Baku.

Territorial Control and Effective Authority

Following the cessation of hostilities among Azerbaijan, the Nagorno-Karabakh Armenians, and Armenia in the spring 1994, NK had secured uncontested effective control and authority. To date, NK demonstrates greater territorial control than the other secessionists. The Karabakh Armenians occupy and control approximately 12 percent of Azerbaijan in addition to the territory they claim for their new republic, effectively creating a buffer zone connecting Nagorno-Karabakh to Armenia.[161] NK leaders attempted to use the additional territory as a bargaining chip, offering the territory's return in exchange for recognition and independence. So far, that strategy has not yielded fruit. Also, given that the de facto regime in Karabakh is a military regime, the level of control and authority it maintains over the population is decisive.

Armenia and NK have a number of functional linkages but are not politically integrated. Indeed, some suggest that it is the Karabakh Armenians who influence Armenia proper, not the other way around. Armenian Deputy Prime

---

[160] Those territories include Kelbajan, Gubadly, Zangilan, Jabrayil, and part of Fizuli and Agdam.
[161] In 1994, Armenian forces controlled approximately 14 percent of Azerbaijan, only 5 percent of which was claimed by Nagorno-Karabakh.

Minister Leonard Petrosyan was previously the president of Nagorno-Karabakh, for example. Moreover, Karabakh politics play an important role in Armenian politics. Armenian President Levon Ter-Petrossian was forced to resign in 1998, in part because he was too willing to compromise on the issue of Nagorno-Karabakh.

In 1995, NK established redevelopment and economic reform plans for the republic, strengthening its claim as the effective government, independent of both Azerbaijan and Armenia. Its economic redevelopment and liberalization during the 2000s was particularly strong.[162] One observer noted that in 2007, despite the significant damage during the war, "downtown Stepanakert [was] almost completely rebuilt."[163]

Still, Karabakh's governance might be questioned because of its failure to create independent institutions. For instance, rather than implementing its own currency, Karabakh has adopted the Armenian *dram* as its monetary unit. Further, NK did not adopt an independent constitution until December 2006.

Popular Legitimacy

Support for Nagorno-Karabakh's de facto regime was strong among the Karabakh Armenians. In May 1995, open and reportedly fair elections were held for Karabakh's parliament. Turnout was 71 percent and nearly 80 percent in two respective rounds of voting.[164] This high participation rate suggests that the Karabakh Armenians supported the secessionist government, at least insofar as they viewed the Karabakh elections as a legitimate means of political expression. The July 2007 presidential election also had high turnout, at around 77 percent. Significant progress toward democracy within NK was made during its independence; still, the homogeneity of its population and the lack of a truly contested political space with an active opposition limited the credibility of its claim to be a liberal government.

Within Armenia, popular support for an irredentist claim to Nagorno-Karabakh was far greater than it was with its leaders. The Armenian government did not claim Nagorno-Karabakh for itself, nor did it recognize Azerbaijan's authority over the territory.[165] Instead, the government insisted that NK's declaration of independence granted it a status equivalent to, but separate from, Azerbaijan. Yet Armenian authorities did not recognize Nagorno-Karabakh's statehood. According to one expert, Nagorno-Karabakh was so

---

[162] Kolstø and Blakkisrud (2008, p. 495).

[163] Ibid. Though the authors go on to say that the rebuilding was geographically constrained to the city.

[164] As a result, Russian parliamentary figures began to call on Azerbaijan to extend full diplomatic recognition to Nagorno-Karabakh in order to bring the conflict between the two to a resolution. Higher-level Russian authorities did not make the same proposal.

[165] The Armenian government agreed as early as September 23, 1991, to renounce territorial claims to Karabakh.

important to the Armenian populace across the border because it allowed them to create a more desirable national identity. Whereas the old national narrative was one of "victimization" from the Armenian genocide, NK's success shifted the narrative to "self-defense" and "victory."[166] As a result, the Armenian people were and remain invested in the fates of those in NK. And this was not only important psychologically; numerous tangible benefits transferred from the Armenian diaspora into Nagorno-Karabakh.

Projected Viability

Nagorno-Karabakh's internal stability is likely to remain for the foreseeable future; indeed, it has persevered for more than 20 years so far. In that sense, the state is viable. On the other hand, the regime depends on Armenia for monetary support and military control. For example, Armenia provides an "'interstate loan' to NK that covers 75–80 percent of its needs [each year]."[167] The Azeri blockade and embargo of Nagorno-Karabakh, which began in 1989, also strongly impacted the local economy. The final impediment to Karabakh's viability is the additional, occupied territories. The situation presents a catch-22 of sorts because Karabakh's internal viability is imperiled without a durable, territorial connection to Armenia and its external viability is imperiled so long as hundreds of thousands of Azeris remain displaced from their homes within the occupied territories. NK can likely survive under the current conditions, but the status quo conditions are undesirable long term.

One other factor deserves mention regarding viability – Azerbaijan's increased military spending and military posture toward NK. Recent years have raised fears of preventive Armenian war over NK because, although Armenia's military is currently more capable than Azerbaijan's, it may not remain that way for long.[168] In 2009, Azerbaijan's defense budget was $1.4 billion USD, more than three times Armenia's.[169] Furthermore, Azerbaijan no longer accepts NK leaders' participation in peace talks – it is willing to deal only with Armenia.[170]

EXTERNAL INFLUENCE AND INDIFFERENCE

Great Power responses to the post-Soviet secessions varied from movement to movement and power to power. Initially, all of the Great Powers besides Russia abstained from diplomatic or military intervention in the conflicts. The wars were already seen as domestic conflicts, subject only to the young home states

---

[166] Kolstø and Blakkisrud (2008, p. 501).
[167] Lynch (2002, p. 847).
[168] German (2007).
[169] International Institute for Strategic Studies (IISS) (2010).
[170] Caspersen (2008).

and not under the purview of external actors. Great Power leaders were aware that the conflicts might conflagrate into war but took little preventive action.[171] The European powers, the United States, and Russia were critical of the home states' excessively violent responses to the uprisings. However, little more than strong language was brought to bear to stop it.

After the Soviet Union fell, international politics surrounding the secessions shifted. As the conflicts evolved into full-scale wars, the noninterventionist stance maintained by the Great Powers became untenable. The United States and the European powers were suspicious of Russian involvement in the periphery, believing its actions betrayed neo-imperial ambitions. Russia, for its part, developed concerns about the American and European powers' encroachment into its sphere of influence. The Great Powers' past hands-off approach was replaced with engagement and intervention.

The UNSC initiated peacekeeping in Abkhazia, whereas the OSCE played the primary mediating role in Nagorno-Karabakh and South Ossetia.[172] OSCE observers were dispatched to Chechnya as a result of Russia's membership within the organization, but they were later expelled by Moscow and did not return. The international organizations entrusted with maintaining peace in the secessionist regions reflected the external actors engaged in each conflict. Abkhazia attracted the most international attention and interest in its resolution. Europe and Russia took the lead in Nagorno-Karabakh and South Ossetia. And, though there was certainly interest in the Russo-Chechen conflict, Russia prevented much external involvement. Russia, the United States, and the European powers were far more involved in the politics surrounding the post-Soviet secessions than were China or Japan. Though, as in Yugoslavia, China had influence through its role as a permanent member of the UNSC. Among the active powers, Russia and the United States have engaged strategically in the conflicts themselves, whereas the European powers primarily pursued multilateral negotiations.

RUSSIA

Russia was the single most important Great Power player in each of the post-Soviet secessions because of its historical or continuing role as a home state. Its most direct role was that of the home state in the Chechen conflict, though it was centrally involved in the initiation and cessation of hostilities in all of the

---

[171] Lapidus (1998, p. 24) notes regarding Chechnya that "The international community had available to them ample early warning that the conflict was escalating, as well as a broad array of possible responses, but...timely and appropriate responses were not adopted before the intervention by Russian military forces."

[172] The United Nations became involved in Abkhazia at Georgia's request. Tbilisi initially asked Russia to intervene to quell the violence but later decried Moscow's pro-Abkhaz bias. As a result, it asked the UN to take a more active role.

Caucasus wars.[173] Russian interests were importantly intertwined with the fates of the secessionists and the home states. Once Russian authorities reestablished stability within Russia proper following Soviet disintegration, they began working to ensure that their priorities in the near-abroad were met. Russian policy toward Abkhazia oscillated between support for the breakaway republic and its Georgian home state, depending on the perceived friendliness of the Georgian regime in power at the time. Russia's support for the South Ossetians, whom it saw as rightfully Russian, was unequivocal. Finally, Moscow's position on Karabakh was somewhat unclear. Russia wanted Azerbaijan to join the CIS and so courted its favor at times by supporting its efforts in Karabakh. At the same time, Russia was often at loggerheads with Azerbaijan as a result of Caspian oil and its perceived pro-Western orientation. Though importantly engaged in Karabakh, Russian interests were somewhat less at stake there than in Georgia.

South Ossetia and Abkhazia

At the time of its intervention in Georgia, Russia itself was not a unitary actor. At the highest levels, Yeltsin and Russia's Supreme Soviet were making their own independent policies toward the North Caucasus.[174] Likewise, in the field, remnants of Soviet forces determined their own actions within the separatist republics. Regardless, Russia was influential from the start. According to King, "whether prompted by the whim of brigade commanders or by a policy directive of Moscow, Soviet armed forces, later to become Russian Federation troops, were the main suppliers of weaponry (and often soldiers) to [the] separatist groups."[175] The flows of weapons and military equipment from the Former Soviet Union were essential to supplying both the secessionists and their home states during the wars. Whereas the home states could have legally procured the arms, the secessionists would have been much weaker without the illicit supplies. Moscow might not have been responsible for many of its initial violations of Georgian sovereignty because of its own lack of central control. By early in 1993, however, when the Russian Federation dispatched peacekeeping troops to South Ossetia and Abkhazia, the state had reconsolidated its power and conducted a more unified foreign policy.

Russian leaders made no secret of their intention to unilaterally intervene in Georgia, even without the support of the international community. In fact, Russian peacekeepers were dispatched before any international peacekeeping

---

[173] Because Russia's role within the Chechen conflict is that of a home state, its anti-recognition stance is left unexplored except in that capacity (though Russia's status as a Great Power certainly influenced other states' recognition behavior toward Chechnya). In the other secessionist conflicts, Russia's behavior constituted an important external political influence.

[174] Ozhiganov (1997, p. 391).

[175] King (2001, p. 539).

missions had been established. According to one expert at the time, "The UN [found] itself in the delicate situation of facing requests for international legitimization of decisions taken by others."[176] In fact, Russian peacekeeping forces became outright combatants in South Ossetia's conflict after they were fired on by Georgian troops, foretelling their future conflict there. Intervention in the post-Soviet states was not uniquely under Russia's purview, as would be aptly demonstrated in Karabakh, but Russia was the most important and active power in the region. The other Great Powers allowed Russia disproportionate influence over the conflicts because of its special interest, at first. Consequently, both the Georgian government and the rebels came to calculate their behavior with an eye toward Russia's response.

Russian policies in Georgia were a mixed blessing for both sides. On one hand, Russian peacekeepers did help quell the violence between Georgia and the secessionists. On the other hand, Russia was not an impartial arbiter, and its policies often served to increase hostilities and suspicion between the parties. Yeltsin seemed to support Georgia's territorial integrity over Abkhaz independence initially.[177] He reassured Georgian leaders that Russian troops had been dispatched to Abkhazia in order to maintain the peace, nothing more. As time wore on, though, it became clear that Russia had its own interests at heart, rather than altruistic concerns for Georgian stability. Speaking of the problem in South Ossetia, Georgian President Saakashvili, "declared that there is 'no Ossetian problem in Georgia', but 'a problem in Georgian-Russian relations with respect to certain territories.'"[178] Apparently, he had determined that Russia was the principal problem, not the secessionist Ossets.

Russia had significant interests at stake in the near-abroad. Georgia, in particular, held not only two restive separatist regions with favorable views of Moscow, but in Abkhazia, warm water ports on the Black Sea. The ports were strategically and economically attractive. Indeed, Russia only agreed to send peacekeepers to intervene in Georgia conditional on Georgia giving Russia permission to establish military bases there. Moscow maintains an overtly strategic posture there to date.[179]

Between Georgia's two separatist conflicts, Russian support was somewhat stronger for South Ossetia. The Ossets were ethnically and ideologically more similar to Russia than Georgia. Ossetians also saw Russia as their potential future home state. So, not only did Russia have strong identity relations with the Ossets, it stood to increase its territorial control, or at least its influence, if the South Ossetians won independence. In contrast, even though Russia was generally supportive of Abkhazia, its support was more opportunistic and economic

[176] MacFarlane (1997, p. 511).
[177] In a September 3 address, Yeltsin called for Georgia's unity and territorial integrity.
[178] Cited in German (2007, p. 363).
[179] Russia agreed during a meeting of the OSCE in Istanbul, Turkey, in October 1999 to close the Georgian bases.

rather than the result of a consistent interest in Abkhaz independence. Abkhazia and Russia had friendly relations, and Russia routinely violated Georgia's embargo of the region, but Moscow supported Georgia, too, rarely wavering from its insistence that its territorial integrity should be maintained.

Russian support for the secessionists did not arise entirely unprovoked. The Georgian government was also somewhat antagonistic toward Russia, giving Moscow additional justification for backing its challengers. Tbilisi's policies created a dual geostrategic and domestic security concern for Russia. Georgia complicated Russia's conflict with Chechnya by permitting Chechen fighters to enter Georgian territory to evade Russian authorities. Russia also accused Georgian authorities of supplying Chechen fighters with weapons they had procured with the fall of the Soviet Union. Russia believed its own weapons were being used against it in Chechnya.[180] The Georgian government was using the "external security logic" against Russia, attempting to weaken Russia from within by supporting its secessionists. Georgian authorities, for their part, denied aiding and abetting the Chechens, but their claims were not entirely credible. By August 2002, tensions between Russia and Georgia flared into violent conflict. Georgia accused Russia of bombing incursions within Georgian territory west of the Pankisi Gorge. Though denied by Russian authorities, OSCE observers later confirmed Russian responsibility for the bombings.[181] Ultimately, Tbilisi acquiesced to Moscow and arrested a number of Chechen separatists in the region.

Russia played both sides insofar as international law was concerned. It consistently favored a negotiated settlement between Georgia and the secessionists but simultaneously erected some of the largest barriers to compromise. Moscow has also openly flouted traditional practices of international law to the secessionist states' advantage. In 2000, for example, Russia imposed harsh visa restrictions on Georgia. But the standards were not enforced at border crossings with South Ossetia or Abkhazia, affording the secessionists extensive freedom of movement and economic opportunity.[182] Further, Russia eased restrictions on Georgian minorities becoming Russian citizens, not only allowing them to travel more freely, but also providing pensioners with the same benefits a Russian citizen would receive. Finally, Russia's military bases within Georgia, which it agreed to close, remained in place.[183]

The September 11, 2001, terrorist attacks in the United States renewed American interest in Islamism and the unstable, potential terrorist safe havens in the Russian periphery. Since then, Russian authorities have become increasingly suspicious of U.S. intentions in Eurasia. In 2002, American troops arrived

---

[180] Myers (2002b).

[181] Myers (2002a).

[182] Lynch (2002, p. 846); King (2001, p. 541).

[183] King (2004, p. 3). Two Soviet Era bases within Georgia were closed in 2007, but reinforced bases in the separatist enclaves were agreed upon when Russia established full diplomatic relations in 2008 ("Russia to Boost Abkhazia Bases" 2009).

in Georgia to train Georgian military personnel in counterterrorism techniques. In addition, American leaders confessed a special "affection" for Georgian Presidents Shevardnadze and Saakashvili. Saakashvili, who became president in 2003, was educated in the United States and was reform minded. Shevardnadze, against all evidence to the contrary, was also believed to be a liberalizing force. In Moscow, the seemingly sudden American interest in Georgia generated suspicions that the United States was manipulating Georgia's political process. One member of the Russian leadership remarked in 2003, "Time will show whose interests will be guiding the new Georgian leadership [under Saakashvili] – the interests of the United States or the Georgian people."[184] U.S. officials assured Russian decision makers that their presence in Georgia was purely in the interest of maintaining peace and security within the state and, further, that Georgian stability would benefit Russia in its conflict with Chechnya.[185] Those assurances rang hollow in Moscow, perhaps because Russian leaders had repeated a similar justification for their own policies in Georgia. Russo-Georgian-U.S. relations were especially fraught during 2006 and 2007. Saakashvili's government became more assertive with the secessionists, including recognizing an alternative, pro-Tbilisi regime in South Ossetia. At the same time, Georgia was entering into talks regarding NATO membership and leaders in Western capitals seemed to turn a blind eye to the huge popular protests demanding that Saakashvili step down because of corruption.

Domestic opinion within Russia favored support and recognition for the separatist states in both Georgia and Azerbaijan. Russian officers were even known to have defected in order to support the military efforts in the secessionist states.[186] Again as in Yugoslavia, Russian policy was more moderate than public opinion alone would have suggested.

Nagorno-Karabakh

Like Georgia, the new Azeri government's pro-Western orientation stymied Russia's plans for overwhelming influence in the near-abroad. Moscow was importantly involved in the Karabakh war on the Azeri side, and Russia had brokered the NK cease-fire. Consequently, Russian decision makers expected Azerbaijan would join the CIS and acquiesce to Russian policy preferences in the region. But the Azeris chose a more independent course and were often critical of Moscow's policies. Much of Russian diplomacy was, therefore, focused on bringing Azerbaijan back into the Russian sphere of influence, whether with positive inducements or negative sanctions. Russian preferences toward Nagorno-Karabakh reflected Moscow's greater strategy toward Azerbaijan;

---

[184] Mydans (2003).
[185] Weisman (2004).
[186] King (2001).

the specter of NK independence was only sparingly invoked as a tool for Russian influence.

In that vein, Russia consistently preferred an exclusively Russian peacekeeping force for NK to maintain its primacy, but the OSCE rejected this request. The United States and others countered by allowing Russia (under the guise of the CIS) to supply one-third of the peacekeepers. Experiences in Bosnia had deterred any other Great Power's provision of troops. Russia rejected the West's counter offer, so no peacekeepers were deployed at all; the Karabakh Armenians were left with a peacekeeping mission without peacekeepers.

Through 2001, "Russia [continued] to place considerable pressure on Azerbaijan to join the defense arrangements of the CIS, thus allowing them to station Russian military forces in Azerbaijan. President Aliyev... requested assistance from Turkey, the OSCE and the United States in resisting these pressures."[187] Nevertheless, Azeri reticence to accept Moscow's preferences did not translate into strong Russian support of Nagorno-Karabakh.

Russian interests in the secessionist conflicts suggested that Russia preferred recognition to maintenance of the home states' sovereignty for at least two of the three separatist regions. Russian support was especially strong for Georgia's separatists. Formal recognition was withheld, however, as a function of the unambiguous opposition of Western governments, which Moscow was now attempting to productively engage as it transitioned away from the Cold War and toward more liberal democratic government. It was also, perhaps, a result of Russia's own troubles with Chechnya during the 1990s. By 2006, however, most of that domestic security concern had been alleviated, and yet Russia maintained nonrecognition and support for negotiated settlements even after the various Kosovo recognitions in 2008.

THE UNITED STATES

Unlike Russia, American interests were decidedly opposed to the post-Soviet secessions. U.S. relationships with their home states or, more accurately, potential relationships with the home states were too great a sacrifice in the name of support for self-determination and (possibly) democracy. Georgia and, to a lesser extent, Azerbaijan emerged from the Soviet Union with decidedly pro-Western orientations, and those pro-Western views and policy preferences were important to the United States in the wake of Soviet disintegration. They held the possibility of oil resources, strategic footholds in the Caucasus, and later as allies in the war on terror. Similarly, American authorities believed Yeltsin to be a staunch reformer. So although Russia was not a democratic, pro-American ally, it was initially seen as inexorably moving toward that end. The conflict in Chechnya, troubling though it was, threatened to destabilize the Russian Federation and halt Russia's progress. None of the prospective gains to be

---

[187] Minorities at Risk (2009).

made in the post-Soviet states suggested the United States would support the secessionists. Self-determination, heralded as the Soviet Union disbanded, went virtually unmentioned in reference to the secessions in Azerbaijan, Georgia, or Russia.

As time went on, and the secessions became protracted, American support became even stauncher, especially in Georgia. In fact, the United States vocally decried Russian aggression at the outset of the Five Day War even though American intelligence suggested that Georgia had reinitiated the fighting.

Chechnya

The United States supported Russia's territorial integrity but objected to Moscow's means of reasserting control over Chechnya. Fortunately for Moscow, Chechnya was not at the top of the list of U.S. interests regarding Russia. Instead, America's own security interests and ambitions were primary. NATO expansion was planned, the United States needed Russia's support for its missile defense system, and the Clinton administration hoped the Russians would ratify the START II treaty.[188] U.S. policy sought to maintain amicable relations with Russia while calling for restraint and respect for human rights in Chechnya.

Even diplomatic criticism was muted because of Washington's friendly attitude toward Yeltsin and what was perceived to be his democratization project in Russia. Warren Christopher, then secretary of state, said Russia's military campaign in Chechnya was "ill-conceived and badly executed," but he blamed Yeltsin's aides rather than Yeltsin for the failure; they had given him bad advice.[189] Again, Christopher supported Yeltsin's instincts, "It's best in such matters to leave it to the judgment of President Yeltsin; it's a democratic society; it's not the old Cold War. I'm sure he thought through what he was doing before he did it...when he felt he had no other alternative."[190]

U.S. criticism of Russian tactics in Chechnya did not indicate support for Chechen independence. The regime ascending to power in the North Caucasus was no more desirable than the Russian government it would replace. One American expert remarked at the time, "Many of the [Chechen] leaders are gangsters. To argue for our [democratic] ideals would reinforce mob leadership...Thomas Paine produces Al Capone."[191] Other experts indicated contrarily that the U.S. lack of support for Chechen independence hinged not on the regime's criminality, but on its Islamism and potential to spur additional

---

[188] START II aimed to reduce the number of long-range warheads on either side to fewer than 3,500.
[189] Raum (1995).
[190] Interview with Secretary of State Warren Christopher, *McNeil-Lehrer News Hour* aired December 13, 1994.
[191] Les Gelb, cited in Schweid (1995).

separatism.[192] In either case, the United States saw its relationship with Russia as more friendly than that with the Chechens.

Perceptions of Russia shifted somewhat precipitously after the fall of the Soviet Union. Secretary Christopher's statement that Russia was a "democratic society" and this was no longer the "old Cold War" indicates the extent of the change in Washington's perceptions of Moscow. Similarly, American leaders drew parallels between the American Civil War and the Russian war in Chechnya. Again, U.S. decision makers saw a Western, democratic leader in Yeltsin; he was trying to hold on to Chechnya as Lincoln had held on to the Confederacy during the American Civil War.[193] Interestingly, Gorbachev had compared his own situation to Lincoln's in 1990–1991 when he opposed Baltic independence, but Gorbachev's protest fell on deaf ears.[194] Just five years later, Yeltsin was embraced as a champion for democratic leadership.

It was true that Yeltsin was democratically elected, but Russian democracy was far from consolidated. If these perspectives are taken as evidence of Washington's view of Russia, they reflected future aspirations for Russia's domestic politics rather than the reality in the mid-1990s. For the entire period leading up to the second Russo-Chechen war, U.S. interests in Russia's future, and the potential material benefits to be gained from that future, subdued American criticism of Russia and made Chechen recognition highly unlikely. Moreover, Chechnya did not possess the oil or other valuable commodities that might have made recognition more attractive.

South Ossetia and Abkhazia

The United States did not recognize Georgian independence at first because of the chaos surrounding its civil war and Washington's uncertainty about Georgia's democratic aspirations. American leaders quickly abandoned their attempt at conditional recognition for the post-Soviet states, however, in exchange for the more immediate gains in U.S. security and economic interests there. Georgia's decidedly pro-Western orientation promised access to Caspian oil and support for American military initiatives such as the expansion of NATO and the Iraq War. Later, in the early 2000s, Georgia's geography made it an important staging location for U.S. counterterrorism efforts in Central Asia. South Ossetia and Abkhazia claimed democratic aspirations, which might have drawn U.S. sympathy, but so did Georgia. Supporting the secessionists would only contribute to further Georgian instability and offered no potential rewards.

The United States supported Georgia early, beginning during its secession from the Soviet Union. U.S. officials first implied that Georgian recognition depended on Gamsakhurdia's regime improving human rights conditions within

---

[192] Rumer (2002, p. 63).
[193] Lapidus (1998, pp. 34–35).
[194] Ibid.

the republic. But their threat was not credible.[195] At that time, Georgia was an attractive ally because of its pro-Western orientation. Since then, even when Georgia's democratic bona fides were in question, American support remained strong. Following the Georgian civil war, Washington initially supported Shevardnadze, hoping he was a genuine democratic reformer. Corruption, however, was endemic. Once it was clear Shevardnadze was not what the United States had hoped for, it and many U.S. NGOs shifted their support (and bankrolls) to the opposition. As noted before, U.S. engagement fueled Russian suspicions.

As of 2004, the United States had donated a billion dollars in aid to Georgia for the promotion of democracy and development since Georgian independence.[196] American troops trained the Georgian military. Additional American funds flowed to Georgia to stem the growth of Islamic militarism in the Caucasus as part of the war on terror. Over the years, Georgian stability has become vital to U.S. interests in the region. American strategic interests in Central Asia and interests in the East-West energy corridor make them believe Georgia is the centerpiece to stability within the Caucasus.[197] The United States maintains only a limited military presence in Georgia. However, its role there is not without controversy. One of the U.S.-financed military training facilities is near South Ossetia and provoked suspicions of U.S. intentions within the Ossetian community.[198]

Supporters of U.S. policies in Georgia see a triumph in Georgia's peaceful coup (in 2003) and genuine democratic aspirations. But according to Charles King, Georgia might also be seen as a cautionary tale. What the United States created in Georgia might be characterized as a Potemkin democracy. Underneath the veneer of democratic reforms was a deeply fractured state and society. Georgia's borders are not established, nor are its sovereign authorities. Indeed, Georgia might have most appropriately been termed a failed state.[199] But U.S. interests in Georgia were entrenched early on and were unlikely to shift toward the secessionists.

Nagorno-Karabakh

Like Georgia, the U.S. relationship with Azerbaijan is reasonably amicable, making its recognition of Nagorno-Karabakh unlikely from the beginning. At independence, the Azeri government became an important political ally of the United States on a variety of important issues. Even though U.S.-Azeri relations benefited American interests in the region, their relationship is one of strange

[195] "Russia condemns rights violations in Georgia; Georgia creates army" (1991).
[196] More precisely, between $1.2 billion and $1.3 billion (Chivers, 2004); Mydans (2003).
[197] Smith (2004).
[198] Ostrovsky (2005).
[199] King (2004).

bedfellows. The United States and Azerbaijan share little in common beyond their policy preferences. Indeed, American leaders often seem uncomfortable with their decision to pursue economic and strategic interests while sacrificing their supposed dedication to democracy, human rights, and self-determination. U.S. decision makers voiced criticisms of the manner in which Azerbaijan waged its political battles against the Armenian civilians of NK and imposed economic sanctions on Azerbaijan pending the removal of its sanctions of Nagorno-Karabakh. Still, recognition did not come, nor does it seem more likely for the foreseeable future.

By the mid-1990s, Caspian oil was an important American interest in the Caucasus. Its interest was shared, however, by a number of other states as well, namely Russia, Iran, Turkey, Georgia, Azerbaijan, and Greece. The struggle over oil and oil transport took the form of two competing alliances. On one side were the United States, Turkey, Azerbaijan, Georgia, Kazakhstan, and Chechnya. On the other were Russia, Iran, Armenia, Greece, Turkmenistan, Georgia's secessionists, and the Armenians of Nagorno-Karabakh.[200] So, not only did the United States not have economic or strategic reasons to support the secessionists, it actually stood to lose oil access if the separatists gained legitimate control over the resource; all of the secessionists but the Chechens sided with Russia when it came to oil.

Azeri authorities supported the Western alliance regarding oil, and they lent military support to the U.S.-led invasions of Iraq and Afghanistan: "Azerbaijan also grants overflight rights to the American military and is cooperating with a Pentagon-sponsored modernization of a former Soviet airfield that could be used by American military planes."[201] Though the Azeri regime is not democratic, U.S. leaders have overlooked the state's governmental shortcomings in favor of strategic access and energy resources. In any case, Karabakh is seen as similarly authoritarian, provoking little sympathy from American decision makers on its behalf, despite increasing commitments to democratic reforms within the territory that NK leaders believe are important to securing American support.[202] And although Azeri authorities were suspicious of U.S. intentions because of its large domestic Armenian lobby and significant foreign aid to Armenia in the early 2000s, the lobby does not appear to have had much impact on Washington's policies vis-à-vis the conflict.

Domestic politics within the United States remained as they were throughout the Yugoslav secessions. Though the United States had domestic challengers, they were neither strong nor violent and, therefore, played no role in the post-Soviet recognition decisions. An active Armenian lobby rallied some support for Nagorno-Karabakh within Congress, but its influence was limited essentially to a greater provision of humanitarian aid to Karabakh.

---

[200] Minorities at Risk (2009).
[201] Chivers (2006).
[202] Caspersen (2011, pp. 343–344).

THE EUROPEAN POWERS

Whereas the European powers were the primary early actors in the Yugoslav secessions, they took a more moderate diplomatic approach toward the post-Soviet secessions. In part, this was because the European powers' attention was occupied in the Former Yugoslavia throughout the early and mid-1990s. It was also because their interests were much less at stake in the Former Soviet Union. Decision makers in London, Berlin, and Paris were, like those in Washington, preoccupied with the potential instability resulting from Soviet dissolution, but again preferred the use of multilateral institutions in an attempt to resolve the post-Soviet conflicts. The European powers actively involved themselves in humanitarian and conflict resolution efforts. They were particularly welcome in Georgia because Tbilisi saw the EU and the UN as potential counterweights against Russia.[203] It was only in the early 2000s, as EU expansion, oil, and other interests came to the forefront, that the powers began to play a more substantial role.

The Caucasian Secessions

The European powers' response to the Caucasian secessions was similar to that of the Americans'. Russia's transition to democracy took precedence over its unfortunate behavior in the periphery. Once Russia was fully democratic, it would be expected to comply with international law. They were less sanguine about Russian abuses of human rights in Chechnya. European leaders favored Russia's political ends, but not its means of securing them. As the conflict wore on, the European powers grew increasingly critical of Russia's tactics; France and Germany were particularly vocal. In January 1995, French Foreign Minister Alain Juppe, rotating president of the EU at the time, remarked that "a clear disproportion [existed] between Russia's methods and her objectives" and expressed disappointment that a Russian promise to end the conflict was not honored.[204] Russia, because it was a member of the OSCE, was obligated to inform the member states of its impending military actions in Chechnya, but no notice was given. Early in 2000, the European Union halted food aid to Russia in response to its renewed hostilities with Chechnya.

The OSCE actively involved itself in diplomatic efforts to resolve the Chechen conflict. Its members conditioned trade and other agreements on Moscow's concession to OSCE observers in Grozny, including the assured delivery of humanitarian aid and serious negotiations with the secessionists. Similarly, the Council of Europe conditioned Russia's membership on the successful resolution of the conflict in Chechnya.[205] Even with the emergent global interest in

---

[203] German (2007, pp. 364–365).
[204] Smyth (1995).
[205] Lapidus (1998, pp. 39–40).

terrorism in 2001, most European states maintained that both sides' use of terrorism was detrimental to the peace. Still, the European powers opposed Russia's means, not its ends; they upheld its territorial integrity.

The remaining Caucasian conflicts drew similarly little outright intervention from the European powers. Both French and British leaders opposed intervention alongside Russia in Abkhazia. Britain and France played the most active diplomatic role in Nagorno-Karabakh, but again like the United States, Britain had oil interests supported by the Azeri regime and opposed by NK. Consequently, Britain also supplied arms and training to Azerbaijan.[206] European countries' increased energy dependence generally served to strengthen Azerbaijan's hand and mute criticism even though it was the EU's largest regional trading partner.[207] Germany played only a secondary role in NK. France, though it has a large and politically powerful Armenian diaspora, did not support NK so much as it supported conflict resolution. Though the EU had the most leverage in Georgia and Armenia, none of the European powers' interests were significantly imperiled or enhanced by the potential independence of the Caucasian secessionists. Later, in 20006, as EU expansion was considered, under the European Neighborhood Policy (ENP), leaders negotiated partnership action plans with each of the Caucasian states. These plans, however, negotiated with individual EU members, were more about economics and politics than conflict resolution.[208]

France and Britain had domestic unrest, but their conflicts would have only contributed to their already overdetermined support for the home states' territorial integrity. Although German decision makers evidenced significantly more support for self-determination than their European counterparts, their concerns for human rights in Chechnya and the other conflicts did not provoke support for secession when both parties' behavior was condemnable.[209] Finally, European states did not have strong relationships or shared identity with the secessionists. None would consider themselves co-ethnics or coreligionists, though the Abkhaz', South Ossetians' and NK Armenians' protestations of democracy and economic liberalism did represent an ideological affinity. Again, though, Georgia made a similar claim to democratic aspirations, resulting in a wash.

CHINA AND JAPAN

The Asian powers were not involved directly or diplomatically in the Caucasian conflicts. Japan, just transitioning from its role as a powerful regional player to

---

[206] Giragosian in Chorbaijan (2001, pp. 247–248).

[207] German (2007, pp. 359, 360–361).

[208] Ibid., pp. 361–362.

[209] German Chancellor Kohl was the first Great Power leader to publicly criticize Russia's tactics in Chechnya, for example, on January 5, 1995.

one of global influence, had few interests or humanitarian concerns in the Caucasus. Though it had a lingering conflict with Russia, their antagonisms were not strong enough to provoke Japanese support for Chechnya. China was similarly not disposed toward support for the secessionists, and especially not the Chechens, who shared an Islamic character with one of China's Uighur secessionists in Xinjiang. The Chechens' perceived similarity to China's own secessionists made recognition an especially unattractive option; beyond Bejing's general preference that internal conflicts remain that way. According to one expert at the time,

The millions of Muslims in Xinjiang are restive and dissatisfied with Chinese rule. The prospect of having its own "Chechnya" in the western part of the country (indeed, not merely an enclave, as in Russia, but in a region bordering a vast Muslim world that provides moral and material support for separatist ambitions) is a source of acute concern to the Chinese leadership, already harried by separatism in Tibet.[210]

The conflicts in the Russian periphery presented a more direct threat to Chinese territorial security than did Yugoslavia's. Nevertheless, the threat of Chechen independence was not probable, as none of the other Great Powers was disposed to recognize Chechnya.

Japanese decision makers were neither engaged nor, for the most part, interested in the post-Soviet conflicts. Japan did, however, send humanitarian aid. At the urging of the United Nations High Commissioner for Human Rights and the International Committee of the Red Cross, Japan donated humanitarian aid to those displaced by the violence in the North Caucasus in 2000.

Japan also sent dedicated humanitarian aid to Chechnya. The Japanese government commented at the time that it believed Chechnya to be a part of Russia. It was disheartened, though, by the high number of casualties emerging from the second Russo-Chechen conflict, by then a common theme in Great Power rhetoric. Russia and Japan have an outstanding conflict over the Northern Territories, four disputed islands between the two states. That conflict does not seem to have influenced Japanese policy toward the region. According to the Japanese Ministry of Foreign Affairs, the principal issues for Japan, Russia, and the Caucasus states are the strengthening of their bilateral security and economic relations. Chechnya and the other secessionist conflicts are only mentioned in passing.[211]

None of the Caucasian secessions drew serious attention from the Asian powers. Similar to the positions of the others, interest in Chechnya was greatest, but Russia's status and resurgent strength deterred a strong response. For China in particular, deference to state sovereignty and the territorial status quo were forgone conclusions.

---

[210] Rumer (2002, p. 62).
[211] The Ministry of Foreign Affairs of Japan (2004).

DEVELOPMENTS IN CHECHNYA, 1999–2011

The second Russo-Chechen war began in 1999 when Chechen-based Islamists staged incursions into neighboring Dagestan.[212] Russian authorities responded by intervening in early December, ostensibly to push back the Chechen-led invaders and restore order. The military action, though, became much more extensive, encompassing the whole Chechen AO. Within a month of the invasion, Chechnya and Russia were at war again. Moscow was more successful this time; the Chechens were internally divided and Russians were united, better prepared, and with higher morale. The war, which Moscow dubbed a "counter terror" action ended officially in spring 2009.

Two powerful factions arose within Chechnya following the first Russo-Chechen war, affecting the character of the more recent conflict. One was the initial nationalist movement for Chechen independence, whose goal remained unchanged since the first war. The other was an Islamic movement, connected to the Wahhabists, not so much dedicated to Chechen independence as to a worldwide Islamic movement.[213] The second major distinction between the first and second conflict was the manner in which the combatants waged war, as both sides pursued especially violent and unsavory tactics in the latter conflict. Terrorism and violence against civilians became more frequently employed by the Chechens, and those fighting in their name, whereas the Russian military engaged in extensive and indiscriminate civilian targeting, torture, summary execution, and forced disappearances.[214] Additionally, Chechen fighters began terrorist actions including bombings, suicide bombings, and kidnappings, in Russia proper. Extreme measures did not hasten conflict resolution, however. In fact, the political resolution of Chechnya's status seemed further away than ever at the end of 2011 even though Russia had secured a military victory, successfully quashing what remained of the already unstable Chechen separatist regime. The Chechen insurgency had become so weak that sporadic terrorism was virtually the only tactic employed. But the conflict continued.

Postwar Chechnya

Maskhadov's governmental authority languished without external recognition or resolution of the republic's status. The first war ended with the Khasavyurt Agreement that negotiations on Chechnya's final status would occur five years later. Chechens concluded at the time that Russians were merely prolonging Chechnya's inevitable independence. Russian authorities hoped (and planned) that Chechnya's situation would change in the intervening years. Moscow was

---

[212] Evangelista (2002).

[213] Lyall (2009, p. 339).

[214] See Human Rights Watch (2000, 2003, 2006); Lyall (2009). Indiscriminate shelling was also a feature of the first war (see Smith 2006).

right. I in part because of its own policies, Chechnya's circumstances changed for the worse, as did the Great Powers' interpretation of its secession. The Russian government also had a new ally in Akhmad Kadyrov, a former Chechen insurgent turned pro-Russian ally who, in 2003, became president of the Chechen Republic.[215]

Political Islam had important effects on Chechnya's domestic government and on how the Chechens were perceived internationally. One source noted that "Chechnya's period of independence... appears to have been the peak of the transit of fighters, cash and ideology from abroad."[216] Furthermore, a variety of negotiations held under the auspices of international organizations such as the OSCE and UN during the interwar years yielded little effect: "Maskhadov was the target of several assassination attempts in 1998–9, and although he still enjoyed broad popular support, he exercised little effective control."[217] If Maskhadov's control within Chechnya had consolidated, the incursions into Dagestan, led by the Wahhabists in 1999, may very well not have occurred. Instead, the consolidation of political authority occurred on the Russian side.

The Second Russo-Chechen War, 1999–2009

In November 1999, Russian forces captured northern Chechnya and by February 2000, they had occupied Grozny, or at least its remnants.[218] The Chechen resistance was forced to move farther south where mountainous terrain, porous borders, and sympathetic governments precluded Russian forces from gaining control. Rather than stopping the violence in Chechnya and its surrounding areas, Russia's counterterrorism efforts were met with increasing brutality on the part of the Chechen resistance. Chechens adopted the Russian military's violent behavior as their own with devastating consequences for Russian civilians. In 2002, a siege on a Moscow theater killed 129; two Russian passenger planes were downed in 2004 killing 88; and, in the most notorious and controversial Chechen attack, more than 150 schoolchildren (300 total victims) were killed in a botched hostage taking in Beslan in 2004. Terror attacks would continue through 2013, including a potential threat targeting the 2014 Winter Olympics in Sochi, Russia. The primary Islamic group within Chechnya also began using suicide bombing, within both Moscow and Chechnya. For its part, the Russian government's methods in the second Chechen war were characterized as "Stalinist anti-guerrilla tactics."[219]

---

[215] He had become acting head of the pro-Russian government in 2000.

[216] Chivers and Myers (2004).

[217] Estimates suggested there were between 1,600 and 1,800 Chechen rebels (Kramer 2004/5, pp. 7, 12).

[218] Kramer (2004/5) notes that by 2000, Grozny was "almost completely leveled by Russian air and artillery forces" (p. 8). Grozny was "almost uninhabitable." He continues, "Basic services (e.g., running water, electricity, heat, and natural gas) are non-existent or nearly so" (p. 6).

[219] Felgenhauer (2002).

Russian troops used torture, rape, forced disappearances, and summary execution in prosecuting the war.[220]

Unlike anemic troop levels in the first Chechen war, the Russian government said it had as many as 93,000 troops in Chechnya as of January 2000.[221] Nevertheless, the conflict's ultimate outcome remained uncertain. According to one expert in 2004,

It is unlikely the Chechen guerillas will be able to mount a counteroffensive similar to the one they carried out in August 1996. Russian soldiers have maintained a tighter hold on Grozny and most other cities than they did at any point during the earlier war, and they have avoided repeating some of their gravest mistakes, especially with regard to urban warfare. Nonetheless, the seemingly endless conflict has also revealed major weaknesses...In a military sense, an end to the conflict appears as elusive as ever.[222]

But Russia's occupation techniques have only fueled Chechens' hatred of Russians.[223] Before 1999, Chechnya's population rebounded to just over a million. By 2005, the population shrank to 700,000 and tens of thousands of Chechnya's citizens (Russians and Chechens) became internally displaced or international refugees. Human Rights Watch (HRW) estimated between 3,000 and 5,000 people had disappeared between 1999 and 2005. The disappearances were attributed to both Chechen security forces and the Russian military. HRW criticized Moscow's handling of the conflict arguing it "brought suffering to hundreds of thousands of civilians" and "undermined the goal of fighting terrorism."[224] Yet, on multiple occasions, the Putin regime proclaimed vindication in the lack of international condemnation for its tactics.[225]

Russian forces killed Chechen leader Aslan Maskhadov on March 8, 2005.[226] Officials celebrated the operation as a success, but observers on all sides questioned whether and how peace could come to Chechnya without a popular representative of the Chechen people. Indeed, Moscow was even less likely to negotiate a settlement with the Islamists. In comparison, Maskhadov seemed reliable and moderate. He was replaced by Abdul-Halim Sadulayev, who was in office for just over a year before being killed by pro-Russian Chechen forces. Another, relatively moderate rebel fighter, Doku Umarov, became the president of the Chechen Republic of Ichkeria from 2006 until he – in a rather

[220] Human Rights Watch (2000, 2003, 2006).
[221] Felgenhauer (2002, p.159); Kramer (2004/5, p. 5) suggests Russian troops "outnumber the rebels by more than fifty to one." The *New York Times* estimated in 2002 that Russian soldiers in Chechnya numbered 85,000 (Myers 2002b).
[222] Kramer (2004/5, p. 61).
[223] Felgenhauer (2002).
[224] Myers (2005).
[225] Although Russia was censured for its human rights abuses by the UN Human Rights Commission in 2000 and 2001, post-September 11, similar diplomatic sanctions failed to garner sufficient international support.
[226] At the time, it was unclear whether Moscow had assassinated Maskhadov or whether, as Russian officials claimed, police had killed him as he violently resisted arrest.

dramatic ideological shift – resigned from his post in 2007 to become the self-proclaimed emir of the Caucasus Emirate. He further disavowed all of Chechnya's secular laws. Umarov's new, more expansive goal for the insurgency was a Northern Caucasus Islamic state wherein Chechnya was but one of the provinces. Umarov's leadership has overseen the end of any centralized, secessionist government in Chechnya.

Aside from the formal military campaign, Moscow also began consolidating power in Chechnya. In 2000, President Putin chose Akhmad Kadyrov as Russia's primary administrator in Chechnya. Kadyrov had previously fought with the nationalists in favor of Chechen independence, so he was seen as a traitor, especially hated, and he was assassinated by Islamist Chechens in 2004. His successor was Alu Alkhanov, who served until 2007. During Alkhanov's time in office, Moscow moderated its stance toward Chechnya somewhat. Rather than isolating Chechnya and attempting to starve the insurgency, the Russian government began development projects. News reports cited newly paved roads, construction, working electricity, and freshly hung streetlamps. In Grozny, for example, "more than 60 miles of roads have been restored...and the buildings on several main streets are under repair."[227] Still, the government's efforts in Chechnya were uneven and limited. Russia had "not yet addressed the difficult and expensive tasks of restoring sewage lines, gas and flows of potable water" as late as 2006.[228] The extent of work yet to be completed remained daunting. In addition, it was rumored that Russian corruption and theft financed the "good works" underway in Chechnya.

Since 2007, Ramzan Kadyrov, the son of Akhmad Kadyrov and a former guerrilla fighter, has served as the president of the Chechen Republic. The Kadyrov administration has seen the full consolidation of authority in Chechnya and significant, continued rebuilding. Kadyrov's government has been criticized by human rights groups for its repressive policies and human rights abuses – including the continuing use of torture and the extrajudicial killings of Kadyrov's personal enemies.[229] However, many Chechens have come to believe that Chechnya needed an authoritarian leader in order to impose control on the region so divided after so many years of war.[230]

RUSSIAN RECOGNITION AND THE FIVE DAY WAR

The secessionist conflicts in Georgia might have persisted indefinitely as cold wars had it not been for the Great Power politics surrounding Kosovo's independence and a reckless Georgian invasion. The United States had become increasingly critical of Russia's role in Georgia's conflicts but also pressed the

[227] Chivers (2006).
[228] Ibid.
[229] Feifer (2009).
[230] Ibid.

Saakashvili regime to temper its newly aggressive approach toward its domestic discontents, suggesting that NATO and EU membership depended on genuine efforts to peacefully resolve the wars.[231] Nevertheless, as discussed earlier in the chapter, Georgia became increasingly assertive in its relations with South Ossetia in 2006–2007, refusing to negotiate with anyone other than the pro-Georgian authorities. Furthermore, Georgia's taking the Kodori Gorge in 2006 raised fears of reconquest in Abkhazia.

It was around that time that Russia linked the recognition of Kosovo to that of South Ossetia and Abkhazia. According to President Putin, "We need common principles to find a fair solution to these problems for the benefit of all people living in conflict-stricken territories...If people believe that Kosovo can be granted full independence, why then should we deny it to Abkhazia and South Ossetia?" He continued, "I am not speaking about how Russia will act. However, we know that Turkey, for instance, has recognized the Republic of Northern Cyprus...I do not want to say that Russia will immediately recognize Abkhazia and South Ossetia as independent states, but such precedent does exist."[232] Putin's comments suggested a more assertive Russian policy posture toward Georgia, one that would likely face strong opposition from the United States, but also one that could be avoided if the Kosovo conflict reached a settlement based on "common principles."

When the United States, Britain, and France recognized Kosovo's unilateral declaration of independence on February 18, 2008, at least insofar as Russia was concerned, it belied their implacable commitment to international law and the principles specifically agreed to in Security Council Resolution 1244. Still, Moscow did not move to recognize the Georgian secessionists, choosing to preserve coordinated nonrecognition among the Great Powers instead. President Putin's annual press conference, just before the declaration, made plain his perspective on the matter when pressed by a German reporter,

Are you Europeans not ashamed to apply double standards in settling one and the same issue in different parts of the world? Here in this region we have Abkhazia, South Ossetia and Trans-Dniester that exist as independent states. We are always being told that Kosovo is a special case. This is all lies. There is nothing so special about Kosovo and everyone knows this full well. It is exactly the same situation of an ethnic conflict, crimes committed on both sides and complete de facto independence. We need to decide on a common set of principles for resolving such issues. We are not driving the situation into a dead end. We are proposing to our partners that we draw up a common code of conduct

[231] During a visit to Georgia, George W. Bush articulated this view clearly, "Georgia's leaders know that the peaceful resolution of conflict is essential to your integration into the transatlantic community. At the same time, the sovereignty and territorial integrity of Georgia must be respected" (Ostrovsky 2005).
[232] "Russia: Putin calls for 'universal principles'" (2006).

on such matters. Why should we encourage separatism?. . .If we act only out of political expediency and serve only the political interests of particular countries we will undermine international law and the general order.[233]

Though he reveled in his peers' hypocrisy, Putin would not respond by counter-recognizing Russia's clients. The authorities in South Ossetia and Abkhazia, buoyed by the precedent in Kosovo yet feeling increasingly vulnerable about their status within Georgia, responded by asking the members of the UN and CIS for recognition.[234] Their appeals were denied.

   Later that summer, on August 7, 2008, Georgian forces advanced on South Ossetia. The authorities in Tbilisi claimed that they were responding to attacks on them originating on the secessionists' side.[235] However, when the Georgian military killed members of the Russian peacekeeping forces stationed there, Russia responded with force, taking control of South Ossetia and Abkhazia and creating a substantial buffer zone within Georgia proper. Moscow formally recognized the two shortly thereafter, on August 26. The United States and a number of European countries decried Russian aggression against Georgia.[236] In time, Russia pulled back to the status quo ante, but Moscow dedicated itself to realizing the independence and statehood of South Ossetia and Abkhazia – with or without the support of the other Great Powers.[237] As in Kosovo, without the definitive signal of coordinated legitimacy to initiate a recognition cascade, only a handful of states have followed Russia's lead, including Nicaragua, Venezuela, Nauru, Vanuatu, and Tuvalu. Some reaped significant monetary rewards from Russia for doing so.

CONCLUSION: POST-SOVIET HASTE?

Widespread recognition has not come to the post-Soviet secessionists for a variety of reasons, but a lack of domestic sovereignty does not appear chiefly among them. The separatist regimes surpassed a high standard of territorial control by defeating their home states militarily and compelling their retreat even though other indicators of control were exercised to varying degrees. The variance in domestic sovereignty from republic to republic, however, was not

---

[233] Putin (2008).

[234] Caspersen (2008).

[235] U.S. and European intelligence later confirmed that the Georgian forces had planned and initiated the violence.

[236] *BBC News* (2008). "US Condemns Russia over Georgia" (2008). In a statement on September 1, the European Council "strongly condemned" Russia's recognition.

[237] "Giorgi Kandelaki, deputy chairman of the Georgian parliament's foreign affairs committee, said that Abkhazia's campaign for recognition was paid for by the Kremlin: 'The entire campaign to get any miniscule recognition that would go beyond the existing "cohort" – Hamas, Venezuela, Nicaragua, and Nauru – is carried out, co-ordinated, financed and executed by Russia with Russian taxpayer money and using vast networks of Russian diplomacy,' he told the Moscow Times" (von Twickle 2011).

the focus of Great Power attention. Instead, Great Power preferences regarding recognition derived from their own parochial interests.

One could look at the Caucasian de facto regimes and conclude the Great Powers' hesitance in granting recognition has been vindicated by Chechnya's political faltering from 1996 to 1999. Perhaps none of the secessionists could have successfully transitioned to independent statehood; they were and are too weak. To be sure, Chechnya no longer meets the standards set by international law, but this is the result of a self-fulfilling prophecy of international isolation and indifference to Russian methods of regaining authority there. As Chechnya weakened, Russia became more powerful. South Ossetia and Abkhazia, though heavily subsidized by Russia and international humanitarian organizations, and now each with a handful of recognitions, have a powerful opposition in the U.S. and the EU's unequivocal support for Georgia. Finally, Nagorno-Karabakh inhabits an unsustainable region fully surrounded by its increasingly assertive and militarized home state. And for NK, Russian support has become more equivocal since the South Ossetian and Abkhaz conflicts in 2008 as Russia has taken the initiative to break the logjam in the trilateral negotiations.[238]

In the end, we are left with a counterfactual: did the Great Powers' decision not to recognize the secessionists indicate that they could not have been states? Or did the Great Powers' decisions determine that they would not be states, regardless of their potential? I contend that the latter more accurately characterizes the post-Soviet cases presented here.

What the wars of Soviet succession demonstrate most vividly is that although a battlefield victory – perhaps the most unambiguous sign of domestic sovereignty – is usually sufficient to compel external recognition, it is not universally so. State interest, rather than the facts on the ground determine recognition and, collectively, whether the secessionist actor will be admitted full membership in international society. In these cases, most interests aligned with the home states.

Second, even though Russia supported the Georgian secessionists' ambitions – in support of its own interests in undermining Tbilisi, supporting ethnic kin, and forestalling NATO expansion into its periphery – it withheld recognition in part to remain in the good graces of its Great Power peers and in part to ensure stability in the international order, abiding only occasionally to international law, certainly, but maintaining its insistence on a negotiated settlement and the United Nations framework in the face of American and European unilateral recognition of Kosovo. It was not until Georgia's provocative intervention into South Ossetia that Russia saw fit to retaliate and recognize its secessionist friends.

Third, the de facto states will likely fail without the support of the international community. The Soviet Union's legitimate successor states received important material and psychic benefits from system membership. They received loans from institutions such as the World Bank and IMF as well as directly from

---

[238] IISS (2010).

other states. Indeed, Russia was said to have used its international loans to fund its war in Chechnya even while its population was suffering. And President Shevardnadze credited international support for the continued viability of Georgia,

As regards material factors, I would like to say straightaway, without concealing anything, that if it had not been for the assistance, support and financial participation of the Western countries, and especially the World Bank, the IMF and the European Union, we would not have survived. One third of the revenue of the current budget, that is wages, pensions and other things needed for the state, is formed by means of the participation of the West and especially the IMF.[239]

Though the secessionists treat one another as the legitimate authorities within their respective territories, without the recognition of the powerful, they will likely not fare much better than they have in the past.[240] As Michael Ignatieff argued, in the Cold War's aftermath, "huge sections of the world's population have won the right of self determination on the cruelest possible terms: they have been simply left to fend for themselves. Not surprisingly, their nation-states are collapsing."[241] It is likely that the remaining post-Soviet secessions will meet a similar fate.

SELECTED SOVIET SUCCESSOR TIMELINE (1989–2011)

	1989
January	Moscow imposes direct rule over Nagorno-Karabakh and dispatches troops.
March	
18	Mass Abkhaz demonstrations demand independence from Georgia.
June	Georgian SSR nullifies Soviet authority within the republic.
July	
16	First clashes of the Georgian-Abkhaz war begin in Sukhumi.
September	
1	Azerbaijan initiates blockade of Nagorno-Karabakh and Armenia; Nakhichevan blockade is initiated by Armenia in response.
October	
1	Protests begin in South Ossetia over Georgian language laws.
November	
10	South Ossetian Popular Front demands status be upgraded to SSR.
20	Georgian SSR restores Georgian independence (of 1921).
23	Violent clashes reported between Georgians and South Ossetians.

[239] "President Shevardnadze defends concept for strengthening state sovereignty" (1997).
[240] King (2001, p. 542, 2001a).
[241] Ignatieff (1994).

December

1   Armenia's Supreme Soviet calls for reunification with Nagorno-Karabakh.

1990

April

3   USSR Supreme Soviet rules recognized minorities may remain within the USSR even if their SSR secedes.

August

20   Georgian declared the official language of Georgia; Abkhaz and South Ossetian parties banned from Georgian elections.

25   Abkhazia's Supreme Soviet declares sovereignty (remains open to federation); declaration is ruled invalid by the Georgian authorities.

September   South Ossetia declares independence from Georgia.

October

28   Georgian elections yield 54 percent in favor of nationalist parties (first round).

November

27   Chechen-Ingush SSR declares sovereignty (and independence).

11   Georgian elections yield 62 percent in favor of nationalist parties (second round).

14   Georgian SSR elects Zviad Gamsakhurdia president.

16   Georgian SSR sends notification of independence demands to OSCE.

December

9   South Ossetia holds independent elections.

11   Georgia abolishes the South Ossetian Autonomous Oblast; state of emergency declared.

1991

January

7   Gorbachev declares South Ossetia's sovereignty declaration and Georgia's state of emergency unconstitutional.

22   Heavy fighting breaks out in South Ossetia marking the beginning of the war.

March

17   Union Treaty referendum held to determine the future status of the USSR.

          Abkhazia and South Ossetia hold referenda on the Union Treaty though Georgia boycotts.

30   Georgian reinforcements arrive to quell the South Ossetian uprising.

31   Georgia holds a referendum on independence from USSR (90 percent participate, 97.65 percent favor independence). Many in Abkhazia and South Ossetia are not allowed to vote.

April   Russian troops expel 10,000 Armenians from Azerbaijan to eliminate Armenian rebels (not NK Armenians).

9   Georgia declares independence from the USSR.

14   Gamsakhurdia appointed Georgia's first independent president.

July	Ingushetia declares itself an SSR (In Dec. 97% vote for SSR)
August	
1	Rallies and strikes demanding Chechen independence begin.
30	Azerbaijan's Supreme Soviet declares independence from the USSR (receives assurances that Soviet troops will stay in NK first).
September	
15	Ingush rebels declare Ingushetia an SSR, independent of Chechnya.
21	Armenian referendum on secession from USSR (99.3 percent support independence).
23	Armenia declares independence from the USSR.
October	
23	Russia bans political groups intending to violate its territorial integrity.
27	Presidential and parliamentary elections held in Chechnya (Dudayev wins with 85 percent of vote, irregularities reported).
November	
2	Chechnya's parliament declares independence from Russia.
8	Yeltsin declares a state of emergency in Chechnya.
10	Russian parliament denounces Yeltsin's declaration.
26	Azerbaijan revokes NK's autonomy.
December	
10	Nagorno-Karabakh holds a referendum on independence (99.9 percent vote in favor of independence, Azeris boycott).
21	South Ossetia declares independence.
22	Georgian civil war begins between Gamsakhurdia and the opposition.
25	Gorbachev resigns; Soviet Union disbands.
28	Independent elections held in NK.

1992

January	
1	Major hostilities break out in Nagorno-Karabakh.
4	Gamsakhurdia's opposition, having gained control in Georgia, appeals for a cease-fire in South Ossetia.
6	New parliament of Nagorno-Karabakh formally declares independence.
20	South Ossetia holds a referendum on independence; turnout reported to be 90 percent, 98.2 percent vote for independence (Georgians boycott).
March	Each autonomous republic except Chechnya and Tatarstan signs a union agreement with Russia.
10	Eduard Shevardnadze takes power within Georgia.
23	EC and United States recognize Republic of Georgia.
24	Minsk Group is established by the OSCE.
May	
8	Cease-fire negotiated between Azerbaijan and Armenia but is immediately violated by both.

13	Trilateral talks among North Ossetia, South Ossetia, and Georgia begin.
June	Russia recognizes the division of Chechen-Ingushetia; Ingushetia maintains ties to Russia.
8	Heavy fighting breaks out in South Ossetia, part of a massive attack by Shevardnadze regime.
24	Cease-fire is established between Georgia and South Ossetia, the Sochi Agreement (lasts until 2004).
July	
3	Russian-backed settlement talks begin with South Ossetia, North Ossetia, and Georgia.
23	Abkhazia declares independence from Georgia.
August	
14	Georgian-Abkhaz war begins.
September	
2	Nagorno-Karabakh declares independence from Azerbaijan.
3	Russian-backed negotiations between Abkhazia and Georgia yield a cease-fire.
13	Russian-backed cease-fire between Georgia and Abkhazia collapses.
20	NK begins petitioning states for recognition.
October	
1	Abkhaz offensive against Georgia begins.
11	Shevardnadze elected (95 percent); much of Abkhazia and South Ossetia cannot participate.
27	Russian troops become involved in Abkhaz-Georgian violence.
31	Azerbaijan parliament votes against membership in the CIS.
December	
3	OSCE sends mission to South Ossetia.

1993

January	
20	UN mission to Georgia arrives.
26	South Ossetia settlement talks begin under the auspices of the OSCE.
February	North Ossetia recognizes South Ossetia's independence
March	Chechnya adopts a new constitution
May	
14	Georgia and Russia negotiate a cease-fire in Abkhazia.
20	Russo-Georgian cease-fire for Abkhazia takes hold.
July	
12	Russian-backed cease-fire and agreement presented for Abkhazia; both parties reject the plan.
31	OSCE settlement grudgingly approved by Armenia, Azerbaijan, and NK Armenians (NK Armenians later renege on the commitment).
August	
26	Georgian troops begin withdrawal from Abkhazia.
September	
27	Abkhaz forces capture Sukhumi.

October

8   Shevardnadze announces Georgia will join the CIS (does so
           October 23).

November South Ossetia adopts a new constitution

December

1   "Memorandum of Understanding" signed between Georgia and
           Abkhazia under UN auspices (stipulates cease-fire, observers,
           refugee return).

1994

January   President-in-Exile Gamsakhurdia dies.

February

3   Treaty on Friendship, Cooperation, and Peaceful Coexistence signed
           between Moscow and Tbilisi.

April

4   Cease-fire agreed to between Georgia and Abkhazia.

May

9   Bishkek Protocol brokers cease-fire among Azerbaijan, Armenia, and
           NK (violations continue through summer and fall 1994).

14   Second cease-fire agreement signed between Georgian and Abkhaz
           authorities in Russia.

June

16   CIS peacekeeping force deployed to Abkhazia (1,600 troops).

November

30   Abkhazia adopts new constitution reaffirming its sovereignty; Georgia
           calls for sanctions.

December

2   Russian bombardment of Chechnya begins (ground troops follow on
           the 10th).

15   U.S. State Department condemns Abkhazia's declaration of
           sovereignty.

1995

February

17   South Ossetians and ethnic Georgian refugees begin returning to
           South Ossetia.

March

6   Abkhazia announces it will consider confederation with Georgia.

July

19   Formal negotiations begin between South Ossetia and Georgia.

1996

January

24   Russia admitted into the Council of Europe (COE).

April

21   Dzhokar Dudayev killed in Russian missile attack.

May	
28	Truce agreement between Russia and Chechnya signed (breaks in July).
August	
31	Alexander Lebed negotiates the Khasavyurt peace agreement between Russia and Chechnya; final decision on Chechen sovereignty is delayed for five years.
November	
10	South Ossetia holds presidential elections.
December	
31	Russia withdraws its last troops from Chechnya (completed January 5).

1997

January	
27	Maskhadov wins Chechnya's presidential elections (Moscow recognizes Maskhadov).
May	
12	Presidents Yeltsin and Maskhadov sign a formal peace agreement. Yeltsin pledges to never use or threaten force against "the Republic of Ichkeria."[242]

1998–2011

January 1998	Maskhadov announces plans for Shari'a law in Chechnya.
February 3, 1998	Armenian President Ter-Petrossian forced out over his willingness to compromise on NK.
June 23, 1998	Maskhadov declares a state of emergency in Chechnya.
July–September 1999	Russian-Chechen violence intensifies in Chechnya and Dagestan.
September 30, 1999	Russia intervenes in Chechnya in antiterrorist action.
October 1, 1999	Russia recognizes Moscow-based Chechen government, not de facto Maskhadov regime.
February 6, 2000	Putin declares direct rule in Chechnya.
June 2000	Moscow appoints Kadyrov prime minister in Chechnya.
March 2001	Georgia and Abkhazia sign agreement renouncing the use of force.
April 2001	U.S.-brokered talks on Nagorno-Karabakh conclude without progress.
November 2001	Russian-Chechen peace talks held in Moscow.
Spring 2002	American Special Forces train Georgian troops in counterterrorism.
October 2002	Bending to Russian pressure, Georgia takes action against Chechen rebels in Pankisi Gorge region.
November 2003	Shevardnadze ousted in the Rose Revolution in Georgia.

[242] Stanley (1997).

March 2003	Positive referendum on Russian-backed constitution for Chechnya held.
January 2004	Mikhail Saakashvili elected president in Georgia.
May 2004	South Ossetia holds independent, unrecognized parliamentary elections.
October 2004	Abkhazia holds unrecognized presidential elections; opposition non-Moscow-backed candidate wins.
January 2005	President Saakashvili offers South Ossetia autonomy within Georgia. Offer is rejected.
February 2005	Maskhadov calls for cease-fire and peace talks; Russia refuses.
March 2005	Russian Special Forces kill Maskhadov in Chechnya.
July 2005	Russia begins to withdraw from Georgia, closing two Soviet-era bases: the Akhalkalaki base and the Batumi base (completed in 2007).
July 2006	Georgia announces the formation of Abkhazia government-in-exile.
July 2006	Shamil Basie killed in Ingushetia.
September 2006	Georgia and NATO discuss closer relations.
	Georgia takes the Kodori Gorge (previously under Svan control).
November 12, 2006	South Ossetians hold referendum on independence, 99.9 percent in favor.
	A counter-referendum is held in Georgian-controlled territories.
December 10, 2006	Nagorno-Karabakh adopts first independent constitution.
April 2007	President Saakashvili recognizes South Ossetian counter government as potential negotiation partner rather than Kokoity.
July 2007	Nagorno-Karabakh holds presidential elections.
November 2007	State of emergency declared in Georgia; anti-Saakashvili protests held.
February 2008	Dmitry Medvedev elected president of Russia.
February 17, 2008	Kosovo declares independence with U.S. and most EU states' support; Russia and China remain opposed to unilateral statehood.
March 2008	Abkhazia asks UN for recognition.
	Violent clashes break out in Nagorno-Karabakh.
April 2008	NATO defers decision on Georgia entering membership program.
May 2008	Russia sends approximately 300 unarmed troops to Abkhazia.
August 2008	Georgia attempts to retake South Ossetia by force; Russian peacekeepers defend and establish extensive buffer zones around it and Abkhazia.
	France brokers a peace agreement to end the conflict.
	Russia recognizes South Ossetia and Abkhazia.
November 2008	Azerbaijan and Armenia recommit to efforts to resolve NK conflict (negotiations conclude in November 2009 without resolution).
April 2009	Russia declares a formal end to counterterrorism action in Chechnya.
May 2009	NATO military exercises begin in Georgia.
June 2009	UN observers leave Abkhazia-Georgia border after UNSC fails to extend their mandate because of Russia's veto.

September 2009	EU report on Russian-Georgian war lays much of the blame on Georgia.
July 2010	U.S. Secretary of State Hillary Clinton visits Georgia, reasserting support for Georgia's territorial integrity.
May 2011	Protestors in Georgia rally to demand reforms and the resignation of Saakashvili.

7

Conclusions and Substantive Interpretations

> Non-recognition does not affect Nagorno-Karabakh's existence, or its status as an independent state...Nagorno-Karabakh is the same as Azerbaijan, but it is just not recognized![1]

In a 2000 interview, Karabakh Defense Minister Anushavan Danielyan remarked that nonrecognition did not matter; Nagorno-Karabakh's status was the same as that of Azerbaijan, regardless of the international community's judgment. He was wrong. Or rather, he was describing what he hoped to be true, not what NK had actually experienced. External recognition is not merely a rubber stamp confirming what has already been achieved on the ground as far as state emergence is concerned. Instead, mutual recognition is fundamentally important. It constitutes external sovereignty and international system membership. Without extensive external recognition, state-like actors are not offered the status or material advantages reserved exclusively for states. Indeed, Danielyan cannot truly believe his own rhetoric. If he and other Armenian leaders did, Nagorno-Karabakh would compromise its demand for recognition and simply accept the very minimal, everything but recognition autonomous association offered by the authorities in Baku. Nagorno-Karabakh does not merely want to be autonomously governed *apart* from the Azeris, however. The Armenians want to be *a part* of the international community. There is something special about statehood not approximated by self-government alone.

Nonrecognition did not affect NK's existence or prevent its securing de facto authority, but it has certainly stunted the Karabakh Armenians' capacity to thrive. Moreover, according to every member of the international system, even its Armenian patron, NK is not "the same" as Azerbaijan; its status is lesser. So it is for Nagorno-Karabakh, Chechnya, Abkhazia, and South Ossetia, and so it is and has been for the de facto unrecognized regimes outside of the post-Soviet

[1] Lynch (2002, p. 848).

space. What incenses the de facto authorities most is that external recognition has not depended on their domestic-level characteristics or their capacity to govern or, in the NK case, their dedication to democratization. Rather, an international political calculus beyond Armenia and Azerbaijan is dictating the secessionists' status.

External recognition is not only significant for de facto independent regimes left outside of the international community to founder. Its importance is magnified in active, nonfrozen, secessionist conflicts where recognition is pivotal to a movement's success (or failure). For example, in the former Yugoslavia, recognition had a decisively positive effect on Croatia, socially promoting it into the international community of states before it had fully secured its territory. Partially as a result of the accrued benefits of statehood, Croatia was able to legitimately recapture the 30 percent of the territory it lost during the war.[2] Kosovo, with a number of powerful benefactors, is already a member of several prestigious international organizations and the recipient of substantial development loans. Although Kosovo had the weakest claim to functional self-government of the three Yugoslav cases analyzed in this study, it won some international favor as Serbia's relationship with the Great Powers soured. Only in Slovenia, where effective, legitimate authority was secured prior to recognition – and with Serbia's consent – were recognition's effects less palpable.

RESEARCH SUMMARY AND EMPIRICAL FINDINGS

Of the many movements aspiring to independent statehood, what determines which secessionists will receive recognition? The extant literature on statehood in law, international relations, and comparative theory suggests that recognition ought to depend on a movement's domestic-level characteristics. This project did not dispute the importance of domestic-level characteristics such as colonial status, ethno-federative status, and war victory. But, because the existing members of the international system are empowered to grant and withhold recognition, it argued that international-level factors should not be dismissed out of hand. International politics were likely to influence recognition, even if state leaders were attempting to abide by the international norms and laws.

The realities of the international system suggested that not all states would play an equally influential role in recognition. The Great Powers – the strongest members of the international system – play an especially important role in the selection of new states. By virtue of their material capabilities, their interests are the most extensive, they have special roles in international institutions such as the UNSC, and their policy positions serve as focal points for states whose interests are not as extensive. Noting that the Great Powers were often the first movers in recognition, I suggested first that when in concert, their support would

---

[2] The means were not legitimate, but retaking the territory was understood as an act of territorial self-defense.

initiate a cascade of recognition throughout the system. In contrast, when that support was unanimously withheld, it would strongly favor the home state's continued legitimate authority, even if not its effective rule.

Second, I argued that the Great Powers would not be impartial, apolitical arbiters when assigning recognition to their new peers. Each secessionist movement offers state leaders a role in determining whether and when a new peer will enter the international community. Powerful states are likely to form preferences based on the likely effects of recognition and statehood for any secessionist conflict. It would be difficult, if not impossible, to exclude those preferences from being expressed in practice. This was especially true because leaders approached diplomatic recognition as an expression of mutual self-interest and not – as many international jurists would have it – as a matter dictated by international law.

I proposed three major, non-mutually exclusive categories of international-level interests that would influence the Great Powers' recognition decisions: (1) external security or geostrategic, (2) domestic politics, and (3) system stability. I then derived hypotheses based on the logic of those interests vis-à-vis recognition. First, if state leaders recognized based on a concern for their external security or other geostrategic ambitions, recognition could be used as a tool to weaken a state's enemies or support its friends. Second, leaders could be influenced by their own domestic security concerns when conferring recognition; a Great Power destabilized by separatist conflicts of its own, for example, could be reticent to recognize similar movements elsewhere for fear of sending a signal legitimating secession. Finally, I suggested the Great Powers shared a larger, mutual interest in system stability that would predispose them to prefer coordinated recognition among themselves. The constellation of state interests then, rather than individual state interests alone, would best explain the Great Powers' recognition in practice. When in agreement, they would easily collude in favor or against a given secessionist movement. When they could not agree, they would defer indefinitely to the status quo. I argued that breaks from this agreement would rarely occur, and when they did, they would be destabilizing not only for the government and the secessionist movement directly involved, but for the greater international order as well.

To test the international-level interest arguments alongside the more conventional, domestic-level explanations for state emergence, I created a dataset composed of all major secessionist movements and Great Power recognition decisions from 1931 to 2000. Event history analysis offered a number of unique benefits for this project. First, the method ensured that the hypothesized causes were temporally before their anticipated effects. Second, the timing of recognition could be explored. In other words, it permitted an analysis of when the Great Powers were more or less likely to recognize a new member, not only if they were more or less likely to do so.

The quantitative models found significant and robust support for most of the domestic-level hypotheses and all of the international-level hypotheses. Broadly, this means that international politics among the Great Powers have important effects on the likelihood of system membership for aspiring states above and beyond their domestic-level characteristics. Only one specific finding, regarding mutual democracy's effect on the probability of recognition produced unexpected, though still statistically significant, results. Most strikingly, the hypothesized interest in Great Power coordination had an especially large substantive effect on the likelihood of additional recognition. Individual models run for each of the Great Powers also showed distinct patterns of interest from state to state. For example, whereas France and the USSR/Russia were most influenced by geostrategic considerations, China and Britain were most influenced by domestic insecurity in their recognition. So although the drive to coordinate was shared by all of the Great Powers, they otherwise had diverse priorities.

Though Great Power interests were found to have statistically significant, substantively meaningful effects on the likelihood of recognition in a given year, the analysis could not ensure that the quantitative indicators accurately captured what Great Power leaders considered their interests at the time. Nor could it uncover unhypothesized sources of variation or examine the string of events or pattern of causes and effects leading states to recognize. In contrast, each of these aspects could be more effectively studied through careful case studies.

The quantitative analysis also left one more question, unrelated to the inherent limitations of the method. External interests' influence relative to domestic sovereignty considerations remained unexplored because of the unavailability of data on secessionists' effective control and legitimate authority within the territories they claimed. The small N case studies presented an opportunity to explore that relationship. Two clusters of secessionist movements, one in the Former Yugoslavia and one in the post-Soviet states, were selected based on the degree of domestic sovereignty exercised by each movement. In this way, domestic sovereignty's and external interests' relative influence could be isolated.

In the Yugoslav case cluster, Great Power interest played a significant role in leaders' decision calculus. Slovene recognition, which appeared a forgone conclusion according to the domestic sovereignty criteria, was withheld (albeit for a limited time) as a result of the Great Powers' interests in maintaining unanimity within Europe and in achieving a comprehensive settlement. Legally speaking, Croatia's recognition was less certain and in flux. In fact, Croatian authorities did not control a significant portion of the territory they claimed when they first received recognition and they were still actively at war. Though Tudjman's secessionist regime did not unambiguously meet the legal standards, external politics pointed toward recognition. Regarding the relative importance of domestic sovereignty norms for recognition, British Minister of State Douglas Hogg remarked that Croatia was a "special case" where the rules of international law did not apply.[3] Another special case would arise before the end of the decade in the Former Yugoslavia, but this time in Kosovo. Despite Herculean attempts to maintain coordinated nonrecognition over the years, the Great Powers remained divided over Kosovo's final status when Britain and the United States decided that the negotiations would never bear fruit and encouraged the Albanians to unilaterally declare independence. The decision was not a result of Kosovo's achieving effective independence, nor had it enacted the standards pushed by the international community up to that point; when status came, it came as a result of political fiat. Still, unless and until the United States and Europe can convince Russia and China to support Kosovo's statehood, the situation will remain dangerously unstable for regional and international politics.

None of the secessionist regimes in the post-Soviet states has yet received widespread external recognition. Each is (or was) functionally independent for an extended period, but none won external support sufficient to provoke international acceptance. Ironically, on recognition, the secessionists' home states had not secured much more domestic sovereignty than their secessionists. But in the Former Soviet Union, the Great Powers have mostly dedicated their support to the regimes in Baku, Tbilisi, and Moscow, rather than those in Stepanakert, Sukhumi, Tskhinvali, or Grozny. In a possible instance of post-Soviet haste, the international community quickly consecrated the sovereign claims of the Soviet Union's constituent SSRs without first considering alternative scenarios for dissolution in those that were conflict prone. Though the USSR disbanded with relatively little conflict, concentrated violence and enduring conflict did occur in four of the new states. The international community, for its part, knew of the potential for war, instability, and contests over sovereignty, but it preferred nonintervention and immediate gains in security and trade to alternative, longer-term solutions.

Although Chechnya demonstrated a high degree of domestic sovereignty when it compelled the Russian army's retreat in 1996, Great Power recognition was not forthcoming. The Great Powers were unsympathetic to the Chechens' plight. The Cold War had just ended, but Moscow's image had already been completely rehabilitated in the West. The United States and the European Powers now saw in Russia a democratizing, liberal ally whose territorial integrity was in the interest of global stability. Chechens' initial support for extreme ethno-religious politics and their use of terrorist tactics against civilians did not help their cause. In the United States at least, officials were convinced that support for self-determination would only lead to an anti-democratic end. Isolated, Chechnya's domestic sovereignty dwindled along with its prospects for recognition as the decade wore on. Religious nationalism had dashed what little compassion had arisen because of Russia's excessively harsh tactics.

---

[3] Cited in Caplan (2005, p. 65 at n.58) and presented in this analysis on p. 129.

Chechnya's lawlessness was no longer considered an internal Russian affair; its domestic chaos was now seen as a potential international threat. Leaders consequently turned a blind eye to Moscow's Stalinist-era policies there.

Abkhazia, South Ossetia, and Nagorno-Karabakh all had moderate levels of domestic sovereignty throughout the period under study. External interests implied that Abkhazia and South Ossetia would receive more support for independence than would the Karabakh Armenians, however. Russia strongly preferred recognition for Abkhazia and South Ossetia because of its external security interests; identity-based affinity; and interestingly, concern for its own domestic stability. Nevertheless, the constellation of Great Power interests suggested that none of the regimes would actually receive recognition. The United States and Russia, the Great Powers most engaged in the post-Soviet conflicts, had divergent preferences with respect to the secessionists in Georgia. The United States had an opposite, if not equally strong, interest in Georgia's economic and political stability. Similarly, though less hotly contested, the United States supported the Azeri regime – less influenced by its Armenian lobby than Azerbaijan's resources – whereas Moscow sometimes supported the secessionists. As a result, the Caucasian de facto regimes continued on as uncertain states, unable to procure foreign aid, make treaties, trade on international markets, request international loans, or join international governmental organizations. Moscow defied the international consensus by trading with the regimes and providing direct aid, but it did not go so far as to formally recognize. Even when the United States, Britain, France, and Germany recognized Kosovo's unilateral declaration of independence, Russia maintained coordinated nonrecognition for its clients in favor of systemic stability – that is, until the authorities in Georgia attempted to retake South Ossetia by force.

The two clusters of case studies found that the Great Powers routinely pursued their own interests where the recognition of new states was concerned. And this was often despite their explicit acknowledgment that the secessionists fell short on the legal standards but would be recognized (Croatia and Kosovo), or surpassed them but would not be (Chechnya, Abkhazia, South Ossetia, and Nagorno-Karabakh). Despite the Slovenian case's seeming support for the domestic-level contention that international politics do not overturn a *fait accompli*, the Chechen case demonstrated the benefits of membership most compellingly. Perhaps nonrecognition did not lead directly to Chechnya's reincorporation into Russia, but it unequivocally created the permissive conditions for it.

SUBSTANTIVE IMPLICATIONS

Acknowledging international politics' influence over the outcomes of these ostensibly internal, secessionist conflicts promises better understanding of civil conflict dynamics and, ultimately, better models of civil war. In secessionist conflicts, actors are responding to incentives not currently specified in domestic-level models.[4] For example, secessionist movements sensing the potential for political recognition may be encouraged to continue fighting rather than accept seemingly generous settlements from their home states. Perhaps this is why Kosovo Albanians rejected Serbia's offers of "everything but independence" and would accept "nothing but."[5] Their leaders were confident that the United States and Europe would eventually support their statehood and, therefore, refused to compromise. Equally, home states assured that the international community would not recognize their challengers – as was perhaps the case for Russia after the 1996 cease-fire with Chechnya – might feel emboldened to crack down on secessionists and their presumed supporters. In general, many strategies for conflict prevention and resolution exclude external political factors and, therefore, underestimate the role of the international community, as a force for either good or ill. These findings have clear implications for our models and present important new considerations for diplomacy, peacekeeping, and conflict resolution.

Next, state birth may exhibit cohort effects. States emerging into the international system around the same time may share characteristics because of the favorable dispositions of powerful states at that time or the changing composition of the Great Powers themselves. For example, all other things being equal, it may be more difficult for the Great Powers to collude when there are more states whose preferences must coincide or with very different inclinations regarding the international order. This would mean that the same secessionist movement would face different odds of success depending on the number of Great Powers or where there are entrenched differences over fundamental aspects of the international order. A new state's lineage may also have important, long-term effects on international politics. A majority of states in the system today were born in the last past 50 years; they make up a majority of states in the United Nations. Research should explore whether the states of generation X meaningfully differ from those of generation Y and, if so, how those differences might influence world politics. Were states born during the recent period of American primacy different from those born during pax Britannica? Did states that had to fight outside the system as de facto states take on distinct institutions or craft alternative foreign policy dispositions from those socially promoted into the international community? Generally, how important are these formative experiences surrounding state emergence over the long term?

We should also not expect that all states would have a uniform composition across time because different factors will motivate external acceptance during different eras. Colonialism has been thoroughly discredited as an institution of governance and is not likely to reemerge. So whereas ethno-federative status like colonialism dramatically increased the likelihood of external recognition in recent years, it may not do so in years to come should powerful states' interests

---

[4] Fearon (2004a).
[5] Martti Ahtisaari quoted in Rubin (2006).

change. In the most extreme case, the assumption that states are like units, performing a relatively consistent set of functional tasks vis-à-vis their populations, may simply not reflect reality. Or at least, states are not born functionally equivalent; they may only become so over time.

Relatedly, this project's findings mostly reaffirm domestic-level factors' hypothesized associations with state emergence. Yet, the results also make plain the potential limitations of the underlying theories explaining those relationships. According to an international-level interpretation, domestic-level factors are important determinants of state emergence because powerful outsiders believe that they ought to be and not because of their inherent, domestic-level effects. Furthermore, anticolonial, ethno-federal, and war-winning secessionists were found to be more likely recipients of Great Power recognition before their home states conceded to their independence, not only afterward.[6] This effectively defeats the argument that international recognition only occurs after conflicts have already been decided domestically. Moreover, it lends renewed credibility to existing scholarly, international-level arguments suggesting that international norms helped assure the end of imperialism.[7]

This research also shows that the Great Powers, in the service of their own parochial purposes, welcome many more members into the international community than are demonstrably sovereign and viable. The incentives to coordinate usually ensure a modicum of stability among the Great Powers themselves, but these mutually agreeable membership decisions may be short sighted. Unless socially promoted states can secure domestic authority using the various benefits that system membership provides – such as development loans, legal authority, foreign aid, and foreign investment – Great Power leaders may be complicit in the proliferation of weak and failed states.[8] In the opposite case, unless most home states with de facto independent, but unrecognized secessionist challengers can exploit the benefits of statehood to successfully reincorporate those territories, as Russia did with Chechnya, then the Great Powers may also be eroding domestic sovereignty among the system's existing members.

The successful functioning of the interstate system relies on its members being able to assert authority within their borders. Ultimately, when this contract is broken, it will create regional – and possibly global – insecurity as the negative externalities of members' internal anarchy or their inability to consolidate domestic authority spread. Moreover, this will be a particularly persistent problem so long as system members insist on upholding the façade of

---

[6] The structure of the data for this project precluded testing whether recognition was more likely after a settlement between a secessionist movement and its home state.

[7] Though this study did not examine international norms' influence on statehood, it does not deny their demonstrable significance. For important works in this vein, see Fabry (2010); Kornprobst (2008); Mayall (1990); Spruyt (2005).

[8] Of course, social promotion only potentially explains a subset of the universe of state failures and most likely forms an underlying, rather than a proximate, cause.

sovereignty for states that have clearly lost authority on the ground, not allowing them to "die" or otherwise seriously endeavoring to (re)build them.[9]

Finally, returning to the controversial cases that opened this study, it is clear that the Great Powers' political jockeying over the fates of Kosovo, South Ossetia, and Abkhazia is pivotal to whether they will ultimately become full members of the international community. Outsiders could consecrate the secessionists' membership in the international system, but they remain uncertain states because a schism, rooted in the politics between the Great Powers themselves, has precluded a system-wide recognition cascade. Unfortunately, the breaks in coordinated recognition may have far-reaching effects.

The most immediate effect is that Russia and China may now believe that the United States, Britain, France, and Germany are willing to use recognition in a baldly political fashion without consideration for stability among the Great Powers. It is already apparent, in Russia's recognition of Abkhazia and South Ossetia, that Moscow no longer thinks it necessary to defer to its Great Power peers if they are not willing to extend the same courtesy. Historically, cases of overlapping sovereignty like these have been the catalysts of international war. And there are many other ongoing secessionist conflicts. If these conflicts portend future unilateral recognitions or multiple, smaller cascades as secondary states align their recognition with a particular Great Power, then the international order itself may be imperiled.

The break over Kosovo, South Ossetia, and Abkhazia and the results of this study more broadly also call into question international law's efficacy concerning matters of state emergence. The ICJ ruled in 2010 that Kosovo's unilateral declaration of independence was legal – as it broke no existing international law and it was undertaken by those in a capacity outside of the purview of UNSC 1244. Although the ICJ's first finding is unambiguously correct, its second is difficult to reconcile with the facts of the Kosovo case. If the Albanians agreed to negotiate a settlement with Serbia but unilaterally declared independence, it hardly seems to matter whether they were acting in their official capacity when they did so. The court's ruling may have conformed to the letter of the law, but it was not aligned with its spirit. On the other hand, for a long time, the Serbian government was not negotiating in good faith. And the Great Powers that recognized Kosovo's independence did so secure in their belief that justice, if not legal legitimacy, was on their side. Aside from the fact that most secessionist conflicts do not receive a hearing in international courts as Kosovo did, is there a more legitimate way for international law to approach conflicts between states and other non-state actors? Could special tribunals or more permanent institutions do a better job at conflict resolution than the current, ad hoc approach? Would legalizing or outlawing secession improve outcomes? Would new states conforming to Montevideo's recognition prerequisites be better states? If so, is

---

[9] Jackson (1990); Herbst (1996/7, 2000); Fazal (2004, 2007); Atzili (2006/7).

there a way to induce the Great Powers' compliance? Or is the practice of recognition inexorably political?

The power politics of recognition and new statehood have an indelible impact on the membership and character of the international system. Understanding how and why the international community accepts some new members while rejecting most others has the potential to help minimize unnecessary and ineffective civil violence and build stronger and more legitimate new states.

APPENDIX A

Project Codebook

November 2010
    Secession and Great Power Recognition Dataset
    (1931–2000)
    Version 2.0

A Note to Users:
This is the codebook for the Secession and Great Power Recognition Dataset, Version 2.0.

Users of the data should use the following citation:
Coggins, Bridget. (2011). "Friends in High Places: International Politics and the Emergence of States from Secessionism." *International Organization* 65:3, pp. 433–467.

Comments or inquiries regarding this dataset should be directed to: Bridget. Coggins@gmail.com

Definition of a Secessionist Movement:
A secessionist movement is a nationalist group that is attempting to separate from an existing state in order to form a newly independent state.

A secessionist movement is operationally defined as any group that formally declared independence before 1931 and continued on through 1931 <u>or</u> that began after 1931. To be considered a secessionist movement, the group must have <u>all</u> of the following characteristics:

    1. a formal declaration of full independence and intended separation from their home state (in many cases, these declarations are UDIs, or unilateral declarations of independence, signifying that they do not [yet] have the consent of the former governing state),
    2. a national flag,

3. a claim to both territory and population over which the movement presides, and

4. the movement must last at least 7 (24-hour) days, include at least 100 individuals, and claim at least 100 square meters of territory.

A movement is **not** considered to be secessionist if it has any of the following characteristics:

1. It proclaims independence short of national self-government (e.g., autonomy within a state government, independence from other colonial territories short of independence from the colonial government, or other internal civil rights movements).

2. It claims jurisdiction over the entirety of the home state as in the cases of revolution or coup d'état.[1]

3. It attempts to join another preexisting state (this is irredentism).[2] In addition, irredentism is often initiated by the state government hoping to annex a portion of another state, rather than by the individuals within the territory itself.[3]

4. A federation of which it is a part formally dissolves without any contest. One of the two (or more) parties must desire unity under a governing regime in order for a secession to take place.

5. It does not declare independence, but instead is granted it unilaterally (as in the case of the South African Bantustans or the Japanese puppet state of Manchukuo).[4]

6. A claim to territory is made without a population (e.g., artificial/platform islands in the 1960s) or a claim to population is made without a claim to territory (e.g., pirate states).[5]

---

[1] Consistent with Fearon and Laitin (2003), this dataset asserts that the important distinction between civil conflicts lies not in the ethno-religious versus ideological dimension that many scholars use, but rather between wars of autonomy and secession and wars for control of the state apparatus as in elite or social revolutions.

[2] The two exceptions to this rule are the cases of Cyprus and Northern Ireland's separation from the UK. Although many within Cyprus (Greek Cypriots) demanded independence so that a later association with Greece might be achieved, independence was required prior to a voluntary association. In this case, the demand was not straightforwardly irredentist, but rather secessionist. Northern Ireland is now classified as a secession because the Irish government has dropped its claim to the territory.

[3] Horowitz, cited in Moore (1998).

[4] For the purposes of this project, the emergence of a new state agreed to by a colonial government prior to its declaration of independence or demand for independence will not be considered to remain true to the topic. Colonial units that unilaterally declare independence will be considered attempts at secession, however.

[5] These criteria are essential to distinguishing real claims to independence from insincere claims such as those based on tax and/or legal escapism, for example, the Kingdom of Minerva. Established in 1972, Minerva was envisioned by its libertarian founders as a taxless nation. It was located on a Pacific reef off the coast of Tonga only visible above water at low tide. Its founders built up the state's landmass, minted approximately 10,500 Republic of Minerva, $35 dollar coins (Stebinsky 2005), and established a cabinet. Unfortunately, Minerva was invaded and occupied by Tonga,

An attempt to secede is considered to have begun on the earliest date of any of the following acts:

1. A formal declaration of independence is issued.
2. Violent conflict between a group and the home state begins with the stated demand of full independence for the group. A formal declaration of independence must follow. Coding is retroactive in this case.
3. Nonviolent action is taken on behalf of the secessionists with the stated demand of full independence from the home state. Some examples of this might include the formation of separatist political parties and their participation in elections (e.g., the Quebecois in Canada or Lega Nord in Italy) or peaceful public demonstration (e.g., Tibetans in China). A formal declaration of independence must follow. Coding is retroactive in this case.

Qualifications 2 and 3 exclude cases such as Taiwan, which would not be classified as an attempted secession because no formal declaration of independence has followed popular calls for independence there.

A secessionist movement is considered to have ended when any of the following occurs:

1. It formally renounces its claim of independence. The date of renouncement is the end date.
2. It agrees to a settlement short of full independence, implying the renouncement of its secessionist ambition. The date of agreement is the end date.
3. Five years pass without reported secessionist activity (protests, militarized disputes with the home government, negotiations, external appeals for support, etc.). The date of the last recorded activity is the end date.
4. The home government (or occupying government) formally agrees to grant the secessionists independence or grants a plebiscite to determine independence. The date of the agreement is the end date when independence is granted. The date of the referendum, if in favor of independence, is the end date. If the vote is not in favor of independence, an end date will not be assigned unless one of the earlier listed qualities also obtains.

Within the dataset, abbreviations in captions correspond to political parties or activist organizations associated with the secessionist movement. Captioned words may also correspond to current place names of states or regions or to particular ethnic or regional groups associated with the movement.

which had claimed the "land" for itself. Beginning in 2003, a group based in South Carolina revived the Minervan independence cause, changed the governmental structure to a principality (a 22-year-old law student, Prince Calvin, presides over the government-in-exile), and it now sells "Free Minerva" t-shirts and memorabilia online. Though the group has an admittedly impressive website, Minerva has no population and, therefore, does not qualify as a secessionist movement. (Additional curiosity may be sated at minervanet.org.)

Definition of Great Power:

The definition of great power employed in this data comes from the Correlates of War (COW) identification of "major power" states:

At one end of the status or power spectrum, a political entity may have most of the earmarks of statehood but not qualify for system membership, or it may merit inclusion in the system but remain peripheral enough in activity, power, or importance to fail of inclusion in the central system prior to 1920. At the other end of the spectrum, all students of world politics use, or appreciate the relevance of, the concept of "major power." Sharing that appreciation and recognizing its relevance for establishing a wide range of war data categories, we add this smallest sub-system to our classification scheme.[6]

Operationally, Great Powers appearing within the time frame for this dataset were as follows:

> Great Britain (1931–2000)
> United States (1931–2000)
> Union of Soviet Socialist Republics (1931–1991)
> which continued as Russia (1991–2000)
> China (1950–2000)
> France (1931–1940) and (1945–2000)
> Germany (1931–1945) and (1991–2000)
> Italy (1931–1943)
> Japan (1931–45) and (1991–2000)

VARIABLES IN THE SECESSION AND GREAT POWER RECOGNITION DATASETS

Domestic Data

1. case: The unique dataset I.D. number for the secessionist conflict. There are 259 secessionist movements. See Appendix B for case I.D.
2. name: The longhand name for the conflict dyad. Where a conflict between a secessionist–home state dyad recurs or where more than one distinct secessionist movement exists within the same ethnic or geographic region, then roman numerals serve to distinguish the movements, for example, China-Tibet I, China-Tibet II, or place name in parentheses, for example, France–French West Africa (Guinea) or France–French West Africa (Mauritania). See Appendix B for names.
3. homestate: The state from which the secessionist movement is attempting to secede. In some cases, a single secessionist movement attempts to secede from a number of home states as in Kurdistan. Each secessionist–

---

[6] More information is available in the COW appendix: "State System Membership List, Frequently Asked Questions" (Version 2002.1) at http://www.correlatesofwar.org or in Small and Singer (1982).

home state dyad is coded as a separate instance of secession (e.g., Iraq-Kurds, Turkey-Kurds) because it is theoretically possible for one group to succeed in its goal of independence whereas another does not (or fails or compromises whereas the other does not). Coded uses the Correlates of War (COW) country code for the home state.[7]

4. cow: The three-letter Correlates of War data abbreviation for the home state (actor1).

5. ccode1: The three-number Correlates of War data country code for the home state (actor1).

6. year: The calendar year for which observations were coded.

7. distinct: A variable indicating the extent of linguistic and religious differences between the secessionist group and the home state majority. If the two share a language family, the indicator is coded 0, if different, then 1.[8] Religious dissimilarity compares the majority's religion to that of the secessionists'.[9] If the two shared a religion, the indicator is coded 0, if different, then 1. The indicators were then summed together.

   0 group shares both language and religion with majority

   1 group is distinct from the majority on one dimension: religion or language

   2 group is distinct from the majority on two dimensions: religion and language

8. mar: A dummy variable indicating whether the secessionist group is found within the Minorities at Risk (MAR) data in a given year.[10] "At risk" minority groups are those that number at least 100,000 or constitute 1 percent of their home state's total population, suffer discrimination because of their minority status, and are politically mobilized in order to advance or defend the group's interests[11]: 1 = Minority at Risk, 0 = Not a Minority at Risk.

9. colony: A dummy variable indicating whether the secessionist movement is a colony of the home state during each conflict year. Operationally, a *colony* is defined as a jurisdiction (people and territory) governed by a

---

[7] The variable ccode corresponds to the Correlates of War Country Code for the home state where available. For coding rules, see Correlates of War Project (2005).

[8] Language families, of which there are 128 worldwide, were identified using the Ethnologue database (Gordon 2005). If the majority did not share a common language, the national language or language of government was used.

[9] Differences were judged among the five major world religions: Buddhism, Christianity, Hinduism, Islam, and Judaism. This operationalization is close, but not identical, to Huntington's (1993) measure of civilization. An additional religion variable, measuring smaller distinctions such as those among Sunni, Shia, and Sufi Islam or Protestant, Catholic, Orthodox, and other forms of Christianity was also created but was not statistically significant.

[10] Minorities at Risk Project (2009).

[11] For additional criteria, see the Minorities at Risk website: http://www.cidcm.umd.edu/mar/definition.asp. Although it is possible for a MAR group to be politically advantaged by its status, this was not the case for the groups in this study.

state or agents of a state that is neither geographically contiguous nor within 100 miles of its shoreline. Secondary secessions, that is, secession attempts where the home state is a former colony itself, are not coded as colonies even though they reside within units that once were. Emblematically, Bangladesh's secession from Pakistan and Biafra's attempted separation from Nigeria were not considered anti-colonial; 1 = Colony. 0 = Not a colony.

10. ethnicfed: A dummy variable indicating whether the secessionists have a state within an ethno-federal union during each conflict year.[12] *EthnicFed* follows Philip Roeder's (2007) coding but drops all colonial units. For example, Slovenia was a member of an ethnic federation, Yugoslavia, whereas Mozambique was a Portuguese colony; 1 = Ethno-federal union member, 0 = Not an ethno-federal union member.

11. vlevel: The level of violence experienced annually in a given secessionist–home state dyad. The variable comes from the Uppsala Conflict Data Program (UCDP) at the Peace Research Institute, Oslo (PRIO). In a given year, the variable codes
   0 no armed conflict
   1 between 25 and 999 battle-related deaths
   2 at least 1,000 battle-related deaths[13]

12. warwin: A dummy variable indicating the year in which a secessionist movement defeats its home state in a war for independence, taken from the COW intrastate war data; 1 = Secessionist war win, 0 = Conflict is ongoing, ends in a stalemate, or ends in a loss.[14]

13. UN: A dummy variable indicating the year in which a secessionist movement becomes a full member of the United Nations (UN); 1 = UN membership, 0 = Not a member.

14. cowsys: A dummy variable indicating the year in which a secessionist movement becomes a member of the COW System Membership Data; 1 = COW membership, 0 = Not a member.

International Data

1. case: The unique dataset I.D. number for the secessionist conflict. See Appendix B for case I.D.

---

[12] Roeder (2007) considers colonies to be a form of ethnic segment state. Unfortunately, combining the two types of units in this way raises construct validity problems. Colonial administrations were not typically representative of the people; therefore, the posited theoretical mechanism underlying segment state emergence, namely disproportionate bargaining leverage with the state, cannot function in the manner it does in ethnic federations. Further, alternative explanations for the disproportionate success of anticolonial groups and ethno-federal groups exist, distinct from Roeder's, making them equifinal. Consequently, this analysis treats the two as distinct.

[13] UCDP/PRIO (2008).

[14] Secessionist conflicts often remain ongoing after combat ceases.

2. name: The longhand name for the conflict dyad. Where a conflict between a secessionist–home state dyad recurs or where more than one distinct secessionist movement exists within the same ethnic or geographic region, then roman numerals serve to distinguish the movements, for example, China-Tibet I, China-Tibet II, or place name in parentheses, for example, France–French West Africa (Guinea), France-French West Africa (Mauritania). See Appendix B for names.

3. actor1: The state from which the secessionist movement is attempting to secede (referred to as the home state in the domestic dataset). In some cases, a single secessionist movement attempts to secede from a number of home states as in Kurdistan. Each secessionist–home state dyad is coded as a separate instance of secession (e.g., Iraq-Kurds, Turkey-Kurds) because it is theoretically possible for one group to succeed in its goal of independence, whereas another does not (or fails or compromises whereas the other does not).

4. cow: The three-letter Correlates of War data abbreviation for the home state (actor1).

5. ccode1: The three-number Correlates of War data country code for the home state (actor1).[15]

6. year: The calendar year for which observations were coded.

7. ccode2: The three-number Correlates of War data country code for the Great Power state (actor2).[16]

8. dyadid: A unique I.D. number for each secessionist conflict–Great Power dyad.

9. colony: A dummy variable indicating whether the secessionist movement is a colony of the home state during each conflict year. Operationally, a *colony* is defined as a jurisdiction (people and territory) governed by a state or agents of a state that is neither geographically contiguous nor within 100 miles of its shoreline. Secondary secessions, that is, secession attempts where the home state is a former colony itself, are not coded as colonies even though they reside within units that once were. Emblematically, Bangladesh's secession from Pakistan and Biafra's attempted separation from Nigeria were not considered anticolonial; 1 = Colony, 0 = Not a colony.

10. ethnicfed: A dummy variable indicating whether the secessionists have a state within an ethno-federal union during each conflict year.[17] *EthnicFed* follows Philip Roeder's (2007) coding but drops all colonial units. For example, Slovenia was a member of an ethnic federation,

---

[15] The variable ccode corresponds to the Correlates of War Country Code for the home state where available. For coding rules, see Correlates of War 2 Project (2003).

[16] See note 15.

[17] See note 12.

Yugoslavia, whereas Mozambique was a Portuguese colony; 1 = Ethno-
federal union member, 0 = Not an ethno-federal union member.

11. vlevel: The level of violence experienced annually in a given secessionist–
    home state dyad. The variable comes from the Uppsala Conflict Data
    Program (UCDP) at the Peace Research Institute, Oslo (PRIO). In a given
    year, the variable codes
    0 no armed conflict
    1 between 25 and 999 battle-related deaths
    2 at least 1,000 battle-related deaths.[18]

12. warwin: A dummy variable indicating the year in which a secessionist
    movement defeats its home state in a war for independence, taken from
    the COW intrastate war data; 1= Secessionist war win, 0 = Conflict is
    ongoing, ends in a stalemate, or ends in a loss.[19]

13. challengers: A count of the number of ongoing secessionist challenges
    against the given Great Power (actor2) in a given year. Data collected
    from this dataset.

14. challengeh: A dummy variable indicating whether a Great Power
    (actor2) has an unusually high number of secessionist challengers during
    a given year. The variable was created by taking the number of seces-
    sionist challenges for each Great Power home state in each year of the
    dataset and coding 1 for cases in the 90th percentile and above, which
    included those Great Powers with between 10 and 21 challengers in a
    conflict year; 1 = Unusually high number of challenges, 0 = Not an
    unusually high number of challenges.

15. vchallenge: A variable indicating the cumulative level of violence reached
    in a Great Power's (actor2) domestic secessionist challenges in a given
    year. The intensity of violence was measured by summing the levels of
    violence from the PRIO dataset for each Great Power's domestic seces-
    sionist challenges in a given year.[20] The resulting variable ranges from 0
    (none) to 6 (violence equivalent to 3 full-scale civil wars).

16. cwmid: A dummy variable indicating whether a Great Power (actor2)
    and a home state (actor1) initiate a militarized interstate dispute during a
    given year. The variable is taken from the Militarized Interstate Dispute
    (MID) data; 1 = MID initiated, 0 = No MID initiated.

17. mutualdem: A dummy variable indicating that both the Great Power
    (actor2) and the home state (actor1) were stable democracies during a
    given year. The variable is derived from scores provided by the Polity IV
    data. Consistent with accepted practice, states with Polity scores above 7

[18] UCDP/PRIO (2008).
[19] Secessionist conflicts often remain ongoing after combat ceases.
[20] No armed conflict (0), 25–999 battle-related deaths (1), 1,000 or more battle-related deaths (2).
The intensity of violence measure is rather crude. For example, two conflicts causing 300 battle-
related deaths would be coded identically to one conflict with more than 1,000 battle-related
deaths. Unfortunately, no better algorithm is readily available.

were considered democracies; 1 = Mutual democracy, 0 = Not mutual democracy.[21]

18. mutualaut: A dummy variable indicating that both the Great Power (actor2) and the home state (actor1) were stable autocracies during a given year. The variable is derived from scores provided by the Polity IV data. Consistent with accepted practice, states with Polity scores below −7 were considered autocracies; 1 = Mutual autocracy, 0 = Not mutual autocracy.[22]

19. prec: A dummy variable indicating that at least one Great Power had previously granted recognition to a given secessionist movement, collected from this dataset; 1 = Previous recognition, 0 = No previous recognition.

20. precs: A count variable indicating the number of Great Power recognitions granted to a given secessionist movement as of that conflict year.

21. gprecpro: A variable measuring the proportion of the total number of Great Powers that have granted a secessionist movement recognition as of a given conflict year.

22. recyear: A dummy variable indicating the year in which a given Great Power (actor2) grants formal recognition to a given secessionist movement.

---

[21] One or both of the states had Polity scores between −10 and 6, −66, −77, or −88.
[22] One or both of the states had Polity scores between −6 and 10, −66, −77, or −88.

APPENDIX B

Unique Case I.D.

#	NAME
1	USA – Marshall Islands
2	USA – Micronesia
3	USA – Philippines
4	USA – Hawaiians
5	USA – Puerto Rico
6	Canada – Quebec
7	St.Kitts and Nevis – Nevis I
8	Bolivia – Cambas
9	UK – Baluch
10	UK – Rhodesia – Northern Rhodesia – Barotseland (Lozi)
11	UK – Northern Ireland
12	UK – Yemen (FLOSY)
13	UK – Buganda
14	UK – Gold Coast (Ghana) I
15	UK – Jews (Palestine/Israel) I
16	UK – Karen
17	UK – Newfoundland
18	UK – Rhodesia – Northern Rhodesia
19	UK – Rhodesia
20	UK – Scots II
21	UK – Scots I
22	UK – Iraq
23	UK – Egypt
24	UK – Burma (Myanmar)
25	UK – Pakistan (West & East)
26	UK – India
27	UK – Ceylon (Sri Lanka)

28   UK – Jews (Palestine/Israel) III
29   UK – Jews (Palestine/Israel) II
30   UK – Sanusis
31   UK – Sudan
32   UK – Gold Coast (Ghana) II
33   UK – Malaya (Straits Settlements)(Malaysia)
34   UK – Cyprus
35   UK – British Somaliland
36   UK – Nigeria
37   UK – Sierra Leone
38   UK – Tanganyika
39   UK – Uganda
40   UK – Kuwiat
41   UK – Mau Mau (Kenya)
42   UK – Zanzibar (inc. w/Tanganyika)
44   UK – Gambia
45   UK – Guyana
46   UK – Basuotoland (Lesotho)
47   UK – Botswana
48   UK – Yemen (NLF)
49   UK – Mauritius
50   UK – Swazi
51   UK – Fiji
52   UK – Bahamas
53   Australia – PNG
54   UK – Seychelles
55   UK – Rhodesia – Zimbabwe
56   UK – Brunei
57   Netherlands – Netherlands Indies I
58   Netherlands – Netherlands Indies II
59   Netherlands – W. Papua (Iran Jaya)
60   Netherlands – Dutch Guiana
61   Belgium – Flemish
62   Belgium – Belgian Congo
63   Belgium – Burundi (Bezi)
64   Belgium – Rwanda
65   France – Alawites (Hatay)
66   France – Basques
67   France – Brittany
68   France – Casamance
69   France – Corsica
70   France – French Somaliland II
71   France – French Indochina (Laos)
72   France – French Indochina I

73	France – French West Africa RDA
74	France – Syria
75	France – French Indochina (Cambodia)
76	France – French Indochina (Vietnam) II
77	France – Morocco
78	France – Tunisia
79	France – French West Africa (Guinea)
80	France – Mossi (Burkina Faso)
81	France – French Eq. Africa (CAR)
82	France – French Eq. Africa (Chad)
83	France – French Eq. Africa (Middle Congo)
84	France – French West Africa (Cote d'Ivoire)
85	France – French Somaliland I
86	France – French Eq. Africa (Gabon)
87	France – Niger
88	France – French West Africa (French Soudan)(Mali)
89	France – Senegal
90	France – French West Africa (Mauritania)
91	France – Algeria
92	France – Comoros
93	France – Dahomey
94	France – Madagascar
95	France – Monaco
96	France – Savoy
97	France – French Indochina (Pathet Lao)
98	Switzerland – Jura
99	Spain – Basques II
100	Spain – Catalans II
101	Spain – Spanish Guinea
102	Spain – Basques I
103	Spain – Basques III
104	Spain – Catalans I
105	Portugal – Guinea Bissau
106	Potugal – Mozambique
107	Portugal – Sao Tome & Principe
108	Portugal – Angola
109	Portugal – East Timor
110	Portugal – Cape Verde
111	Czechoslovakia – Slovakia
112	Italy – Giulians
113	Italy – Sicily
114	Italy – Italian Somaliland
115	Italy – Padania
116	Italy – Sardinia

117   Italy – South Tyrol
118   Italy – Montenegro
119   Italy – Sanusis
120   Croatia – Serbs
121   Yugoslavia – Albanians (Kosovars)
122   Serbia and Montenegro – Kosovo Albanians
123   Yugoslavia – Bosnia/Herz
124   Yugoslavia – Croatians
125   Yugoslavia – Slovenians
126   Yugoslavia – Macedonia
127   Bosnia and Herz. – Serbs
128   Bosnia – Croats (Muslims 1994–1995)
129   Cyprus – Turkish Cypriots
130   Moldova – Transnistria
131   Moldova – Gagauz
132   USSR – Adzhar
133   USSR – Ajars
134   Russia – Chechnya I
135   Russia – Chechnya II
136   Russia – Dagestanis
137   USSR – Tatars
138   Russia – Tatars
139   USSR – Estonians II
140   USSR – Abkhaz Rep.
141   USSR – Latvians II
142   USSR – Lithuanians III
143   USSR – Armenia
144   USSR – Azeris
150   USSR – Russian
151   USSR – Tajiks
152   USSR – Turkomen
153   USSR – Ukrainians II
154   USSR – Uzbeks
155   USSR – Balkars
156   Czechoslovakia – Carpatho-Rusyns
162   USSR – Lithuanians II
163   USSR – Ukrainians I
164   Ukraine – Crimea
165   Georgia – Abkhazia
166   Georgia – South Ossetia
167   Azerbaijan – Nagoro-Karabakh (Armenians)
168   Azerbaijan – Talysh
169   Denmark – Iceland
170   Denmark – Faeroe Islands

171	Mali Federation – Senegal
172	Senegal – Casamance II
173	Senegal – Casamance I
174	Ivory Coast – Anyi
175	Cameroon – Southern Cameroon
176	Nigeria – Edos
177	Nigeria – Ibos (Igbo)
178	DRC – South Kasai
179	DRC – South Katanga
180	DRC – Stanleyville
181	Uganda – Bankonjo II
182	Uganda – Bankonjo I
187	Ethiopia – Somali I
188	Ethiopia – Somali II
189	Ethiopia – Tigray II
190	Ethiopia – Eritreans
191	Ethiopia – Tigray I
192	Angola – Cabindans
193	South Africa – Inkatha (Kwazulu)
194	South Africa – Namibia
195	Namibia – Basters (Rehoboth)
196	Namibia – Lozi
197	Comoros – Anjouan
198	Comoros – Moheli
199	Morocco – Saharawis
200	Sudan – Southerners I
201	Sudan – Southerners II
202	Iran – Arabistanis (Ahwaz)(Khuzestan)
203	Iran – Kurds II
204	Iran – Kurds I
205	Iran – Azeris
207	Turkey – Kurds II
208	Iraq – Kurds I
209	Iraq – Kurds II
210	Iraq – Kurds III
211	Iraq – Kurds IV
212	Israel – Palestinians I
213	Israel – Palestinians II
214	Saudi Arabia – Asiris
215	Yemen – South Yemen
216	China – Manchukuo
217	China – Uighurs II
218	China – Eastern Mongols
219	China – Southern Mongols

220 China – Tibet I
221 China – Uighurs I
222 China – Hui
223 China – Tibet II
224 China – Tibet III
225 China – Tibet IV
226 China – Uighurs III (Xinjiang)
227 Japan – Shans
228 India – Assam
229 India – Boro/Bodo
230 India – Hyderabad
231 India – Kashmir I
232 India – Kashmir II
233 India – Malayalis
234 India – Meitei
235 India – Mizos
236 India – Nagas
237 India – Sikhs I
238 India – Sikhs II
239 India – Tripuras
240 Pakistan – Baluch
241 Pakistan – Pashtuns
242 Pakistan – E.Pakistan (E. Bengal)(Bengalis)
243 Bangladesh – Chittagong
244 Burma – Arakanese II
245 Burma – Kachins II
246 Burma – Karenni
247 Burma – Karens
248 Burma – Mons
249 Burma – Shans I
250 Burma – Shans II
251 Burma – Arakanese I
252 Burma – Kachins I
253 Sri Lanka – Tamils
254 Thailand – Malays I
255 Vietnam – Chams
256 Malaysia – Singapore
257 Philippines – Mindanao III
258 Philippines – Mindanao I
259 Philippines – Abu Sayyaf
260 Philippines – Mindanao II
261 Indonesia – Acheh I
262 Indonesia – Acheh II
263 Indonesia – Papuans

264 Indonesia – Sulawesis
265 Indonesia – W.Papua (Iran Jaya)
266 Indonesia – East Timor
267 Indonesia – Ambonese
268 Papua New Guinea – Bougainville I
269 Papua New Guinea – Bougainville II
270 New Zealand – Maori
271 New Zealand – Samoa (W. Samoa)
272 Vanuatu – Tafea
273 Vanuatu – Vemeranans
274 Solomon Islands – Guadacanal
275 United Arab Republic – Syria

References

Anderson, Lisa. (2004). "Antiquated Before They Can Ossify: States That Fail Before They Form." *Journal of International Affairs* 58:1, pp.1–16.

Arbatov, Alexi, Abram Chayes, Antonia Handler Chayes, and Lara Olson (Eds.). (1997). *Managing Conflict in the Former Soviet Union: Russian and American Perspectives* Cambridge, MA: MIT Press.

Ashley, Richard. (1984). "The Poverty of Neo-Realism." *International Organization* 38:1, pp. 225–286.

Atzili, Boaz. (2006/7). "When Good Fences Make Bad Neighbors: Fixed Borders, State Weakness, and International Conflict." *International Security* 31:3, pp. 139–173.

Auerswald, Philip E., and David P. Auerswald. (2000). *The Kosovo Conflict: A Diplomatic History through Documents*. Cambridge, UK: Kluwer Law International.

Ayoob, Mohammed. (1995). *The Third World Security Predicament*. Boulder, CO: Lynne Rienner Publishers.

Ayres, R. William. (1998). "Strategies and Outcomes in Post-Soviet Nationalist Secession Conflicts." *International Politics* 35, pp. 135–163.

Ayres, R. William. (2000). "A World Flying Apart? Violent Nationalist Conflict and the End of the Cold War." *Journal of Peace Research* 37:1, pp. 107–117.

Bakke, Kristin, John O'Laughlin, and Michael D. Ward. (2011). "The Viability of *de facto* States: Post-War Developments and Internal Legitimacy in Abkhazia." Working paper presented at the Annual Meeting of the American Political Science Association. September 1–4, 2011, Seattle, Washington.

Baranovsky, Vladimir. (2000). "Russia: A Part of Europe or Apart from Europe." *International Affairs (Royal Institute of International Affairs 1944–)* 76:3 (July), pp. 443–458.

Barkin, J. Samuel, and Bruce Cronin. (1994). "The State and the Nation: Changing Norms and the Rules of Sovereignty in International Relations." *International Organization* 48:1, pp. 107–130.

Barnett, Michael, and Martha Finnemore. (2004). *Rules for the World: International Organizations in Global Politics*. Ithaca, NY: Cornell University Press.

Bartkus, Viva Ona. (1999). *The Dynamics of Secession*. Cambridge, UK: Cambridge University Press.

243

Bearce, David. (2002). "Institutional Breakdown and International Cooperation: The European Agreement to Recognize Croatia and Slovenia." *European Journal of International Relations* 8:4, pp. 471–497.

Beck, Nathaniel, Johnathan Katz, and Richard Tucker. (1998). "Taking Time Seriously: Time Series Cross-Sectional Analysis with Binary Dependent Variable." *American Journal of Political Science* 42:4, pp. 1260–1288.

Beissinger, Mark R. (2002). *Nationalist Mobilization and the Collapse of the Soviet State.* Cambridge, UK: Cambridge University Press.

Bellamy, Alex J. (2002). *Kosovo and International Society.* New York: Palgrave MacMillan.

Bennigsen, Marie. (1999). "Chechnia: Political Developments and Strategic Implications for the North Caucasus." *Central Asian Survey* 18:4, pp. 535–574.

Berger, Mikhail. (1997, May 20). "Bankers Give Recognition to Chechnya." *Independent Press, The Moscow Times.*

Betts, Richard. (1994). "The Delusion of Impartial Intervention." *Foreign Affairs* 73:6 (November/December).

Bhatty, Robin, and Rachel Bronson. (2000). "NATO's Mixed Signals in the Caucasus and Central Asia." *Survival* 42:3, pp. 129–145.

Biersteker Thomas J., and Cynthia Weber. (Eds.). (1996). *State Sovereignty as a Social Construct.* Cambridge, UK: Cambridge University Press.

Bookman, Milica Zarkovic. (1992). *The Economics of Secession.* New York: St. Martin's Press.

Boucher, David. (1998). *Political Theories of International Relations.* Oxford, UK: Oxford University Press.

Bowley, Graham. (2008, March 2). "Declaring Something a Lot Like Dependence." *New York Times*, available at http://www.nytimes.com/2008/03/02/weekinreview/02bowley.html?pagewanted=all&_r=0.

Box-Steffensmeier, Janet M., and Bradford S. Jones. (1997). "Time Is of the Essence: Event History Models in Political Science." *American Journal of Political Science* 41:4, pp. 1414–1461.

Box-Steffensmeier, Janet, and Christopher J. W. Zorn. (2001). "Duration Models and Proportional Hazards in Political Science." *American Journal of Political Science* 45:4, pp. 972–988.

Box-Steffensmeier, Janet M., and Bradford S. Jones. (2004). *Event History Modeling: A Guide for Social Scientists.* Cambridge, UK: Cambridge University Press.

Bozic-Roberson, Agneza. (2004). "Words before the War." *East European Quarterly* 38:4 (Winter), pp. 395–408.

Bradbury, Mark. (2008). *Becoming Somaliland.* London: Progressio.

Brancati, Dawn. (2006). "Decentralization: Fueling the Fire or Dampening the Flames of Ethnic Conflict and Secessionism?" *International Organization* 60:3, pp. 651–685.

Brady, Henry E., and David Collier. (2004). *Rethinking Social Inquiry: Diverse Tools, Shared Standards.* New York: Rowman & Littlefield.

British Broadcasting Company (BBC) Monitoring Europe – Political. (2006, February 14). "Envoy Assures Kosovo President of British Support on Final Status Issue," available at http://www.lexis-nexis.com.

British Broadcasting Company (BBC) News. (2009, August 12). "Russians to Boost Abkhazia Bases," available at http://news.bbc.co.uk/2/hi/8196974.stm.

British Parliamentary Debate. (2004, February 4). "Development Aid for Somaliland" *Transcript*.

Brooke, James. (1991, October 2). "As Centralized Rule Wanes, Ethnic Tension Rises Anew in Soviet Georgia." *The New York Times* Section A, p.3.

Browlie, Ian. (1990). *Principles of Public International Law*, 4th ed. Oxford, UK: Oxford University Press.

Brownlie, Ian. (1983). *System of the Law of Nations: State Responsibility*. Oxford, UK: Clarendon Press.

Bucheit, Lee C. (1978). *Secession: The Legitimacy of Self-Determination* New Haven, CT: Yale University Press.

Buckley, Neil, and Arkady Ostrovsky. (2005, January 26). "Georgia Offers Power-Share Plan to South Ossetia." *Finiancial Times*, available at http://www.ft.com/cms/s/o/9dd61b56-6f43-11d9-94a8-00000e2511c8.html#axzz1ZMmCjE7r.

Bull, Hedley. (1977). *The Anarchical Society* New York: Columbia University Press.

Bunce, Valerie. (1999). *Subversive Institutions: The Design and Destruction of Socialism and the State*. Cambridge, UK: Cambridge University Press.

Burns, Nicholas. (1997, January 6). "U.S. Support for Elections in Chechnya." *Press Statement: U.S. Department of State*.

Bush, George H. W. (1991, September 2). Presidential News Conference. Kennebunkport, ME.

Bush, George H. W. (1992, March 16). "Remarks to the Polish National Alliance in Chicago, IL."

Buzan, Barry, Charles A. Jones, and Richard Little.(1993). *The Logic of Anarchy: Neo-Realism to Structural Realism*. New York: Columbia University Press.

Byman, Daniel, Peter Chalk, Bruce Hoffman, William Rosenau, and David Brannan. (2001). *Trends in Outside Support for Insurgent Movements*. Santa Monica, CA: RAND, National Security Research Division.

Cain, Kenneth L. (2003, December 14). "Suspended Nationhood." *New York Times Magazine* 6:1, p. 93.

Campbell, Edwina S., and Jack M. Seymour Jr. (1997). "France, Germany, and the Yugoslavian Wars," in Constantine P. Danopoulos and Kostas G. Messas (Eds.), *Crises in the Balkans*. Boulder, CO: Westview Press.

Caplan, Richard. (2005). *Europe and the Recognition of New States in Yugoslavia*. New York: Cambridge University Press.

Carment, David, and Patrick James (Eds.). (1997). *Wars in the Midst of Peace: The International Politics of Ethnic Conflict*. Pittsburgh, PA: University of Pittsburgh Press.

Cagorovic, Ljubinka. (2005, October 14). "Montenegro PM Says No Delaying Independence Vote." *Reuters*.

Caspersen, Nina. (2008). "Separatism and Democracy in the Caucasus." *Survival* 50:4, pp. 113–136.

Caspersen, Nina. (2012). *Unrecognized States: The Struggle for Sovereignty in the Modern International System*. Cambridge, UK: Polity.

Central Intelligence Agency. (2006). "Georgia." *World Factbook Online*, available at https://www.cia.gov/library/publications/the-world-factbook/.

Cherkasov, Alexander, and Tanya Lokshina. (2005). "Chechnya: 10 Years of Armed Conflict." *Helsinki Monitor* 2, p. 144.

Chivers, C. J. (2004, August 15). "Threat of Civil War Is Turning the Abkhaz into Russians." *New York Times*, available at http://www.nytimes.com/2004/08/15/

world/threat-of-civil-war-is-turning-the-abkhaz-into-russians.html?pagewanted=all
&src=pm.

Chivers, C. J. (2004, August 17). "Georgia's New Leader Baffles U.S. and Russia Alike." *New York Times*, available at http://www.nytimes.com/2004/08/17/world/georgia-s-new-leader-baffles-us-and-russia-alike.html.

Chivers, C. J. (2006, April 23). "Azerbaijan Leader, Under Fire, Hopes U.S. Visit Improves Image." *New York Times*, available at http://www.nytimes.com/2006/04/23/world/europe/23azerbaijan.html?pagewanted=all&_r=0.

Chivers, C. J. (2006, May 4). "Signs of Renewal Emerge from Chechna's Ruins." *New York Times Online*, available at http://www.nytimes.com/2006/05/04/world/europe/04chechnya.html?pagewanted=all.

Chivers, C. J., and Ellen Barry. (2008, November 7). "Georgia Claims on Russia War Called into Question." *New York Times*, available at http://www.nytimes.com/2008/11/07/world/europe/07georgia.html?pagewanted=all&_r=0.

Chivers, C. J., and Steven Lee Myers. (2004, September 12). "Chechen Rebels Mainly Driven by Nationalism." *New York Times*, available at http://www.nytimes.com/2004/09/12/international/europe/12russia.html.

Chorbajian, Levon (Ed.). (2001). *The Making of Nagorno-Karabakh: From Secession to Republic*. New York: Palgrave.

Chopra, Jarat. (2003). "Building State Failure in East Timor" in Miliken, Jennifer (Ed.). *State Failure, Collapse, and Reconstruction*. Oxford, UK: Blackwell.

Christopher, Warren (U.S. Secretary of State). (1994, December 13). "Interview." *McNeil-Lehrer News Hour*. [Transcript]

"Chronology for Ossetians (South) in Georgia." (2004). *Minorities at Risk*, available at http://www.cidcm.umd.edu/mar/chronologies.asp?regionId=2.

"Chronology for Armenians in Azerbaijan." (2000). *Minorities at Risk*, available at http://www.cidcm.umd.edu/mar/chronologies.asp?regionId=2.

Clark, Bruce. (1997, November 14). "Chechen Chief Takes Struggle to Washington." *The Financial Times Limited*.

"Clinton Assures China Ties Unchanged by Taiwan President's Visit." (1995, June 9). *Associated Press*, available at http://www.apnewsarchive.com/1995/Clinton-Assures-China-Ties-Unchanged-by-Taiwan-President-s-Visit/id-b5b18da640595771eedb16bbe545472a.

"Clinton Seen Moving toward Kosovo Independence." (1999, April 1). *Paris Le Monde in French, World News Connection*.

Cobban, Alfred. (1969). *The Nation State and National Self Determination*. New York: Crowell.

Coggins, Bridget. (2011). "Friends in High Places: International Politics and the Emergence of States from Secessionism." *International Organization* 65:3, pp. 433–467.

Connelly, Matthew. (2002). *A Diplomatic Revolution: Algeria's Fight for Independence and the Origins of the Post-Cold War Era*. New York: Oxford University Press.

"Convention on the Rights and Duties of States (Inter-American)." (1933, December 26). In *Treaties and Other International Agreements of the United States of America 1776–1949*. Compiled under the direction of Charles I. Bevans LL.B., Assistant Legal Advisor, Department of State, Volume 3, Multilateral 1931–1945 Department of State Publication 8484, Washington, DC: Government Printing Office, 1969.

Cornell, Svante. (2001). *Small Nations and Great Powers: A Study of Ethnopolitical Conflict in the Caucasus.* Surrey, UK: Curzon Press.

Correlates of War Project. (2005). "State System Membership List, v.2004.1," available at http://correlatesofwar.org.

Crawford, Beverly. (1996). "Explaining Defection from International Cooperation: Germany's Unilateral Recognition of Croatia." *World Politics* 48, pp.482–521.

Crawford, James R. (1979). *The Creation of States in International Law.* Oxford, UK: Clarendon Press.

Crawford, James R. (2000). "State Practice in International Law in Relation to Unilateral Secession" in Anne F. Bayefsky (Ed.), *Self-Determination in International Law: Quebec and Lessons Learned.* The Hague, The Netherlands: Kluwer Law International.

Dahl, Robert. (1957). "The Concept of Power." *Behavioral Science* 2, pp.201–218.

"Daily Report: Eastern Europe." (1992, August 27). *Tanjug, World News Connection.*

Danopoulos, Constantine P., and Kostas G. Messas (Ed.). (1997). *Crises in the Balkans: Views from the Participants.* Boulder, CO: Westview Press.

David, Stephen R. (1997). "Internal War: Causes and Cures." *World Politics* 49:4, pp. 552–576.

"Deserters face deportation to Croatia." (1994, February 4). *RFE/RL Daily Report (Bulgaria) World News Connection.*

Ding, Wei. (1991). "Yugoslavia: Costs and Benefits of Union and Interdependence of Regional Economies." *Comparative Economic Studies* 33:4, pp. 1–26.

"Dniester region to hold referendum if Kosovo gains independence." (2006, February 27). *ITAR-TASS in English* World News Connection.

Dugger, Celia. (2005, October 13). "Poverty and Inequality Decline in Former Soviet Union, Study Finds." *New York Times*, available at http://www.nytimes.com/2005/10/13/international/europe/13russia.html?pagewanted=print&gwh=0D71EE66B985B8270B5FE4FD44B458D0.

Duncan, Raymond W., and G. Paul Holman, Jr. (Eds.). (1994). *Ethnic Nationalism and Regional Conflict: The Former Soviet Union and Yugoslavia.* Boulder, CO: Westview Press.

Dunlop, John B. (2000). "How Many Soldiers and Civilians Died during the Russo-Chechen War of 1994–1996?" *Central Asian Survey* 19:3/4, pp. 329–339.

Dunlop, John B. (2002). "Russia: The Forgotten War." *Hoover Digest Online* 1(Winter), available at http://www.hoover.org/publications/hoover-digest/article/6631.

Duursma, Jorri C. (1996). *Fragmentation and the International Relations of Micro-states: Self-Determination and Statehood.* Cambridge, UK: Cambridge University Press.

"EU downplays comments on Kosovo independence." (2006, March 1). *AFP (North European Service), World News Connection.*

Eckstein, Harry. (1975). "Case Study and Theory in Political Science," in Fred Greenstein and Nelson Polsby (Eds.), *Handbook of Political Science*, Vol. 7. Reading, MA: Addison Wesley, pp. 79–138.

Eide, Asbjørn. (2001). "Chechnya: In Search of Constructive Accommodation." *Leiden Journal of International Law* 14, p. 442.

Elbadawi, Ibrahim, and Nicholas Sambanis. (2001). "How Much War Will We See?" *Journal of Conflict Resolution* 46, pp. 307–334.

Emerson, Rupert. (1960). *From Empire to Nation: The Rise to Self-Assertion of Asian and African Peoples*. Cambridge, MA: Harvard University Press.

"Envoy Assures Kosovo President of British Support on Final Status Issue." (2006, February 14). BBC International Reports Monitoring, available at http://www.lexis nexis.com.

Evangelista, Matthew. (2002). *The Chechen Wars: Will Russia Go the Way of the Soviet Union?* Washington, D. C.: Brookings Institution Press.

Eyal, Jonathan. (1993). *Europe and Yugoslavia: Lessons from a Failure*. Whitehall, London: The Royal United Services Institute for Defence Studies.

Fabry, Mikulas. (2010). *Recognizing States*. Oxford, UK: Oxford University Press.

Falk, Richard. (1975). "A New Paradigm for International Legal Studies." *Yale Journal of Law* 84.

Fawcett, J. E. S. (1968). *The Law of Nations*. London: The Penguin Press.

Fawn, Rick, and Jeremy Larkins. (1996). *International Society after the Cold War: Anarchy and Order Reconsidered*. New York: St. Martin's Press.

Fawn, Rick, and James Mayall. (1996). "Recognition, Self-Determination and Secession in Post-Cold War International Society," in R. Fawn and J. Larkins (Eds.), *International Society after the Cold War*. London: Macmillan in association with *Millennium Journal of International Studies*, pp. 193–219.

Fazal, Tanisha. (2004). "State Death in the International System." *International Organization* 58:2 (April), pp. 311–344.

Fazal, Tanisha. (2007). *State Death: The Politics and Geography of Conflict*. Princeton, NJ: Princeton University Press.

Fearon, James D. (2004a). "Separatist Wars Partition and World Order." *Security Studies* 13:4 (Summer), pp. 394–415.

Fearon, James D. (2004b). "Why Do Some Civil Wars Last So Much Longer Than Others?" *Journal of Peace Research* 41:3, pp. 275–301.

Fearon James D., and David Laitin. (2003). "Ethnicity, Insurgency and Civil War." *American Political Science Review* 97:1, pp. 75–90.

Feifer, Gregory. (2009) "The Price of Progress: Life in Kadyrov's Grozny Permeated by Fear" Radio Free Europe/ Radio Liberty, available at http://www.rferl.org/content/The_Price_Of_Progress__Life_In_Kadyrovs_Grozny_Permeated_By_Fear/1797452.html.

Felgenhauer, Pavel. (2002). "The Russian Army in Chechnya." *Central Asian Survey* 21:2, pp. 157–166.

Fink-Hafner, Danica, and John R. Robbins (Ed.). (1997). *Making a New Nation: The Formation of Slovenia*. Brookfield, VT: Dartmouth Publishing Company Limited.

Finnemore, Martha. (1996). *National Interests in International Society*. Ithaca, NY: Cornell University Press.

Finnemore, Martha, and Kathryn Sikkink. (1998). "International Norm Dynamics and Political Change." *International Organization* 52:4 (October), pp. 887–917.

Franck, Thomas. (1990). *The Power of Legitimacy Among Nations*. Oxford, UK: Oxford University Press.

Frantz, Douglas. (2000, December 21). "Russians Send a Message to Georgians: Toe the Line." *New York Times*, available at http://www.nytimes.com/2000/12/21/world/rus sians-send-a-message-to-georgians-toe-the-line.html.

Fukuyama, Francis. (1992). *The End of History and the Last Man*. New York: Free Press.

Gellner, Ernest. (1983/1993). *Nations and Nationalism*. Ithaca, NY: Cornell University Press.

George, A. L. (1979). "Case Studies and Theory Development: The Method of Structured Focused Comparison," in Paul Gordon Lauren (Ed.), *Diplomacy: New Approaches in History, Theory and Policy*. New York: Free Press.

George, A. L., and Andrew Bennett. (2004). *Case Studies and Theory Development in the Social Sciences*. Cambridge, MA: Belfer Center for Science and International Affairs.

"Georgia lifts state of emergency in South Ossetia." (1991, November 25). *Agence France Presse – English, available at* http://www.lexisnexis.com.

German, Tracey C. (2007). "Visibly Invisible: EU Engagement in Conflict Resolution in the South Caucasus." *European Security* 16:3–4, pp. 357–374.

Ghosn, Faten, and Scott Bennett. (2003). "Codebook for the Dyadic Militarized Interstate Incident Data, Version 3.0," available at http://correlatesofwar.org/COW2 Data/MIDs/MID_v3.0.codebook.pdf.

Ghosn, Faten, Glenn Palmer, and Stuart Bremer. (2004). "The MID3 Data Set, 1993–2001: Procedures, Coding Rules, and Description." *Conflict Management and Peace Science* 21, pp. 133–154.

Gibler, Douglas M., and Meredith Sarkees. (2002). "Coding Manual for v3.0 of the Correlates of War Formal Interstate Alliance Data set, 1816–2000." *Typescript*.

Gill, Bates, and James Reilly. (2000). "Sovereignty, Intervention and Peacekeeping: The View from Beijing." *Survival* 42:3, pp. 41–59.

Gladwell, Malcolm. (2000). *The Tipping Point: How Little Things Can Make a Big Difference*. New York: Little, Brown and Company.

Glaser, Charles. (1997). "The Security Dilemma Revisited." *World Politics* 50 (October), pp. 171–201.

Gleditsch, Kristen. (2002). *All International Politics Is Local*. Ann Arbor: University of Michigan Press.

Gleditsch, Nils Peter, Peter Wallensteen, Mikael Eriksson, Margareta Sollenberg, and Havard Strand. (2001). "Armed Conflict 1946–2001: A New Dataset." *Journal of Peace Research* 39:5, pp. 615–637.

Goble, Paul A. (1996). "Dangerous Liaisons: Moscow, the Former Yugoslavia and the West," in Richard H. Ullman (Ed.), *The World and Yugoslavia's Wars*. New York: Council on Foreign Relations.

Goebel, Julius, Jr. (1915). *Recognition Policy of the United States*. New York: Columbia University Press.

Goertz, Gary. (2005). *Social Science Concepts: A Users Guide*. Princeton, NJ: Princeton University Press.

Goldgeier, James M., and Michael McFaul. (2003). *Power and Purpose: U.S. Policy Toward Russia after the Cold War*. Washington, DC: Brookings Institution Press.

Goldsmith, Jack L., and Eric A. Posner. (2005). *The Limits of International Law*. Oxford, UK: Oxford University Press.

Gordon, Raymond G., Jr. (Ed.). (2005). "Ethnologue: Languages of the World, 15th ed." Dallas, TX: SIL International, available at http://www.ethnologue.com.

Gourevitch, Peter. (1978). "The Second Image Reversed: The International Sources of Domestic Politics." *International Organization* 32:4, pp. 881–912.

Gow, James. (1997). *Triumph of the Lack of Will: International diplomacy and the Yugoslav War*. New York: Columbia University Press.

Grant, Thomas D. (1999a). "Defining Statehood: The Montevideo Convention and its Discontents." *Columbia Journal of International Law* 37, p. 403.

Grant, Thomas D. (1999b). *The Recognition of States*. Westport, CT: Praeger.

Grant, Thomas D. (2000). "Current Development: Afghanistan Recognizes Chechnya." *American University International Law Review* 15, p. 869.

"Guidelines on the recognition of new states in Eastern Europe and the Soviet Union" and "Declaration on Yugoslavia" (1991, December 16). *EPC – European Community*, available at http://207.57.19.226/journal/Vol4/No1/art6.html and http://207.57.19.226/journal/Vol4/No1/art7.html#TopOfPage.

Gurr, Ted Robert. (2000a). *Minorities at Risk: Origins and Outcomes of Ethno Political Conflicts*. Washington, DC: United States Institute of Peace Press.

Gurr, Ted Robert. (2000b). *Peoples versus States: Minorities at Risk in the New Century*. Washington, DC: United States Institute of Peace Press.

Hannum, Hurst. (1990). *Autonomy, Sovereignty and Self-Determination: The Accommodation of Conflicting Rights*. Philadelphia: University of Pennsylvania Press.

Hale, Henry E. (2000). "The Parade of Sovereignties: Testing Theories of Secession in the Soviet Setting." *British Journal of Political Science* 30:1, pp. 31–56.

Halperin, Morton H., David J. Scheffer, and Patricia L. Small. (1992). *Self-Determination in the New World Order*. Washington, DC: Carnegie Endowment for International Peace.

Hanson, Alan. (2000). "Croatian Independence from Yugoslavia, 1991–1992," in Melanie C. Greenberg et al (Eds.), *Words over War: Mediation and Arbitration to Prevent Deadly Conflict*. New York: Rowman and Littlefield, pp. 76–108.

Henderson, Errol A., and J. David Singer. (2002). " 'New Wars' and Rumors of 'New Wars.' " *International Interactions* 28, pp. 165–190.

Heraclides, Alexis. (1990). "Secessionist Minorities and External Involvement." *International Organization* 44:3, pp. 341–378.

Herbst, Jeffrey. (1996–7). "Responding to State Failure in Africa." *International Security* 21:3 (Winter), pp. 120–144.

Herbst, Jeffrey. (2000). *States and Power in Africa: Comparative Lessons in Authority and Control*. Princeton, NJ: Princeton University Press.

Herbst, Jeffrey. (2004). "Let Them Fail: State Failure in Theory and Practice," in Robert Rotberg, *When States Fail: Causes and Consequences*. Princeton, NJ: Princeton University Press.

Hobsbawm, Eric. (1977). "Some Reflections on the 'Break-up of Britain.'" *New Left Review* 105.

Hoffmann, Bruce. (1996). "Yugoslavia: Implications for Europe and for European Institutions," in Richard H. Ullman (Ed.), *The World and Yugoslavia's Wars*. New York: Council on Foreign Relations.

Holbrooke, Richard. (1998). *To End a War*. New York: Random House.

Hollis, Duncan B. (1995). "Accountability in Chechnya – Addressing Internal Matters with Legal and Political International Norms." *Boston College Law Review* 36.

Hopf, Ted. (2002). *Social Construction of International Politics: Identities & Foreign Policies, Moscow, 1955 & 1999*. Ithaca, NY: Cornell University Press.

Horowitz, Donald L. (1985). *Ethnic Groups in Conflict*. Los Angeles: University of California Press.

Horowitz, Donald L. (1998). "Structure and Strategy in Ethnic Conflict." *World Bank Conference on Development Economics*, Washington, DC. April 20–21.

Human Rights Watch. (1996, January 1). "Human Rights Watch World Report 1996 – The Russian Federation," available at http://www.unhcr.org/refworld/docid/3ae6a8c47.html.

Human Rights Watch. (2000). " 'Welcome to Hell': Arbitrary Detention, Torture and Extortion in Chechnya," available at http://www.hrw.org/reports/2000/russia_chechnya4/.

Human Rights Watch. (2003, April 7). "Human Rights Situation in Chechnya." *Human Rights Watch Briefing Paper to the 59th Session if the UN Commission on Human Rights*. Geneva, CHE.

Human Rights Watch. (2006). "Human Rights Watch World Report 2006." New York: Human Rights Watch.

Huntington, Samuel P. (1993). "The Clash of Civilizations?" *Foreign Affairs* 72:3, pp. 22–49.

Ignatieff, Michael. (1994). *Blood and Belonging: Journeys into the new Nationalism.* Toronto: Viking Press.

International Crisis Group. (2007). "Abkhazia: Ways Forward." *Europe Report*, No.179, available at http://www.crisisgroup.org/~/media/files/europe/179_abkhazia___ways_forward.ashx.

International Crisis Group. (2011, February 8). "Armenia and Azerbaijan: Preventing War." Europe Briefing, No. 60, available at http://www.crisisgroup.org/~/media/Files/europe/caucasus/B60%20Armenia%20and%20Azerbaijan%20—%20Preventing%20War.

International Institute for Strategic Studies. (2010). "The Military Balance, 2010." *Routledge*, 110: 1.

Isayev, Sayed. (1997, October 8). "Chechnya to Issue Passports, despite Non-recognition." *ITAR-TASS News Agency.*

ITAR-TASS. (2006, February 27). "Dniester Region to Hold Referendum if Kosovo Gains Independence." ITAR-TASS in English, *World News Connection.*

"Ivanov: Russia Will Withdraw from Independent Kosovo." (2000, March 23). *Moscow, ITAR-TASS in English, World News Connection.*

Jackson, Robert H. (1987). "Quasi-States, Dual Regimes and Neo-Classical Theory: International Jurisprudence and the Third World." *International Organization* 41:4 (August), pp. 519–549.

Jackson, Robert H. (1990). *Quasi-States: Sovereignty, International Relations and the Third World.* Cambridge, UK: Cambridge University Press.

Jackson, Robert H. (Ed.). (1999). *Sovereignty at the Millennium.* Oxford, UK: Blackwell Publishers.

Jackson, Robert H., and Alan James. (1993). *States in a Changing World: A Contemporary Analysis.* New York: Oxford University Press.

James, Alan. (1986). *Sovereign Statehood: The Basis for International Society.* London, UK: Allen and Unwin Publishers.

James, Alan. (1999). "The Practice of Sovereign Statehood in Contemporary International Society." *Political Studies* 47:3, pp. 457–473.

Jervis, Robert. (1976). *Perception and Misperception in International Politics.* Princeton, NJ: Princeton University Press.

Jervis, Robert. (1993). "International Primacy: Is the Game Worth the Candle?" *International Security* 17:4 (Spring), pp. 52–67.

Jones, Daniel M., Stuart A. Bremer, and J. David Singer. (1996). "Militarized Interstate Disputes, 1816–1992: Rationale, Coding Rules, and Empirical Patterns." *Conflict Management and Peace Science* 15:2, pp. 163–213.

Judah, Tim. (1997). *The Serbs: History, Myth & the Destruction of Yugoslavia.* New Haven, CT: Yale University Press.

Judah, Tim. (1999). "Kosovo's Road to War." *Survival* 41:2 (Summer), pp. 5–18.

Judah, Tim. (2001). "Greater Albania?" *Survival* 43:2 (Summer), pp. 7–18.

Kahler, Miles. (1984). *Decolonization in Britain and France: The Domestic Consequences of International Relations.* Princeton, NJ: Princeton University Press.

Kalashnikova, Marina. (1997, June 17). "Chechnya Achieves International Status, but Only for Its Airport in Grozny." *Russica Information, Inc. – RusData DiaLine, Russian Press Digest.*

Kaplan, Robert D. (1993). *Balkan Ghosts: A Journey Through History.* New York: St. Martin's Press.

Kaplan, Robert D. (1994). "The Coming Anarchy." *Atlantic Monthly* 273:2 (February), p. 44.

Kaplan, Robert D. (1997). *The Ends of the Earth.* New York: Vintage Books.

Kaufman, Joyce P. (2002). *NATO and the Former Yugoslavia: Crisis, Conflict, and the Atlantic Alliance.* New York: Rowman & Littlefield.

Kaufman, Stuart. (1997). "The Fragmentation and Consolidation of International Systems." *International Organization* 51:1, pp. 173–208.

Kaufmann, Chaim. (1996). "Possible and Impossible Solutions to Ethnic Civil Wars." *International Security* 20:4, pp. 136–175.

Keohane, Robert. (1984). *After Hegemony.* Princeton, NJ: Princeton University Press.

Ker Lindsay, James. (2012). *The Foreign Policy of Counter Secession: Preventing the Recognition of Contested States.* Oxford, UK: Oxford University Press.

Khachican, Arthur. (2001). "Multilateral Mediation in Intrastate Conflicts: Russia, the United Nations and the War in Abkhazia," in Levon Chorbajian (Ed.), *The Making of Nagorno-Karabakh: From Secession to Republic.* New York: Palgrave.

King, Charles. (2001a). "The Benefits of Ethnic War: Understanding Eurasia's Unrecognized States." *World Politics* 53 (July), pp. 524–552.

King, Charles. (2001b). "Eurasia's Nonstate States." *East European Constitutional Review* 10:4 (Fall).

King, Charles. (2004). "A Rose Among Thorns: Georgia Makes Good." *Foreign Affairs* (March/April).

King, Charles. (2008). "The Five Day War: Managing Moscow after the Georgia Crisis." *Foreign Affairs* (November/December), pp. 2–11.

King, Gary, Robert Keohane, and Sidney Verba. (1994). *Designing Social Inquiry.* Princeton, NJ: Princeton University Press.

King, Gary, and Langche Zeng. (2001). "Logistic Regression in Rare Events Data." *Political Analysis* 9:2, pp. 137–163.

Kolstø, Pål, and Helge Blakkisrud. (2008). "Living with Non-recognition: State and Nation-building in South Caucasian Quasi-states." *Europe-Asia Studies* 60:3 (May), pp. 483–509.

"Kosovo: Opinion Poll Shows Support for Rugova." (1997, February 17). *Belgrade BETA in Serbo-Croatian, World News Connection.*

"Kosovo: Rugova Calls for International Protection, Independence." (1998, August 5). *Tirana ATA in English, World News Connection.*

"Kosovo: The Beginning of Negotiations." (2006, February 23). *BETA Week, World News Connection.*

Kornprobst, Markus. (2008). *Irredentism in European Politics: Argumentation, Compromise and Norms.* Cambridge, UK: Cambridge University Press.

Kramer, Andrew E. (2013, July 3). "Militant Vows to Attack Winter Olympics." *New York Times Online,* available at http://www.nytimes.com/2013/07/04/world/europe/Russsias-most-wanted-militant-vows-to-attack-winter-olympics.html.

Kramer, Mark. (2004/5). "The Perils of Counterinsurgency: Russia's War in Chechnya." *International Security* 29:3 (Winter), pp. 5–63.

Krasner, Stephen. (1982). "Structural Causes and Regime Consequences: Regimes as Intervening Variables." *International Organization* 36:2, pp. 185–205.

Krasner, Stephen. (1999). *Sovereignty: Organized Hypocrisy.* Princeton, NJ: Princeton University Press.

Krasner, Stephen D. (2009, March 30). "Who Gets a State, and Why? The Relative Rules of Sovereignty." *Foreign Affairs,* available at http://www.foreignaffairs.com/articles/64872/stephen-d-krasner/who-gets-a-state-and-why.

Kreptul, Andrei. (2003). "The Constitutional Right of Secession in Political Theory and History." Seattle, WA: Mises Institute Working Paper, Seattle University School of Law.

Kurtulus, Ersun N. (2002). "Sovereign Rights in International Relations: A Futile Search for Regulated or Regular State Behavior." *Review of International Studies* 28, pp. 759–777.

Lacina, Bethany, and Nils Petter Gleditsch. (2005). "Monitoring Trends in Global Combat: A New Dataset of Battle Deaths." *European Journal of Population* 21:2–3, pp. 145–166.

Lake, David A., and Donald Rothschild (Eds.). (1998). *The International Spread of Ethnic Conflict: Fear, Diffusion and Escalation.* Princeton, NJ: Princeton University Press.

Lalonde, Suzanne. (2002). *Determining Boundaries in a Conflicted World: The Role of Uti Possidetis.* Montreal, Quebec: McGill-Queen's University Press.

Lapidus, Gail. (1998). "Contested Sovereignty: The Tragedy of Chechnya." *International Security* 23:1 (Summer), pp. 5–49.

Lapidus, Gail W., and Victor Zaslavsky, with Philip Goldman (Eds.). (1992). *From Union to Commonwealth: Nationalism and Separatism in the Soviet Republics.* Cambridge, UK: Cambridge University Press.

Larrabee, F. Stephen. (1997). "US Policy in the Balkans: From Containment to Strategic Reengagement," in Constantine P. Danopoulos and Kostas G. Messas (Eds.). (1997). *Crises in the Balkans.* Boulder, CO: Westview Press.

Lauterpacht, Hurst. (1947). *Recognition in International Law.* Cambridge, UK: Cambridge University Press.

Layne Christopher. (1993). "The Unipolar Illusion: Why New Great Powers Will Rise." *International Security* 17:4 (Spring), pp. 5–51.

Lehning, Percy. (Ed.). (1998). *Theories of Secession.* London: Routledge.

Lewis, Ioan M. (2010). *Making and Breaking States in Africa: The Somali Experience.* Trenton, NJ: The Red Sea Press.

Libal, Michael. (1997). *Limits of Persuasion: Germany and the Yugoslav Crisis, 1991–1992.* Westport, CT: Praeger.

Licklider, Roy. (1995). "The Consequences of Negotiated Settlements in Civil Wars, 1945–1993." *The American Political Science Review* 89:3, pp. 681–690.

Lieberman, Evan S. (2005). "Nested Analysis as a Mixed-Method Strategy for Comparative Research." *American Political Science Review* 99:3 (August), pp. 435–452.

Lieven, Anatol. (1998). *Chechnya: Tombstone of Russian Power*. New Haven, CT: Yale University Press.

Lustick, Ian S., Dan Miodownik, and Roy J. Eidelson. (2004). "Secessionism in Multicultural States: Does Sharing Power Prevent or Encourage It?" *American Political Science Review* 98:2, pp. 209–229.

Lyall, Jason M. K. (2006). "Pocket Protests: Rhetorical Coercion and the Micropolitics of Collective Action in Semiauthoritarian Regimes." *World Politics* 58:3, pp. 378–412.

Lyall, Jason. (2009). "Does Indiscriminate Violence Incite Insurgent Attacks?: Evidence from Chechnya." *Journal of Conflict Resolution* 53:3 (June), pp. 331–362.

Lynch, Colum. (2007, March 21). "UN Mediator Calls for Kosovo Independence." *The Washington Post*, available at http://www.washingtonpost.com/wp-dyn/content/article/2007/03/20/AR2007032001795.html.

Lynch, Dov. (2002). "Separatist States and Post-Soviet Conflicts." *International Affairs* 78:4, pp. 831–848.

MacFarlane, S. Neil. (1985). *Superpower Rivalry and Third World Radicalism: The Idea of National Liberation*. Beckenham, Kent, UK: S. Neil MacFarlane.

MacFarlane, Neil S. (1997). "On the Front Lines in the Near Abroad: The CIS and the OSCE in Georgia's Civil Wars." *Third World Quarterly* 18:3 (September), pp. 509–526.

Mahoney, Jim, and Gary Goertz. (2004). "The Possibility Principle: Choosing Negative Cases in Comparative Research." *American Political Science Review* 98:4, pp. 653–669.

Markedonov, Sergey. (2010, November). "Radical Islam in the North Caucasus: Evolving Threats, Challenges, and Prospects." *CSIS Russia and Eurasia Program*. Washington, DC: Center for Strategic and International Studies.

Martell, Peter, and Adrian Blomfield. (2011, January 9). "Sudan Referendum: Birth of a Failed State." *The Telegraph* available at http://www.telegraph.co.uk/news/worldnews/africaandindianocean/sudan/8248001/Sudan-Referendum-birth-of-a-failed-state.html.

Matthews, Jessica. (1997). "Power Shift." *Foreign Affairs* 76:1, pp. 50–67.

Maull, Hans W. (1995–6). "Germany in the Yugoslav Crisis." *Survival* 37:4, pp. 56–80.

Mayall, James. (1990). *Nationalism and International Society*. Cambridge, UK: Cambridge University Press.

Mayall, James. (1999). "Sovereignty, Nationalism, and Self-Determination," in Robert Jackson (Ed.), *Sovereignty at the Millenium*. Oxford, UK: Blackwell Publishers, pp. 52–80.

Mearsheimer, John J. (1990). "Back to the Future: Instability in Europe After the Cold War." *International Security* 15:1 (Summer), pp. 5–56.

Mearsheimer, John J. (2001). *The Tragedy of Great Power Politics*. New York: W.W. Norton.

Menon, P. K. (1994). *The Law of International Recognition in International Law: Basic Principles*. Lewiston, NY: Edwin Mellen Press.

Mesic, Stipe. (2004). *The Demise of Yugoslavia: A Political Memoir*. New York: Central European University Press.

Minahan, James. (1996). *Nations Without States: A Historical Dictionary of Contemporary National Movements*. New York: Greenwood Publishing Group.

Ministry of Foreign Affairs of Japan. (2004). "Diplomatic Bluebook 2004: The Russian Federation, Central Asia and the Caucasus," available at http://www.mofa.go.jp/region/europe/russia/index.html.

Minorities at Risk Project. (1999). "Minorities at Risk Dataset, version MARv899." College Park: Center for International Development and Conflict Management, University of Maryland.

Minorities at Risk Project. (2009). "Minorities at Risk Dataset," College Park, MD: Center for International Development and Conflict Management, available at http://www.cicdm.umd.edu/mar/data/asp.

Monahan, Patrick J, and Michael J. Bryant with Nancy C. Cote (1996). "Coming to Terms with Plan B: Ten Principles Governing Secession." no.83 (June) Toronto: CD Howe Institute Commentary, available at https://apps.osgoode.yorku.ca/osgmedia.nsf/0/826DDAC19C5431C3852571A9006512A3/$FILE/comingtoterms.pdf.

Moore, Margaret (Ed.). (1998). *National Self-Determination and Secession*. Oxford, UK: Oxford University Press.

Morgenthau, Hans J. (1985). *Politics Among Nations*, 5th ed. New York: Knopf.

Mueller, John E. (1970). "Presidential Popularity from Truman to Johnson." *American Political Science Review* 64:1 (March), pp. 18–34.

Mueller, John. (1990). *Retreat from Doomsday: The Obsolescence of Major War*. New York: Basic Books.

Mueller, John. (2004). *The Remnants of War*. Ithaca, NY: Cornell University Press.

Musgrave, Thomas. (1997). *Self-Determination and National Minorities*. Oxford, UK: Claredon Press.

Mydans, Seth. (2003, November 28). "Georgia and Its Two Big Brothers." *New York Times*, available at http://www.nytimes.com/2003/11/28/world/georgia-and-its-two-big-brothers.html.

Mydans, Seth. (2003, December 2). "Secessionists from Georgia Hold Talks with Russia." *New York Times* available at http://www.nytimes.com/2003/12/02/world/secessionists-from-georgia-hold-talks-with-russia.html.

Myers, Steven Lee. (2002a, August 24). "Georgia Moves against Rebels and Accuses Russia of Airstrikes." *New York Times*.

Myers, Steven Lee. (2002b, October 5). "Russia Recasts Bog in Caucasus as War on Terror." *New York Times*, available at http://www.nytimes.com/2002/10/05/world/russia-recasts-bog-in-caucasus-as-war-on-terror.html.

Myers, Steven Lee. (2005, March 25). "Rights Group Reports Thousands of Disappearances in Chechnya." *New York Times*, available at http://www.nytimes.com/2005/03/22/international/europe/22chechnya.html?_r=0.

Myers, Steven Lee. (2006, May 28). "Ukraine Battles Smugglers as Europe Keeps Close Eye." *New York Times* 1: 4.

"No foreign backing for Chechen independence bid without Russia's consent – OSCE." (1997, February 1). *British Broadcasting Corporation, BBC Summary of World Broadcasts*, Interfax News Agency, Moscow.

O'Connell, Mary Ellen. (1992). "Continuing Limits on UN Intervention in Civil War." *Indiana Law Journal* 67:4, pp. 903–913.

Onuf, Nicholas. (1994). "The Constitution of International Society." *European Journal of International Law* 5:1, pp. 1–19.

Oppenheim, Lassa. (1955). *International Law: A Treatise*, 8th ed. London: Longmans, Green and Company.

Orentlicher, Diane F. (1998). "Separation Anxiety: International Responses to Ethno-Separatist Claims." *Yale Journal of International Law* 23:1, pp. 1–78.

Organization for Security and Cooperation in Europe (OSCE). (2011, January 25). "Republic of Azerbaijan: Parliamentary Elections." OSCE/ODIHR Election Observation Mission Final Report, available at www.osce.org/odihr/elections/azerbaijan/75073.

Osiander, Eric. (2001). "Sovereignty, International Relations and the Westphalian Myth." *International Organization* 55:2 (Spring), pp. 251–287.

Österud, Öyvind. (1997). "The Narrow Gate: Entry to the Club of Sovereign States." *Review of International Studies* 23, pp. 167–184.

Ostrovsky, Simon. (2005, May 10). "Bush Treads Sensitive Ground with Offer to Help Georgia's Separatist Conflicts." *Agence France Presse – English* available at http://www.lexisnexis.com.

Owen, Elizabeth. (2006, November 16). "South Ossetia: Where Memories of the Pre-Conflict Era Are Fading." *Eurasia Insight*, available at http://www.eurasianet.org/departments/insight/articles/eav111706.shtml.

Ozhiganov, Edward. (1997). "The Republic of Georgia: Conflict in Abkhazia and South Ossetia," in Alexi Arbatov, Abram Chayes, Antonia Handler Chayes, and Lara Olson (Eds.), *Managing Conflict in the Former Soviet Union: Russian and American Perspectives*. Cambridge, MA: MIT Press.

Paul, T.V., G. John Ikenberry, and John A. Hall (Eds.) (2003). *The Nation State in Question* Princeton, NJ: Princeton University Press.

Parker, Jeffery. (2001). *Europe in Crisis, 1598–1648*. Oxford, UK: Blackwell Press.

Pegg, Scott. (1998). *International Society and the De Facto State*. Aldershot, UK: Ashgate University Press.

Peterson, M. J. (1982). "Political Use of Recognition: The Influence of the International System." *World Politics* 34:3, pp. 324–352.

Petrossian, E. (1991). "Act on Referendum Conducted in the Nagorno-Karabakh Republic on December 10, 1991." *Office of the Nagorno-Karabakh Republic in Washington, DC*, available at http://www.nkrusa.org/nk_conflict/declaration_independence.shtml#two.

Petrovic, R. (1992). "The National Composition of Yugoslavia's Population, 1991." *Yugoslav Survey* 33:1, pp. 4–13.

Philpott, Daniel. (1995). "Sovereignty: An Introduction and Brief History." *Journal of International Affairs* 73.

Philpott, Daniel (2001). *Revolutions in Sovereignty: How Ideas Shaped Modern International Relations* Princeton, NJ: Princeton University Press.

Pond, Elizabeth. (1981, August 5). "Nationalism That Surfaced in Kosovo Protests Ripples across Yugoslavia." *The Christian Science Monitor*, p. 14.

Posen, Barry. (1993). "The Security Dilemma and Ethnic Conflict." *Survival* 35:1, pp. 27–47.

Posen, Barry. (2000). "The War for Kosovo: Serbia's Political-Military Strategy." *International Security* (Spring) 24:4, pp. 39–84.

Potier, Tim. (2001). *Conflict in Nagorno-Karabakh, Abkhazia and South Ossetia: A Legal Appraisal*. The Hague, The Netherlands: Kluwer Law International.

"President Shevardnadze Defends Concept for Strengthening State Sovereignty." (1997, April 17). *BBC Summary of World News Broadcasts NTV, Moscow.*

Principality of Minerva On-line. (2005, June 25). http://www.minervanet.org.

Prunk, Janko. (1997). "The Origins of an Independent Slovenia," in Danica Fink-Hafner and John R. Robbins (Eds.). *Making a New Nation: The Formation of Slovenia*. Brookfield, VT: Dartmouth Publishing Company Limited.

Pusic, Vesna. (1992). "A Country by Any Other Name: Transition and Stability in Croatia and Yugoslavia." *East European Politics and Societies* 6: 3.

Putin, Vladimir. (2008, February 14). "Transcript of Annual Big Press Conference." Available at http://archive.kremlin.ru/eng/speeches/2008/02/14/1011_type82915_16 0266.shtml.

Quaye, Christopher O. (1991). *Liberation Struggles in International Law*. Philadelphia: Temple University Press.

Radan, Peter. (1999). "Yugoslavia's Internal Borders as International Borders: A Question of Appropriateness." *East European Quarterly* 33:2, pp. 137–155.

Radan, Peter. (2002). *The Break-up of Yugoslavia and International Law*. London: Routeledge.

Ramet, Sabrina Petra. (1993). "Slovenia's Road to Democracy." *Europe-Asia Studies* 45:5, pp. 869–886.

Ratner, Steven R. (1996). "Drawing a Better Line: Uti Possidetis and the Borders of New States." *American Journal of International Law* 90:4, pp. 590–624.

Raum, Tom. (1995, January 13). "Clinton Respects Russian Rule in Chechnya but Wants Bloodshed Stopped." *Associated Press*, available at http://www.apnewsarchive.com/ 1995/Clinton-Respects-Russian-Rule-in-Chechnya-But-Wants-Bloodshed-Stopped/id-b3deoa8ba1be4cb8a4db04df54343020.

Redman, Michael. (2002). "Should Kosovo Be Entitled to Statehood?" *The Political Quarterly*, pp. 338–343.

Regan, Patrick M. (2000). *Civil Wars and Foreign Powers: Interventions and Intrastate Conflict*. Ann Arbor: University of Michigan Press.

REGNUM News Agency. (2006, January 30). "Vladimir Putin: 'Decisions on Kosovo Should be of Universal Nature,'" Available at http://www.regnum.ru/english/581342. html.

Rezun, Miron. (1995). *Europe and War in the Balkans: Toward a New Yugoslav Identity*. Westport, CT: Praeger.

Rich, Roland. (1993). "Recognition of States: The Collapse of Yugoslavia and the Soviet Union." *European Journal of International Law*, 4:1, pp. 36–65.

Rittberger, Volker (Ed.). (1993). *Regime Theory and International Relations*. Oxford, UK: Oxford University Press.

Roeder, Philip. (2007). *Where Nation States Come From: Institutional Chance in the Age of Nationalism*. Princeton, NJ: Princeton University Press.

Rosecrance, Richard N. (1999). *The Rise of the Virtual State: Wealth and Power in the Coming Century*. New York: Basic Books.

Rubin, Alissa J. (2006). "Serbia, Kosovo Remain Split on Independence." *Los Angeles Times*, available at http://articles.latimes.com/2006/jul/25/world/fg-kosovo25.

Rumer, Boris. (2002). "The Powers in Central Asia." *Survival* 44:3 (Autumn), pp. 57–68.

"Russia." (2006). *CIA World Factbook Online*, available at http://www.cia.gov/cia/publications/factbook/geos/rs.html.

"Russia condemns rights violations in Georgia; Georgia creates army." (1991, September 10). *Associated Press* available at http://www.lexisnexis.com.

"Russia: Putin calls for 'universal principles' to settle frozen conflicts." (2006, February 1). *Radio Free Europe* RFE-RL, Inc., *World News Connection*.

"Russia: Russian foreign minister opposes independence for Kosovo." (1998, June 23). *Moscow Interfax, World News Connection*.

"Russia to Boost Abkhazia Bases." (2009, August 12). BBC News, available at http://news.bbc.co.uk/2/hi/8196974.stm.

"Russia: UK against Kosovo gaining independence." (1999, April 20). *Moscow, ITAR-TASS World Service in English, World News Connection*.

Saideman, Stephen M. (1997). "Explaining the International Relations of Secessionist Conflicts: Vulnerability vs. Ethnic Ties." *International Organization* 51:4 (Fall), pp. 721–753.

Saideman, Stephen M. (1998). "Is Pandora's Box Half-Empty or Half-Full? The Limited Virulence of Secession and the Domestic Sources of Disintegration," in David A. Lake and Donald Rothchild (Eds.), *The International Spread of Ethnic Conflict: Fear, Diffusion, Escalation*. Princeton, NJ: Princeton University Press, pp. 127–150.

Saideman, Stephen M. (2002). "Overlooking the Obvious: Bringing International Politics Back into Ethnic Conflict Management." *International Studies Review* 4:3 (Fall), pp. 63–86.

Saideman, Stephen M. (2002a). "Discrimination in International Relations: Examining Why Some Ethnic Groups Receive More External Support Than Others." *Journal of Peace Research* 39:1 (January), pp. 27–50.

Saideman, Stephen M. (2002b). "Thinking Theoretically about Identity and Foreign Policy," in Michael Barnett and Shibley Telhami (Eds.), *Communal Identity and Foreign Policy in the Middle East*. Ithaca, NY: Cornell University Press.

Sambanis, Nicholas. (2003). "Expanding Economic Models of Civil Wars Using Case Studies." *World Bank*, available at http://politics.as.nyu.edu/docs/IO/4744/ns1110.pdf.

Sarkees, Meredith Reid. (2000). "The Correlates of War Data on War: An Update to 1997." *Conflict Management and Peace Science*, 18:1, pp. 123–144.

Sarkees, Meridith Reid, and Frank Wayman. (2010). *Resort to War: 1816–2007*. Washington, DC: CQ Press, available at http://correlatesofwar.org.

Schelling, Thomas. (1971a). "Dynamic Models of Segregation." *Journal of Mathematical Sociology* 1, pp. 143–186.

Schelling, Thomas. (1971b). "On the Ecology of Micromotives." *Public Interest* 25, pp. 61–98.

Schreuer, Christoph. (1993). "The Waning of the Sovereign State: Towards a New paradigm for International law?" *European Journal of International Law* 4, pp. 447–471.

Schoiswohl, Michael. (2004). *Status and (Human Rights) Obligations of Non-Recognized and De Facto Regimes in International Law: The Case of Somaliland*. Leiden: Brill Academic Publishers.

Schweid, Barry. (1995, May 17). "Administration Powerless to Stop the Fighting in Chechnya." *Associated Press*, available at http://www.apnewsarchive.com/1995/

Administration-Powerless-To-Stop-the-Fighting-in-Chechnya/id-
4458e2cefofdabcad402a0e8013c7e58.

Schweller, Randall. (1996). "Neo-Realism's Status Quo Bias: What Security Dilemma?"
Security Studies 5:1, pp. 90–121.

"Serbia and Montenegro." (2006). *CIA World Factbook Online: 2006*, available at
https://www.cia.gov/library/publications/the-world-factbook/geos/pk.html.

"Serbia's Draskovic says UK Straw's comment on Kosovo violates international law."
(2006, March 12). *AFP (North European Service), World News Connection.*

Shannon, Vaughn. (2000). "Norms Are What States Make of Them." *International
Studies Quarterly* 44:2 (June), pp. 293–316.

Shepsle, Kenneth. (1992). "Congress Is a 'They' Not an 'It': Legislative Intent as an
Oxymoron." *International Review of Law and Economics* 12, pp. 239–256.

Silber, Laura, and Allan Little. (1996). *Yugoslavia: Death of a Nation.* TV Books, Inc.
distributed in the USA by Penguin Books.

Simms, Brendan. (2002). *Unfinest Hour: Britain and the Destruction of Bosnia.* London:
Penguin Books, Ltd.

Singer, J. David. (1972). "The 'Correlates of War' Project: Interim Report and
Rationale." *World Politics* 24:2 (January), pp. 243–270.

Skakov, Alexander. (2005). "Abkhazia at a Crossroads: On the Domestic Political
Situation in the Republic of Abkhazia." *Iran and the Caucasus* 9:1, pp. 159–186.

Slaughter, Anne-Marie. (1995). "International Law in a World of Liberal States."
European Journal of International Law 6:1, pp. 503–538.

"Slovenia's self-defense." (1991, July 6). *The Economist* 320:7714, p. 46.

Small, Melvin, and J. David Singer. (1982). *Resort to Arms: International and Civil Wars,
1816–1980.* Beverly Hills, CA: Sage Publications.

Smith, David J. (2004, August 6). "Saakashvili in Washington." *The Washington Times*,
available at http://www.washingtontimes.com/news/2004/aug/5/20040805-083048-
3256r/.

Smith, Graham. (1999). *The Post-Soviet States: Mapping the Politics of Transition.* New
York: Oxford University Press.

Smith, Sebastian. (1997, January 27). "Big Turnout for Chechnya's Landmark Post-War
Elections." *Agence France Presse – English*, available at http://www.lexisnexis.com/.

Smith, Sebastian. (2006). *Allah's Mountains: The Battle for Chechnya.* New York: I. B.
Tauris.

Smyth, Patrick. (1995, January 13). "French Make 'Neglected' Mediterranean a
Priority." *The Irish Times, City Edition*, p. 12.

Sorensen, Georg. (2001). *Changes in Statehood: The Transformation of International
Relations.* New York: Palgrave Press.

"South Ossetia forms national guard." (1991, December 1). *Agence France Presse*,
available at http://www.lexisnexis.com/.

"South Ossetia mobilizes." (1991, December 23). *Agence France Presse*, available at
http://www.lexisnexis.com/.

Spencer, Metta. (1998). "The Breakup of Yugoslavia," in Metta Spencer (Ed.),
Separatism. Lanham, MD: Rowan and Litlefield.

Spruyt, Hendrik. (1994). *The Sovereign State and Its Competitors.* Princeton, NJ:
Princeton University Press.

Spruyt, Hendrik. (2005). *Ending Empire: Contested Sovereignty and Territorial
Partition.* Ithaca, NY: Cornell University Press.

Srivastava, Virendra, and David Giles. (1987). *Seemingly Unrelated Regression Equation Models: Estimation and Inference.* New York: Marcel Dekker.

Stanley, Alessandra. (1997, May 13). "Yeltsin Signs Peace Treaty with Chechnya." *New York Times,* available at http://www.nytimes.com/1997/05/13/world/yeltsin-signs-peace-treaty-with-chechnya.html.

Stebinsky, George. (2005, June 19). "Coin Comment." *The Columbus Dispatch* H6:C1.

Stern, Jessica Eve. (1994). "Moscow Meltdown: Can Russia Survive?" *International Security* 18:4 (Spring), pp. 40–65.

Strang, David. (1990). "Anomaly and Commonplace in European Political Expansion." *International Organization* 45:2 (Spring), pp. 143–162.

Sturzo, Luigi. (1927). *Italy and Fascismo* London: Faber and Gwyer.

Tanner, Marcus. (1997). *Croatia: A Nation Forged in War.* New Haven, CT: Yale University Press.

Tappe, Trent N. (1995). "Chechnya and the State of Self-Determination in a Breakaway Region of the Former Soviet Union: Evaluating the Legitimacy of Secessionist Claims." *Columbia Journal of Transnational Law* 34.

"Text of Peace Agreements, Rebel Leader Comments." (1996, September 3). *British Broadcasting Corporation, BBC Summary of World Broadcasts,* adapted from Russian Public TV, Moscow, in Russian 4pm GMT September 1, 1996.

"The National Composition of Yugoslavia's Population, 1991." (1992). *Yugoslav Survey* 33:1, pp. 4–13.

"The Road to War" (1991, July 6). *The Economist* 320:7714, p. 2.

Tilly, Charles. (1992). *Coercion, Capital and European States, AD 990–1992.* Cambridge, MA: Wiley-Blackwell.

Toft, Monica Duffy. (2003). *The Geography of Ethnic Violence.* Princeton, NJ: Princeton University Press.

Toft, Monica Duffy. (2010). *Saving the Peace: The Durable Settlement of Civil Wars.* Princeton, NJ: Princeton University Press.

Twigg, Judyth. (2005, December). "Differential Demographics: Russia's Muslim and Slavic Populations." PONARS Policy Memo No. 388, available at http://www.ponar seurasia.org/memo/differential-demographics-russias-muslim-and-slavic-populations-judyth-twigg.

Uppsala Conflict Data Program/International Peace Research Institute (UCDP/PRIO). (2008). "UCDP/PRIO Armed Conflict Dataset Codebook, Version 4-2008," available at http://www.pcr.uu.se/research/ucdp/datasets/ucdp_prio_armed_conflict_dataset/.

Ullman, Richard H. (Ed.). (1996). *The World and Yugoslavia's Wars.* New York: Council on Foreign Relations.

United Nations. (1960). Declaration of the Granting of Independence to Colonial Countries and Peoples. Available at http://legal.un.org/avl/ha/dicc/dicc.html.

United Nations. (2001). *Transcript.* Third Committee Meetings, 56th Session of the United Nations General Assembly/SHC. Available at http://www.un.org/ga/56/third/index.html.

United Nations. (2003). "Charter of the United Nations," available at http://www.un.org/aboutun/charter.

United States, Department of State. (2008). "The Case for Kosovo," available at http://www.state.gov/p/eur/ci/kv/c24701.htm.

United States, Department of State. (2009). "2008 Human Rights Report: Georgia," available at http://www.state.gov/g/drl/rls/hrrpt/2008/eur/119080.htm.

"US Condemns Russia over Georgia." (2008, September 4). *BBC News*, available at http://news.bbc.co.uk/2/hi/europe/7597336.stm.

Usborne, David. (1991, September 20). "EC Pulls Back from Sending Troops to Yugoslavia." *The Independent*.

Van Evera, Stephen. (1997). *Guide to Methods for Students of Political Science*. Ithaca, NY: Cornell University Press.

"Vedrine Rules Out Partition, Independence for Kosovo." (1999, April 12). *Paris, Agence France Presse in French, World News Connection*.

Vodopivec, Peter. (1992). "Slovenes and Yugoslavia, 1918–1991." *East European Politics and Societies*, 6:3, pp. 220–241.

Von Glahn, Gerhard. (1992). *Law among Nations*, 6th ed. New York: MacMillan Publishing.

von Twickle, Nicholas. (2011, September 22). "Abkhazia Boasts IKEA Goods and Pricey Cars, but no ATMs." *Moscow Times*, available at http://www.themoscowtimes.com/mobile/article/abkhazia-boasts-ikea-goods-and-pricey-sports-cars-but-no-atms/444121.html.

Walt, Stephen. (1985). *The Origins of Alliances*. Ithaca, NY: Cornell University Press.

Walter, Barbara. (1997). "The Critical Barrier to Civil War Settlement." *International Organization* 51:3, pp. 335–364.

Walter, Barbara. (2002). *Committing to Peace: The Successful Settlement of Civil Wars*. Princeton, NJ: Princeton University Press.

Walter, Barbara. (2003). "Explaining the Intractability of Territorial Conflict." *International Studies Review* 5:4, pp. 137–153.

Walter, Barbara. (2006a). "Building Reputation: Why Governments Fight Some Separatists but Not Others." *American Journal of Political Science* 50:2, pp. 313–330.

Walter, Barbara. (2006b). "Information, Uncertainty, and the Decision to Secede." *International Organization* 60:1, pp. 105–135.

Walter, Barbara. (2009). *Reputation and Civil War: Why Separatist Conflicts are So Violent*. Cambridge, UK: Cambridge University Press.

Walter, Barbara, and Jack Snyder (Eds.). (1999). *Civil Wars, Insecurity and Intervention*. New York: Columbia University Press.

Waltz, Kenneth. (1979). *Theory of International Politics*. New York: Random House.

Watson, Adam. (1992). *The Evolution of International Society: A Comparative Historical Analysis*. New York: Routeledge.

"We are always ready for war, Abkhaz minister tells Russian newspaper." (2004, August 4). *BBC Monitoring International Reports, Global News Wire – Asia Africa Intelligence Wire. World News Connection*.

Weber, Max. (1919/2004). *The Vocation Lectures: Science as a Vocation, Politics as a Vocation*, Rodney Livingstone (Trans.). Indianapolis, IN: Hackett Publishers.

Weisman, Steven R. (2004a, January 25). "Powell Calms the Russians on U.S. Intent over Georgia." *New York Times*, available at http://www.nytimes.com/2004/01/25/world/powell-calms-the-russians-on-us-intent-over-georgia.html.

Weisman, Steven R. (2004b, January 27). "Powell Displays Tough U.S. Stance Toward Russians." *New York Times*, available at http://www.nytimes.com/2004/01/27/world/powell-displays-tough-us-stance-toward-russians.html.

Weisman, Stephen R. (2005, May 20). "US Is Seeking to Speed Up Talks on Kosovo's Status." *New York Times* A:1, p. 7.

Weller, Marc. (1992). "The International Response to the Dissolution of the Socialist Federal Republic of Yugoslavia." *The American Journal of International Law* 86:3 (July), pp. 569–607.

Wendt, Alexander. (1999). *Social Theory of International Politics.* Cambridge, UK: Cambridge University Press.

Wendt, Alexander. (2004). "The State as Person in International Relations Theory." *Review of International Studies* 30:2, pp. 289–316.

Wight, Martin (Ed.). (1977). *Systems of States.* Leicester, UK: Leicester University Press.

Wight, Martin. (1991). *International Theory: Three Traditions.* Leicester, UK: Leicester University Press.

Willoughby, W. W. (1896). *An Examination on the Nature of the State: A Study in Political Philosophy.* New York: MacMillan.

Wilson, Woodrow. (1918, January 8). "War Aims and Peace Terms" (Fourteen Points Speech), SEN-RG46. Washington, DC: Records of the United States Senate, National Archives.

Wood, Nicholas. (2006, May 22). "Montenegrins Elect to End Union with Serbia." *New York Times,* available at http://www.nytimes.com/2006/05/22/world/europe/22cnd-monte.html.

World Data Analyst. (2006). Encyclopædia Britannica, Inc., available at http://corporate.britannica.com/library/online/wda.html.

Xhudo, Gazmen. (1996). *Diplomacy and Crisis in the Balkans.* New York: St. Martin's Press.

Yalowitz, Kenneth, and Svante E. Cornell. (2004). "The Critical but Perilous Caucasus." *Orbis* (Winter), pp. 105–116.

Yannis, Alexandros. (2001). "Kosovo Under International Administration." *Survival* 43:2 (Summer), pp. 31–48.

"Yugoslavia's rebel republics prepare to go it alone." (1991, October 1). *Agence France Presse, World News Connection.*

Zellner, A. (1962). "An Efficient Method of Estimating Seemingly Unrelated Regression Equations and Tests for Aggregation Bias." *Journal of the American Statistical Association* 57, pp. 348–368.

Zellner, A. (1963). "Estimators for Seemingly Unrelated Regression Equations: Some Exact Finite Sample Results." *Journal of the American Statistical Association* 58, pp. 977–992.

Zickel, Raymond (Ed.). (1991). *Soviet Union: A Country Study.* Washington, DC: Federal Research Division, Library of Congress.

Index

democracy, 96
  criteria for statehood, 30
  in Abkhazia, 198
  in Georgia, 157, 195, 198
  in Nagorno-Karabakh, 185, 198
  in post-Soviet states, 164
  in Russia, 192, 194, 197, 219
  in Slovenia, 91
  in South Ossetia, 198
  mutual, 58, 74, 75, 76, 218
dissolution, 7
distinct
  operationalization, 68
distinctiveness, national, 50
domestic authority. *See* sovereignty
domestic security motive, 9, 47, 217
Dudayev, Dzhokhar, President of Chechen
    Republic of Ichkeria, 155, 156, 157,
    168, 173

Eagleburger, Lawrence, US Deputy Secretary of
    State, 123
East Germany. *See* Germany
East Pakistan. *See* Bangladesh
East Timor, 10, 23, 54
EC standards. *See* Badinter Commission
Emerson, Rupert, 41, 64
English School, 8, 26
Eritrea, 6, 62
Eshba, vyacheslav, Abkhazia Defense Minister,
    177
ethnic conflict, 18, 59, 61
ethnic federation, 51, 69
ethnicfed
  operationalization, 68
European Community (EC), 38, 78, 85
  recognition guidelines. *See* Badinter
  Yugoslavia engagement, 112,
    114, 116
European Neighborhood Policy (ENP), 198
European Union (EU)
  Chechnya engagement, 197
  Five Day War, reponse to. *See* Five Day War
  Georgia engagement, 198
  Kosovo engagement, 1, 112, 133, 134
  Nagorno-Karabakh engagement, 198
  post-Soviet engagement, 150, 165
  Yugoslavia engagement, 85, 120
external legitimacy
  statehood and, 8
external security motive, 9,
    46, 217

Five Day War, 2, 193
  response to, 2
Foreign direct investment (FDI), 34
France, 54, 75, 223
  Abkhazia engagement, 198
  Chechnya engagement, 197
  Croatia recognition, 130
  Kosovo engagement, 132
  Kosovo recognition, 204, 220
  Nagorno-Karabakh engagement,
    198
  patterns of recognition, 58, 73, 75,
    76, 218
  secessionism in, 137
  Serbia relations, 138
  Slovenia recognition, 130
  Yugoslavia engagement, 113, 114, 120, 130,
    136, 138
fraternities and sororities, 27
French-Indochinese War, 6
frozen conflicts, 1, 62

Gamsakhurdia, Zviad, President of Georgia,
    160, 161, 176, 194
Gellner, Ernest, 41
Genscher, Hans-Dietrich, Foreign
    Minister and Vice Chancellor of
    Germany, 121, 122
George, A. L., 82
Georgia, 13, 138, 145, 151, 192
  European relations, 2
  Five Day War in. *See* Five Day War
  independence of, 160
  minorities in, 159, 160
  nationalism in, 143
  NATO and, 138
  Russian relations, 2
  Soviet rule in, 149, 159
  United States relations, 2
Georgian, ethnicity
  Georgianization, 157, 159
  in Abkhazia, 158, 176, 180
  in Georgia, 158
  in South Ossetia, 158
Georgian-Abkhaz War, 167, 176, 177
geostrategic motive. *See* external security
    motive
Germany, 223
  Chechnya engagement, 197, 198
  Croatia recognition, 130
  Kosovo recognition, 220
  Nagorno-Karabakh engagement, 198

Lightning Source UK Ltd.
Milton Keynes UK
UKOW04f1513230717
305852UK00001B/72/P